Centered on Majesty

Susan League

Christian Faith
PUBLISHING

ISBN 978-1-0980-8415-8 (paperback)
ISBN 978-1-0980-8416-5 (digital)

Christian Faith Publishing, Inc.
832 Park Avenue
Meadville, PA 16335
www.christianfaithpublishing.com

Cover & Text Design and Cover Photo: Beach City Publishing

Printed in the United States of America

Enthroning Him Testimonials

Jennifer Smalley Bonds
I was given *Enthroning Him* as a gift from my Dad. This book has been a gift that keeps on giving. I have gone through *Enthroning Him* at least twice and each time I have been challenged and blessed. Between the pages there is an obvious anointing and a sweetness that I cannot explain. I would encourage everyone to read this book if they can as it is good at stirring up the spirit and one's Faith.

MaryBeth Cleland
The *"Enthroning Him"* devotionals deeply touched me. It revealed truths deep in my soul I never understood until "God's powerful Word" and the "Enthroning series" collided in My heart. I began to cherish "the next day" so I could eagerly dive in to this divinely inspired devotional which helped to open my eyes on a daily basis. Praise Jesus for this amazing, complicated, and often painful journey called Life!" What a gift having the *"Enthroning Him* series" to help navigate the daily road ahead.

Maria VanDiepen
"Enthroning Him" has become a part of my daily life. It was written by a precious woman of God that I love dearly. It has become my 'go to' morning encouragement. Each truth is portrayed in a story or real-to-life reference which makes me feel like I'm having coffee with a friend and inspires me to follow Christ closely. Thank you Susan for sharing your beautiful gift!

Wayne and Sharon Farlee
Reading Enthroning Him as a morning devotion became a tradition after breakfast each day. Susan has a God-given talent to connect in her writings what is portrayed in the scriptures; as it can relate to our daily lives. We really appreciate and enjoy what Susan has done in the past, and are looking forward to reading her new book. May God richly bless you in all your future endeavors.

Cody Robinson

I found Susan League's daily devotional, "*Enthroning Him*", to be an excellent read, inspiring, uplifting, and very encouraging. Amazed that anyone could come up with a new message every day for a year containing such wonder, spiritual quality and insight, I had to envision the Lord watching over her shoulder and whispering in her ear as she wrote. I also really liked that she backed up every message with a scripture, in that way sharing not just her thoughts, but more importantly, our Father God's. In short, I highly recommend "*Enthroning Him*" for anyone serious about their Christian walk!

An Anonymous Missionary

Just wanted to tell you something special. My mother, who I have been praying for her salvation for more than 20 years, told me she is a Christian (but she doesn't read the Bible or go to church, she does pray though) so I bought your devotional book for her when I was at the network conference. What I really liked about it is that you have the verses written out! This is great for her since she hasn't learned to read the Bible for herself!

Anyways, since I gave it to her she has been reading it every morning! And then she tells me what it says and how it applies to her! I am so blown away as I have never seen this side of my mother before! On the day my dad and mom drove me to the airport she took a picture of the devotional and told me to read it! She said it was perfect for today! I asked her how. It was April 24th. The verse was the prayer of Jabez! She said my ministry in missions was God's way of extending my borders and he would keep me from harm! Anyways, it was the first time she has expressed understanding our call to missions! I was shocked but so grateful! Thank you so much for writing this book!

Dedication

For Todd
Husband, Father and Pastor

In Memory

Sandi Age
Wife, Mother and Co-Publisher

Preface

Sometimes in life, we are faced with opportunities
that become avenues for God to use us unexpectedly.
This is absolutely true of **Centered on Majesty**.

This book was written as an encouragement for all of us from a
place that only the Holy Spirit could know in each of our lives. I
am convinced that no two people will be affected in the same way
as you read through these devotionals. Even in my recent days of
editing, I have been overwhelmed at the divineness of the words
that I was humbly able to record. It is my prayer that the presence
of the Lord will minister to you in a powerful way as you entrust a
few moments of each day here with Him. Open your heart to hear
His voice, listen carefully and realize that you are deeply loved.

In the navigation of your life, many things will attempt to
get your attention and focus but may the anchor of being
centered on the Lord Jesus sustain you and help you grow in
your journey. May you be kept, safely **Centered on Majesty**.

In His love,

Susan League

Introduction

As the publisher of this second masterpiece of writing and sharing from Susan's heart, we are blessed to get this next book into your hands. I have seen so many daily Bible reading books in my time, and there are many. But when we came across the writings that she has been writing for years, we had to come forward and convince her that her words needed to be in print. We believe, these are words and scriptures given to her from our Lord. The first book (**Enthroning Him**) was the beginning of her writings, you will hear her words and they may be slight incontent at times, but they are large in thought. The space that you will find on some pages, will give you a great chance to journal your thoughts, and there will be many. Enjoy this next book (**Centered on Majesty**) We will, prayerfully, start working on her third devotional book (**Unending Covenant**) as soon as the Lord provides. We pray that these words will resonate within your heart as you start your busy days. But also read the scriptures she has shared with you to really bring it from what God has put into her heart. You will be truly blessed as we were, and we hope and pray these words will resonate in your spirit and lead you into a day of reflections and peace with the Word of God.

I would like to add something that we had not foreseen in the endeavors of publishing this book. After 7 years of fighting cancer, my wife of 42 years was called home as we were preparing to publish this amazing devotional. Sandi was my co-publisher in this endeavor and will always be with me in spirit and I know that she has met our Lord and Savior, Face to Face.

Barry Age
Sandi Age
Beach City Publishing

Lord of All

Jesus is the King of kings and the Lord of lords,
He is Majesty.
We can be centered on Majesty as this New Year begins.
Not a resolution, but a life decision.
May we not strive to make Jesus first, but to make Him
central to our life, because when we do, He will be first!
We will be walking with Him and talking with Him, constantly.
Our life will be encompassed by His Spirit
From here we will be poured
into and out of the centrality of Jesus in us.
We have never been an item on God's "to do list".
He has always been centered on us,
centered on ways to show His love to us.
He is all about finding ways to display His care and grace.
Centering our heart on Majesty is taking
one more step toward Him.
One step, one day at a time, closer toward His purposes.
Centered on Majesty is letting everything else in our life
flow out of where He is in us.

Isaiah 12:2
**Surely God is my salvation; I will trust and not be
afraid. The LORD, the LORD himself, is my strength
and my defense; he has become my salvation.**
Matthew 6:21 ♥ Isaiah 26:3

Our Heart

When centering our life, the very first and
most crucial issue is centering our heart.
Have you ever been like a little rubber duck, meant for a bathtub,
but felt as though you are out on the high seas?
That little rubber duck is no match for the massive waves
and swells that the sea naturally invokes. In the same
way, it is mere foolishness to think that somehow, in
ourselves, we can stand in combat without Jesus.
There must come a moment in our life in Christ when we realize
that we are no match for the schemes of the enemy without Jesus.
He is our anchor. He is the One that God provided to fight for us.
He is not only a viable opponent for the enemy of our
soul but He is a VICTORIOUS warrior. When we stop
trying in our "rubber duck" ability to weather the waves,
and take refuge in Him, we will find victory.
Of course we are not a rubber duck are we?
No! We are children of the Most High God,
who He has made more than conquerors in Christ Jesus, our Lord.
We've been made victorious through the blood of Jesus Christ.
Faith is the necessity to letting God be God, in centering our heart.
Faith agrees with the Word of God, as we walk in obedience,
letting God fight the battle that we can never win without Him.
It is submitting to His authority.
Centering our heart on Jesus is paramount to living in victory.

2 Chronicles 20:15

And he said, "Listen, all Judah and inhabitants of Jerusalem and King Jehoshaphat: Thus says the LORD to you, 'Do not be afraid and do not be dismayed at this great horde, for the battle is not yours but God's.

Ephesians 1:15-23 ♥ Ephesians 6:12 ♥ Psalm 61:2-4

Our Family

The greatest blessing from God, second to our salvation is
our family. It's a treasure that must be guarded and cherished.
We must protect and become more and more aware
of the world's threat to its health and well-being.
If the enemy can keep peace from our home,
he will do whatever it takes to do so.
From dishes and dirty laundry, to sarcasm and attitudes,
The tiny issues become as mountainous as Mt. Everest!
Centering our family on Jesus is easier said than
done, but with His help, it is possible!
The enemy, though, might attempt to bully and
intimidate us into thinking that our family or loved
ones are too far gone for the Lord to intervene.
Perhaps we have unintentionally fallen into the trap of
believing that irreparable damage has been done.
I want remind you that the Word of God is the truth that
we must center our family on. He is a God of miracles and
restoration. He is God, the ultimate Authority on reconciliation!
No family is too far gone, and in faith, we can stand in the gap
and believe God to do what only He can do. When we
recognize who we are in Christ and the redemptive power
of the blood of Jesus, we can know that He is able.
May His peace and merciful grace reside within our family
with joy and the happiness that can only be found in Jesus.

2 Corinthians 5:19

*Now all these things are from God, who reconciled us to Himself
through Christ and gave us the ministry of reconciliation, namely,
that God was in Christ reconciling the world to Himself, not
counting their trespasses against them, and He has committed
to us the word of reconciliation. Therefore, we are ambassadors
for Christ, as though God were making an appeal through
us; we beg you on behalf of Christ, be reconciled to God.*

Jeremiah 32:27 ♥ Ephesians 3:20

Our Home

Whether we are married or single, old or young,
we must have Christ as the center of our
most important relationships.
If you're looking for Mr. or Miss Right, or if you've
found the love of your life, the love that Christ has for
each of you, must be the substance for your hearts.
Loving without Christ being the center of our home is like
expecting a body to survive without a healthy heart.
You may be able to "get by", but the essence of your life will
be weak and without Christ, never as strong as it could be.
Love that is not 'Christ' centered can sadly, become 'self' centered.
Unrealistic expectations that put undue pressure on the one
we love so deeply, can wreck even the best of relationships.
Physiologically, an unhealthy heart will begin to become
unproductive, it begins to quiver and misfire without adequately
meeting the needs of the body. It steadily grows weak.
Imagine attempting to sustain such an expectation imposed
on us by that one we love? We might be able to undertake
for a while but it will be short-lived because the depth of a
heart's need for God is deeper that any human can satisfy
or fulfill. That place was intended for God so why would
we expect that a person, as great as they might be, to have
the capacity to be what only God can be in our life?
Jesus is the author and the finisher of our faith and His
desire is that we would be bound together by His love!

Psalm 73:26
*My flesh and my heart may fail, but God is the
strength of my heart and my portion forever.*
Hebrews 12:1-2 ♥ 1 John 3:1 ♥ 1 John 4:10
Romans 8:32 ♥ John 15:13

Growing Up

When I was a little girl, I remember that when people asked
me how old I was, I would always answer in "halves"!
"I'm 5 and ½" or "I'm going to be 10 on my next birthday".
I remember just wanting to be older and to grow up.
At that time, I couldn't see or understand
the sweetness of childhood.
We can seldom see the process of growing as sweet or purposeful,
we just want to "be there!"
Part of growing is to understand the depth of power
that is ours in the name of Jesus. It is one thing to
know it, but living in it is something else. It requires a
growth that returns our heart to child-like faith.
The reality of Him being the source that holds us together is a
truth that will help us. It will come as we align our heart with
His word and center our life in the majesty that only belongs to
Jesus. As we grow in Christ, we are changed from glory to glory.
Growing doesn't happen overnight, it's a process and
sometimes all we want to be is, "All-grown up".
It's pretty interesting that growing is continual, no matter how long
we've been walking with Jesus. No matter our age, growing never
stops and knowing Jesus is an ongoing joy. We know that He has so
much in store for us, but that's not just for our future, it's for today!
He is majesty and wants to show Himself so strong in our life.

2 Corinthians 3:13-18

*Since we have such a hope, we are very bold, not like Moses, who
would put a veil over his face so that the Israelites might not gaze at
the outcome of what was being brought to an end. But their minds
were hardened. For to this day, when they read the old covenant,
that same veil remains un-lifted, because only through Christ is it
taken away. Yes, to this day whenever Moses is read a veil lies over
their hearts. But when one turns to the Lord, the veil is removed.
Now the Lord is the Spirit, and where the Spirit of the Lord is, there
is freedom. And we all, with unveiled face, beholding the glory of the
Lord, are being transformed into the same image from one degree of
glory to another. For this comes from the Lord who is the Spirit.*

Jeremiah 10:6 ♥ John 1:3 ♥ Colossians 1:17

Our Work

I've heard it said, "I'd rather have a job than be looking for a job". Life without work is not realistic. For most, a paying job is vital and most become accustomed to a lifestyle based on their wages. Even for wealthy people, work is still necessary, though it may come in a different form. From volunteer work to construction, work gives us a sense of accomplishment and purpose. We must always remember, though, that the Lord is our source and God, is Jehovah Jireh, our Provider. He will lead and guide us even in our work and helping us there. Without being centered on Him, we will never operate at our highest potential. Our work opens so much that is God's purpose in our life. He pays attention to how we work and what our attitude is about it. Sometimes we grumble at having to work, but our work is a way that God can bless us and be a blessing to others. When we start to see our work as a way that others can see our life, we will begin to see that work is not all about us. Even on the days we stumble or make a mistake, still the grace of God is with us. Did you know that the Bible has a lot to say about working? Many look forward to retirement, no more going to work! But most find that they still want to do something because there is something the Lord put in us that causes us to want to be purposeful in our life. You may not find yourself working for an employer at that stage in life, but there will be other things that will take our focus. It may be working in a garden, building or wood-carving. My dad loved working in his little shop after retirement. Helping in a community center or volunteering at the church or a local hospital, is a way that people find that need fulfilled. Whatever our work, may we see that being centered on Jesus, means that whatever we do, we are doing in His name, for His pleasure in us. Anyone can work and have a bad attitude, always grumbling but what does that convey? As we are centered on Jesus, may we reflect Him while we work? May the Lord take pleasure in us, even in our work and may our attitude bless Him. In all things let us remember to give Him thanks and praise, as we are centered on Majesty?

Psalm 90:17
Let the favor of the Lord our God be upon us, and establish the work of our hands upon us; yes, establish the work of our hands!
Matthew 5:16 ♥ Proverbs 16:3 ♥ Philippians 2:14-18
Philippians 4:13 ♥ Colossians 3:23-24

In Storms

I've heard it said that boats are most generally safe in the harbor and while this is true, that is not what boats are made for. Navigating a boat on a big lake doesn't seem like it would be too difficultand on most days that is true. Until a storm comes, then it's a whole other ballgame. Navigating the storms of life is one of the most difficult issues we face, because the waves can be so unpredictable. Thankfully we are not left helpless or without hope because Jesus is in the boat! He is our navigator and captain we just have to let Him have the wheel. He is working His plan and as we believe Him for greater things, we can rest assured that He will make a way and bring us safely to the other side of the storm. Resisting the "bullying" of the enemy is step one, then get into the Word of God and realize who your Father is! He has given us all we need and He will make a way as we stand strong, not in ourselves but in Him. The disciples were in a boat with Jesus and they didn't realize that all they had to do was call on Him to help. They waited until they thought they were going to die before they called out to Him. They maneuvered their boat as long as they could before they woke Him and even then, instead of asking for His help, they accused Jesus of not caring about them. May we realize that He is for us, and the lies of the enemy are just that, "Lies". Remain centered on Jesus in your storm, He is with you.

Luke 8:22-25

One day he got into a boat with his disciples, and he said to them, "Let us go across to the other side of the lake." So they set out, and as they sailed he fell asleep. And a windstorm came down on the lake, and they were filling with water and were in danger. And they went and woke him, saying, "Master, Master, we are perishing!" And he awoke and rebuked the wind and the raging waves, and they ceased, and there was a calm. He said to them, "Where is your faith?" And they were afraid, and they marveled, saying to one another, "Who then is this, that he commands even winds and water, and they obey him?"

Romans 8:31 ♥ Hebrews 11:6 ♥ James 4:7

When You Call

Most of us have a telephone of one kind or another.
Even for folks without a cell phone, they
still maintain a land-line phone.
Sometimes when we call people, they don't answer.
Other times, their line goes to voicemail requiring
us to leave a message or call back later.
It can be frustrating when you have an urgent matter and
you are unable to reach that person you are calling.
At times we view prayer as one of those calls we place and feel as
though no one is there on the other end. We feel as though God
is too busy or perhaps He can't hear us calling Him. But, dear
friend, He is always there and He always hears us when we call.
Most often, for us, when our children call, if
it's at all possible, we answer their call.
Honestly, I can't help but believe that it's the same with God.
When we call on Him for help, His attention
is immediately drawn to us.
As our heart remains centered on Him, even when we don't
immediately hear His answer, we can have confidence that God
is with us. We are His children and let us never succumb to the
enemy's lies about who God is and how much He loves His own.
Staying centered on Him when we call on His
name is the faith that touches His heart.

Jeremiah 33:3
**'Call to Me and I will answer you, and I will tell you
great and mighty things, which you do not know.'**
Psalm 18:6 ♥ Psalm 55:16 ♥ Psalm 116:2

Trustworthy

When you are faced with a difficulty, without a solution,
that's when we should relinquish our striving to the strength of
Jesus' covering. He holds us and when we are at our "wits end",
and overwhelmed, may we find our way to the "Rock" of Christ
Jesus for our security. This is the place where we can stand,
as we rest in the assurance that He is there with us.
He is trustworthy but we might not ever experience it if we
allow the circumstance to keep us from centering on Him.
He leads as we trust Him.
He helps as we seek Him.
He holds us as we run to Him.
He guards what we entrust to Him!
God is great and more trustworthy than we could ever imagine.
You can trust Him with what you are facing today.

Psalm 20:6-8
Now I know that the LORD saves His anointed; He
will answer him from His holy heaven
With the saving strength of His right hand.
Some boast in chariots and some in horses,
but we will boast in the name of the LORD, our God.
They have bowed down and fallen, But we have risen and stood upright.
Psalm 125:1 ♥ 2 Timothy 1:12 ♥ Job 36:26

Life

Without question we can all agree that life is a gift.
When life enters the world, it is nothing
short of a miraculous event.
From the emerging of a butterfly to the birth of a newborn baby.
Life takes our breath away as we reflect on how
wonderful and awesome our Creator God is.
Life never happens apart from God.
He is The Creator and life cannot be sustained without Him.
Living can sometimes be the focus of our life.
It seems to be human nature to pursue the best life
we possibly can, but do we realize that the best life we
can live is a life that is centered on our Creator?
Not just knowing that He is, but knowing WHO He is.
The God who, not only created you, but
the God loves you so deeply.
He is the God who formed you in your mother's womb.
He is the God who designed and fashioned
you to be the person you are.
When we choose life on our own, without seeking to
ask God what His plans are for us or what purpose He
had in mind when He created us, we will live a life that
might be good, but it will not be our best life.
Making a choice to pursue the life God
has intended for us means not
relying on ourselves but relying on God. It is focusing on His
plans and instead of our own. Imagine you building a new
invention and then someone else comes along to use it but they
do not ask you what it was made for or anything about it. That is
sometimes how we are with our own lives. We forget to ask God,
who created us what His purpose and design for our life is.

John 10:10
**"The thief comes only to steal and kill and destroy. I came
that they may have life and have it abundantly."**
Jeremiah 1:5 ♥ Genesis 1:27

On Purpose

Tattling is nothing new. I remember it well from my growing up years with three sisters and a brother. Time and time again, children run to parents to declare the intentions of their siblings. "He did it 'on purpose'", they insist. It is one thing for someone to do something hurtful by mistake or an accident, but when it's intentional or "on purpose", that's a whole other story. Even as we grow and gain understanding, intentional injustices are very hard to grasp and come to terms with.

On the other hand, there are so many wonderful people who intentionally do good Intentionality is to do something "on purpose". I can't help but see the wonder about God's love for us and how it is the most extreme display of intentionality that has the potential to dramatically impact every human life. Intentionality happened on the very first day of creation when God said, let there be light followed by the word to make man in His image, and then woman. The heart of God was never without love for humanity. Even when Adam and Eve disobeyed and His heart was undoubtedly crushed, on purpose, God made a way for us to have a relationship with Him. The plan of redemption cost Him dearly and the price was an injustice in every way but it was the only way. The plan required that Jesus would die a very cruel and undeserved death on the cross. Even though it was an injustice to crucified Jesus, it was absolutely "on purpose". It wasn't ever out of God's control; He was absolutely always in control. The plan of redemption was a plan of intention to make a way for man to have a relationship with Him through His son Jesus. God loved us on purpose with an unending and persistent love!

John 3:16
For God so loved the world, that he gave his only Son, that whoever believes in him should not perish but have eternal life.
Romans 5:8 ♥ Ephesians 5:2

Remembering

There are times when the Lord has done the
most precious things for me or shared a nugget
that spoke such a volume of His love to me.
At the time, I've not taken the time to write it down, knowing
that I would surely be able to recall its impact for years to come.
Sadly, before I knew it, the memory faded
and I had to work to remember it.
The Lord does things for us each day and as we
focus on them, little or big, we will find our hearts
are more and more centered on His Majesty.
It takes being intentional, and refusing to let
situations and circumstances take center stage. That
place belongs to One, and His name is Jesus.
Remember today what He has done for you,
even if it's only one thing that comes to mind.
Maybe it happened last week, last month, or last year.
Give Him praise and worship Him for His goodness.
Center your heart on remembering Jesus' faithfulness
and His faithfulness will become our center.

Proverbs 3:3
*Let love and faithfulness never leave you; bind them around
your neck, write them on the tablet of your heart.*
Hebrews 10:23 ♥ Deuteronomy 11:18

Friendship

One of the greatest blessings I have known has been
the friends that the Lord has brought into my life.
I couldn't even begin to count the precious people
that He has given me to call my friends.
Some people underestimate the worth of friendship
and think that they don't need friends.
The fellowship and friendship we have in each
other is no less than a gift from God.
He made us to need each other and to be
strengthened when we live life together.
Friendship brings a fullness to life that nothing else can.
True friendship cannot be purchased and is priceless.
As Christ brings us together, He brings us to Himself.
As our heartstrings are tied and knitted together,
we begin to understand the "knitted-ness" of where Jesus
wants to be at an even deeper level of our heart and life.
Centering on Him and that place of His friendship at a far more
significant depth, we will just begin to tap into His awesomeness.
The deep of Christ calls to the deep in us,
He has given His life that we might know the
greatest level of friendship in our life.
I believe this is what David, the Psalmist meant when He said, "He
calls me friend". Abraham experienced his relationship with God
at such an intimate depth, that it exceeded all other friendships.
May our relationship with God surpass any
other relationship in our life?
True friendship with God cannot be
purchased, it is priceless and eternal.

James 2:23
*And the scripture was fulfilled that says, "Abraham believed God, and it
was credited to him as righteousness," and he was called God's friend.*
John 15:13-15 ♥ Proverbs 27:9 ♥ Psalm 42:7

Sweetness

One of the things I miss about living in Africa is the mangoes.
Before I went to Mali, I had never even tasted a mango but since,
they are my all-time favorite fruit!
Describing them is difficult but they are so good.
They are sweet and bursting with amazing flavor.
Since coming back to the states,
I have tried countless times to find mangoes
here that taste like the mangoes in Mali.
Again and again, I have been disappointed because
there just aren't any and there probably won't be.
If I want to have those mangoes,
it will take me going back to Mali to do so.
When we taste the goodness of God,
we have tasted a sweetness that cannot be compared to any other.
Many taste of God's goodness, then for whatever reason,
they walk away from Him and find themselves in
places of attempting to find that same sweetness.
They try and try but searching, fueled by a false hope,
brings them disappointment again and again.
When we are purposefully centered on Him and
His majesty, we will know the greatest sweetness.
The wavering search will be subsided and
we can settle into His purposes.
The longer we are deceptively led away to find fulfillment
apart from Jesus, we will be disappointed.
He is the sweetest sweetness there is.
There is a blessing for us as we take refuge in His sweetness.

Psalm 34:8
***Oh, taste and see that the LORD is good! Blessed
is the man who takes refuge in him!***
Psalm 119:103 ♥ Psalm 63:3

In His Love

During the time we lived in Mali,
I had the joy of spending some time at an
orphanage for abandoned newborns.
These children's greatest need was to feel love and to be held,
so we held them and loved on them whenever we went.
Love is the theme of so many stories and causes.
Love is the greatest of all our needs. Feeling
loved and accepted by others gives us a sense of
confidence. The power of love is so significant.
It has been proven that babies without the touch
of love are severely impaired and often die.
The need for the love of others is great, but the
need for God's love is even greater.
Nothing we seek for or look to can fill that need in our heart.
We are severely impaired and empty when
God's love is not a part of our life.
Just as I held those tiny babies, we are held in His arms.
We are loved and cared for by Him always,
regardless of the love we know or feel from others.
The love that God has for us does not depend on the situation,
it is constant and sustaining.
His love has been communicated by the gift
of Jesus to us for our salvation.
We are not left abandoned because of the circumstances of our life,
we have been reconciled with God by the gift
of salvation through Jesus our Savior.
There is no greater love and no greater gift.

1 John 4:9-10

*In this the love of God was made manifest among us, that God sent
his only Son into the world, so that we might live through him.
In this is love, not that we have loved God but that he loved
us and sent his Son to be the propitiation for our sins.*

John 15:9 ♥ John 3:16-17 ♥ Jeremiah 31:3

His Covering

How are you today? Are you where you want to be with Jesus? If you are just going through the motions, wishing instead of believing for the changes you desire in your walk with Him, today can change all that. New beginnings begin with a new day and a call to your heart to make a conscious decision for a conscious change. When I was a young Christian, I remember hearing those older than I was, pleading the blood of Jesus over situations, family members for protection, and it became a practice in my own walk with the Lord. However, just recently as I was praying and pleading the blood of Jesus over my family, my children, my home, my marriage, my finances, my coworkers and job, over my nieces and nephews, etc., I sensed the sweet voice of the Holy Spirit gently say, "there's more to it than that, I am calling you to walk in the direction and obedience that you are pleading the blood of Jesus for." For instance, if I plead the blood of Jesus over my finances, rebuking the devourer, will I be obedient when Jesus calls me to spend differently. Am I willing or will I just keep spending without applyingthe principles of His word to that area of my life. It's the same with our marriage. Maybe you've been waiting for a change in your spouse, and as you plead the blood of Jesus over your marriage, perhaps He is calling you to bless your spouse in a way you never have before, etc. While we have the awesome privilege of pleading the blood of Jesus and knowing that His blood surpasses the onslaught of the enemy, may we carefully walk in the direction of what we are asking Jesus to do on our behalf. May we resist the temptation to pray our prayer and not walk in obedience to His word and His will. There is a powerful covering in the blood of Jesus for us to abide under.

Pleading the blood of Jesus is not the superstitious application of a magic formula of words. Rather, a spiritual dynamic is being applied. The power of the blood of Jesus Christ is greater than both the energy of our own humanity and that of our Adversary. The power that saves is also the power that releases, delivers, and neutralizes the enterprises of hell and the weaknesses of the flesh. The appropriation of the power of the Blood in tough situations is intended for every believer in Christ to know, to understand, and to employ.—Pastor Jack Hayford

1 Peter 1:18-19
For you know that it was not with perishable things such as silver or gold that you were redeemed from the empty way of life handed down to you from your forefathers, but with the precious blood of Christ, a lamb without blemish or defect.

Revelation 12:11 ♥ *Ephesians 2:13* ♥ *Hebrews 9:14*
Hebrews 10:19-22

Faithfulness

Basing our expectation of the faithfulness of God is not
dependent on how much or how little we have known faithfulness.
The faithfulness of God exceeds what we can see or feel.
He is not a man. He is always faithful.
The emotion of each day does not dictate the depth of
His commitment to us. He is constantly faithful!
When faced with unfaithfulness, from someone else or even
our own heart, trust is difficult to regain. There is, however,
One that is forever faithful and constant. His name is Jesus.
We may not have always been faithful,
and faithfulness may be an area where some are growing into.
Step by step, it takes walking in Christ and constantly centering our
faith on the process. As we grow in faithfulness to the heart of God,
our life will begin to mirror His faithfulness.
It occurs when we trust His ways before we trust our own.
"Faithfulness" means "steadfastness, firmness, fidelity.
Discouragement tends to take the wind out of our sail when
we face failure in the area of faithfulness to what our heart longs for.
That longing is driven by our soul's desire to be as close as we
possibly can to Jesus. But don't let that discouragement keep
you from pressing on and pressing into His faithfulness.

Lamentations 3:23-24
**Because of the Lord's great love we are not consumed, for his compassions
never fail. They are new every morning; great is your faithfulness.**
2 Timothy 2:13 ♥ *Psalm 119:89-90*
1 Thessalonians 5:23-24 ♥ *Romans 3:3*

Wholeheartedly His

The world around us and the culture we live in
can be described as primarily "self-involved".
If we are not careful, we can easily fall into the trap of
putting ourselves before our relationship with Christ.
It can happen innocently and subtly.
Tenacity is paramount to avoid the pitfalls of this lifestyle.
When we are primarily pursuing the things
that our flesh desires and wants,
we will not and cannot pursue the things of
the spirit with our whole heart.
Tension will take up residence because God will not
share you willingly with the desires of the flesh.
He will constantly and consistently pursue, not just your heart,
but your wholehearted devotion.
He calls us to Him first before anything or anyone else in our life.
There is treasure to be found in Jesus that we will never know
if we never pursue Him and let Him have our whole heart.
And at the same time, there is a treasure in you that He
placed there before the foundations of the world that will
never be realized without Him holding all of your heart.
It is His love and mercy that causes Him to
want to completely captivate us.

Matthew 22:37-38
*And he said to him, "You shall love the Lord your God with
all your heart and with all your soul and with all your
mind." This is the great and first commandment.*
Colossians 3:2 ♥ Matthew 6:21

To Him

In Psalm 136, again and again, we are called to center on "Him".
The writer calls us to give thanks "to Him", who...alone does great wonders
by wisdom and understanding made the heavens stretched out the earth
upon the waters made the great lights, the sun and the moon smote Egypt
and brought Israel out from captivity divided the Red Sea into parts and
made Israel to pass through shook off and overthrew Pharaoh led His people
through the wilderness smote great kings and gave their land as a heritage
earnestly remembered us in our low estate imprinted s on His heart rescued
us from our enemies gives food to all mankind Each of these verses ends
with…"for His steadfast love endures forever." Forever! His mercy doesn't end
with our mistakes or our situation. His loving-kindness leads us closer and
closer to His side and His covering.

Its truths were realized long before it was written and for centuries since.
May we realize today, that centering on His Majesty is our calling. He has
done great things! He rescues us from our enemies and leads us through the
wilderness that feels barren and endless. We may not see the end but the Lord
our God does and He is leading! We are written on the heart of our God!

If you were to write a Psalm today, what would it say?
What can we recall to our own hearts about all that the Lord has done for us?
Even if It's only a few verses, recall the goodness of God to you and your life.
"Give thanks to Him, for His steadfast love endures forever".

Psalm 136

Give thanks to the Lord, for he is good, for his steadfast love endures forever.
Give thanks to the God of gods, for his steadfast love endures forever.
Give thanks to the Lord of lords, for his steadfast love endures forever;
to him who alone does great wonders, for his steadfast love endures forever;
to him who by understanding made the heavens, for his steadfast love endures forever;
to him who spread out the earth above the waters, for his steadfast love endures forever;
to him who made the great lights, for his steadfast love endures forever;
the sun to rule over the day, for his steadfast love endures forever;
the moon and stars to rule over the night, for his steadfast love endures forever;
to him who struck down the firstborn of Egypt, for his steadfast love endures forever;
and brought Israel out from among them, for his steadfast love endures forever;
with a strong hand and an outstretched arm, for his steadfast love endures forever;
to him who divided the Red Sea in two, for his steadfast love endures forever;
and made Israel pass through the midst of it, for his steadfast love endures forever;
but overthrew[a] Pharaoh and his host in the Red Sea,
for his steadfast love endures forever;
to him who led his people through the wilderness, for his steadfast love endures forever;
to him who struck down great kings, for his steadfast love endures forever;
and killed mighty kings, for his steadfast love endures forever;
Sihon, king of the Amorites, for his steadfast love endures forever;
and Og, king of Bashan, for his steadfast love endures forever;
and gave their land as a heritage, for his steadfast love endures forever;
a heritage to Israel his servant, for his steadfast love endures forever.
It is he who remembered us in our low estate, for his steadfast love endures forever;
and rescued us from our foes, for his steadfast love endures forever;
he who gives food to all flesh, for his steadfast love endures forever.
Give thanks to the God of heaven, for his steadfast love endures forever.

In His Shadow

Have you ever seen a child play in their shadow? It's
very cute and it doesn't take them long to realize that
they cannot get away from it. In their shadow, their
image is much larger than their physical stature.
Being in the shadow of someone or something bears to it
a sense of being hidden. It's a place of protection and covering.
As we are hidden in the shadow of Christ, His image is
projected beyond ours. At the same time, when we walk
in the shadow of our Savior, we project His image.
The overshadowing of the identity of Jesus means,
He is seen in a greater measure in our life.
His shadow over us is a projection of the image of who He is.
He is greater than we can ever be, and we will only know the
greatness of His image as we walk in the shadow of His covering.
Walk, dance, abide, rejoice, and live in the shadow of the Almighty.
We can desire to walk with Him and never
truly take a step with the Lord.
We can talk about walking with Jesus, but our words may
only be words without action. To truly walk in His shadow
requires faith to trust that His presence is the covering we
need. Are we willing to let Him be seen instead of us?
Are we excited to let Him be our identity in humility
instead of allowing our pride to overshadow our life?
There are many things that may attempt
to overshadow our life but only in the shadow
of Almighty God will we find strength and security.
May His shadow be seen over us today!

Psalm 36:7
*How precious is Your lovingkindness, O God! And the
children of men take refuge in the shadow of Your wings.*
Psalm 91:1 ♥ Isaiah 51:16 ♥ Psalm 121:5
James 1:17

Clarity

Knowing the direction of the Lord for a season in our life
can so often feel like an enormous challenge. As the challenge
mounts, we can sometimes feel more and more overwhelmed
by it. In our spirit, we may have sensed Him leading us in a
certain direction but we are hesitant, not wanting to make a
mistake. Our desire is to be completely obedient to His leading.
Taking time to hear His voice is very important but worry, anxiety
and fear should not be our motivator. We can trust in His ways and
the provision of God who loves us and holds us in His tender care.
We are His!
Faith is walking in His leading.
He doesn't want us to be filled with frustration and confusion.
The Lord is with us and with each step we take, we can know that
He is faithful to continue to lead us. His righteous right hand
holds us as we yield to His plan and avoid over-rationalization.
May we not miss the clear and obvious by being overly
focused on the obscure and subjective? As we develop our
relationship with Jesus, He will lead us into His purposes.
Those things that attempt to take us from His presence can
wait, stay with Him a little longer in that quiet moment.
When we do, we will find His presence giving us more clarity.
So forgo the hours of worry.
Wait in His presence and then walk in His
clarity as you center on Jesus.

Jeremiah 33:3
*Call to me and I will answer you, and will tell you great
and hidden things that you have not known.*
John 6:63 ♥ John 10:27 ♥ Psalm 32:8
Isaiah 30:21

Steps

God desires to be more involved in our life than we can imagine.
He doesn't want us to be led away by the romance
of the flesh, things that entice us to indulgence,
but He longs for us to be enveloped in Him.
When a baby learns to walk, they begin
by taking steps and pretty soon,
when those steps are added together, they
become what we call, "walking".
Walking with someone is taking steps together, not walking
ahead of them or behind them. While it is true that the
Lord calls us to follow His ways and His leading,
He so desires for us to walk with Him. Sometimes we think
God is way ahead of us or far behind us, when all the while,
He is right beside us, waiting for us to step into His stride.
God never expected us to walk in life alone, without Him.
We can see so many instances in God's word of His involvement
in the lives of those He loved. Mary, the Children of Israel, Noah,
Abraham, John, Esther, Ruth and Naomi, David, Joseph, Paul,
the 3 Hebrew children and so many more. He was very involved
with their lives and those examples and instances have been
recorded for us to see. They are there for us to know that His ways
are much higher than ours and He has so much in store for us.
Taking steps toward Jesus and with Jesus is walking together.
Center your stride in His. Talk to the Lord throughout
your day, through the challenges and the joys, which way
you should take, what is His best. He longs to be a part of
more than just our difficulties and struggles but involved
in every way and every area of our daily life, moment by
moment. Listen to the counsel of the Holy Spirit and rest
in peaceful assurance, that you are walking with Him.

Psalm 16:11
You make known to me the path of life; in your presence there is
fullness of joy; at your right hand are pleasures forevermore.
Proverbs 8:20 ♥ Matthew 7:13

Remembering

Do you have a favorite memory?
I think we all probably have more than one!
Remembering takes us back to the places of God's faithfulness.
It strengthens our trust in Him and causes
us to realign our heart to His.
As we remember, it gives us cause to dream for things ahead and to
believe God to work again or to continue what He has begun in us.
Work is something that requires more than just one day.
Imagine the projects of our life.
Building a home, painting a masterpiece, writing a book, etc.
Time is a necessary requirement,
and the same is so as God works in and through our life.
Excitement fills our spirit and joy begins to bubble
up in our soul as we recall who He is and what
His work is determined to accomplish!
May we continue in the plan of God,
pursuing kingdom purposes for His glory and for our good!

Matthew 28:18-20

*And Jesus came and said to them, "All authority in
heaven and on earth has been given to me. Go therefore
and make disciples of all nations, baptizing them
in the name of the Father and of the Son and of the Holy Spirit,
teaching them to observe all that I have commanded you.
And behold, I am with you always, to the end of the age."*

Isaiah 43:1

*But now thus says the LORD, he who created you, O Jacob,
he who formed you, O Israel: "Fear not, for I have redeemed
you; I have called you by name, you are mine.*

The Indelible Love of God

Our choice in loving God is just that, our choice.
We can make a decision to love Him, serve Him and walk with Him
but the decision of our choice does not change His love for us.
Sometimes we think and act as if God's
love is based on us and it is not.
We can choose to love or walk away from this incredible, indelible
love. As we are centered on the immense love of God, it cannot
do less than compel our soul and draw us into His heart.
Escaping God's love is impossible because no matter
where we are or where we go, it is always there because
ultimately His love desires fellowship with each of us.
That fellowship and place of belonging is for today and for eternity.
His love for us is indelible, the decision of knowing it, is our choice.
We love Him, because He first loved us.
It is the Love of God our Heavenly Father, it is the Love
of Jesus, His Son who came to be our redemption and it
is the Love of the Holy Spirit who walks with us each day
to show us and demonstrate His love in our lives.
May the love we have for God become
more indelible than ever before.
We must choose to love Him with an
inerasable and deepening choice.
One that does not waver.

Ephesians 3:14-19

For this reason I bow my knees before the Father, from whom every family in heaven and on earth is named, that according to the riches of his glory he may grant you to be strengthened with power through his Spirit in your inner being, so that Christ may dwell in your hearts through faith—that you, being rooted and grounded in love, may have strength to comprehend with all the saints what is the breadth and length and height and depth, and to know the love of Christ that surpasses knowledge, that you may be filled with all the fullness of God.

Romans 8:35-39 ♥ Isaiah 49:16 ♥ Song of Solomon 8:6

Blessings!

Some may know an old song called, "Count Your Blessings".
The lyrics go like this...

"Count your blessings name them one by one,
count your blessings see what God has done,
count your blessings...name them one by one,
count your many blessings, see what God has done!"

Sometimes it's easier to see the bad and not the good.
It's interesting that people even seem to enjoy sharing bad news
more han good news. Have you ever noticed how contagious
the two are? Hang out with a negative person for long enough
and it won't be long until you become negative too.
We can't, of course, stick our heads in the
sand to the difficulties of life,
but the Word of God calls us to give thanks in everything.
This is the day the Lord has made, let us rejoice and be glad in it!
Everyday has troubles of its own, but the Lord, He is faithful!
May we be the ones who infect others by our gratitude to God?
He is wonderful! He is faithful! We have so much to be thankful for.
It takes energy and ambition to be centered on our blessings.
But I believe there's a reason that the Lord calls us to do so.
Hidden in gratitude is contentment, and hidden in
thankfulness, generosity flourishes from our life.
It may take retraining our words and changing our
mindset but if we will take the time to look, we will see
how full of blessings our life truly is. May we live and
glorify God from the fullness of our blessings!

Lamentations 3:22-23
The steadfast love of the Lord never ceases;
his mercies never come to an end;
they are new every morning; great is your faithfulness.
Isaiah 12:4-5 ♥ *Colossians 3:15-17*

Mercy

I once heard someone say that the reason God gives
us new mercies each morning is because He knew that
we would need new mercy for every new day.
I think that is absolutely true! However, may we also realize
that the mercy of God carries His faithfulness? For the
times when we might feel as though we have used
up the new mercy that was extended to us, for the day at hand.
Defeat and frustration attempt to plague us, to the point
of us feeling as though we'll have to wait until we have access to
tomorrow's portion of mercy to be right with God again.
We sometimes perceive that enduring the rest of the
day in defeat is somehow our punishment for not
measuring up and hitting the mark as we should.
It's probably happened to all of us more times than we care to admit.
While it is true that God's mercies are new every morning,
the remainder of the verse says, "GREAT is His faithfulness!"
We don't have to wait until tomorrow to
know the newness of His mercy,
in fact we don't have to even wait a moment!
The Lord's mercies flow out of His great love for us and
He is continually near to those who call on His name.
May we not attempt to limit His God mercy based on our humanity
or allow the lies of the enemy to isolate us from them.

Lamentations 3:22-23
The steadfast love of the Lord never ceases;
his mercies never come to an end;
they are new every morning;
great is your faithfulness.
Psalm 86:5 ♥ Ephesians 2:4 ♥ Hebrews 4:16
1 Peter 1:3

Light

In and of itself, darkness has the potential of causing fear
in the majority of people. Even when nothing else is wrong,
there is something about the dark that can be troubling to us.
Living in darkness can change a person's perception and
it is not until the darkness is overcome by light that we can
clearly see where we are and what is happening around us.
After I was married and had moved from the home where I
spent much of my growing up years, we went back for a visit
with my parents. It was a home I was very familiar with but
one night I got up for a drink of water. On my way back to go
to sleep, I walked down a long hall and it was very dark.
Before reaching the room where I was staying,
there would be a bend in the hallway.
In the darkness, I turned too soon and you guessed
it, I walked right into the wall, full stride! In the
morning, I had a black eye as a reminder.
The light of Christ in us is what dispels so
much of the darkness around us.
Allowing His light to shine in and through
us, is like turning on a light switch.
When light overtakes darkness that has been overwhelming,
peace is felt and a calmness can prevail. What if we have the
love and light of Jesus in us but never let it shine? It would
be like coming into a dark room and leaving the light off.
Let your light so shine before men, that they may see your good
works and glorify God! Jesus said we are the light of the world.
May His light in us not be covered by situations and circumstances
that occur each day. But let them be the channel for His light
to shine! They are where the light of Christ is most needed.
In the everyday, in the moments of life.
The more we center our life on the light of Christ,
the more He will shine in and through us.

Proverbs 4:18
But the path of the righteous is like the light of dawn,
which shines brighter and brighter until full day.
Matthew 5:14 ♥ Matthew 5:16 ♥ Ephesians 5:8

Believing

To believe something simply means to have
confidence in the truth, the existence, or the reliability
of something, without any visible proof.
We will only act purposefully if we truly believe in something.
Imagine the heart of God who dared us to simply
believe Him for the answers to our life and for
miracles that He could do on our behalf.
We don't have to work anything out, that's His job.
We don't have to do the miracles, because that's His part.
God has only required that we believe that He
will do what He promised in His word.
His word is the basis for our believing faith and
when we do it, that is an act of our faith.
It is ingredient to make God's plan of prayer work.
God ventured to believe that men would simply believe Him.
Believe that He is good. Believe that He
is able to keep His word to us.
We did not initiate such a plan, God did this and
we need only to simply believe Him!
Is there something you've half-heartedly entrusted to God?
Is there something you're still trying to figure out or control
for a certain outcome? Trust Him today and release your
plan to His miracle working power with anticipation.
Lay your despair, no matter how small, down
today and be assured that God is able!

*The prayer power has never been tried to its full capacity…if we want
to see mighty wonders of divine power and grace wrought in the place
of weakness, failure and disappointment, let us answer God's standing
challenge, "Call unto me, and I will answer thee, and show thee great
and might things which thou knowest not." ~ J. Hudson Taylor*

Matthew 7:7
**Ask, and it will be given to you seek, and you will
find; knock, and it will be opened to you.**
*Mark 11:23-24 ♥ 2 Corinthians 9:8 ♥ Philippians 4:19
Philippians 4:7*

Steadfastness

Some people spend their lives waiting for steadfastness
to prevail in their life. It can seem like an elusive
pursuit and yet we cannot help but pursue it.
What can keep us from steadfastness?
Feelings and distractions have the capacity and great potential
to cause a wandering that brings us just close enough to God,
but yet leave us "feeling" at arms' length away from Him.
One dominating thought that prevents a steadfast heart is an
ongoing perceived need, that can seem real but in reality it is just
like a mirage. An example is the person who spends their life,
trying to "find themselves", when all the while our foundness
can only be in Christ Jesus. However, it can truly seem like a
mirage in a desert, unless we decide to rest confidently, without
fear upon God and His word and know that we are only whole
in Him. It is the solidity for our feet to walk upon, but feelings
will continually take us wherever the whim of the day directs.
Christ Jesus never intended for us to live in such a state of turmoil.
He is the Prince of Peace for our life! He is
the Rock on which we can stand!
He is the Light for our path!
We can confidently rest in Him and our
heart can know steadfastness.
We were created to live in steadfastness but
that steadfastness is not found,
and cannot be known apart from Christ because it is
only when we are found, completely surrendered to His
ways and not our own that we will find we can rest.
When we understand it, we can decide and say to our heart, as the
Psalmist said, "my heart is steadfast". In other words, "my heart is
confident in God, my heart trusts in Him alone, not in my feelings.
It's essential for us and as we set our heart to be centered on the
steadfastness of Christ, we will find our soul comforted in Him.

1 Corinthians 15:58
Therefore, my beloved brothers, be steadfast, immovable,
always abounding in the work of the Lord,
knowing that in the Lord your labor is not in vain.
Psalm 108:1 ♥ Psalm 57:7 ♥ Psalm 112:7

Thirst

Being thirsty is a natural part of life. We even see that Jesus had times of being thirsty. We get to peek at Jesus' life as His word opens a curtain when He comes for a drink of water. He was so thirsty that He takes His disciples through a "part of town" that was viewed as unthinkable. But He goes and while He was there He meets a woman, in the middle of the day. She comes at this time because it is a time of day when others do not come. She was a woman of shame. She came for water but what she really needed was Jesus. As He approaches the well, He asks her for water for Himself. The Bible never says that He ever got the drink He was thirsty for, instead He begins to share with this woman about the water that would satisfy her deeper need. The well of her souls' troubles and despair was deep, but water from the well of Jesus could minister to that deep place in her. He forgoes His physical need to minister to her greater spiritual need. We see the same thing happen when David, in battle says to his men, "I long for a drink, oh if only someone could break through the battle and get to the well of Bethlehem". Someone does go and brings him the water he asks for, and instead of drinking it, he pours out as an offering before the Lord. Isn't that a crazy thought, why would David, being so thirsty, ask for a drink and then not drink it? What would cause him to pour it out and forgo satisfying the physical need that was screaming within him? Perhaps it was the same for David as it was for the Samaritan woman. An anguish and need that they each had, was deeper than the physical. The well of Bethlehem! Jesus! Our need for Jesus is deeper than any physical needs that are felt. Unfortunately for us, our physical needs often dictate and dominate our life and focus. We give credence to their demands instead of centering our hearts on the well of Bethlehem. The gift of the well of Bethlehem and the water that only Jesus can give us, remains adequate to quench every thirst within each of us.

1 Chronicles 11:17-18

And David longed, and said, Oh that one would give me drink of the water of the well of Bethlehem, that is at the gate! And the three brake through the host of the Philistines, and drew water out of the well of Bethlehem, that was by the gate, and took it, and brought it to David: but David would not drink of it, but poured it out to the LORD.

Psalm 42:1 ♥ Psalm 63:1 ♥ John 4:13-15

In His Strength

Strengths and weaknesses are a part of our culture.
In interview situations or application processes, we are
often asked to list our strengths and/or weaknesses.
When we answer, we attempt to downplay our weaknesses
and highlight the strengths that are our gifts and talents.
Fear is associated with exposing our weaknesses.
Strength is regularly equated with how strong a person is.
If we are weak in a certain area or way, we naturally try to
compensate for those weaknesses to become stronger.
While we all have weaknesses and God has given us each strengths,
we sometimes displace the Lord's influence for the people He has
created us to be. We are fearfully and wonderfully made, designed
marvelously by His heart! May we not live life in a defeated state
because our weaknesses seem to meet us coming and going!
As we look to Jesus for the power of His grace and
purpose for our life, we will find renewed strength.
While our culture has a certain rhetoric for what strengths
and weaknesses mean, God's economy is far different.
Centering on His strength brings us to the place where
Paul's heart called the believers at Ephesus, to be strong
in the Lord and empowered by His might. The word of
God tells us that when we are weak, He is strong on our
behalf. Centering on His strength and not our own will
lead us out of turmoil and into His grace and peace.

Ephesians 6:10
Finally, be strong in the Lord and in the strength of his might.
Nehemiah 8:10 ♥ Joel 2:23 ♥ Psalm 59:17

Personal Godliness

The pursuit of personal godliness can sometimes be thought
of as an option. The more accurate and loving call from our
Heavenly Father is a mandate that the enemy would love for
us to dismiss for another day or season. What might cause
us to shrink back from such a mandate? If we only knew the
implications, if we could only grasp the Father's purpose, perhaps
we would be more inclined to entertain His heart's request for us.
We are those, whom He created and formed with His own hands.
We are those, who He gave all to have a relationship with us.
We are those whom the quest of His love pursues.
We are the object of His immeasurable affection.
So why personal godliness? It is His best
for us, it is His best for our good.
Living a life that pleases God is not about working to earn salvation,
we know that is an impossibility. But it is an obedience
of gratitude and worship that leads to an unparalleled
relationship with our Savior. The sweetest presence we will
ever know are the quiet moments we share with Him.
Yielding to the personal discipline of pursuing godliness
will lead us to a greater love that floods us, not to legalism,
but to centering all that we are on His Majesty.

*Prayer—secret, fervent, believing prayer—lies at the
root of all personal godliness.* ~Williams Carey

Psalm 1:1-3

**Blessed is the man who walks not in the counsel of the wicked, nor
stands in the way of sinners, nor sits in the seat of scoffers; but his delight
is in the law of the Lord, and on his law he meditates day and night.
He is like a tree planted by streams of water that yields its fruit in its
season, and its leaf does not wither. In all that he does, he prospers.**

1 Timothy 4:8 ♥ Micah 6:8 ♥ 1 Timothy 6:6

Innermost Place

Abundance in Christ is found as we allow Him into the
innermost place of our hearts and lives. Sometimes we are
pretty focused on everything outward and perceive its influence
in our life more than the secret place that the Lord God
alone occupies within us. It is not out of the outward, but it is
of the heart where the Spirit of God, in us, will flow out of.
If we attempt to live in abundance that flows from the external
parts of our lives, we will find an ongoing deficit. We have things
just a little turned around, because the Lord has designed our
hearts to flourish when His is in the innermost place of who we are.
It is out of Him that abundant life is known. Sadly, though,
the external often bombards our attention. It demands to be
tended. As a result, we can sometimes fail to see the value and
importance that is paramount. It is that secret place and our
innermost being where Christ continually desires to tend in us.
It is out of our innermost being that Jesus said,
rivers of living waters would flow. Those rivers of living water
are of the very water, He offered the broken woman at the well.
A devastated life changed and transformed. He is still offering
to give us that water, not only that we would drink of it, but that
it would flow out of us into a devastated world around us.
It will never flow out of the external of our life, only
from the deepest influence of Christ in us. We must
center the innermost place of our heart on Jesus!

Matthew 7:38
**Whoever believes in me, as the Scripture has said, 'Out
of his heart will flow rivers of living water.'**

Psalm 91:1
**He who dwells in the shelter of the Most High will
abide in the shadow of the Almighty.**

Compassion

Compassion is costly. When we see someone in need
and compassion begins to well up in our heart, we can be
overwhelmed by it. We think immediately about our resources
in terms of time, finances and personal responsibility.
Within a moment, we estimate a determined cost. Do
we have anything to give, anything to spare?
That momentary calculation determines our
response to the compassion in our heart.
But, what if, when we experience compassion,
we stop and look to Jesus.
What resources does He have, is He limited by time?
Is He able to do miracles through us? What has our prayer been?
Have we been asking Him to use us and to lead us? Yes!
May fear not grip us when compassion stirs us, but
may faith in the resources of Jesus overwhelm us to the
point of being compelled with His compassion.
Compassion moved Jesus when He walked the earth and it still
moves Him today. His compassion is as needed now as it was then.
Compassion can be given and lived out in so many ways to touch
people who are in need. Living out compassion is beautiful, it is
comforting, and it brings a sense of worth to us and to others.
Centering on His compassion to be lived out through us
will bring great purpose to our life. It takes courage and
faith, but the reward of being His vessel of compassion
carries a great reward and fulfilling love.

Matthew 9:36-38

*When he saw the crowds, he had compassion for them,
because they were harassed and helpless, like sheep
without a shepherd. Then he said to his disciples,
"The harvest is plentiful, but the laborers are few; therefore pray
earnestly o the Lord of the harvest to send out laborers into his harvest."*

Mark 8:2 ♥ Matthew 9:12-13

For the Joy

As a child, and even as an adult, there is something special about knowing we have brought pleasure to our parents. For me and many others, we remember wanting our dad to be proud of us. Bringing joy to our father is an unspoken, yet intense desire. Some spend their whole lives trying to attain the joy of pleasing their earthly father. We can imagine the joy of His heart and how Jesus must have felt when God, the Father opened heaven and announced, "This is my beloved Son, in whom I am well pleased." Joy is a treasure without price and without finding the priceless treasure of Christ, the quest for it is futile. Christ, Himself, showed us the key to knowing true joy and it is only found in doing the will of our Father in heaven and living closely with Him. It is dependence and assuring trust in His capacity to be all that we need. This is the place where Jesus lived. He knew what true joy was and that it was only found in fellowship and His relationship with the Father. Even though Jesus endured so many hardships and even dying on the cross, that agony did not compare to the joy He knew He would experience by His obedience to the Father. True and sustaining joy is for each of us and though we are not Jesus, He is the example of resisting the temptation of being overly swayed by distractions and urgency. The longing joy of every heart is found in the contentment that only Christ brings when we are joined by Him to the Father. It's ongoing and full of precious interaction. It's more than just one heartfelt prayer when we receive the gift of our salvation. Joy is a super-natural result of walking and centering on Jesus and doing the will of our Heavenly Father. It's nothing we will ever truly understand without surrendering and living it out.

Romans 15:13
May the God of hope fill you with all joy and peace as you trust in him, so that you may overflow with hope by the power of the Holy Spirit.
2 Corinthians 8:2 ♥ Isaiah 61:10 ♥ Romans 12:1-2
Psalm 27:6 ♥ Philemon 1:7 ♥ Isaiah 9:3

Centered By Majesty

Did you see the little word change?
What a difference such a little change can make...
today, "by" in place of "on".
How does that change us?
To be centered by Majesty not just on Majesty?
Centered by Christ and His influence almost takes
us to another level in our trust and faith.
Even Christians can find themselves wandering from time to time,
in search of God's wisdom and direction for certain seasons.
Our dependence in being anchored must be established
not only on Him but by Him. Attempting to steer our lives
to be on track must be governed by the Holy Spirit.
Stopping to surrender to Him.
Stopping to ask for His help.
Stopping to lean in and learn by His ways.
Being centered by Majesty allows Him to steer
and guide our life and decisions.

Isaiah 58:11
*Now to him who is able to do far more abundantly than
all that we ask or think, according to the power at work
within us, to him be glory in the church and in Christ Jesus
throughout all generations, forever and ever. Amen.*

Psalm 16:11
*You will make known to me the path of life;
In Your presence is fullness of joy;
In Your right hand there are pleasures forever.*

Psalm 32:8
*I will instruct you and teach you in the way which you should go;
I will counsel you with My eye upon you.*

Yearnings

Have you ever had to take a detour in a certain direction because there was a road block of one kind or another? That yellow caution tape warning that it would be dangerous to proceed, even though doing so might be the very thing we so long for? Feelings are definitely important but can be a fury to manage if left to their whims! They want and they yearn, don't they? The wrestling of our yearnings internally, between our flesh and spirit, can be easy one day and almost impossible the next, so it seems or feels. But God does not change and our feelings should not be so entertained to the point that they take on a life of their own, or be allowed to play the leading role in our lives. Our feelings matter to God and He truly cares about the issues of our lives, but as we look at what truth is, then suddenly what we find ourselves standing on, turns from shifting sand to a concrete foundation. May we change our centeredness, and view the feelings of our life through the truth of His word. That's where we can stand and be effective, that's where we can be confident! As long as we attempt to stand on shifting sand, we will be consumed with our own life, just trying to stand without falling down.

If God has been calling us out of something or if He has placed caution tape around a certain situation and given us a detour, then why, oh why do we yet long to go there anyway? Take the way out!

There are times that we have asked God to bring closure to something and yet when He does, we let our feelings bring it back to life and we find that the yearning returns us to wrestling. We know very well that our best is in His hands and not our own. Our hands must be held in His hands and our feet must be directed with the Light of His word. Center your yearnings on Christ alone.

John 16:13

"But when He, the Spirit of truth, comes, He will guide you into all the truth; for He will not speak on His own initiative, but whatever He hears, He will speak; and He will disclose to you what is to come.

Galatians 5:26 ♥ Romans 8:26-27 ♥ Isaiah 59:21

Uncontainable

When we fill a container, there is a certain comfort in knowing it is full. We can rest just knowing that we are not in danger of running out. Containers hold things. Some containers are small, some are large and some are quite extended as in "containment fields". To contain something carries the understanding that it can be held within something else. Something contained, would be to say that it is limited. Of course, we know that our God cannot be contained in any container. But do we recognize that He chooses to allow us to be vessels that hold Him? It's up to us, just how full we are for there is no lack of Him. The Lord does not withhold Himself in any way. Some people live just above empty, not realizing they can live in fullness. Imagine living life, never eating an entire meal, but instead just having a bite to eat here and there. That person never knows what fullness is and the same is true spiritually. If we've never been full then we cannot understand or realize the joy of His fullness. Or perhaps we've lived being contained by so many other things, and we've only allowed God to be a portion of our fullness. We can easily be filled with so many things, but we will never know true fullness until we are empty of those things and He fills us from the inside out. God is not contained in us, but we are contained in Him because He is uncontainable. His word tells us that the whole earth is full of His glory. That's not past tense, but it is now and always full. The glory of God does not run out or decrease with time but He is continually full. There is no containing the glory of God. It is all around us and there is more than enough for each one of us. One of my favorite verses in the Bible is Ephesians 6:10, in the amplified version, which says, "In conclusion, be strong in the Lord [draw your strength from Him and be empowered through your union with Him] and in the power of His [boundless] might." His strength and grace, His love and mercy are full. The enemy doesn't want us to realize the boundlessness of our God. He is ever abounding in His sufficiency to us. Let us be centered on His uncontainable glory and goodness.

Isaiah 6:3
And one called to another and said: "Holy, holy, holy is the LORD of hosts; the whole earth is full of his glory!"
Psalm 72:19 ♥ Habakkuk 2:14 ♥ Romans 15:13
Psalm 16:11

All About Him

In a narcissistic culture that imposes that life is or should be all about us, we can easily be swayed into living within this mindset. We can focus life on ourselves or we can consciously decide to turn our hearts toward the One who gave us life. A life limited to our wants, our desires, and our pursuits will be a life that becomes stagnant and unfulfilling. However, being "all about Him" centered changes everything. It changes what we pursue and the life we live has greater impact and greater purpose. As we make Jesus our center, we welcome Him in. The misconception may be that Jesus will just come in and find His place in our hearts and life. We assume that it will just happen and life will automatically be all about Him. Fear can impair the "all" portion of our life being about Jesus, and we can be reluctant to truly surrender ourselves completely. Removing "self" from the throne of our heart and life is the beginning of letting our life be all about Him. We find in doing so, we become all about Him and His place in us is sweeter and more precious. It takes us from reluctant surrender to willfully abandoning all that we are for all that He is. When we see self-serving and self-influenced lives it is usually not a pretty sight, but a life consumed by Jesus is a beautiful life that reflects a love and grace that cannot flow out by any other means. We are mistaken if we ever think that life that is "all about Him" will be the demise of who we are and what a life can be. My friends, the opposite is quite true. Allowing Him prominence in our life gives Him the freedom to move more mightily in us than ever before!

2 Corinthians 12:9
But he said to me, "My grace is sufficient for you,
for my power is made perfect in weakness."
Therefore I will boast all the more gladly of my weaknesses,
so that the power of Christ may rest upon me.
John 3:30 ♥ Matthew 16:24 ♥ 1 Corinthians 2:6-12

Our Source

The purest form of anything is found nearest its source.
The more removed from the source, the greater the
chances are of finding a more and more diluted form.
When determining the root of a matter or situation, we
can spin our wheels or follow endless rabbit trails until
we realize that those origins are getting us nowhere.
This futility will only lead us to frustration and
will be repeated until we realize that the source
of all truth is Christ Jesus, our Savior.
He is the Way, the Truth and the Life...no one can come
to the Father except through and by Him. So often in our
sophisticated society, we put our human intellect above truth,
above Jesus. He is Our Source. In Him all truth is found and
resonates because it is who He is, not just what He represents.
When we seek peace, direction and comfort, we don't have to
wander around lost, because the He is the source of all we need.
He is our Peace, He is our Provider, and He is our Rescuer. Why
look elsewhere? Doing so only prolongs the agony of turmoil
that gleefully captivates our mind and pervades our thoughts.
Centering on our source, Christ Jesus, brings us to
the most undiluted and pure truth that can be found.
May we refuse to settle for anything less!

Isaiah 40:28-31

*Have you not known? Have you not heard? The everlasting God,
The LORD, the Creator of the ends of the earth, doesn't faint,
neither is weary; there is no searching of his understanding. He
gives power to the faint; and to him who has no might he increases
strength. Even the youths shall faint and be weary, and the young
men shall utterly fall: but those who wait for The LORD shall
renew their strength; they shall mount up with wings as eagles;
they shall run, and not be weary; they shall walk, and not faint.*

John 14:6 ♥ Psalms 119:57a ♥ 1 John 4:4
Philippians 4:8

Led In Righteousness

Christ stands ready to lead us moment by moment and step
by step, each and every day, without fail. Our part is the work
of being mindful of Him and His intentions in our life.
We can be sure that there is a leading that is paramount
to His labor in us. It is that we would grow in the ways of
Christ and be filled more and more with His the character.
Leading involves following from one place to another, from
somewhere to somewhere else! We cannot stay where we've
always been and be led in all righteousness. David prayed the
prayer of being led because he knew full well the dangers that
prowled for him if he was not being led by the Spirit of God.
Being "led" by the Lord in any area can seem ambiguous to
us but picture this thought. My great aunt will be 99 years
old this week, she is completely blind and has been so for
some time. For her to maneuver, she needs someone to lead
her. Her eyes cannot help her. She must rely on the eyes of
someone else. She is not helpless and can maneuver in some
astounding ways but often miscalculates distances and objects.
Being led in God's righteousness is relying
on His eyes and not our own.
It is dependence on His vision and plan.
May we be led in righteousness, to more of Him and out of the
cumbersomeness that has cluttered His place in our heart.

Psalm 5:8
**Lead me, O LORD, in your righteousness because of
my enemies; make your way straight before me.**
Proverbs 8:20 ♥ John 16:13

Transition

Every day, we are constantly moving from one thing to the next. There are transitions that we maneuver through. Getting up each morning, transitioning from sleep to waking up and beginning a new day. Getting to work and beginning our day, we finish and go home and transition from work to what will follow. Transitioning is part of life. Some transitions are less noticeable than others. Even the transitions mentioned above may not even appear to be transitions but they are. Transitioning can be frightening and the Lord knew that, depending on how drastic the transition is.

Moving from one place to another…transition.

Moving from school to the workplace…transition.

Singleness to marriage…transition.

Becoming a parent, or homeowner…transition.

Working to retirement…transition.

The empty nest…transition.

Throughout God's word, He conveys his nearness to us for each and every transition we will face. There won't be anyplace or anything we will face, that the Lord, our God will not be there with us to help us. Nonetheless, some transitions bring us to a crisis and in those moments we must actively look to God as our help. He is ever present. He knows full well the transitions of our days and of our lives. Transitions can catch us by surprise but they never catch God by surprise. Often the transitions that we face are the channels He has purposed so that we will become more established and dependent upon Him. He is drawing us nearer, He lovingly calls us closer. The Lord holds us in the palm of His hand!

Ephesians 3:17-19

So that Christ may dwell in your hearts through faith—that you, being rooted and grounded in love, may have strength to comprehend with all the saints what is the breadth and length and height and depth, and to know the love of Christ that surpasses knowledge, that you may be filled with all the fullness of God.

Joshua 1:9 ♥ Ecclesiastes 7:8-11 ♥ Philippians 4:6-7

Embracing Discipline

The word "discipline" can carry a negative implication because
it is generally associated to a time of failure that required some
form of punishment. But discipline is also a defining of the
boundaries that can often become out of balance in our life.
Centering on Jesus begins with acknowledging
our need for the discipline of walking as a disciple
which contains the same meaning.
The prayer of our heart that yields to His discipline in our life
carries with it an invitation. It is an invitation for Jesus to,
in a way, restructure us spiritually.
Voluntarily allow Him in to cut out the
indulgences in many areas of our life.
It is like cropping a picture that contains too much background.
Can we honestly look at our life as a photograph?
Who is that in the background? Isn't He supposed to be out front?
Yes! But it takes discipline.
When we take away the background, suddenly
the image is bigger and clearer.
The image of Christ then fits more
appropriately in the frame of our life.
May we embrace and center our heart on His discipline and
carefully look at the areas that we have indulgenced in.

Colossians 2:6-8

*Therefore, as you received Christ Jesus the Lord, so walk in him, rooted
and built up in him and established in the faith, just as you were taught,
abounding in thanksgiving. See to it that no one takes you captive by
philosophy and empty deceit, according to human tradition, according
to the elemental spirits of the world, and not according to Christ.*

Matthew 6:33 ♥ Romans 12:2 ♥ John 3:30

Value

As children grow, their abilities change, and
their creativity advances. Young works of art that
we display on the family refrigerator or
our office cubicle, are not always the masterpiece that could
be displayed in a great museum. As a parent, those works of art
are far more valuable to us than they may be to someone else.
What is of value to us and what holds value to God? There
is often a pretty big difference between what He views as
valuable and what we see as invaluable. When He begins to
show us things of value in the gifts we have been given, we can
easily tend to dismiss them as unimportant. We may see the
developed gifts of someone else and compare what we have
to offer with what others are already doing. Discouragement
looms like a dark cloud and we dismiss the prompting of the
Holy Spirit's stirring. But when we yield to Him and place our
gifts in His hands, we will see the miraculous take place.
You see, our gifts will never be significant until we see the
significance of their origin. Born in us from the heart of God!
Will we take them and say, "not my will, but Yours be done"?
Giving them to the Lord will prove our reliance on Him.
He makes it a masterpiece, but we first have to allow Him control.
He takes what we deem as small and says, "I can do great things
with that!" And that's when we get to stand back and watch
Him be God! No one glories more in those moments that the
relinquisher of the gift because they know full well every limitation
and challenge, every weakness and deficiency. We hold things
that we view are worthless but when we put them in God's hands,
they become great, not because of us but because of Who we give
them to. Our goal is to value Him as the center of our gifts,
and as we do, we might just be surprised what He does with them.
What is He challenging you to put in His hands today?

John 6:9
*"There is a lad here who has five barley loaves and two
fish, but what are these for so many people?"*
*1 Corinthians 1:27-29 ♥ Zechariah 4:10 ♥ Isaiah 54:2-3
Luke 11:13 ♥ 1 Samuel 17:40*

Great Love

Today is a day that love is celebrated and it reminds me of a quote I once found in a church some years ago that read, "You give without loving, but you cannot love without giving." It is quite true that ultimate love is a love that demands an expression of more than just words. We find that God's love for us and love for all humanity was not given in only words but it was given by a dramatic expression. John 3:16 is the basis for an expression we find difficult to truly understand. "God so loved the world, that He gave His only begotten son, that whosoever believes on Him would not perish but have everlasting life". The love of God is a love that draws us because of the measure of its immeasurable giving to us. Its monumental exploits, that God intends, to profound our understanding are given with a deeper purpose than our human eyes can behold or our hearts can understand. It came to capture us and lead us to a place of safety and protection. It came to silence the accusations of our enemy and from the regrets of our past. Centering on God's great love takes our focus off of external to the supremacy of what only God is able to be in our life. True and abounding love! A love that is greater than our sin, lavished upon us for the pure joy of the Father in bringing us to redemption through Christ. God wanted to make a way for us and Jesus is the only adequate probability. All others fail miserably at bringing peace and redemption. Our Father paid in full when He gave Jesus to be our Savior. Through His love, He makes us His own. There is no greater love known to man than the love of God. God is love and in Him is the source of true love and all love is known best. Outside of God, love is diluted because He is the ultimate origin.

C.H. Spurgeon wrote it this way: "Behold it, wonder at it and never cease to admire it! Is it not one of the greatest marvels that even God, Himself, has ever worked that we should be called the sons of God?"

Galatians 2:20

I have been crucified with Christ. It is no longer I who live, but Christ who lives in me. And the life I now live in the flesh I live by faith in the Son of God. who loved me and gave himself for me.

John 3:20 ♥ Romans 5:8 ♥ Ephesians 2:4-5

Restorer

When items such as cars, trucks, dressers, armoires, pianos, etc. get old they can either be discarded or restored. To restore something means to "return it to its original state". Aren't you glad that the Lord never discards us? Daily He acknowledges His great love for each of us. No matter the circumstance, God is faithful and He rescues us when we are overwhelmed.

I recently heard a minister preaching on the 23rd Psalm. It was an amusing moment as the orator questioned the Psalmist's words in verse 4, "Yeah", though I walk through the valley of the shadow of death." He goes on to question, who, when walking through the valley of the shadow of death says, "yeah"?

His question made me smile as I realized how many times I have read that passage, and never considered that word in the context as he had during his message. It led me to ponder what was stated just above, that the Lord is our Shepherd, gives us cause to want for nothing. He leads us beside still waters and restores our soul.

Walking through difficulty is not something we want to embrace or welcome. The opposite is usually true, we more generally resist such seasons. Just before verse 4, we find a place of restoration for our soul in God's presence.

The assurance of restoration by the presence and peace of God, in spite of what we will go through, is a comfort that the Lord wants us to realize.

Not just after such episodes but before we face them. We are preserved for His glory if we will look to Him for grace and strength.

We have assurance that He will restore the devastation with the gifts of what only His grace can bring.

Psalm 23:1-4

The Lord is my shepherd; I shall not want. He makes me to lie down in green pastures; He leads me beside the still waters. He restores my soul; He leads me in the paths of righteousness for His name's sake. Yea, though I walk through the valley of the shadow of death, I will fear no evil; For You are with me; Your rod and Your staff, they comfort me.

Isaiah 40:29 ♥ Isaiah 1:18 ♥ 2 Corinthians 5:17

Might

At one time or another, all of us have attempted to pick
up something that was far too heavy for us alone.
Maybe we were able to pick it up but carrying it was another
story altogether. With all our might, we struggle and strain,
with a deep determination to do it. Sometimes we succeed
but other times, we must find some help. Some of us are
a bit more stubborn than others and are so reluctant to
ask for the help we need for whatever we are trying to
do. What a relief it is when help comes to our aid.
Often we are handling life and the weights of the world on our own,
thinking that we don't need God to help us at all.
We think, "He's too busy, I'm fine". But His might
and strength are for you today. The longer we
carry life on our own, the heavier it gets,
until suddenly we are overwhelmed and find that taking one
more step is almost too much for us.
The Lord, our God is a very present help in times of trouble,
and His might calls us to cast our cares on
Him because He cares for us.
We aren't imposing on God when we ask Him to carry our burdens,
it is His pleasure to do so. May we not forget who our God is!
He spoke the universe into being and there is no one above Him.
He is great and as close as the whispered prayer of your heart.

Isaiah 40:29
***He gives power to the faint, and to him who
has no might he increases strength.***
*Psalm 56:3 ♥ Ezekiel 43:2 ♥ Psalm 55:22
1 Peter 5:6-7*

He Cannot Fail

Failure can be devastating, no matter what our age. It can become monumental and debilitating. They can become the source of our discouragement and even become a barrier to the future God has for us. As we sometimes let failure overtake us, today, I pray that the one thing that God fails at, will overshadow our whole being, our whole life and the circumstances of our life. God cannot fail, it is His only failure, it is the only thing He cannot do! Our imagination often gets the best of us and instead of realizing that God cannot fail, we base our perspective on what our abilities are. We try and struggle and yet, all the while, God is strong enough and has all the necessary resources to take care of the greatest needs we have. We wonder and worry about outcomes instead of standing on the firmness of who God truly is. He, my friends, cannot fail. Not, He might not, or probably won't, or doesn't want to, He cannot. It is impossible for Him to fail, He is unable! It's not an option, so when we put our life and our heart, our trust and our confidence in Him, we are placing it in the most capable of hands. Far more capable than our own, or the hands of even the person on this earth that we love the most. I wonder if He isn't just waiting for us to center on Him and take Him at His word. To live with a faith that matches His impossibility to fail us.

Deuteronomy 7:9
Know therefore that the LORD your God is God; he is the faithful God, keeping his covenant of love to a thousand generations of those who love him and keep his commandments. What if some were unfaithful? Will their unfaithfulness nullify God's faithfulness?
Numbers 23:19 ♥ Titus 1:2 ♥ Romans 3:3

Greatness of Our God

Every day, we use things to help us accomplish the things we do.
From a computer to a potato peeler, even a saw or crane,
we all have tools for different tasks, depending on our calling
and work. Our list could go on and on. Without the tools, our
efforts can be near impossible as we think about what abilities
we have and how quickly our responsibilities can be done. We
use these objects throughout our day and in much the same
way we are held in the hands of God for His purposes.
From time to time, accolades are given for a job well done.
We rejoice at the goodness of God and
His help and faithfulness to us.
We are so inadequate for any situation or job without the
help of the Lord and the guidance of the Holy Spirit.
Our caution is to always realize where our help comes
from and Who our hearts should long to please.
May we not live for the applause of people but to please the One
who gives us His strength and Who helps us each and every day.
The Lord can use each and every one of us for His
greatness to be accomplished. What pleasure He takes
in our willingness to be the instruments He uses.

*"It is not great men who change the world, but
weak men in the hands of a great God."*
-Brother Yun, *The Heavenly Man: The Remarkable
True Story of Chinese Christian Brother Yun*

Psalm 18:2
*Lord is my rock and my fortress and my deliverer, my
God, my rock, in whom I take refuge, my shield,
and the horn of my salvation, my stronghold.*
*Galatians 1:10 ♥ Proverbs 16:7 ♥ John 12:43
1 Thessalonians 2:4*

Really

I often think about how incredible God
is and marvel at the way He
loves us. It's amazing to think that the God who created the
universe would be mindful of us. A sweet friend recently
shared with me of a situation she had finally began praying about
instead of worrying about it. Within just a short few days, the
situation began to change and she is seeing God begin to work in it.
"I don't know why it took me so long to give it to the Lord", she said.
Do we realize how great a love He has for us? He is really,
really, really concerned about the things that touch our
lives and He really, really, really cares about you.
He is our most intimate Friend.
The One who we can share all our deepest heart with.
The Lord, our God, embraces us and there we are held in His
hands. Doubts and feelings can be such thieves that attempt
to rob us from understanding and living in this truth. Perhaps
these thieves have not only been working on your heart
and mind, but maybe they've been working overtime!
The word of God tells us that when we submit to God,
we can resist the devil and he will flee.
Not maybe, or hopefully, but the devil will flee...
he literally runs away because of the presence
of God we take shelter in.
We know that God is great, we know that He is able,
and we know that He loves us. As we walk in that truth,
our faith is more sound and our trust
becomes stronger and stronger.

Isaiah 41:10
*Fear not, for I am with you; be not dismayed, for I am
your God; I will strengthen you, I will help you, I will
uphold you with my righteous right hand.*
1 Peter 5:8 ♥ James 4:7 ♥ Proverbs 18:24

Go with Him

Centering on God is like following a compass or GPS.
We are never forced to follow the automated directions,
but the likeliness of arriving at the correct destination is far higher
if we do. Once I drove alone to a huge city for a conference out of
state. In the downtown metropolis of what seemed like hundreds
of freeways, I relied more than I ever thought I would on the GPS
that meticulously guided me. From exit to exit, and freeway to
freeway, to what seemed like a series of circles more than anything.
I remember, at one point wondering if I was just getting lost.
But the thought of not listening and giving credence to the little box
was even more distressing. I made it through the maze of freeways,
right on time, to my conference and praised God for the invention!
When God told Moses to lead the people
of Israel, he did not have a GPS.
No map and no compass… God just told
him to go and to rely on Him.
Moses was extremely hesitant and asked the Lord, "who are you
going to send with me". And God said, "my presence will go with
you". Moses replies and it is one of my favorite verses in the Bible
when he says, "Lord, if your presence doesn't go with me I don't
want to go!" Isn't that just how we are? There are plenty of things
that are presented to us, avenues we can take, directions we could
go, but if God doesn't go with us, or if it's not His plan, we shouldn't
want to go there. Relying on His direction is vital in such a time
as this. God's direction is beyond even the latest technology that
we often turn to for direction. May we not attempt to replace the
wisdom of God with our educated intelligence. We need Him so
very much, not just lead us but, that we would not go without Him.
Often there is a caution that we sense in our heart or
spirit and we disregard it, only to realize later that we
should have heeded it. Centering on Majesty is giving God
preference over our own desires and directions. May we
trust Him more today than we even did yesterday!

Exodus 33:15
**And he said to him, "If your presence will not go
with me, do not bring us up from here".**
Psalm 43:3 ♥ James 1:5

Miracle of Life

"Tiny fingers and tiny toes, match the delicate little nose.
From head to toe, God's touch, we see and know.
Little sparkling eyes looking to and fro,
So curious and mindful given to watch and grow.
Little one full of squeaks and coos, little miracle, no words will do."
God is amazing in His infinite gentle love in the joy
of seeing a new baby but will we stop today and still
marvel at the life we each have to live and hold.
The miracle of God's love is for a life time, not just a moment.
The joy of His presence, the kindness of His grace,
the comfort of His nearness. The faithfulness of God is ours.
May we be awed again at all that He is. so
worthy of our praise and honor.
How overwhelmingly magnificent is our God.
The life we hold is the life He has given. Find joy in your life today!
Center on Him, for that is where you will find it.

Jeremiah 1:5
Before I formed you in the womb I knew you, and
before you were born I consecrated you;
I appointed you a prophet to the nations.
Psalm 139:15 ♥ Jeremiah 31:3 ♥ Psalm 118:24

The Word

Have you ever longed in your heart to know God more,
to experience Christ in a deeper way?
Is there something inside that stirs you to know
there is more to Him than you've known?
He has pursued your heart to be all His.
If we long to know Him, we can find all that we could
ever attempt to grasp as we look to His word.
This surrender and hunger will lead us to the Word of God and
it is in His word that we will find the heart of God.
Don't stop hungering for Him, pursue His word.
In His book, "*In His Presence*", E.W. Kenton writes,

"The Word illumined by the Holy Spirit is God's light on life's pathway.
The Word is a part of Himself.
You can lean on the Word as you would lean on Him.
You can rest in the Word as you would rest in Him.
You can act on the Word as you would act
if He had just spoken to you."

Centering on Majesty is centering on the Word.
He is there to be found by you.

Psalm 18:30
As for God, his way is perfect:
The Lord's word is flawless;
he shields all who take refuge in him.
Psalm 119:105 ♥ Hebrews 4:12 ♥ James 1:22

Plenty

The plenty of Jesus' sufficiency is finding
that He is more than enough.
In His sufficiency there is abundance. However, it
supersedes the physical issues of life and impacts
those things and areas that we cannot see.
How does or how can this practically
influence our walk with Christ?
How can we find this resting place for our soul
when turmoil or issues attempt to take over and
dominate our thinking and reasoning?
The Psalmist said in Psalm 23,

"The Lord is my shepherd,
I shall not want, He makes me to lie down in green pastures,
He leads me beside quiet waters,
He refreshes my soul."

Stay in the green pasture of plenty, and let Him shepherd you there.
The green pasture is the Word of God. It is the place that His spirit
calls and draws us to. It is in this place that there is a green pasture
for us to not only eat from but to rest in. The Word of God is our
sufficiency but so many other things and influences attempt to keep
us away from the very place where our strength and hope is found.
We somehow think that another pasture will prove better.
But in this passage where the writer describes
the Lord to be our Shepherd,
we know that a shepherd's job is to care for his sheep. To
make sure they are safe and to be sure they have enough
to eat. The place of God's word are both of those things
for us today. May we stay centered on the Word of His
provision, in His pasture of plenty and sufficiency.
That is where there is rest and where we will find His peace.

Psalm 23:1-3
The Lord is my shepherd; I shall not want. He makes me to lie down
in green pastures: he leads me beside the still waters. He restores my
soul: he leads me in the paths of righteousness for his name's sake.
2 Corinthians 12:9 ♥ Matthew 11:28 ♥ John 10:10

Our Wellspring

Defined by Webster, *a wellspring is a source of continual supply.*
This little word has been rolling over and over in my heart
and has brought me to a greater understanding of God's
goodness. His goodness reaches out to us continually
and it is through salvation that we experience it. The word
"well-spring" is somethings only thought of in terms of
a well related to water, a place to draw deeply from.
But the true meaning is rooted more in the meaning of a
"spring". The well-spring of our salvation is God, Himself.
When we consider a well, we know it's deep and often
the water in it can be difficult to access. This depth,
does in every way represent the depth of God.
It is His love, His grace and mercy to us, however when we
attach it to the meaning of a "spring", we have the opportunity
to realize the accessibility that is extended to us.
A spring bubbles up and bears an endless
supply that is always fresh and alive.
It is accessible to us continually, a free gift from God through
His son Jesus, when we make Him the Lord of our life.
The writer of Proverbs uses the word to describe our hearts and the
necessity of guarding our hearts. Guarding how? Guarding what?
We must guard our heart from allowing it to be contaminated
by things that we need to resist and forsake. Guarding what
we do and say, our attitude and pursuits. Many will dismiss
the necessity of guarding ourselves but when we are serious
about knowing Christ, we must be ever-attentive.
As we center on the well-spring of our salvation,
may it cause us to more diligently guard the gift we have
so freely received, and may we be generous to share it
with others. May we generously give and love, share
and encourage with kindness and compassion.

Proverbs 4:23
Keep your heart with all vigilance, for from it flow the springs of life.
Isaiah 12:2-3 ♥ Proverbs 16:22

Advancing Forward

Moving ahead and moving forward from a place that has been secure may be one of the most difficult things the Lord calls us to do. Staying put is more familiar than advancing and will often keep us from experiencing the fullness of what God has for us. Advancing requires our faith and dependence on God. As He stirs our hearts, we can be sure that He is faithful to lead us as we seek His direction. Fear can be crippling and keep us from getting up, getting out, and getting on with the call of God. The Holy Spirit is the key that brings us to yield to the gentle whisper of the Father. To hear a whisper, we must be quiet, we must listen attentively. Chances are that the whispering of the Holy Spirit to a person's heart has been happening long before they ever begin to hear it. Many stay in places of infancy in their walk with Christ because they have refused His drawing to delve in deeper and pursue Him more intimately. The truth of the matter is that the Lord is not limited by our inabilities or insecurities. When He calls and draws us deeper, He equips us into greater things, but we may never experience such places without moving forward and advancing toward Him. In my walk with Christ, I often reflect on a season when I knew there had to be more in Him. Something was stirring in my heart and when I shared this place with a dear friend, he encouraged me and said these words, "whatever you do, don't stop hungering for Jesus". Advancing forward in Him is to not stop hungering. I have shared those words countless times with others who have been where I was, and the Lord often brings them back to my own heart as He calls me to face challenges that are not always easy, but I know they are His leading to bring me to a greater purpose. Centering toward Christ is to set your heart toward His heart. Placing your hand in His hand, surrendering your will to His will, and to walk away from the mountain you've been circling long enough.

Exodus 14:15
The Lord said to Moses, "Why do you cry to me?
Tell the people of Israel to go forward".
Isaiah 6:8 ♥ Proverbs 4:25 ♥ Deuteronomy 1:6

Our Barrier

One of the most quoted scriptures in the Bible, is one of my favorites as well. Found in Isaiah, chapter 59, verse 19:

"So shall they fear the name of the Lord from the west, and his glory rom the rising of the sun. When the enemy shall come in like a flood, the Spirit of the Lord shall lift up a standard against him."

What a comfort to know that there is a place of refuge and safety when we feel completely overtaken by the flood waters of life. In another way, I have been realizing that the Lord is a barrier and restraint for our lives when He has kept us from walking into areas that could have been so detrimental to our life. The Lord is our Guide and Protector when the enemy comes in like a flood and attempts to overtake decision and discipline in our life. Instead of being swept away, the restraint of God keeps us firmly anchored. May our hearts realize how gracious the Lord has been to us and for us! How much He loves us and is for our good and not our demise. He is not waiting idly by without concern or aid. God is faithful, one of those things that He doesn't just do, it's a part of who He is! The Holy Spirit has been our Barrier and Restraint in more ways and instances than we will probably ever realize. The flood of the enemy is no match for Him!

2 Chronicles 20:15

And he said, "Listen, all Judah and inhabitants of Jerusalem and King Jehoshaphat: Thus says the LORD to you, 'Do not be afraid and do not be dismayed at this great horde, for the battle is not yours but God's.

Philippians 4:13 ♥ 2 Timothy 1:7

Possible

This is faith, not just to know or believe that God is able, but to trust He is. Trust Him to the point, that regardless of the outcome, we are confident of His goodness. When His answers may not be our preference and when the outcome doesn't make sense. He remains our foundation. The foundation of Christ and the solidity of it never, ever changes even when we do. We might never understand why a situation unfolded as it has, but we can know that through the difficulty, God is still God of all. How did the Psalmist know that God reigned so powerfully? It was because he experienced the power and strength of God, and nothing that happened in his life could deter him. Do you think anyone could ever talk you out of the fact that the sky is blue or that water maintains life or that cats purr, dogs bark and babies cry? No way! We know all those things are true, there may be variations of them, but ultimately they are true. May we be so sure, above even these certainties, that God is who He said He is. While we may not understand His ways, understand and remain certain that God is God. We never have to doubt it, regardless of whether or not we understand. God is ultimately in charge and He gets to make the hard calls. He doesn't need our permission to be who He is, but often people have this unspoken attitude. Our part is to pray and trust! Know and believe! He is God and He is ever, ever faithful and good. He loves deeper than our finite minds can comprehend. Center your heart in Him, all things are possible!

Genesis 18:14
Is anything too difficult for the LORD? At the appointed time I will return to you, at this time next year, and Sarah will have a son.
2 Corinthians 4:7 ♥ Psalm 93:1

Mindful

Being mindful of something is to be aware, alert and attentive. Mindful of important things can become challenging when life gets busy. Sadly, self and busyness really love to have center-stage! Beware of not being aware of the important issues that the Lord is working on in your life and speaking to you about.
When life gets busy, we tend to set those things on the back burner and let them simmer. The danger is that our attention wains from centering on Jesus and allows other things take precedence in our life.
It's an amazing thought that the Lord God, our Father is ever mindful of us. Nothing has deterred His affection and nothing will. He says to us; cast your cares on Me because I care for you. He cares so deeply and so passionately for you today!
Imagine the galaxies and how enormous they are. They are important to God but man on planet earth is His ultimate concern. The spiritual condition of our heart outweighs all else to Him. Who are we that God would love us so? How can it be when we have disappointed His heart again and again? It is one of the most amazing realities to know that He continues to call us to Himself no matter how far we stray.
His love is greater than our mistakes or failure.
Change your mindset to being mindful of Him today. The Lord has so much for us! As we center on being mindful of Him, we will find that it will require us shifting our stance and resetting our heart to where He is. It requires effort to move Him from the peripheral to the center of our thoughts and focus. He is the example of being mindful of man, He can help us to be more mindful of Him.

Job 7:17
hat is mankind that you make so much of them,
that you give them so much attention?
Hebrews 2:6 ♥ Psalm 8:3-4

Fragrance

Smells can be good, and they can be really bad! Consider…if the character, attitude and compassion of Christ conveys the most wonderful fragrance, we might want to ask ourselves, "how do I smell"? Some will answer, "with my nose!" But seriously, if Jesus is the most wonderful fragrance that our life can emit, and our old selfish and prideful nature has another odor, is His fragrance filling our life?

Fragrance can be very expensive and there is fragrance that is very inexpensive that some try to pass off as the authentic. The imitation of fragrance is not genuine and leaves quickly as not having a genuine heart of Christ's love.

There is a fragrance that is intangible that comes from our life when the love of Christ is not only seen but felt by our life. We don't have to say a word for it is noticed without a word. Each of us have the opportunity to pour the fragrance of our lives out as an offering of worship to the Lord as we bless Him by blessing others.

In the Word of God, a woman came and poured expensive perfume on the feet of Jesus. She was a disrespected woman but her heart was filled with genuine worship. It was more than just the expensive perfume that filled the room, it was her humility, her gratitude, and her worship as she came with selflessness to His feet. The woman didn't care about ridicule or what others thought, her heart had to be poured out and she refused to let anything stand in the way. May we be so centered on Jesus that we are driven to pour out our worship and gratitude in selflessness.

Ephesians 5:1-2
Therefore be imitators of God, as beloved children; and walk in love, just as Christ also loved you and gave Himself up for us, an offering and a sacrifice to God as a fragrant aroma.

John 12:32 ♥ 2 Samuel 24:23-25
2 Corinthians 2:14-15

Listen

Have you ever been talking to someone and they were looking at you and attentive, but in some way you knew they weren't really hearing you. They were hearing but not really listening? How many times have we tried to talk to our children or spouse and they later say, "I didn't hear you say that?" It can be frustrating to say the least, for both parties! Sometimes, we're the ones saying, "When did you say that?". Often spouses tune each other out and kids become "mommy & daddy deaf". It is referred to as "selective hearing". Communication is definitely a challenge that has always been a part of life. Throughout the Word of God, we find instances when God spoke in various ways and His people were called to not only listen, but to "harken" to His voice. Meaning: "To listen; to lend the ear; to attend to what is uttered; to give heed; to hear, in order to obey or comply". John 10:27 tells us, "My sheep hear my voice, and I know them, and they follow me". The Lord calls us each day to not only take time to hear Him, and the leading of the Holy Spirit but to follow His instructions. We might hear but if we don't ever move in the direction He is leading, it is of little good that God speak to us. Have you ever heard the old proverb, "you can lead a horse to water but, you can't make him drink?". The same is true of many of us! God wants to do so much in our lives and He's speaking, in fact, He's been speaking for a long time and we've pushed His leading aside, just like little kids who become accustomed to their mom's voice and we declare they've become "mommy deaf". We often have selective hearing when it comes to what we do or do not want to do in regard to what we hear God telling us! May the Lord ignite us with the joy and excitement of knowing Him. May we pursue Him with a heart that is anxious to hear His voice and be obedient! Center the ears of your heart on listening to His voice today.

Psalm 95:6-9

Oh come, let us worship and bow down; let us kneel before the Lord, our Maker! For he is our God, and we are the people of his pasture, and the sheep of his hand. Today, if you hear his voice, do not harden your hearts, as at Meribah, as on the day at Massah in the wilderness, when your fathers put me to the test and put me to the proof, though they had seen my work.

Matthew 13:8 ♥ Matthew 11:15 ♥ Mark 4:9
Mark 4:23 ♥ Deuteronomy 27:9

Consideration

When a person considers a situation, a motive, or decision, there is usually a bias to their views. The longer we are away from allowing the Word of God to influence our day to day agenda and course, the further away from His influence we will obviously be. We will remain in this state and, an uncertain emptiness will pervade even the most seemingly successful endeavors. Consider God as you center on Him. Consider His ways or His concerns, or His plan and purpose. We can have the mind of Christ, but it will not be our first thought if He remains in the peripheral of our life. Considering the heart of God is a process of surrendering our plans and rationale to His.

Will we release and allow Him to be the dominating influence for the decisions of each day? Fullness is found and emptiness is filled when we know we are walking in His plan instead of our own. It happens when we know we have pleased His heart with our attitude and intentions, instead of taking pleasure in ourselves or the accolades of others.

Considering the ways of God is a position of contrition and humility that establishes holy strength. It breaks the dominion of fear and doubt. It brings peace and assurance that He is in control and we have only to trust in Him.

Galatians 1:10
For am I now seeking the favor of men, or of God? Or am I striving to please men? If I were still trying to please men, I would not be a bond-servant of Christ.

Haggai 1:7 ♥ Galatians 6:8 ♥ Psalm 51:16-17
1 Thessalonians 4:1

Breath of God

Life cannot be sustained without breathing. We know that when a new baby is born that they "gasp" for that first breath of air so that their lungs can be filled. It is safe to say that life is given by God and it is His breath in us that sustains life. A person with a diminished ability to breathe will struggle and life will be hard. Being "short of breath" or living with a chronic lung illness limits everything we do. It's heartbreaking to see someone struggle for breath as they attempt to walk a short distance or do a small task. In severe incidents, when people cannot sustain their own respirations, they are put on "life support". The breath of God is our life in both a natural and spiritual sense. If our bodies are healthy, we can breathe without a thought, it is innate, an automatic or parasympathetic physiological attribute. In a spiritual sense, when our capacity for the breath of God in our lives diminishes, everything we attempt to do will be laborious. We may begin to feel as though life is xhausting and that some supplemental oxygen for our spirit might help, so we start to look in a variety of places to find help because we need to breathe. The only problem is that our spirit needs the breath of God and not a counterfeit or artificial means for better air exchange. Our spirit longs and pants for the breath of God! Imagine it this way…you are a deep sea diver. The tank of air you are diving with is provided and has been filled by God, the giver of life. As you breathe underwater, He is the air you are breathing. You enjoy the diving experience for several hours, until an alarm on your respirator begins to signal that your tank is getting low. The warning compels you to resist the temptation to continue on, regardless of how exciting or intriguing the underwater scenery has become. You know that you must get back to the surface, and an urgency begins to compel you upward. Our need for the breath of God in our spirit is much the same. Breathe Him in as you center your heart today.

Psalm 42:1
As a deer pants for flowing streams, so pants my soul for you, O God.
Job 32:8 ♥ Psalm 119:131 ♥ Job 33:4
Psalm 84:2 ♥ Psalm 33:6

Greater Things

Glancing at a recent church newsletter, I saw
the caption... "Greater Things".
I remembered the emphasis and paused what I was doing to
whisper a prayer asking God to do greater things in my life,
and that I might truly believe Him for them. Suddenly, like
lightening, the thought came to me, that if God isn't doing
greater things in our personal lives, He probably won't be doing
greater things through our life. It begins in our personal, quiet,
and private time with Jesus. We must be inviting Him in that place,
not just asking for a public display of the greater things as we live.
How imperative that we honestly trust and believe here first!
By allowing His power dominate our purpose, we will then see
Him do the greater things in the deep places of our life. Then they
will overflow out of that place and be evident through our life.
We sometimes dismiss God's desire to do greater things in the
deep places of our life, believing that those things are for someone
else. Perhaps an insight, strength in faith or witnessing, perhaps
certain wisdom, speaking up or speaking out on behalf of others.
Believing that our relationships will change or that our finances will
be healed by His direction and provision...greater things happen
when we make Him not only first, but the center of all we do.
Greater things in you will spill out through
you by the power of who Jesus is!

John 14:11-13
*Believe me when I say that I am in the Father and the Father is
in me; or at least believe on the evidence of the works themselves.
Very truly I tell you, whoever believes in me will do the works I
have been doing, and they will do even greater things than these,
because I am going to the Father. And I will do whatever you
ask in my name, so that the Father may be glorified in the Son.
You may ask me for anything in my name, and I will do it.*
1 Samuel 17:47 ♥ Zechariah 4:6

Gifts

We are all given gifts and talents by the Lord. Some look at their lives and discount their gifts because they are looking at them with their own eyes or through the muddied waters of doubt and fear given as a filter by the enemy. Our gifts may seem ordinary so therefore we marginalize their potential. But what if we started looking at them with the eyes of God? What He places in us is for His purpose and their potential far exceeds what we can imagine. Paul told Timothy to stir up the gift within his heart. What was the gift and why did it need to be stirred up? It was the gift of God that was in Timothy. When my precious mother in law makes orange juice, she puts the juice in a container and then puts it in the refrigerator so it doesn't spoil…this is where so many are in their life… God has saved us and we are walking with Him, living a Christian life that professes Him. That orange juice is in the refrigerator, available if anyone wants it. So when someone comes along to use it, if they pour directly from the bottle, all the pulp of the juice is at the bottom of the container, what they pour out is almost clear, like water. If they want the full benefit of the juice, they must shake it up! It must be stirred and we must be stirred up too. First it takes us changing our mind…that is what Paul was telling Timothy. He was saying stop diminishing your God given gifts, Timothy! Stop just going through the motions, doing what you've always done, the way you have always done it. Stir up the gifts and see what God will do, furthermore, see why God put them there! Never were they placed to lie dormant or to be partially used. There are some pretty ordinary people who have done some EXTRAordinary things in their life, simply because they believed what God put in their heart to do was from Him and they never estimated that it had anything to do with themselves. It was all about God! He has proven that His abilities to be God are without limit! Then He invites us to be a part of it. We can sit on the sidelines, and let the days continue to roll by us, believing the lie that we aren't good enough or someone else who has better gifts and talents will step up. The Holy Spirit is urging us to stir up the gifts that God has given us. Your gifts are centered in Christ, given by God!

1 Peter 4:10
**As each has received a gift, use it to serve one another,
as good stewards of God's varied grace.**
2 Timothy 1:6-7 ♥ Romans 12:6

Identify

Following a season, long or short, of pain
or illness has an interesting phase.
We often need to process the pain and experience
by verbalizing it with others.

The need to recount the episode, whether pain or sickness,
and its impact on us feels compelling. Whether we whisper it
to the Lord or talk to a friend or our family, we have a need for
others to identify with us and they need us, as they process the
issues of their life. Some experiences are physical, and many are
emotional but always they contain the element of trauma or pain.
The Lord, our God, is keenly aware of this
need in us because He created us.
We may not have even thought of it as a need but, indeed
it is. There are few people I have met that have undergone
a heart attack that when the issue is brought to light, that
they don't have the need of recounting its details, etc.
What a precious Savior we have who has, Himself, faced
suffering and when He did, it was for us. His suffering
also brought the greatest measure of identifying with
us that exceeds the identification of others.
We are reminded that Jesus bore or experienced our sicknesses
and diseases. He knows what we face and its impact on
us. But He also wants us to know that He brought healing
to us when He endured the cross. His suffering not only
brought us healing but also strength for our weaknesses.

Hebrews 4:14-16

*Therefore, since we have a great high priest who has passed through the
heavens, Jesus the Son of God, let us hold fast our confession. For we
do not have a high priest who cannot sympathize with our weaknesses,
but One who has been tempted in all things as we are, yet without sin.
Therefore let us draw near with confidence to the throne of grace, so
that we may receive mercy and find grace to help in time of need.*
Isaiah 53:3-5 ♥ *Matthew 8:16-17*

Obedient

In this day and age of culture, being obedient wars against the mentality of our "rights". People often believe that their "right" is the ultimate measure regardless of what they are called to obey. Some have a very difficult time being compliant, especially if they have never known boundaries. One definition of obedience is: willing to do what someone tells you to do or to follow a law, rule, etc.: willing to obey. If we know what obedience is, then we can also consider what disobedience is. It is most generally equated to an attitude of rebellion. We know that disobedience that goes unchecked can become destructive. The call to obey God's word is part of His love and protection for us. There are times that the Lord whispers to our heart about a certain thing in our life and we might not know the outcome, but we do know what He is asking of us. Obedience to God holds blessing! It's an act of worship that requires faith and trust that He knows better than we do. The hardest times to obey the Lord are when we have a formulated plan and desire, especially, if it has already been put into motion! The longer we hold onto our ways and refuse to trust Him, the more that little root of rebellion can deepen in our heart. Have you ever been pulling weeds and you come upon a little one and give it a tug only to find it incredibly strong? You give it another tug, just a bit harder this time. Then with all your might, you get determined and pull the weed out. Little on the top but once it is out of the ground, the root is very long and has been rooted much deeper than we imagined. Many times, there is an unspoken whisper of the enemy to us that declares, "it's no big deal" and that "it's just a small issue." While we delay obedience to the Lord, the influence of rebellion grows stronger and draws us away from Him. A scary issue is that we can be drawn away by the disobedience of others, and we can draw others from God by our disobedience. Centering our obedience on the Lord brings blessings we cannot imagine, however, they cannot be known without surrender!

Proverbs 10:17
Whoever heeds discipline shows the way to life, but whoever ignores correction leads others astray.
Jeremiah 7:23 ♥ Joshua 1:8 ♥ James 1:22
Jeremiah 38:20

Blessed

In the document known as the "Declaration of Independence", these words were penned: "We hold these truths to be self-evident, that all men are created equal, that they are endowed by their Creator with certain unalienable rights, that among these are Life, Liberty and the pursuit of Happiness." The pursuit of happiness is a powerful and dominating quest. It is interesting as we shift to consider what the Bible tells us about happiness, we find that another word for happiness is "blessed". As we look at the very words of Jesus, and knowing that He is the Way, the Truth and the Life, may it arrest our heart to realize that there is a blessing of happiness that we can know in Him alone.

It won't be found in the pursuit of money or status,
not in getting our way or from emotional gratification.
It is found when love becomes our motivation.
The virtues of Christ will ultimately bring
blessing and lead to reward.
They give us promises. The opposite of blessing
is misery, so it would be wisdom that draws our
heart to be led in the ways of blessing.

It's a little hard to grasp so I am sharing the Message version of our passage to help us. Ultimately, facing hardship is not always a bad thing, it may be the very thing that leads us closer to Christ. As we become more in love with Him, that causes us to be more generous with our own love. As His love flows through our life, the trickle becomes a stream that grows into a river of love and it is out of that place that true happiness is known.

Matthew 5:3-12

"Blessed are the poor in spirit, for theirs is the kingdom of heaven. "Blessed are those who mourn, for they shall be comforted. "Blessed are the [d]gentle, for they shall inherit the earth. "Blessed are those who hunger and thirst for righteousness, for they shall be satisfied. "Blessed are the merciful, for they shall receive mercy. "Blessed are the pure in heart, for they shall see God. "Blessed are the peacemakers, for they shall be called sons of God. "Blessed are those who have been persecuted for the sake of righteousness, or theirs is the kingdom of heaven. "Blessed are you when people insult you and persecute you, and falsely say all kinds of evil against you because of Me. Rejoice and be glad, for your reward in heaven is great; for in the same way they persecuted the prophets who were before you.

Hope

The search for hope is an internal necessity.
In our world today, we see people becoming more and more
desperate for hope. Hopefulness, when unfulfilled can cause
us to become distressed even feeling a little frantic.
But before we begin to allow this condition to reel out of
control and bring dominating fear, may we realize from the
"get-go", that we already hold the greatest hope of the universe
in the comfort and powerful name of Jesus, our Redeemer.
Redeemer, Rescuer, Strong-Tower, Deliverer, and so much more!
His word tells us that He is our Hope.
Despite the condition of our situation or the condition of the world,
He does not change!
The Lord, our God remains faithful and constant!

Psalm 3:2-5
Many are saying of me,
"God will not deliver him."
But you, Lord, are a shield around me,
my glory, the One who lifts my head high.
I call out to the Lord,
and he answers me from his holy mountain.
I lie down and sleep;
I wake again, because the Lord sustains me.

Romans 8:24-25 ♥ Romans 12:12 ♥ 2 Corinthians 4:16-18
Proverbs 24:14

69

Patience

How many of us need patience? Probably most of us, but we're not very brave when it comes to asking God for it! We silently think that praying for patience is just setting ourselves up for frustration, that we may or may not be prepared to handle.

One of the most quoted passages in all of God's word is 1 Corinthians 13. It's referred to as the "Love" chapter. While that is so true, may we see that from cover to cover, His word is about His love. His interceptive love. His faithful love. His sacrificial love. His abundant love. The chapter resounds with the words: "Love is patient and kind." And while we know that God's love is kind, do we realize how patient His love has been in our lives? Sometimes we expect God to be patient with us, but we forego being patient with each other. Matthew 25:40 reminds us, that when we have done it for the least of these, we have done it unto Him. This is a sobering reminder that our actions and attitude not only affect others, but they touch the heart of God. The Lord has a way of leading us in patience with His patience. He paves the way and the more we acknowledge what His patience has meant to us personally, the more evident it will become. So if you find that patience is lacking in your heart and life, but you're afraid to pray for it, just spend some time remembering and reflecting on what His patience has meant in your life. You'll find that the reservoir of patience in your life will begin to increase. Centering on His patient love is the beginning of finding patience!

Ephesians 4:2
Be completely humble and gentle; be patient, bearing with one another in love.
1 Corinthians 13:4-5 ♥ *Psalm 27:14* ♥ *Romans 12:12*

Offering

Can you imagine someone who would go into a jewelry store to purchase an expensive gem with a meager amount of money? The purer the gem, the higher the price tag is. It's worth and value is obvious. But regardless of the firm price tag, a negotiation ensues by the buyer. The seller refutes with explanation of the gem's value and quality. Nonetheless, the attempted buyer puts down an amount of money that is an insult to the true value of the gem. The jeweler shakes his head in disbelief at the buyer's ignorance of truth. I share that illustration to help us understand the story of two men in the Bible, they were brothers named Cain and Abel. God provided a way for their sin to be covered through a specific acrifice. This sacrifice was outlined by God very clearly to Adam and Eve who carefully taught their children. When Cain and Abel grew into men, the time came for them to bring a sacrifice to God. Abel brought an offering to God that was the best he could bring; it was the best he could obtain to give to the Lord. Cain on the other hand, thought surely God would like his offering and instead of adhering to what God had asked, he came up with his own idea. God accepted Abel's offering but not Cain's. Then like us, Cain got mad because when he brought an unacceptable offering that was rejected. Have you ever done a job that was not your best but you tried to pass it off as if it were? That's what Cain did, but what is often overlooked is that God had not given him instruction that was unattainable. Cain just chooses to do it his way instead of God's way, and then attempted to blame God for his disobedience. How often do we choose the way of Cain, attempting to bring a gift of our worship that is less than what we know God is requiring of us and then attempt to pass it off as our best? Sadly disobedience is the way of man. So often refusing to bring the sacrifice which God asks, and instead they bring what they want. Thinking all the while, it's good enough for God. He doesn't mind, after all He loves us. In the Old Testament, the priests were required to go through such rituals of cleansing before they could ever even attempt to bring an offering to God. And while we have the grace of Jesus' ultimate sacrifice, we are still required to live purely before Him as an act of worship. When the Lord invites us to bring our pure worship to Him, it's more than His requirement of us. It's His loving invitation for us to come into a place with Him that is intimate and deeper than we will ever find through our superficial and carnal worship. That's why He keeps calling and urging us to come, it's why we sometimes don't feel satisfied in our spirit. He is calling to come away, without true surrender and pure worship. May we center on the wonder of Him today and adore Jesus with our honest worship and love.

2 Corinthians 9:6-7

The point is this: whoever sows sparingly will also reap sparingly, and whoever sows bountifully will also reap bountifully. Each one must give as he has decided in his heart, not reluctantly or under compulsion, for God loves a cheerful giver.

Hebrews 11:4 ♥ Romans 12:1 ♥ Jude 1:11
Genesis 4:4 ♥ 1 John 3:12

Daylight Savings

Approximately 70 countries around the
world observe "Daylight Savings".
It usually means that time changes and clocks are turned ahead.
The theory is that by turning clocks ahead will allow extra
evening daylight. Some people like it and some don't, but
regardless we must adhere to the change. It's not an option.
We know that we can't save time and often we do our best to
make the most of our time, so much so that we often neglect
to even rest. In some places, when daylight savings is observed,
it also serves as a reminder to recharge batteries in things like
smoke detectors and flashlights. These are things we often
don't think about until we need them to work. Sometimes,
years go by and we don't realize that our batteries are dead.
May today, and for every "daylight savings" day in the future, be a
reminder in a spiritual sense. Take time to recharge your batteries
and rest in the presence of Jesus. Continuing without true rest
and without refueling in Him will leave us frustrated and depleted
spiritually. Sometimes we think of these things as an option
and we can choose to neglect them, but when we do, we run a
great danger of neglecting the most important area of our life.
The physical things take most of our attention because we can
see them but really, the things we cannot see are paramount.
First, is our relationship to Jesus, and then
our relationship with others.
It's things like kindness, love and forgiveness.
We will never have these things to give if we
never receive them from Christ.
Centering on Him and allowing His light to save our day
will bring a radiance that cannot compare to any other.

Psalm 23:3
*e restores my soul; He guides me in the paths of
righteousness For His name's sake.*
Isaiah 40:30-31 ♥ Psalm 51:10-11 ♥ 2 Corinthians 4:16

Indecision

The necessity of decision fills each and every day. Moment by moment, we are faced with making all sorts of decisions from the moment we wake up. Making a decision puts things into motion while indecision leaves us idling. An example is the little boy who stands in front of the ice cream counter with his pennies to buy an ice cream cone. Everything is in place for him to have this treat, but he must decide what flavor of ice cream he will choose. So often we sense the Lord leading us in a certain direction, but we simply cannot make the decision to pursue His direction. We keep weighing the options and circling the decision of whether or not to trust what God has been urging in our spirit. Jesus, in the garden, is the example of a man who had to surrender the suffering of His physical body to the call of God. Jesus prayed, not My will but Thine be done. Most often the decision of pursuing God will call us to choose Him over ourselves. We may be ready to fully surrender and trust that He has our best and our good in His plan. In our indecision we continue to discount the wisdom of God, instead of really trusting that He is good and He cares for us. The reason that turmoil continues to dominate our heart is because more than any other desire of our life, our soul desires to follow after God. His ways are our ultimate desire regardless of any physical necessary surrendering that He is calling us to. We may realize the strong grasp of the physical desires of our life, not wanting to give up certain things, but ultimately our soul bids us to decide to follow Jesus and to yield to His calling for every decision.

Psalm 19:8
The precepts of the Lord are right, giving joy to the heart. The commands of the Lord are radiant, giving light to the eyes.
Philippians 4:8 ♥ Proverbs 2:6 ♥ James 1:5

Mercy & Peace

Somethings just go together, like bacon and
eggs or peanut butter and jelly.
What about chips and salsa or salt and pepper.
We could each probably make a pretty long list.
Mercy and peace are two of these things.
When we extend mercy, peace is given and known. When
we receive mercy, peace is ours. It is the desire of God
that we would have both mercy and peace in our life.
We will not know true peace until we
experience true mercy and grace.

Releasing our attempts to "fix" our self or others is the open door
for mercy and grace to come in and for peace to follow. In His
commentary, Matthew Henry states it this way, "The mercy of
God is the spring and fountain of all the good we have or hope
for; mercy, not only to the miserable, but to the guilty. Next to
mercy is peace, which we have from the sense of having obtained
mercy. From peace springs love; Christ's love to us, our love to him,
and our brotherly love to one another." In our passages today, it's
clear that there was a mandate that these writers expressed from
heaven and the heart of God to live in and extend abundance
here. It was written to the readers first! What do we hold back
from God that prevents our peace and keeps us from His mercy?
He is gentle and kind in that He stands at the door and knocks
(Rev 3:20). But when we decide to let Him in and take control,
the battle becomes His and our peace is found in His shelter.
2 Chronicles 20:15b, New Living Translation: "This is what
the LORD says: Do not be afraid! Don't be discouraged by
this mighty army, for the battle is not yours, but God's."
The Lord desires more than we can understand or fathom,
for us to live in His mercy and abundant grace and peace.
The supply is not limited to our understanding but is
unlimited by His love for us. The only key is opening the
door and giving Him access to our heart and life.

2 Peter 1:2
*Grace and peace be yours in abundance through the
knowledge of God and of Jesus our Lord.*
1 Timothy 1:2 ♥ Galatians 6:16 ♥ Jude 1:2

Prayers

Prayer is a beautiful invitation from God. Did you know that the Bible actually encourages us to pray without stopping? How is that possible? It's the inward and constant heart communication with God, at every turn and in each and every instance of our day. The beauty is knowing that, not only are we given an invitation to talk to the Lord constantly, but we are reminded again and again in His word of how constant His concern is for us. Prayer opens the door for us to hear from God, to share our deepest needs, and to express our heart's overwhelming adoration for who He is in our life. It happens in a whisper and it can last seconds or hours. We have endless opportunity every day to be in touch with God. As we do, we find that He blesses us with His presence. We walk away having received so much more than we even knew we needed. His presence produces trust and assurance that He is with us and we are in His hands. One key makes all the difference and it's us. God never changes, He is ever constant. But we, on the other hand, must be careful that we "pray" prayers and not just "say" prayers. Prayer is so much more than mindlessly saying a formulated set of words, while our mind wanders elsewhere. Focusing can be hard at times, especially when trouble or worries attempt to hijack our time with Jesus. But be diligent in pursuing Him, and let the things of the world grow strangely dim in the light of His glory and grace. As we do, we will find our heart re-centered and anchored by faith.

Philippians 4:6-7

Do not be anxious about anything, but in every situation, by prayer and petition, with thanksgiving, present your requests to God. And the peace of God, which transcends all understanding, will guard your hearts and your minds in Christ Jesus.

1 Thessalonians 5:16-18 ♥ Philippians 1:6 ♥ James 1:17
Psalm 138:8

Attentive

In school, or from our parents, we have all probably heard theexclamatory words, *"pay attention"*! Being attentive takes a certain amount of determination and diligence, otherwise we naturally wander in thoughts and feelings. As young drivers learn to drive, the most important words of advice are that they would not be distracted and inattentive to their own driving or to other drivers around them. It's easy to let things take our attentiveness away from so many areas in our life.

March 17

First and foremost, the most important part of our life that we must guard is our walk with Christ. So many other things, good or bad, attempt to draw our attention from the greatest Love of our life. The things of most value are the things that the enemy will attempt to draw us from. Sadly, many do not see the tactics for what they are, and allow inattentiveness to draw them away from their spouse, parents, children, and other precious relationships.

In the two small books in the Bible called Timothy, Paul gives Timothy, a young pastor the warning to be attentive 3 times. Timothy loved the Lord, his heart was called and focused on ministry, so why would Paul be so repetitive? Is it because like you and me, inattentiveness happens gradually and so often, without notice? What was the implication? Not to be careless with the gift God had given him. May we hear Paul's urgent warning and not dismiss it as inapplicable to us.

Paul encourages Timothy "to guard", inferring that what is to be guarded is of great value, not something to be casually inattentive to. Sometimes we need someone to say, "hey, that's really valuable! Don't lose it". Inattentiveness can rob so much from us. In prayer, may we take the time to bring our inattentiveness to Jesus with a surrender from our pride, to allow Him access to re-center our attention fully on Him.

1 Timothy 6:20

O Timothy, guard what has been entrusted to you, avoiding worldly and empty chatter and the opposing arguments of what is falsely called "knowledge"-

2 Timothy 1:14 ♥ *2 Timothy 4:14*

Convinced

Consideration of the awesome hand of God moving in our life,
seeing redemption work in us and transformation happen in our
thinking, it's no wonder we can stand and know that our Savior
is who He said He would be. Being convinced that our God is
faithful, changes uncertainty into security. When we refuse to
give way when a flood of doubts attempt to assail our faith, and
we lift up our head and heart in adoration to His greatness, we find
our faith strengthened against every discouragement and fear.
Stand in the certainty of Jesus and freedom from darkness. There
is nothing that can separate us from the love of God. This truth
always remains. Friends, He does not change! The issue is our
being convinced of it! That is what makes the difference and
causes our heart to know that no matter what may come in this
life, we belong to the King of kings that He is ours and we are His.
If we continue to refuse to be convinced, we will never
stand in the strength and power of what He intended for
us to live in as His beloved. We can never understand the
immeasurable love of God but just because we are not able
to completely grasp it, cannot determine its being. Often
people allow their faith to be based on what they can grasp
with their intellect. That will always be deficient.
Our place of stature is in Christ alone. We can never earn His favor
or mercy, We must only acknowledge our great need, and allow
His grace to penetrate every part of our life and attitude. Then
rest assured that He is big enough to lead us through hardship
to blessing, holding firm, refusing to doubt. Be centered in
confidence, and completely convinced of God's love for you today.

Hebrews 6:17-18

*So when God desired to show more convincingly to the heirs of the
promise the unchangeable character of his purpose, he guaranteed
it with an oath, so that by two unchangeable things, in which it is
impossible for God to lie, we who have fled for refuge might have
strong encouragement to hold fast to the hope set before us.*

Psalm 54:4 ♥ Romans 8:38-39

Passion

Desire for God is fueled when we realize His passion for us. The passion of God, our Father, has always been fervent and unrelenting. Remembering all that Jesus endured as He prepared for His crucifixion is probably the most vivid display of the passion of God for humanity.

Do you know Jesus as your Savior? We have all sinned, and we are all in need of being saved. The only One who can save us from the effects of the sins of this life is Jesus, God's only son. We are the reason He came to earth, born to walk where we walk. His life afforded Him the opportunity of experiencing life as a man. His life was touched with hardship and suffering. Through it all, the passion of God's heart compelled His determination. Nothing could quench His passionate love to rescue each and every one of us.

Do we realize what kind of strength and power true passion carries with it? What kind of power and strength might our passion for Jesus enable us to do or be? When we follow His example of not allowing anything to stand in His way of His passionate love, not even suffering to the point of death, we will begin to realize by it that ultimate life is found in our passion for Him and nowhere else.

As His passion for us dominated the life of Jesus, may our passion for Jesus dominate our life. May we be captivated by our passion because of His passion. May we be driven and refuse to allow passion to be an option in our life. He was driven from a passion within Him. May we love Him with all of our heart, being centered in passionate love for Jesus.

Ephesians 5:2
And walk in love, as Christ loved us and gave himself up for us, a fragrant offering and sacrifice to God.
Matthew 5:6 ♥ Matthew 22:37-40 ♥ John 17:26

Advocate

Another word for advocate is "activist". It is someone who stands up for what is right and defends a victim when they are unable to defend themselves. The inference is to refute injustice on behalf of someone else. This is the season that we remember the day referred to as "Palm Sunday". It is the day that Jesus was celebrated as He rode into Jerusalem. It was a celebration of not who He was, but who the people wanted Him to be... King on earth, to bring them a new life. His plan exceeded their earthly life into the life we now live and an eternal life. Their celebration was one of pride for what they wanted and what their understanding could grasp. Only a few days later, Jesus would be charged and sentenced to death, as was God's plan that His Kingship would provide the sacrifice for the sins of the world and bring salvation to humanity. He was King on earth but He is also King of the earth. His role is not only to be King and Savior but our High Priest. Jesus is our Advocate! He intercedes on our behalf daily at the right hand of God. He is not just king for a day or a lifetime but for all eternity. Hosanna was the cry of those that lined the Jerusalem streets that day and it is the cry of heaven's angels night and day around the throne room. Jesus refused to let the accolades of men and their applause distract Him from the ultimate call of His life. May His example encourage our hearts to see beyond the moment of just today. As we center on Jesus, may we let Him be the King of our earthly and eternal life. This is a day of true celebration for we know that what happened on the streets of Jerusalem, it's just a glimpse of how things should have been for more than a day. Our genuine joy is almost uncontainable because we know who Jesus is! We have experienced His presence! He has rescued us and redeemed us! What a day to celebrate and be ever so glad that we have an Advocate with our Heavenly Father, our Creator. We are the object of His love, may He be the object of our complete dedication and love. Blessed is He who comes in the name of the Lord!

March 20

Hebrews 4:15
For we do not have a high priest who is unable
to sympathize with our weaknesses,
but one who in every respect has been tempted as we are, yet without sin.
Revelations 17:14 ♥ Matthew 21:1-11

Inheritance of Grace

Perhaps the greatest of all miracles done in the life of any man is the work of redemption. It may seem like a simple decision in our heart to turn our life over to God, but the work of grace goes beyond that decision. The miracle of grace is an inheritance that affords us a wealth that cannot compare to earthly treasurers.

One of the most incredible displays of compassion is to see a family engage in the adoption of a child. Nothing is more moving to see unfold, than a family who opens not only their home but their hearts. To the child, the sentiment is conveyed: "We choose you!" This family opens their home and arranges a place or a room, and the child becomes a part of the family. Something happens in their hearts and a bond is created. Adoption papers are filed and a court appearance takes place when a judge declares the adoption final.

Do you realize that we have been adopted, chosen by God, embraced by His heart and love. Our inheritance is His grace, it is the wealth of our future, it is the key that holds everything else we will ever need. Some think that the greatest inheritance is in the form of money, but the greater inheritance is to realize what grace truly is. It is our freedom from eternity separated from God and judgement.

It is a gift of the greatest proportion.

The decision of acceptance is the beginning of our love to Him.

The papers have been filed, you are His and He is yours, we are His heir and beloved child.

Be centered today in your place in Jesus' heart as you realize that you are His.

Romans 8:15

For you have not received a spirit of slavery leading to fear again, but you have received a spirit of adoption as sons by which we cry out, "Abba! Father!"

John 8:34-36 ♥ 1 John 3:1-2 ♥ Galatians 4:7-9

Godly Courage

In centering our heart, we face a requirement of reigning in our emotions within the context of our circumstances. Often times, we allow our circumstances to dictate the center of our heart and emotions. Jesus shows us such a clear example in His days leading up to the cross. We can easily see that things changed so very drastically for Him, from casual daily walking with the disciples, and teaching them with His gentle sheparding ways. Now, He was literally facing death. Even though Jesus had overcome everything else and ultimately would over-come death, nonetheless, it was a place He had to go through. In consideration, may we not diminish the enormity of what He was facing. We learn from the Word of God, that Jesus, in His humanity, plead for another way to accomplish the will of God, but there was no other way. Today, sometimes, we must face certain situations with Godly courage, knowing that we are standing in the will of our Father. There may not be a way around the mountain you are facing, and it may not move when we pray. But ultimately if we must go through it, or more accurately over it, we can be strengthened to know that the Lord will help us with each and every step up the steep terrain of it. Facing a mountain usually causes most to want to turn the other way, find another route, or abandon the quest all together. Those are our emotions at work and they are very normal feelings, but those feelings do not always line up with the will of the Lord. As we think about Jesus, the Son of the Creator of the Universe, and realize that in all He suffered, He did so for us to know that there is nothing we will face that He is not acquainted with. The suffering and pain, His agony and heart-wrenching loneliness, in it all, gives us such hope that we can make it through. We may not face being crucified on a cross and we are certainly not Jesus, but what we must remember is that Jesus needed the strength of God to go through what He was facing, and we are His! The Word of God tells us: He is ever making intercession for us at the right hand of God our Father. He is not ashamed to call us family. He is our strong tower and refuge. He is the light for our path. He restores our soul. He gives the oil of joy for mourning and the garment of praise for a spirit of heaviness. Why would He tell us He is all these things if we didn't need Him to be so? He is amazing and He is great! He is with you and for you, so stand strong and know that greater is He that is in you, than he that is in the world. Center your heart on Jesus and let Godly courage be yours today.

Psalm 27:1
The Lord is my light and my salvation; whom shall I fear? The Lord is the stronghold of my life; of whom shall I be afraid?
Ephesians 6:10 ♥ Psalm 31:24 ♥ Joshua 1:7-9
Deuteronomy 31:6

Impact of Kindness

At one time or another we have all been the recipient of kindness. Sometimes kind-ness is expected and sometimes it comes as a surprise. It is usually most impactful when we know we don't deserve it. When we surmise and reflect upon our own life and perhaps our walk with Jesus, we cannot help but see how wonderfully kind the Lord has been to us. It has been His kindness that has drawn us closer and closer through Christ's steadfast love and patience. His kindness surpasses our sin and it causes us to finally collapse in His arms of mercy. As the impact of Christ's kindness has such a profound impact on us personally, I am inclined to wonder just how powerful our kindness can be as we share and give as generously as He has. Is there someone with a hard heart in your life, a relationship that perhaps you wring hands over? Kindness touches something in us and it also touches through us. It has the power to be the channel of God's love to brokenness. If kindness has the potential to reconcile the heart of a man back to God, how significant can the kindness of Christ be through our life? I cannot help but remember and ponder the demonstration of a kindness by Jesus in the garden. He was being arrested, ARRESTED, even though He was innocent! He knew He was on His way to the cross to face death. Think of the place Jesus' emotions could have been. In the heat of the moment, in an attempt to defend Jesus, Peter cuts off the ear of the high priest's servant. And as automatic as taking His next breath, what did Jesus do? He put it back on and healed the man…what kindness! He didn't say, "you deserve that", and he didn't leave the man broken. We all wonder where the kindness of Jesus left the heart of that man that day. Often we are so tempted to withhold kindness because of our pride or "right", our opinion or status, but Jesus has called us to be kind to one another because of the great underserved kindness we have known from Him. This quote by Mother Teresa puts it this way: "Let no one ever come to you without leaving better and happier. Be the living expression of God's kindness: kindness in your face, kindness in your eyes, kindness in your smile."

Luke 6:35

But love your enemies, and do good, and lend, expecting nothing in return; and your reward will be great, and you will be sons of the Most High; for He Himself is kind to ungrateful and evil men.

Romans 2:4 ♥ Ephesians 4:32

Ransom

I don't know if I have ever thought of myself in terms of needing to be ransomed. This term is most generally understood for us today for someone who has been kidnapped and held for a sum of money. It's honestly a terrifying thought that something of this nature happens. I am sure that if someone we loved was in such a situation, we would do whatever we could to supply the ransom. Suddenly the preciousness of their life becomes the most important thing and money loses its weight. As we think about the day that Jesus faced the reality of the cross, He prayed in the garden. The Bible says that He was in so much agony that He actually began to sweat drops of blood. I cannot imagine such pressure, unless, someone I loved so dearly was being held hostage. That would probably bring any of us near to such a state. Have we even considered that each of us were a prisoner in need of being ransomed? Jesus was the only sufficient price.

That day, in the garden, when there was no other way, Jesus surrendered His will because of love. No cost was too much for our ransom! Imagine, that in spite of our faults, and failures, Jesus said no price is too high to pay for our freedom from the clenches of death and destruction. A ransom defined: "a sum of money or other payment demanded or paid for the release of a prisoner." Do you see the value that you hold in the eyes of our Heavenly Father today? The greatest issue of the heart of God is to seek and save that which is lost or held captive. He's trying to urge us again and again to share His loveand to tell those that are held that a ransom for them has been paid. Freedom and eternal life is not held for only a few, but Jesus came that through Him the world might be saved. May we re-center the deeds of our life and the purpose of our focus on the ransom that has been paid, Jesus. What a gift, what a love, and what an incredible message we have to share.

1 Timothy 2:6
For there is one God, and one mediator also between God and men, the man Christ Jesus, who gave himself as a ransom for all, which is the testimony given at the proper time.
Psalm 49:7-8 ♥ 1 Corinthians 7:23 ♥ Job 33:24
Isaiah 51:11

Our Deliverer

Today, is a day to remember the footsteps that Jesus took on our behalf as He walked, after being cruelly beaten, up a steep hill to face His own death. His body endured so much pain, that scholars tell us He was almost unrecognizable. Was it turning out to be more than He imagined in terms of physical pain and anguish? It makes us wonder as we know Jesus could have called 10,000 angels to rescue Him. But, if He had, He would have been discounting and disregarding the mandate of God, our Father. His display of faith on this day was the greatest display of faith we can find in the history of the world. We don't often recognize the faith of Jesus, but as we read the Word of God, we find it again and again. This day was paramount; it was the pinnacle of what it means to have faith in God. Jesus has never encouraged us to have a faith that He has not walked within. Have we realized the faith that Jesus had in the plan of God? Think of the times Jesus prayed, those were simply Him trusting God with the same kind of faith that we do whenever we find a quiet place to pray or stand in prayer for a loved one who is ill, when we believe for a broken marriage or wayward child. We often face issues and situations that seem impossible and beyond our ability and strength. The Word of God tells us that when we are weak, He is strong and what a display of that is portrayed on the day Jesus walked to the cross. He walked there because of faith, knowing that in doing so, He would be our Deliverer. The moment in time that Jesus faced the cross would impact humanity for eternity. His faith encourages us today to know that we are loved beyond measure and our deliverance was His life's purpose. May His faith encourage our faith out of weakness and into powerful strength in our wonderful Lord who is able to do exceedingly abundantly, above all that we ask or think on our behalf!

Psalm 34:4
I sought the Lord, and he answered me and delivered me from all my fears.
Psalm 107:6 ♥ 2 Samuel 22:2 ♥ 2 Peter 2:9
Romans 5:8 ♥ Psalm 40:17

Exaltation

Throughout the Word of God we are encouraged to exalt the Lord.
Is that just our praise or is there more? Commentaries tell us
that to exalt is to "esteem highly", or "to prize". Exalting God is
when our soul sings with a deep gratitude that is love-filled
for Jesus, our Savior. It's a song that we may sing through
kindness to others and it may be a song we sing at the top
of our lungs as we drive on our way to work. It may be a quiet
song that is sung in our innermost heart in a room filled with
commotion and people. Sometimes, it's speaking up and standing
for truth, or sharing a testimony with a friend in need of hope.
Exalting the Lord is not just one thing; it's a matter of
our heart and the place we give the Lord in our life. It
is not just an outward display but our esteeming highly
and prizing who Jesus is from our inner-most being.
Maybe your song is small right now, but as your desire to
truly and honestly exalt the Lord in the deepest part of
your heart deepens, the song of exaltation for Him to be
more esteemed in your life than ever before will grow.
Today let your little song grow just a bit louder and longer.
Pretty soon it will be a symphony of your heartstrings to the One
more worthy to be exalted that you can contain. Then it will begin
to spill out and it will negate so much stress and strife from you. It's
turning your eyes to Jesus, the founder and perfecter of our faith,
who for the joy that was set before him endured the cross, despising
the shame, and is seated at the right hand of the throne of God.

Isaiah 25:1
*O LORD, You are my God; I will exalt You, I will give
thanks to Your name; For You have worked wonders,
Plans formed long ago, with perfect faithfulness.*
Psalm 118:28 ♥ Deuteronomy 32:3 ♥ Psalm 34:3
Psalm 99:9 ♥ Exodus 5:2

Constant Hope

When you lose someone dear, there is a certain solace in being able to go to where they have been laid to rest, whether in a cemetery or forest, or at the edge of a mountain ridge. Even though we know they are not truly there, there is something about going where they are buried that brings closure to many questions that surround death. Early in the morning, after Jesus had died, the Bible tells us that the women, presumably Mary and others who followed Him, went to the tomb. They had lost all hope and they went to see if they could linger near where they had at least laid His body in a borrowed grave. Today, we might take flowers, but they took spices as was their custom. They went to the grave that morning because they were so deeply saddened. Their hope was gone and they were distraught, trying to make sense of all that had happened.

They didn't have the understanding to put Jesus' promises in perspective; they only knew He was dead. They didn't know what else to do. They went to find Jesus in the only place they knew to go.

When they arrived, that morning, as they had likely gone the morning before too, they found that Jesus was gone. Realizing that He had been there the day before and was now gone, helps us feel the impact of what happened when they arrived even more. When they found the empty tomb, they also found two angels who said to them, "why are you looking for the living among the dead". When hope is gone, despair can carry us all sorts of places. Sometimes we simply don't know what else to do because disparity can be so misleading. It's important that we stop and ask our hearts in honesty, "Are we looking for hope in places where there is only death?" May we realize that though Jesus died, He rose! He has risen and in that we have constant hope that is unconstrained by life's issues. Jesus is alive and His life gives us unending hope. Being centered on our hope in Jesus is what brings life where there was once death.

Luke 24:1-6a

But on the first day of the week, at early dawn, they went to the tomb, taking the spices they had prepared. And they found the stone rolled away from the tomb, but when they went in they did not find the body of the Lord Jesus. While they were perplexed about this, behold, two men stood by them in dazzling apparel. And as they were frightened and bowed their faces to the ground, the men said to them, "Why do you seek the living among the dead? He is not here, but has risen.

Nearness

Regardless of how you might be feeling or what your current situation may be, there is no one nearer to you than the Lord. He is as near as the mention of His name. The Word of God tells us that He is the friend that stays closer to us than a brother. The implication is that brothers have a special bond and relationship. His nearness calls us to a response. "Will you also come near?" "I'm here, and I want you to know how much you are loved and cared for". Responding to the Savior's nearness is a heart matter. It is letting down our guard and being drawn into His presence. Nearness goes beyond physical proximity in this matter, it is also a level of interaction and sharing with the Lord the issues of our heart.

We can be in a room filled with people and commotion, and still know that the nearness of the Lord is closerthan those closest to us in that place. He requires that we are honest with our hearts and bring our sins to Him that we might be made clean. If we attempt to be clean by following a list of rules we will never find His nearness. It only comes when He cleanses us and then that barrier is dissolved and we will find ourselves closer and closer to Him. The more we love someone, the closer we want to be to them. The Lord already loves us beyond measure and we can know for certain that He DOES want to be closer to us than we can imagine. His nearness is your invitation today.

Psalm 73:28
But as for me, the nearness of God is my good; I have made the Lord GOD my refuge, That I may tell of all Your works.
Psalm 145:1 ♥ James 4:8 ♥ John 15:10
Psalm 119:151

Praise

Athletes train for their sport. Runners run miles to get into shape, basketball players spend hours shooting hoops. Soccer players practice tirelessly to maneuver the ball with their feet. They can develop their skill to a certain place within their individual capacity and talents, but without the influence of a mentor or a wise coach, most will not reach their full potential. A coach provides motivation to build stamina and to reach further and higher. He/she helps an athlete fine tune their gift and they are built up to be stronger than they might be on their own. Coaches are paid huge salaries in professional settings. Life coaches are helping people to grow stronger in their potential. Our praise to God, for His goodness, is an unsung coach for our life, placed there by God, Himself. If applied, it carries the power to help us to be stronger than we are without it. When we function within our own abilities and gifts, we are limited. But when praise is added, it somehow "coaches" our heart in faith and we are strengthened in our spirit. We begin to remind our own heart of God's faithfulness and we know that we are made more than conquerors through Jesus. One of the most devastating things an athlete will ever face is defeat. It's tough to overcome and the same can be true for believers. So realizing the power of our praise is vital. Defeat must go in the presence of praise to Jesus. We may know it, but it may not always be easy to do. That is when we offer Him the sacrifice of our praise and He takes it and blesses us. The blessing we offer to the Lord suddenly becomes the avenue for His presence to minimize our circumstance and give us the strength to face it with determination and greater faith. We may not know the answer but we know the One who is the Answer! Let your heart be centered in praise today, to Jesus and be strengthened by Him.

Psalm 34:1
**I will bless the Lord at all times; his praise
shall continually be in my mouth.**
Acts 16:23-29 ♥ Psalm 149:6 ♥ Hebrews 13:15

Author

Have you ever read a book that was so intriguing that you could hardly put it down? Late, knowing you need to get up early the next day, you think, "just one more chapter"! Written from a perspective that is not our own brings a greater dynamic into a story. The author holds the power of writing the story because an author is obviously the writer. They are the determiners of its content. They hold the pen. The writer of Hebrews encourages us to keep our eyes on Jesus as we live this life, because He is the author and finisher of our faith. He is the writer of our faith. He has a specific plan for each of our lives. I wonder how often we attempt to take the pen from His hand because we so desire to be the writer? For many of us, we are like the Israelites as He continues to interrupt our day to day tasks so that He can write and reveal Himself in our life. Sadly we just keep bumping into the Rock and attempt to push it out of our way, instead of seeing His attempt to interrupt our pursuits. Will we see Him and not just our agenda for Him? Jesus doesn't want us to be His ghost writer; He wants to be the only authentic author of our faith. He has a beautiful plan for each and every one of us, but sometimes we want the story He is writing for someone else. We think it's more exciting, or more glamorous, maybe more honorable and on and on. When we try to be in control, we will miss Him every time. Imagine the story He is really writing as the author of your faith. He is an amazing and creative Author. It's a much better story than we could ever be able to write. May we just gently lay down the pen and let Him pick it up to be the author of His story in us, for His glory.

Hebrews 12:1-2
Therefore, since we are surrounded by so great a cloud of witnesses, let us also lay aside every weight, and sin which clings so closely, and let us run with endurance the race that is set before us, looking to Jesus, the founder and perfecter of our faith, who for the joy that was set before him endured the cross, despising the shame, and is seated at the right hand of the throne of God.
Romans 9:30-33

Carried Away

A fact published by the CDC Emergency Safety
Department says, "2 feet of rushing water can carry away
most vehicles, including SUV's and pick-up trucks."
It's an alarming fact to consider and one that we probably haven't
ever really thought too much about. Maybe some never even
knew that this was a possibility. Many people probably think
that it would take a much deeper amount of rushing water to
carry a vehicle away. The fact above serves as a warning for us.
It's a warning that we can apply to our spiritual walk as well.
There's a high incidence of being carried away spiritually.
It's surprising how many scriptures address this very
issue, warning us. Why are these scriptures there? Because
of the probability that we will not realize how easily we
can be carried away from the principles of God.
There are cautions placed in God's word from His heart to
warn us of our vulnerability. There is an underestimated
danger in what can easily carry us away.
As we center our heart on Jesus, our prudence is vital
and we must be diligent, letting Him be strong in our weaknesses.
Going with the flow is easy; we must refuse the current
and be strong in Christ. Our determination to remain
in Him will keep us from being carried away.

Ephesians 4:14
**Then we will no longer be infants, tossed back and forth by the
waves, and blown here and there by every wind of teaching and by
the cunning and craftiness of people in their deceitful scheming.**
2 Peter 3:17 ♥ Hebrews 13:9 ♥ 2 Corinthians 1:21

Foolish

Today's a big practical joke day called "April Fool's Day".
Light hearted fun is the order of the day
literally all around the world.
I remember living overseas when one of our colleagues played the best
April Fool's joke on us ever, we totally bought
the story, hook, line and sinker!
He roared in laughter as the April Fool's joke was on us and I can tell
you that we felt so foolish! But that was entirely the point…at any rate,
when we realized we'd been had, we were stunned! His story was
SO, and I mean SO convincing, but all along it wasn't true. The goal
of this day is to get someone to believe something that isn't true,
that's the joke! And…that's exactly what the devil tries to do to us
every single day, all day long! He tries to get us to believe that his
lies are truth. What comes with the lies that he implies are truth are
all other kinds of things that range from fear, anger, resentment,
bitterness, selfishness, pride and on and on the list goes. All the
while he sits back and watches us fall for his convincing story
and the last thing we ever realize is that we are being foolish.
May we be so wise by the presence of the Holy Spirit at work in our life!
May we question, "Lord, where is this coming from"? May we
wonder, "Does God's word support this attitude or mindset"? As
we allow the mirror of God's word to be our filter for everything,
we will save ourselves so much heartache and frustration. He calls
us to unmask the felon in our life and rest confidently and securely
in Truth. There is danger in being spiritually foolish, but gratefully
we don't have to remain there. The Word of God tells us that if we
lack wisdom we can ask of the Father who gives to us generously.
It is an ever diligent pursuit to discern the world's truth from God's
and we can only do it with the continual help of the Holy Spirit.
Center your heart on the correct Truth and be wise in Christ.

April
1

James 1:5-6
*If any of you lacks wisdom, let him ask God, who gives generously
to all without reproach, and it will be given him. But let him
ask in faith, with no doubting, for the one who doubts is like
a wave of the sea that is driven and tossed by the wind.*
Romans 1:20-23 ♥ Proverbs 1:5-7 ♥ 1 Corinthians 3:19
1 Corinthians 1:26-31

Completely Infinite

The infinity of God is complete, there is nothing
lacking in it. Because this is who God is, it gives us a
dramatic and fundamentally soundness for our life and
faith. He is beyond the comprehension of man.

He is…
Great
Abundant in strength
Understanding
The Beginning and End
Worthy to be praised
Unsearchable
Above all nations
Above the heavens
Enthroned on high
Unfathomable
Infinite!
In other words, He is limitless.
Now, may we realize that in His greatness, we are His beloved.
He loved us before the foundations of the
earth. He created us and knows us.
I have a few sweet friends who are expecting a baby. They know
that little one is growing but there's an incredible expectation that
they can hardly contain as they wait for the baby's arrival. They
already love that little one! They are planning and rearranging
their lives to prepare for this new member of the family.
God's love for us is even greater, as He has prepared
so much for us out of His infinite greatness.

Psalm 147:5
Great is our Lord and abundant in strength;
His understanding is infinite.
Revelation 1:8 ♥ Psalm 145:3 ♥ Psalm 113:4-6
Ephesians 3:8

Magnet

What's that tug on your heart?
Is that something a pull toward God or away from Him?
Maybe you've been wrestling with Him
about it, trying to make sense of it.
Our soul's greatest need is to be "right" with the Lord.
It is to have peace with Him.
In practical terms, we may feel the pull of the Holy Spirit
in us against the pull of life, it's temptations or worry.
Few can resist the intrigue of playing with a magnet.
Its scientific mystery is mesmerizing. We know that there are
different strengths of magnets and the same is true of the pull
of the things that attempt to draw us away from the Lord.
The power of a magnet is greatest when you are closest to it.
May we rest assured today that God has the greatest pull
if we will surrender to Him.
If we find ourselves drawn away easily, perhaps we are
living too close to the tug of another "magnet".
God will be strong in our weakness and help us
to break away from the attraction of it.
We are assured in scripture that if we draw
near to God, He will draw near to us.
May He be the magnet we center our life on today.

Isaiah 55:6-7
*Seek the LORD while He may be found; Call upon Him while He
is near. Let the wicked forsake his way And the unrighteous man
his thoughts; And let him return to the LORD, And He will have
compassion on him, And to our God, For He will abundantly pardon.*
Hebrews 10:19-22 ♥ James 4:8 ♥ Psalm 145:18

Glory to Glory & Strength to Strength

The phrase "glory to glory" may sound a
bit heavenly when we hear it.
As we read God's word, we must be mindful of that
the words, penned by men, are from the heart of God
for us, not just for a time ago, or a time in the future.
The word of God is applicable for each day.
These words are found in 2 Corinthians 3:17-18, and seem a
bit lofty or something kept for "Just over in the Gloryland",
as the old song goes. But it is a hope for us as we live today.
In essence, it is us growing and finding the character of Christ,
then allowing it to become our character. It is His changing us to
be more like Him, in our actions, words, attitudes and thoughts.
In Psalm we find a similar phrase, as the Lord encourages us,
knowing that the more we trust Him, the more we will grow from
strength to strength. There is so much of Him that He desires
for us to know and contain. It is simply a process of knowing
Jesus more and yielding to the direction He leads us in.
Sadly, in today's culture, instead of moving from glory to glory
and strength to strength, the world is moving from crisis to
crisis and drama to drama. The Lord has so much more for us.
These things distract us from Him and His place in our life.
Sometimes we are led by many other things and opinions,
but "glory to glory" and "strength to strength" will come
as we center our hope, faith and trust in God.

2 Corinthians 3:17-18

*Now the Lord is the Spirit, and where the Spirit of the Lord is,
there is liberty. But we all, with unveiled face, beholding as in a
mirror the glory of the Lord, are being transformed into the same
image from glory to glory, just as from the Lord, the Spirit.*

Psalm 87:4

They go from strength to strength, till each appears before God in Zion.

Listen to That!

There are so many sounds around us every day. Sounds
that are there but we don't always hear them. Birds
singing, TV or radio on, or the neighbor's rooster.
Sometimes we hear them, but often we
don't, though they are still there.
Why is that? Perhaps it's because we are not listening for
them. Listening takes effort and attentiveness. Have you
ever been talking to someone, but you could tell they were
elsewhere in thought, that they weren't really listening.
Faith is our calling. Faith is a call to trust and a call to
rest. It's a call to peace, refusing strife and discord.
But, the Word of God tells us, we must listen before we can trust.
(Romans 10:17) The Lord wants us to be strong in Him but we can't
attain it without His word. If we have His word but are not listening,
our strength is very limited by our own capacities, instead of the
capacity that God has for us in Him. Have you ever had to learn
something new? It wasn't optional, you had to learn it. As a mentor
or teacher gave the instruction, you carefully and attentively listened.
Perhaps you took notes and studied after the session of instruction.
This attentiveness is necessary for us to truly listen to the Word of God.
So many things will distract us and they seem good or innocent but
the ploy of the enemy is to keep us from truly listening, keeping us
weak and powerless in our faith. What if we started to truly listen
to what God is telling us in His word about how He wants us to
live and how amazing His strength is? What if we started to truly
trust Him and live in the strength He promises for our weaknesses?
I venture to say that we would be so much stronger. And that my
friend, is what the enemy fears most. It is the reason he attempts
to keep us distracted with deaf ears to the Word of God.
May we center our attentiveness to listening to His Word today.
Let it be the fuel for your faith in Jesus!

1 Thessalonians 2:13
**And we also thank God continually because, when you
received the word of God, which you heard from us, you
accepted it not as a human word, but as it actually is, the
word of God, which is indeed at work in you who believe.**

Romans 10:17 ♥ Romans 10:17 ♥ Hebrews 4:2

Where is Your Joy Found?

Self-gratification is our attempt to find contentment outside of God. It's often so sugar-coated as "innocent" and it doesn't always appear to be a host of danger. But, we find it's the thing that we put a lot of effort into concealing from others and God. Disguised as happiness or joy, we pursue it, letting it become more and more engrained in our heart or life. Sadly, that takes up some pretty optimal real-estate in our life that belongs to God. It's why He continues to draw us from it and bring us closer to His heart. Self-gratification is an enemy of God that keeps us self-absorbed, instead of consumed by the Holy Spirit. True joy and contentment is only found when we lay these things at the feet of Jesus and release our grip on them. It is saying to Him, "I trust You more than I trust me". From TV to food, to shopping, gossip, competition and on and on our list could go. All kinds of things can attempt to take His place. We must be watchful and diligently aware of the place they attempt to gain in our life. Personal victory through Jesus is attainable because of the cross where He conquered death, hell and the grave to bring us His victory. May we see clearly that selfish pursuits are a disguised counterfeit for the real and true place of contentment. Large or small, it doesn't matter, His call and our surrender will bring us the true joy we desire.

1 John 2:1-6

My little children, I am writing these things to you so that you may not sin. But if anyone does sin, we have an advocate with the Father, Jesus Christ the righteous. He is the propitiation for our sins, and not for ours only but also for the sins of the whole world. And by this we know that we have come to know him, if we keep his commandments. Whoever says "I know him" but does not keep his commandments is a liar, and the truth is not in him, but whoever keeps his word, in him truly the love of God is perfected. By this we may know that we are in him: whoever says he abides in him ought to walk in the same way in which he walked.

1 John 2:16 ♥ 1 Peter 2:11 ♥ Philippians 4:13

Through

I have so many dear friends who have faced hardship
that seemed unbearable and difficulties that were so
overwhelming. Time and again, I have been near enough
to hear them say, "I don't know if I'll ever get over this".
There are things in life that we might never get over,
but God has given us a way in Christ that will bring us
"through" life's trials. He walks beside us and is the
strength for each step we take in the process.
I remember the song, "Hold on My child, joy comes in
the morning!" "The Joy of the Lord is my Strength". It is
in His presence we find His strength that fosters a joy that
cannot be explained and a calm peace that sustains us.
There is nothing we will face that Jesus has not already known,
no heartache that He is not acquainted with, which lets us know
that as we whisper His name, He is there to hold us and help!
May we not, though, remain in such a state but allow
His gentle, shepherding, leading, bring us through.

Psalm 28:6-8
**Blessed be the LORD, Because He has heard the voice of my
supplication. The LORD is my strength and my shield; My
heart trusts in Him, and I am helped; Therefore my heart
exults, And with my song I shall thank Him. The LORD is their
strength; And He is a saving defense to His anointed.**
*Psalm 30:5 ♥ Deuteronomy 31:8 ♥ Joshua 1:9
Exodus 33:14 ♥ John 16:33*

Gifts

Recently I was preparing a special gift for
someone I love and as I did,
I realized how excited I was for them to have the gift.
I couldn't wait to give it and for them to open it. I hoped
they would like it and that its meaning would be felt. As
I was wrapping and tying a bow, I thought of the gifts

that the Lord has given to each of us every day.
When we give gifts, it is our attempt to
convey something to a person.
"You are special to me or you are important to me." I wonder how
God's heart feels as He prepares something so special for us.
I can imagine His reaction when we are
filled with joy by His gesture.
Do we realize that through the blessing of His gifts,
that they are all means of Him expressing His love
to us? There is so much beyond the gift!
When the Lord hears our whispered prayers and makes a way.
When He sees our faith and blesses us, it conveys
an overwhelming sense of His covering.
May we center our heart beyond His gifts into His love.

Jeremiah 29:11

*For I know the plans I have for you, declares the Lord, plans for
welfare and not for evil, to give you a future and a hope.*

Luke 12:6-7

*Are not five sparrows sold for two pennies? And not one of them
is forgotten before God. Why, even the hairs of your head are all
numbered. Fear not; you are of more value than many sparrows.*

1 Corinthians 2:9

*But, as it is written, "What no eye has seen, nor ear heard, nor the heart
of man imagined, what God has prepared for those who love him".*

Enough

Have you ever been near and seen someone
struggling to carry something that was too heavy
for them? You offer to help, but they refuse.
It's so hard to watch, so you attempt to help again.
They refuse, feeling they can or should do it themselves.
You become more insistent and finally they relent
and surrender to your offer to help.
We find ourselves filled with joy to help and they so
completely relieved, have a heart filled with gratitude.
We've all probably been there, on both sides of that story.
The weight of your life may feel pretty heavy.
Somedays we attempt to carry the weight of the world.
Sometimes we face impossibility, and we struggle to make things
work or find a way. Resting in the care of Christ is possible
but only after we surrender to His sufficiency. Coming to the
end of our rope and realizing there is no more left, we can
continue to "hold-on" or we can trust and let our faith in Jesus
be the sufficiency it is. He is faithfully there, every moment.
When He's all you've got, He's all you need.
When holding it all together becomes impossible,
He wants you to let Him hold you and your life.

2 Corinthians 9:8
*And God is able to make all grace abound to you, so that having all
sufficiency in all things at all times, you may abound in every good work.*

Philippians 4:19
*And my God will supply every need of yours according
to his riches in glory in Christ Jesus.*

2 Peter 1:3
*His divine power has granted to us all things that pertain
to life and godliness, through the knowledge of him
who called us to his own glory and excellence.*

Generosity

I recently read a quote that says,
*"When God increases your income,
don't increase your standard of living,
increase your standard of giving".*
The natural tendency is to begin to rely on ourselves instead of
God, on so many levels. He is calling us to give and trust Him more.

The danger is becoming more self-reliant
instead of growing more God-reliant.
This is not just in a monetary way, though it does have its place.
Generosity is about living and giving to others
in ways that exceeds our money.
It's a helping hand, a kind smile, an encouraging
word, putting someone else before ourselves.
Thinking outside of what I need to do for me,
to what can I do on behalf of the Lord for someone else.
Generosity is one of the most beautiful expressions of God's love.
Sharing is precious to watch, gentleness is so soothing to a worried
situation. Lay up your treasures in heaven for someday these
earthly ones will be gone. Only what we do for Christ will last.
He has been so generous to us!!
To our souls by His grace, to our hearts by His
mercy, and to our life by His love. Oh, that we would
be a reflection of Jesus to those around us.
May we look for those who need it most.

Proverbs 11:24
*One gives freely, yet grows all the richer; another withholds
what he should give, and only suffers want.*
Matthew 10:42 ♥ 1 Timothy 6:17-19 ♥ Acts 20:35

Infallible

One of the attributes of God is that He is infallible.
It means that He is unable or incapable of making a mistake.
He cannot be wrong, nor can He ever fail, He is always effective.
Other words to help us understand this characteristic of God are:
Unerring, unfailing, faultless, flawless, impeccable, perfect, precise,
accurate, meticulous and scrupulous.

Why should we realize that today? Why does it matter for us?
Because He is the One who draws us near and pursues us
continually. His ways are perfect and His heart is more pure
than any other. His greatest desire is for us to realize how
very much we can trust Him. We can rest in the ways of God
because He cannot be wrong. We, on the other hand, have every
potential to be wrong apart from His leading, His word and
the voice of the Holy Spirit. As we realize the love story found
in God's word of His undying love for each of us, we must also
be aware that there are things He calls us away from and other
things He draws us toward for our good and well-being.

God is infallible
His word is infallible.
His love is infallible.
His grace is infallible.
His mercy is infallible.
His strength is infallible.

Psalm 12:6
**And the words of the LORD are flawless, like silver
purified in a crucible, like gold refined seven times.**
*Psalm 92:15 ♥ Deuteronomy 32:4 ♥ 2 Samuel 22:31
Psalm 18:30*

The Mirror

April 12

As most of us wake up and start our day, there are things to do here and there around the house. Our devotions, prayer time, morning news, coffee and breakfast. But when it's time to go out for the day either for errands or work, we take special attention to consult the one thing in our home that will reveal to us what our outer appearance looks like. Some take more time than others in front of the "looking glass" as it was called once upon a time. Making sure our hair is in place, make up and clothes in order. We'd never even consider not looking in the mirror before heading out. It's part of our life and how we look is important to us. We wonder what would people think if our hair wasn't just so, etc? Imagine going days without looking in a mirror, and when we finally do the sight is usually worse than we imagined. But is there a mirror for the soul of men? What is it that can help us look inside to see what is truly there? You see, we spend lots of time looking in a mirror at our physical appearances and there's nothing wrong with that. However, the more important matters to God are not the external but the motives and intentions of the heart. His word is the mirror that shows us exactly what is going on in our soul. Oh the danger of neglecting to read the word of God and let it reflect just what our heart holds. We sometimes underestimate what grip unforgiveness can have, as well as bitterness and pride. The enemy will continue to whisper that you can read your Bible later, or that it doesn't really matter if you spend time in His word. He might say, it's too hard for you to understand, but the reality is that this is what he wants you to believe. The word of God is the mirror to show us exactly what is in the depth of our heart and soul. It shows us what we need to relinquish to Him alone. Beware of the danger of not attending to the Word of God. It is the light for our path.

Hebrews 4:12

For the word of God is living and active, sharper than any two-edged sword, piercing to the division of soul and of spirit, of joints and of marrow, and discerning the thoughts and intentions of the heart.

Psalm 119:105 ♥ Ephesians 5:13 ♥ Proverbs 6:23

Integrity

If we realize that blessing follows integrity, we will be less tempted to believe that integrity will follow blessing. Imagine it this way, would we reward our children for doing something wrong or would we reward them doing what is right? It's the same with God in our life, what others see is not what the Lord sees and our integrity is not based on the perception of men but the reality of the pureness in our heart. Story upon story in the Bible of the lives of people who loved God, we see how their integrity preceded the blessings of God, Daniel, Noah, Esther, and Naomi just to name a few. We can be tempted to think that our outward appearances are all that God sees, but the Word of God tells us that He looks at the heart. Many things cause us to work very hard on making the "right" impression to others and that drive can cause us to make Jesus second in line. When we are more concerned about what people think than what the Lord thinks of us, the Holy Spirit pricks our heart, and reveals that to us. We have two choices at that point, we can either dismiss that conviction or pray for the Lord to help us grow in Him, out of that tendency. It will get easier but often, depending on our personality, we can quickly fall back into that same pattern. All the good and kind deeds we do, impressive generosity means nothing if our motives are for the accolades and praise of men. Centering our motives on Jesus and asking the Holy Spirit to set us free from pride will bring us into His likeness. He will help us walk in the humility and strength of the One who matters most in our life. Blessing follows integrity and we have the resurrection power of Christ that makes it possible. Our decision to flee from sin and do all we can to eradicate it from our life is the first step in walking in the integrity we are called to as believers.

1 Samuel 16:7
But the LORD said to Samuel, "Do not consider his appearance or his height, for I have rejected him. The LORD does not look at the things people look at. People look at the outward appearance, but the LORD looks at the heart."
Proverbs 21:3 ♥ Luke 16:15 ♥ Proverbs 16:2
1 Chronicles 28:9

Define

A definition is the communication to describe or explain the meaning of a certain word, idea, or object. There are a variety of ways to describe or define the same thing because most people have different perspectives. We see this played out in various games in which someone attempts to communicate a certain thing or idea as others attempt to guess what it is. It's so fun and I wonder why we don't play them as much anymore. Have you ever considered what defines you and your life? Our lives are so multifaceted that it may be hard to narrow it down. Think for a moment how others might define you? A list of adjectives probably come to mind ranging from your occupation to your looks. For some it may be their gifts that define them or their attitude or personality. But is that what really defines us? Or more appropriately, is that what we want to define us? What defines your life in Christ? Does He define who you are? Is He the center from which everything else pours from and trickles into every vein of your life, influence and existence? This hit home to me recently as the Holy Spirit nudged my heart as I prayed to know Jesus more. This question of definition came from Him and has settled down for me to reckon with. From this place He immediately led me to continually make the first and greatest commandment the priority in my life. I believe it is the essence of knowing Jesus more. To love the Lord, my God, with all my heart, with all my soul, with all my might and with all my strength. Oh, that this would be what defines our lives.

Matthew 22:37
And he said to him, "You shall love the Lord your God with all your heart and with all your soul and with all your mind."
Luke 10:27 ♥ Deuteronomy 6:5

Deserving

We've all been there at one time or another.
Maybe because of a failure or situation, an attitude or regret.
Feeling unworthy or undeserving can become our identity
if we are not careful. May we see this place of "deserving"
through the eyes of Christ and refuse all others.
The essence of worth can sadly weigh heavily on misguided
and illusionary observation. People launch comparisons
and judgements based on bias and familiarity. Some
of those contrasts are heaped upon others while some
are multiplied within the heart that strives to attain
justification. To those we may deem undeserving, whether
ourselves or someone else, the implication may try to
imitate righteousness. In light of the kindness and mercy
of Christ, we can refuse to entertain such notions.
The depth of forgiveness we can joyfully give, stems from the true
and honest reflection of what Jesus has done for us personally.
He has been more than generous, unbelievably so, for most every
one of us. Understanding the complete work of redemption is to
realize that He never demands that we be deserving of the gift
of salvation. Jesus only calls us to receive and open the gift He
prepared for us out of the rich treasure of His royalty. May we
never believe the lie of the enemy that undermines faith to cause
us to wonder whether or not we are deserving or if someone
we love can still be reached by His grace. Evil whispers every
failure and disappointment to equate to being undeserving,
but Jesus' love shouts that He loves us with an unending love
if we will simply believe and surrender our attempts to be
deserving of something that no one could ever deserve.

Ephesians 2:4 & 6
**But God, being rich in mercy, because of the
great love with which he loved us,
even when we were dead in our trespasses, made us alive together
with Christ—by grace you have been saved—and raised us up with
him and seated us with him in the heavenly places in Christ Jesus.**
Romans 8:1 ♥ Ephesians 1:5-6 ♥ Philippians 1:6

Above All

First things first. Going back to the beginning is our call.
Above all, love one another, deeply and genuinely.
Bitterness, resentment and unforgiveness can very
often attempt to jockey for the first place in our life
toward others and sometimes toward God.
It's a challenge at times to remember that the essence of all
forgiveness originates from genuine love. It covers and it heals.
Finding fault is easy.
Being negative and resentful is not generally a pretty sight.
Loving is not always easy but it is always beautiful.
It is our call, regardless of our feelings.
God is love, He sent us His son to be the propitiation for our sin.
Jesus is the love of God that covers our sin.
He wants to be that covering in our lives to others.
If God is love and lives in us, then we have the
capacity to love as He has called us to.
Above all.

1 John 4:8
Above all, love one another deeply, because
love covers over a multitude of sins.

Proverbs 10:12
Hatred stirs up conflict, but love covers over all wrongs.

1 Peter 1:22
Now that you have purified yourselves by obeying the truth so that you
have sincere love for each other, love one another deeply, from the heart.

1 Corinthians 13:4
Love is patient, love is kind. It does not envy,
it does not boast, it is not proud.

No Comparison

In markets around the world you can find all kinds of goods.
There are places you are able to purchase "look
alike" items and some of them are so near the
genuine product, it's hard to tell them apart.
From diamonds to purses, shoes and watches, imitations can
be found. The one thing about imitations is that generally, they
cost much less and their quality is inferior to the real thing.
Around the world, there are religions and beliefs that are
no comparison to the real life we are given in Christ. They
may have some similarities, but ultimately they are lacking
in quality to the point of poverty. The cost of our salvation
was an extremely high price. No other can compare to the
greatness of the power and ultimateness of the blood of
Jesus. His death at Calvary was necessary only one time and
it covers our sins without any need of being repeated.
There is no comparison to the life we have been given in Jesus.
He paid our ransom with His very life when no one else could.
His sacrifice is as superior as the bountiful promises and gifts He
gives to us through His resurrection. Others may try to compete
with the love of God and the power of the cross but they are
merely imitations, attempting to mask their inadequacies.
Jesus is more than adequate and more than sufficient.
He is genuinely perfect and above Him there is no other.

Isaiah 45:5-6
*I am the Lord, and there is no other, besides me there is no God; I
equip you, though you do not know me, that people may know, from
the rising of the sun and from the west, that there is none besides me;
I am the Lord, and there is no other.*

Deuteronomy 32:39 ♥ Psalm 18:31 ♥ Isaiah 43:10

Process

Going through a process isn't always fun,
especially if we are a direct person.
The process for achieving a certain goal may not make sense
to us in the place where we are, but eventually, usually not
until the thing is complete, will we see the benefit of it.
Not long ago, we went through a difficult process to help our
daughter find a place to live in another city. We didn't think it
would be hard and we thought the "process" would be much
quicker than it turned out to be. But, if we hadn't gone through
the process, we would have never found the place God had for her.
It was frustrating at the time and we prayed desperately, all the
while the Lord was leading us and directing our footsteps, thus,
the process to help us get to the place He had for her. At the time
we were very confused but the Lord never left our side in it all.
A process takes us through established steps to help us arrive
at a certain destination designed by God. Some processes are
difficult and some are longer than others, but God has a purpose
in the process at hand. We can rest in faith because He has
proven again and again His faithfulness. Sometimes the process
is about God's timing for a certain season we are in. Always,
though, the process is to show us His incredible love for us. Rest
is trust and trust is faith that He knows better than we do.
Often all we can see is the end and getting there, but the process is
much more important to God. The process is where He teaches us
and shows us things we would have never known about Him if we
hadn't gone through it. We must be careful not to fight against the
process He is leading us through for our good. Rest in Him today!

Isaiah 43:19
*Behold, I am doing a new thing; now it springs forth, do you not perceive
it? I will make a way in the wilderness and rivers in the desert.*
Psalm 125:1-2 ♥ Psalm 37:3-6 ♥ Philippians 1:6

Where Are You

Whenever I call my children, I'm always so curious to know where they are and what they are doing. I usually ask, "where are you?", wondering if they are at work, or busy visiting, etc. I remember when my children were little and things got a little too quiet in the house. I would look around and call their names, until I found them. In a shopping mall or in the neighborhood playing, we would call their names, "where are you?" Sometimes panic sets in, as a parent, when we are unsure of the whereabouts of our children. I imagine that the same feeling can rush upon the heart of God, as we are made in His image. Does it happen when He knows we're nearing or in a place of danger or separation from Him? The Holy Spirit is launched from the heart of God to track us down and bring us back to where we should be. Sadly, some resist and even ignore the gentle whisper of His spirit.

"Where are you?" can be a question that inquires more than a physical location. It can represent a deeper inquiry about the condition of the proximity of our relationship with the Lord. In Genesis, the Bible tells us that God, the Father called out to Adam and said, "where are you?" In that question, the Lord was asking so much more than the location of Adam and Eve. Today, He is still calling to each of us, "where are you?" If we could but hear His love in the question! Today we can listen and let Him search us out in the reserved places of our heart to find out where we really are with Him.

Genesis 3:9
But the LORD God called to the man and said to him, "Where are you?"
John 10:27 ♥ Proverbs 1:33 ♥ Matthew 11:28-29

Courage

Having courage is sometimes easier said than done!
It is especially true when we feel a bit overwhelmed
and when we can't "fix" a situation or problem.
Having courage is a call from the Lord, our God, who loves us and
is able to do exceedingly, abundantly above all that we ask or think.
Having courage doesn't mean having the answer or solution,
it is our faith in the One who does. The proclamation
of our faith is courage that is honored by God. As we
choose His strength over our weaknesses, His heart
takes notice. When we refuse to believe our feelings, and
stand on His promises, He sees our reliance on Him.
God is faithful!
He always has been and always will be!
Regardless of what the enemy may whisper
or what our feelings imply.
We must look above and beyond what is before us
to God, our righteous King and Strong Tower.
In Psalm 144, David wrote of the Lord,

*"my Rock, my keen and firm Strength, My Steadfast Love,
my Fortress, my High Tower, my Deliverer, my Shield."*

2 Timothy 1:7
*For the Spirit God gave us does not make us timid,
but gives us power, love and self-discipline.*

1 Corinthians 16:13
Be on your guard, stand firm in the faith, be courageous; be strong.

Psalm 27:14
Wait for the LORD; be strong and take heart and wait for the LORD.

Psalm 31:24
Be strong and take heart, all you who hope in the LORD.

Contagious

Last year, I took a hazardous materials class for emergency preparedness for my job. I learned about various dangerous substances and importantly, I learned about the process of decontamination. The greater the contamination, the more difficult the decontamination and the greater the risk becomes to higher populations of people.

Have you ever been near someone or a group of people who were laughing so much that you began to laugh too? Or perhaps you were the unfortunate person who got sick after caring for a loved one who was sick? Maybe you've been near a negative person who caused you start carrying a negative attitude. It can happen with our speech, or it can get into our thoughts and take root in a way that surprises us. Life is contagious in so many ways; in good ways and in bad ways. We must be on guard so that we are not contaminated by influences that are contrary to those attitudes Christ calls us to. The Lord can help us and lead us by His wisdom to detect those things that are not healthy for our spirit. Our part is to ask Him to show us and be our guide. When we carry His love and grace, it is truly contagious in a wonderful way.

Giving encourages giving.
Loving encourages loving.
Faith encourages faith.
Hope encourages hope.

1 John 3:2-3

Beloved, now we are children of God, and it has not appeared as yet what we will be. We know that when He appears, we will be like Him, because we will see Him just as He is. And everyone who has this hope fixed on Him purifies himself, just as He is pure.

1 Thessalonians 5:21-22 ♥ Philippians 4:8 ♥ 1 Peter 2:12
1 Peter 4:8

Details

Sometimes it's the little things that make all the difference.
When we look around at creation, the
magnitude of it all is incredible.
A dear colleague of mine just hiked the Grand Canyon. As she
showed me her pictures, I couldn't help but awe at the magnitude of
God's handiwork. I remember my own such experience as well as

others. When I saw Niagara Falls for the first time, when I stand
on the beach and watch powerful waves crash on the shore, the
experience of feeling like an ant at the base of giant redwood trees
and being overwhelmed by the Swiss Alps. Those are incredible
moments, but then to stop and see the tiny flower or butterfly nearby,
so delicate and intricately formed by the heart and hand of God,
causes me to marvel in an awe of the same magnitude because of
His concern for details. Why did God not stop with the awe striking,
with the impressive booming displays that leave us speechless?
Why go on from there? Isn't it just like God to not leave something
out, incomplete or undone! He was just adding frosting to the
cake so to speak…but do you wonder why, like I do sometimes?
Why the vivid colors of thousands of species of birds alone?
Could it be that He wanted us to know that if He
took such care to create these details then we would
know how deeply He cares and loves us.
Could it be that He hoped that when we saw such
things, we wouldn't feel small and insignificant in a
huge, action packed, scary, intimidating world?
Could it be that His details were planned all along, not just to be the
icing on the cake but to be a message to our heart from His? "You are
loved and I see you!" "I care about you and the details of your life".
Look for the Lord today in the little details and I believe you will find
Him there. Right beside you, letting you know that not only does He
want you to be centered on Him, but He is already centered on you.

Romans 1:20
*For since the creation of the world God's invisible qualities-his eternal
power and divine nature—have been clearly seen, being understood
from what has been made, so that people are without excuse.*
Psalm 145:10 ♥ Isaiah 40:28 ♥ Psalm 19:1
Acts 14:17

Valuable

What is valuable to God is not always easy to describe. The things He sees as important may not be what we might typically consider to hold worth. In an attempt to communicate to us, the importance He places on us, Jesus tells us that if He is concerned about little sparrows that have little value then He surely cares a great deal for us because we are extremely important to His heart. The Lord has a premise for this counsel to us. It is to take our focus off of worry and place it on Him. Worry and fear go hand in hand but the Lord our God, again and again, reminds us that we are not to worry but to have faith and trust in Him. In two of the four Gospels, Jesus' words are recorded because He knew we would be tempted frequently to let circumstances regulate our faith. Not only does He tell us that we are so much more important to Him than little sparrows that He keeps watch over, but the detail of His love doesn't just "see" us, He knows every detail of us, down to how many hairs are on our head. It takes effort to refuse to engage in worry and it takes discipline to tell your heart that God is faithful. It's not just a one-time event, sometimes it's daily, and other times it can be moment by moment.

We often see sparrows flitting around in the trees. They are there and then gone, off in flight to who knows where. Their importance is minute compared to the value God places on us and yet, He knows the exact whereabouts of each and every one of them. May this reality help us realize that we matter to God. He cares so much for you and all the details of your life. Let that be your center in Christ Jesus today. He is your Savior!

April
23

Matthew 10:29-31
Are not two sparrows sold for a cent? And yet not one of them will fall to the ground apart from your Father. "But the very hairs of your head are all numbered. "So do not fear; you are more valuable than many sparrows".
Luke 12:5-6 ♥ Luke 12:24 ♥ Luke 12:27

Challenge

When a challenge is presented, we have several options. We can run and hide, pretending it's not really there. Denial and avoidance are not the best tactics to wining a challenge because the longer we avoid it, the more difficult the challenge becomes. We can try to get someone else to take care of it. Delegation is a good thing, right? Yes, but placing blame is not being responsible for what is ours. Thirdly, we can face the challenge, and when we do, we can know that there is One who goes before us. The Lord, our God, is near to help and guide in any challenge we face. He doesn't want us to shrink back in fear but stand up in His name in faith. It is not in our own strength that we will overcome a challenge or make it through. This is first reality we must grasp, otherwise we will probably fail. Many fail and are overtaken by challenges simply because they attempt to stand in their own strength. But that is not what God is calling us to do, He is calling us to stand in His strength. Pride says, "I can do this without God's help". Fear says, "I'm too afraid to face this, what if God doesn't help me or make a way? Then what?" We sabotage God's ability to work when we take on these stances in the face of a difficult challenge. I love the story of David and Goliath. It's a story of a guy so sure of who God was. In his heart, the size of Goliath was never an issue. David made God his focus instead of Goliath. How many times are we faced with a challenge and suddenly it's all we can think about? Instead, what if, when we were faced with a challenge, we were able to really see it for what it truly was, in light of how amazing our God is?

Center on God today, not on the Goliath in your life. God is your strength and He will fight every giant in your life as you let Him. He will use us, just as He used David but we will never be an overcomer if we run and hide in fear. David had to step out in the faith in God that was in His heart, or all of Israel would have been overtaken by the Philistines. God has so much more for us in freedom, than for our lives to be overtaken by giants!

Isaiah 41:13
For I, the Lord your God, hold your right hand; it is I who say to you, "Fear not, I am the One who helps you."
Psalm 27:1 ♥ I Samuel 17:32-37

Sealed

The thought of being sealed in Christ brings me to remember
His burial after the cross. We know that He was buried in a
tomb and the entrance of the place was sealed with a large
rock. However, we gloriously rejoice in the reality that Jesus did
not stay in the tomb but was resurrected through the power
of God. Not only was Christ Jesus sealed in the tomb after He
died, but death was sealed in that tomb. When He rose, He
brought life to us and freed us from the grip of eternal death.

Our salvation seals us in Him and our future is eternal
life, not eternal separation from His love. We have reason to
rejoice to know that we are sealed in Him and through His
resurrection God, through Christ, has given us an amazing
and abundant life for today and for all of eternity.
His sealing is a seal that cannot be broken by human hands,
just as the stone that sealed death in the tomb was not removed
by human hands. The sealing of God is true and is not able to
be penetrated by even the most intense power of the enemy.
We can have rest and peace in knowing that we are sealed by
the Holy Spirit in Christ Jesus, our Redeemer and Savior. His
love seals us, His grace seals us, His mercy seals us and by His
blood we are sealed. May we realize the power of His love, that so
seals us but also keeps us as we will continually walk with Him,
resisting the things of this world that try to overtake our heart.
I am my Beloved's and He is mine.

Ephesians 3:13-14
**In him you also, when you heard the word of truth,
the gospel of your salvation, and believed in him,
were sealed with the promised Holy Spirit,**
*Song of Solomon 6:3 ♥ 2 Corinthians 1:21
Romans 22 6:5 ♥ John 11:25-26*

Take Part

Every day we have opportunities to participate or take part in many things. We can participate in things that are good or not so good. Being a participant can sometimes mean training or preparation. Sometimes it's just being included in an invitation. It's so exciting to know that when we receive Christ, we receive an invitation to be a partaker or to take part in His divine nature.

It is His divine nature that liberates us from the stronghold of sin. While there is none perfect and good except God, He has extended to us the inheritance of His nature. We are no longer dominated by our old nature but, becoming a child of God brings us out of that nature and into His divine nature. It's interesting that as long as we are convinced by the enemy that we do not have any actual rights to the divine nature of God, we will continue to live as a slave to sin; even if we are born again. We must realize what Christ has given us as our inheritance. His inheritance is ours today because Jesus already died on the cross. His death and resurrection activated our right to His nature; all we have to do is realize it is ours. We don't have to be bound any longer by sinful strong holds because Jesus is mighty and demolishes their ability to hold us if we will step into His nature. As long as we leave the inheritance "in the bank" so to speak, we will live impoverished. His inheritance has made us free. We have been adopted by the King of kings and the Lord of lords. Be a partaker today in what is already yours by the precious gift of your salvation through Jesus, our Savior. He is the resurrection and the life! He is your resurrection and your life!

1 John 3:9
No one born of God makes a practice of sinning, for God's seed abides in him, and he cannot keep on sinning because he has been born of God.
2 Peter 1:3-7 ♥ Ephesians 5:1-11 ♥ Romans 6:6

Beatitudes

Attitudes carry a great deal of influence. It happens when we encounter a variety of attitudes of others. At the same time, our attitude has a far greater impact on the lives of others than we probably realize. Attitudes are generally a representation of something within our heart. It is out of the heart that attitudes are seeded. If we find that our attitude is not in line with the Word of God, we can know that bringing it to the Lord, and to His word is the first step in making a change. Have you found yourself critical, negative, judgmental, apathetic, jealous, angry, etc. If so, we have the assurance that the Lord is able to help us, but, it will take surrendering those attitudes for His attitudes. In Matthew, we find a list of what has been labeled, "The Beatitudes". I love the first part of the word, "be". It conveys that the Lord wants us, in our "present" moment, to "be" in Him. When issues and circumstances invade our heart and life, we know from the words spoken by Jesus Himself, there is an attitude that is pleasing to God. I love that in each one, they are preceded by the word, "blessed"! We all want to be blessed and to walk and live in the blessing of God. May I say to you today, look no further…the blessings are listed before us. Sometimes when we find ourselves in these kinds of places, we "feel" anything but blessed. However, our ways are not His ways and His perspective overshadows the perspective of this current age and culture. To give us an understanding of what Jesus was telling us, the Message Bible translation is here for you… Matthew 5:3-12. May we find strength in the reality of being in Him so that out of our innermost being, His attitude will be found and seen.

"You're blessed when you're at the end of your rope. With less of you there is more of God and his rule. "You're blessed when you feel you've lost what is most dear to you. Only then can you be embraced by the One most dear to you. "You're blessed when you're content with just who you are—no more, no less. That's the moment you find yourselves proud owners of everything that can't be bought. "You're blessed when you've worked up a good appetite for God. He's food and drink in the best meal you'll ever eat. "You're blessed when you care. At the moment of being 'care-full,' you find yourselves cared for. "You're blessed when you get your inside world—your mind and heart—put right. Then you can see God in the outside world. "You're blessed when you can show people how to cooperate instead of compete or fight. That's when you discover who you really are, and your place in God's family. "You're blessed when your commitment to God provokes persecution. The persecution drives you even deeper into God's kingdom. Not only that—count yourselves blessed every time people put you down or throw you out or speak lies about you to discredit me. What it means is that the truth is too close for comfort and they are uncomfortable. You can be glad when that happens—give a cheer, even!—for though they don't like it, I do! And all heaven applauds. And know that you are in good company. My prophets and witnesses have always gotten into this kind of trouble."

Luke 6:45
The good person out of the good treasure of his heart produces good, and the evil person out of his evil treasure produces evil, for out of the abundance of the heart his mouth speaks.

Reminders

Some of us couldn't live very productively if we didn't have gadgets to remind of things that are important. In fact, we'd probably miss a lot of wonderful things, lose things and forget things. Have you ever made a list of the things you needed to do on a certain day. Perhaps you made a list for what you needed at the grocery store. If we forget the list, we may remember some of the things, but the likelihood that we will forget part of the list is pretty high. In such moments, we come to realize very quickly the importance of our list. Throughout scripture, it's interesting to see how many times God repeats certain things to us. How much He loves us, the importance of walking out of a life dominated by pride or the place of where our heart should be and so many other things that are necessary for us to live whole. The repetition is the significance.

It's as if He is saying, "be reminded again"! The reprise of God's word is His way of helping us because life can often take our focus elsewhere. It can cause us to remember that He is near and so very mindful of our tendency to forget the things He has spoken to us. These are the things that are essential to being centered on Jesus. Without reminders, we will forget spiritual principles God has called us to that are so important. These reminders serve as a means of encouraging our faith to remember the greatness of Jesus. To follow in His ways are what lead us to our good for His glory in our lives. Reminders are necessary because we so easily forget how very near and present the Lord our God is.

2 Peter 1:12
Therefore, I will always be ready to remind you of these things, even though you already know them, and have been established in the truth which is present with you.
Philippians 3:1 ♥ 2 Peter 3:1 ♥ 1 John 2:21

Speech

Do our words matter? Does God really mind what our speech is?
Does He care that much? The words that we share carry influence and
influence carries impact. Another word for influence is guidance.
Wow! Perhaps this is why the Word of God is filled
with caution regarding our speech. Joy is a side effect
of speech that is encouraging and enriching.
Proverbs warns us that life and death are
in the power of the tongue.
What we say really does matter.
It's not hard to grasp this concept when we consider how affected
we are by the things that other people say to us. Just imagine for
a moment about how you are affected by the encouragement
of a friend or family member. Equally, we can be so impacted
by negative words that are filled with pride and arrogance.
I love a prayer found nestled in Psalm 141:3 that pleads,

*"Set a guard, O Lord, over my mouth; Keep
watch over the door of my lips".*

We can all probably recall a time when we said something we
wish we could take back. Nothing feels worse than to be in that
place. No joy comes from it, but I dare say sadness and misery.
These moments call for quick repentance and apology. May we
never let them become our way of life, dismissing their impact.
O friends, we have such an amazing opportunity to "speak life"
and to "speak hope"! Your words have the incredible potential
to change the course of a situation or relationship. May grace
and mercy season our words as we reflect on the amazing love
of God that has been lavished upon us. May we extend to others
the same kindness that we have needed from Him. As our
words are centered on Him, they have far-reaching influence
to enrich the lives of others and bless the heart of God.

Ephesians 4:29
**Let no corrupting talk come out of your mouths,
but only such as is good for building up,
as fits the occasion, that it may give grace to those who hear.**
*Ecclesiastes 10:12 ♥ Colossians 4:6 ♥ Romans 14:19
Proverbs 15:23*

Kindness

Kindness is love displayed.
It's putting someone else's needs before our own.
It's going out of our way to make a difference.
Here's a sweet story that shares it so well.

When I was seven, my family drove to the Grand Canyon. At one point, my favorite blanket flew out the window and was gone. I was devastated. Soon after, we stopped at a service station. Moping, I found a bench and was about to eat my sandwich when a biker gang pulled into the station. "Is that your blue Ford?" a huge, frightening man with a gray-and-black beard asked. Mom nodded reticently. The man pulled my blanket from his jacket pocket and handed it to her. He then returned to his motorcycle. I repaid him the only way I knew how: I ran up to him and gave him my sandwich.
Zena Hamilton, United Kingdom

Kindness can happen more and more, and the Love of God can be manifested through our lives into the lives of others. God is the essence of kindness. He is the One who calls us and woos us to be selfless and giving. Kindness doesn't happen without our willingness to give. The kindness of God has so touched my life in so many ways. More times than I can count, through many, many people. I am overwhelmed, as maybe you are, by the kindness that is given unconditionally just because of the love inside the heart of the giver. We all know the Lord has done far more for us than we could ever deserve. May our gifts of kindness be determined by generous selflessness. Together, because of the love of God, His kindness can be poured out everywhere we go, in more ways than we can imagine. May we be led to share the kindness of Christ, as selflessly as He gave it to each of us.

Ephesians 4:32
Be kind to one another, tender-hearted, forgiving each other, ust as God in Christ also has forgiven you.
Hebrews 6:10 ♥ Galatians 5:22-23 ♥ Luke 6:35

Continual Praise

Imagine the throne room of God for a moment. In Revelation chapter 4, we can find its brilliant description. It's a place that written words cannot truly communicate. It's more wonderful and magnificent than our imagination can fathom. Within its splendor, day and night, praise and worship to the King of kings and the Lord of lords continues without ending. As heavenly beings never stop lifting their praise to Him saying, *"Holy, Holy, Holy is the Lord God, the Almighty-the One who always was, who is and who is still to come."*

Revelation 4:9-11

Whenever the living beings give glory and honor and thanks to the one sitting on the throne (the one who lives forever and ever), the twenty-four elders fall down and worship the one sitting on the throne (the one who lives forever and ever). And they lay their crowns before the throne and say, "You are worthy, O Lord our God, to receive glory and honor and power. For you created all things, and they exist because you created what you pleased."

I try to imagine this amazing place but I know I'll never be able to truly grasp it for now. We have a greater cause to worship the Lord, a reason far more impacting than even angels do. Life can cause us to be busy and forget from time to time just how amazing God is and how incredible His grace has been in our life. Consider our salvation and what the inheritance of His love means. He hasn't just done one thing for us, He's done EVERYTHING for us. The more we allow the reality of where we would honestly be without Christ to be our center, praise will rise out of our gratitude. With David, the writer of Psalms, may His praise ever be on our lips! May our thanksgiving be so contagious that it encourages others to hope in Christ and trust Him. Indeed, our praise is a reflection of our gratitude but it is also a reflection of our faith. May we no longer waver so easily but may we get a firm grip on our faith, with steadfast assurance, and unshakeable confidence in who God truly is. I am my Beloved's and He is mine.

Psalm 34:1

Of David, when he changed his behavior before Abimelech, so that he drove him out, and he went away. I will bless the LORD at all times; his praise shall continually be in my mouth.

Song of Solomon 6:3 ♥ 1 Thessalonians 5:18 ♥ Psalm 145:1 Psalm 71:6

Everything

Songwriters have written a plethora of songs about the sufficiency of Christ. They are born out of a sense that without the love of the Father, we are completely bankrupt. Here are some of their words: "In Him we live and move and have our being". "If I have You, I have everything, but without you I am nothing". "He's all I need, He's all I need, Jesus is all I need". "I'm desperate for You and I'm lost without You. This is the air I breathe". "More of You, more of You, I have all but what I need is more of You, of things I've had my fill and yet I hunger still, empty and bare, Lord, hear my prayer for more of You." "I need You more, more than yesterday, I need You more, more than words can say, I need You more than ever before, I need You more, I need You more, more than the air I breathe, more than my next heartbeat."* The words go deep into our hearts as we find them so true in our own life. If we have Him, we have everything. As that becomes more a reality in our heart today, may we rearrange the pursuits of our life. Let other things and issues take their place behind and not before Him. As we seek Him first, everything else will come together. (Proverbs 3:5-6) Submitting to His ways and His will must come first. Christ is the key for every locked door and situation. The wisdom of God is the light we need for the darkness around us. Center on Him as your everything today. May we change our view from feeling as though we need to hold all of Him, or get it all together, and instead let Him hold all of us.

May 2

Acts 17:24-25
He is the God who made the world and everything in it. Since he is Lord of heaven and earth, he doesn't live in man-made temples, and human hands can't serve his needs—for he has no needs. He himself gives life and breath to everything, and he satisfies every need.

Job 7:17
What is mankind that you make so much of them, that you give them so much attention,

John 15:5 ♥ Romans 8:32 ♥ Matthew 7:11
Song credits: Kent Henry, Kari Jobe, Alvin Slaughter, Michael W. Smith, Gaither Vocal Band, Kim Walker-Smith

Be Still

Life and culture encourage an ongoing momentum of busyness.
We are daily thrust into activity, demands and responsibilities.
When I was little, I remember well the old merry-go-rounds that
we would get on and then someone would start it to spinning.
The name of the playground apparatus was "merry"-go-round.
While it was fun for a short time, the "merriness" suddenly
became not so fun as we called out for it to stop. Why? Because
a continuation of such a fast circular momentum was sure to
make us sick, and not only that, but the longer and faster
it spun, the more difficult it became to hold on. Then, as it
stopped, depending on how long we'd been on, would determine
how long we walked without balance because the spinning
had changed our internal ability to be centered properly.
Today, kids and adults alike are calling out for someone to stop
the merry-go-round that has them so busy and overwhelmed.
And thankfully there is Someone great who can and who wants
to! The Lord, our God, has a place that is calm and protected in
Him. Life is busy and there are demands we must tend to, but it
shouldn't be furiously spinning out of control to the point we feel
as though we are barely able to hold on. May we see that there is
balance and rest in Christ, as we wait on Him in a place that is
quiet and still in our heart of hearts. Our heart will be "merry"
in Him alone and not in an over busy life that crowds the Lord,
our precious God, into a place that limits all He wants to be in
our life. Center on being a little more still in His presence, and
you will find balance and peaceful rest for each busy day.

Luke 10:38-42

*As Jesus and his disciples were on their way, he came to a village
where a woman named Martha opened her home to him. She had
a sister called Mary, who sat at the Lord's feet listening to what he
said. But Martha was distracted by all the preparations that had
to be made. She came to him and asked, 'Lord, don't you care that
my sister has left me to do the work by myself? Tell her to help me!'
'Martha, Martha,' the Lord answered, 'you are worried and upset
about many things, but few things are needed-or indeed only one. Mary
has chosen what is better, and it will not be taken away from her.*

Psalm 46:10 ♥ Romans 12:2 ♥ Mark 6:31

Teachable Moments

Who needs directions?
"Some assembly required".
Most surmise, "We can figure this out, who
needs to consult the instructions?"
How hard can it be, after all, it looks so simple.
Opening the box with this mindset is much like facing every
day without asking God to help us, to teach us and to lead us.
Sometimes offering to help and show someone an easier or
better way to accomplish a task or handle a situation can be
met with opposition. Some people are more inclined to ask for
help than others. Some want to "figure" it out on their own.
Have you ever watched someone struggle with something that
if they would allow you to help or show them, it would be so
much easier, but yet they struggle on to the point of frustration?
Many times, we are in way over our head and heart before
we stop and ask the Lord to help us or show us His ways.
Pride hardens, but having a teachable spirit or attitude softens,
allowing us to unclench our fist and let God help us. If we
are hardened against others and against God, we will likely
be overrun by stress and anxiety. The moment we surrender
all we know to the Lord, ask Him to show and teach us, is
when we will find rest and peace, because He is faithful!
At the same time, may we have a heart to give and
share the wisdom God has given us to someone who
might be in need of direction and encouragement.
Lending a helping hand to someone as we walk together in this life
is a beautiful example of the love of Christ. May we be determined
to resist pride and surrender and soften our heart before Him today.

James 3:17
*But the wisdom from above is first of all pure, then peaceable, gentle,
accommodating, full of mercy and good fruit, impartial, and sincere.*
Matthew 7:7 ♥ James 1:5 ♥ Proverbs 2:6

Consumed

"May I not be consumed with this life, but instead with
my life in Christ". This filled my heart in prayer today!
It's for each of us from a heart of love from the Lord.
So many things can attempt to consume us.
Even the littlest things, like a poor grade on a test, someone
cut you off in traffic, a cross word we spoke in haste. Suddenly,
those small incidents or other things take on a life of their
own in a way. What we focus on, becomes consuming.
What if, instead of being consumed by this life, we become
consumed with our life in Christ? What if, regardless
of the distractions and incidents of our life, we let Jesus
be who consumes us instead of those moments.
What would that look like lived out?
What a thought!
What a call and challenge to us.
He is big enough to outshine and overshadow even
the most difficult issues we face and are trying to
maneuver through. Moment by moment, it's the constant
re-focusing, like an automatic camera lens.
With a camera, there is something we are
usually attempting to capture
or take a photo of. That main thing is what fills the lens and
the rest is just scenery or background. Though it takes effort
and discipline, we must let Jesus be the center of our focus.
May we let our lens be consumed by Him and let the other
things take their place behind Him in the background.

Hebrews 12:28-29
**Therefore, since we are receiving an unshakable kingdom, let
us be filled with gratitude, and so worship God acceptably
with reverence and awe. For our God is a consuming fire.**
*Deuteronomy 4:23-24 ♥ Psalm 42:1 ♥ Psalm 63:1
Psalm 84:2*

Time

What time is it?

That's one of the most frequently asked questions of our life. We are usually aware of what day or month it is, but time has a way of ticking by rather quickly. So much so, that we are continually looking at the time or asking what the time is.

Why does time matter to us so much?

What is it about time that causes us to hurry or rest in relief? Time can push us in a positive way. It can help us to realize where we are in our day and also in our life. While time should not be our focus, the Bible encourages us to be watchful and to not be foolish about time. We should make the most of the opportunities the Lord has given us.

There are opportunities around us that we often think are unending, but those opportunities can change more quickly than we realize. Moments to be with Jesus, to talk to Him, to give and share His love, come and go like exits on a freeway. Has someone done something special for you that required the sacrifice of time? The gift of time is precious. May we take the time to pursue those moments instead of being too caught up in the pursuit of time. While tasks and our responsibilities are important, may we realize that we have time. We have time to let Jesus be our center instead being driven by time.

Ephesians 5:15-17
Look carefully then how you walk, not as unwise but as wise, making the best use of the time, because the days are evil. Therefore do not be foolish, but understand what the will of the Lord is.

Psalm 90:12
So teach us to number our days that we may get a heart of wisdom.

Colossians 4:5
Walk in wisdom toward outsiders, making the best use of the time.

Our Best

Our best is always our potential.
But there is an even greater potential when we put our best
in the hands of the Lord. Being a Christian doesn't replace a
good work ethic, it is why we have a good work ethic. Being
a Christian doesn't replace integrity, that is where integrity
originates, becoming reality and more than words.
Doing our best blesses the heart of God. When my children were
little and even now, I could tell when they would give their best
or just do what had to be done to "get by". God is our wonderful
and loving Heavenly Father, who knows us and He sees all
that we do. He never stops loving us, even when we don't do
our best, just as we don't stop loving our children when they
could do better. It's true that if we are not careful, laziness can
get the best of all of us from time to time. We must be diligently
watchful and aware of how counterproductive mediocre is.
Do we realize that we grow and become stronger as we give
Jesus our best? When we do not, we become weaker and more
despondent to how the Lord would have us to live. When we
give our best, we are doing so in faith, knowing that it is the
Lord we are serving. He is our example of selflessnessand
kindness. Let us be ever diligent because as we serve others,
it becomes an act of worship and praise to the Lord.

Ecclesiastes 9:10a
Whatever your hand finds to do, do it with your might.
Colossians 3:23-24
**Whatever you do, work heartily, as for the Lord and not for men,
because you know that you will receive an inheritance from the
Lord as your reward. It is the Lord Christ you are serving.**

Ephesians 6:7
Serve with good will, as to the Lord and not to men,

Gifts of Love

Children are gifts to their parents, and
parents are gifts to their children.
Friends and colleagues touch our lives every day.
Fathers are a covering in their families.
Mothers are the heart of their families.
The gifts of those in our lives far exceed our biological families.
In many instances, those who father and those who mother
go way beyond the limits of earthly born children.
I have known of such gifts in my life.
They have deeply impacted not only my life but the lives of others.
As we remember Mother's Day, we must realize that the gifts
we have known are from the hand of our heavenly Father.
We need each other and we have the opportunity,
moment by moment to bless each other.
The nature of every parent is intrinsically from the heart of God.
Often misguided, sometimes underestimated, but His
goodness is in the essence of His gift. As we celebrate
special occasions let the gifts we have and have
known be traced to the goodness of the Giver.

James 1:17
*Every good gift and every perfect gift is from above,
coming down from the Father of lights with whom
there is no variation or shadow due to change.*

Matthew 7:11
*So if you who are evil know how to give good gifts to
your children, how much more will your Father in
heaven give good things to those who ask Him!*

Aim

A dear friend of mine is an archer.
She is not just an archer; she's a champion archer, winning
many tournament awards and trophies. Her discipline of
practice is what led her to such an achievement. It didn't
happen overnight and it wasn't without some agony.
Her form and inward stability is paramount. Without
it, she'd just be shooting arrows in the wind. She has
to keep her aim and diligently keep her stance.
As she strains and focuses her eyes, may we also see that
we are urged with an urgency by Paul in many instances,
to keep our stance, and to remain diligent and stable in
Christ Jesus our Savior. There is earnestness in his words,
from the heart of God, for us to be steadfast and to live a life
that pleases the Lord. We cannot afford to waver or let our
guard down. The more deeply we are rooted in His grace, in
His word and in His love, the stronger we will become.
Keep your aim friends. Keep your stance sure in
Christ. Diligently be centered in the only place that is
definite for your life, in Him, who alone is God.

1 Thessalonians 4:1
*Finally, then, brothers, we ask and urge you in the Lord Jesus,
that as you received from us how you ought to walk and to please
God, just as you are doing, that you do so more and more.*

2 Corinthians 13:11
*Finally, brothers, rejoice! Aim for perfect harmony,
encourage one another, be of one mind, live in peace.
And the God of love and peace will be with you.*

Ephesians 4:1
*As a prisoner in the Lord, then, I urge you to walk in a
manner worthy of the calling you have received:*

Philippians 1:9
*And this is my prayer: that your love may abound more
and more in knowledge and profound insight,*

1 Thessalonians 3:12
*And may the Lord cause you to increase and overflow with love for
one another and for everyone else, just as our love for you overflows.*

His Will

Jesus knew the purpose of His life on earth before He ever left
the beauty of heaven. He came to be our Salvation and in that,
there was a requirement of an ultimate sacrifice of His life. He
knew it was right, He knew it was the purpose and yet, there was a
moment when He said to God the Father, "Not my will but Yours
be done". As close as He was to the Father, their wills differed
for a moment. "Isn't there another way?" Even Jesus faced a time
when He had to surrender His will to the will of the Father.

Every day we are faced with choices of doing our will or the
will of the Father. We sense His leading in many different
situations. We decide in a split second how we will proceed, in
His will or ours. May we begin to lay our will at the feet of Jesus
because His ways are perfect, and our ways are full of fault.
Ways we think are right are not right at all,
even when we try to make them right.
May we constantly center our heart on the will of God,
always being mindful that He is working,
and that there is a plan that is outside of our will and inside of His.
We can pray the prayer of Jesus today in surrender,
"not my will but Yours be done".

Luke 22:42
"Father, if you are willing, remove this cup from me.
Nevertheless, not my will, but yours, be done."

Matthew 26:39
Going a little farther, He fell facedown and prayed, "My Father, if it is
possible, let this cup pass from Me. Yet not as I will, but as You will."

Deuteronomy 32:4
The Rock! His work is perfect, For all His ways are just; A God of
faithfulness and without injustice, Righteous and upright is He.
2 Samuel 22:31 ♥ Psalm 18:30 ♥ Psalm 19:7

"Is" Faithful

The word "is" is important in the word of God.
It carries a meaning that we sometimes
overlook and read right over.
"Is"
Notice where there is an "is", it is not a "was" or "will be".
That means that today, right now, God "is" faithful.
In your present situation, question, and circumstance
God "is" faithful. He "is" with you. You already have the
assurance that you need for each moment you are in.
May we resist the temptation to think that God is away
somewhere, and that we are unnoticed by Him. Our faith
acknowledges the Lord, our God in each detail of our life.
In joy, in sorrow, in hardship and provision,
may we see how very, very faithful God "is".
"Is" is for our "now".
In His greatness, in His mercy, in His love, in His grace,
in His provision, in His strength, in His power,
in His glory, in His presence, and in His covenant...
He "is" faithful!

1 Corinthians 1:9
**God, who has called you into fellowship with His
Son Jesus Christ our Lord, is faithful.**

1 Thessalonians 5:24
One who calls you is faithful, and He will do it.
2 Thessalonians 3:3 ♥ Deuteronomy 7:9

Side Effects

In the medical field, we know the reality
of what side effects can mean.
The goal for any treatment or medication is good side effects and
not bad or adverse ones. The premise of every medical intervention
is to improve a person's health or condition, not make it worse.
As medications and procedures have different side effects,
living life has side effects as well. Living for God and letting
His will prevail in our life carries a blessing for us. Many
of us have heard the term, "garbage in, garbage out".

Living and making ungodly choices, having ungodly priorities
and ambitions will not lead us to the blessings of the Father.
Instead, we will see the side effects of such a life and what those
choices can bring. However, if we make Jesus our mark, and set
our focus on His ways, then we will have Godly assurance.
Think of it this way, what you feed will grow. It's a simple
principle in that, if we cater and feed our "fleshly" desires without
reservation, they will dominate our spirit. The opposite is also
true! With the help and strength of Christ in us, if we pursue
His ways, then our spirit will grow in strength. As we walk out
of the desires of our flesh, we walk into His best for our life.
The Lord, our God, is our Rock and sure foundation.
He is dependable and we can know that the ways
He has established for us are stable and will bring
stability to our life as we center on Him.

1 Peter 2:11
Beloved, I urge you as foreigners and exiles, to abstain from
the desires of the flesh, which war against your soul.
Galatians 4:29 ♥ Romans 13:14 ♥ Galatians 5:24-25
Psalm 37:23

Pleasing to God

Have you ever wondered what pleases God?
What is it that matters to Him?
He calls us to love Him with all of our heart, soul and mind. There
are so many ways we can please the Lord and so many ways we can
displease Him too. In reading about Paul, there was a depth to his
faith that caused him to surrender himself completely the cause of
Christ. In the Bible, Paul declares himself to be a "bond-servant" of
Christ. What did that mean or entail? A bond-servant is someone
who voluntarily gave themselves, and their rights to serve,
becoming one who is subservient to, and entirely at the disposal
of his master; a slave. It meant that they no longer belonged to
themselves; instead, they willingly bound themselves to their master
as a slave. Wow! That's what Paul did because he realized that life
apart from serving Christ would be empty and meaningless.
There are many things that can enslave a person, even today.
Many things are unseen and kept hidden in the hearts of men and
women, but nevertheless, they are there. Sometimes, it's our own
ambition and pursuits. Often we find ourselves trying to "hold
onto" things instead of, laying them down in faith. Fear can grip
our life as we wonder if we can manage without those things that
have become a way of life. Honoring and pleasing God is to resist
those enslavements and entanglements to become a voluntary
bond-servant and to stop serving counterfeit masters that only
become more and more cruel and deplete our lives of joy and rest.
In Christ is where peace lies, in Him there is wholeness and joy.
As we wonder how to get there, Paul encourages us to
start "throwing those things off". In a prayer of surrender,
we can ask the Lord, who loves us, to help us.
A life that pleases God is a life that is richer
than we could ever imagine.

Galatians 1:10
*For am I now seeking the favor of men, or of God? Or am
I striving to please men? If I were still trying to please
men, I would not be a bond-servant of Christ.*
*1 Corinthians 7:22 ♥ Romans 6:22 ♥ 1 Timothy 2:1-3
2 Corinthians 5:9*

Faithful

We are welcome in the steadfastness of God's faithfulness every day. The invitation is for us today. It's ours even if we failed Him in some way yesterday. The lie of the enemy is that we must somehow fix ourselves before we can come to Him. But the truth is, that Jesus is the only one who can make things right and the sooner we come to Him, we will find Him faithful in spite of our faithlessness. Remember when Adam and Eve sinned in the garden? They hid from God and attempted to make a covering for themselves out of leaves because they knew they were naked. In that condition, the last thing they wanted to do was stand before God. They wanted, more than anything to be right before Him again somehow and they did the only thing they could do. But it was an inadequate fix. God was merciful to them and He made a covering for them. He made a covering for our sin, that was a "once and for all" covering, when He sent Jesus to the earth to be our Savior. His blood is the only covering that is adequate and it is the only way we can stand before Him, and not be naked and bare. We must know that He is faithful! Sometimes, we let our inadequate and faithlessness be the measurement of where we are with God. He is faithful even when we are not, He is truly the measurement. Our measurement cannot be ourselves or the life of someone else, it can only be Jesus, He alone is completely faithful.

Deuteronomy 7:9
Know therefore that the LORD your God, He is God, the faithful God, who keeps His covenant and His lovingkindness to a thousandth generation with those who love Him and keep His commandments;
1 Corinthians 1:9 ♥ Romans 3:3 ♥ 2 Timothy 2:13

New Life

Our life in Christ is the new life that He has given to us. It replaces the oldness and emptiness we once knew. His life in us is the restoration that brings wholeness to our fragmented state. New life is receiving the gift of salvation and the daily newness that knowing Him brings. Daily, Jesus is our newness. Continually, He is our source and strength. Sometimes we give an amount of attention to our relationship with Jesus and then put Him on the "back-burner", so to speak. We know He'll be there if we need Him, but that's not the place He desires to hold in our life. May He be at the forefront and may we let everything else take second place to Him.

"The moral miracle of Redemption is that God can put into me a new disposition whereby I can live a totally new life."—Oswald Chambers

The Lord, our God has a new life for each of us that we cannot conceive as we trust in Him. He is leading us to make new choices for the new life He is bringing into being in us. This new life comes from a place of calling out for more of Him. Lyrics of a great worship chorus by Kim Walker-Smit say,

*I need you more, more than yesterday, I need
you more, more than words can say,
I need you more, than ever before, I need you more, I need you, Lord.
More than the air I breathe, more than the song I sing, more than
the next heartbeat, more than anything and Lord, as time goes by,
I will be by your side, cause I never want to go back to my old life.*

Oh that last line, "cause I never want to go back to my old life!" May we decide each and every day to continue to walk into new life in Christ, refusing to go backwards or become complacent in Him. May we sing out, "Jesus, I need You more!"

Romans 6:6
We know that our old self was crucified with Him so that the body of sin might be rendered powerless, that we should no longer be slaves to sin.
*Isaiah 43:19 ♥ Ezekiel 36:26 ♥ 2 Corinthians 5:17
Colossians 3:9*

Beauty

What is beautiful to you?
It has been said that beauty is in the eye of the beholder.
It's true of so many things:
A mate, clothing, vehicles, pets and on the list could go.
What one person sees as beautiful, another may not, not at all!
When we think about what God sees in us, we may ask,
"Lord, I don't get it, what do you see in me? How can you love me?"
In our ordinariness, we are more precious
to the Lord than we realize.

I am reminded of a young boy who was the baby of the family.
He didn't appear to be anything special at all, at least
to those around him. But, God saw something great in
the young boy named David, who tended sheep. You see,
God saw a king in David. God saw potential that was far
beyond what even David, himself, could conceive.
You are beautiful and precious to God. He sees in you what you
cannot see in yourself. He chose you to be His and you were created
by the very hands of God. You are the object of His deep affection.

1 Samuel 16:7
*But the LORD said to Samuel, "Do not look on his appearance
or on the height of his stature, because I have rejected
him. For the LORD sees not as man sees: man looks on the
outward appearance, but the LORD looks on the heart."*

Psalms 139:14
*I praise you, for I am fearfully and wonderfully made.
Wonderful are your works; my soul knows it very well.*

Ecclesiastes 3:11
*He has made everything beautiful in its time.
Also, he has put eternity into man's heart,
yet so that he cannot find out what God has
done from the beginning to the end.*

Without

Living without some things is often quite difficult. "To go without", can carry a negative implication because we have such a strong desire to "have". What is it that might be healthy for us to give up, or to live without? Certainly we know that according to the word of God, the Lord, Himself, has given us access to all spiritual gifts. He wants us to have life and life abundant. So, what is the "without" we should consider? It is living without sin, without selfish ambition and pride. It's refusing to be a part of talk that is not pleasing to the Lord, or indulging in what seems okay but still we know in our heart that we are not being obedient to the voice of the Holy Spirit to live without.

Living without indulging in ungodliness brings a measure of blessing in our life that often is underestimated. The Lord has so much in store for us, but it will only be seen in its fullness when we decide to live without the things that oppose Him in our life. We are all tempted every day to live in these indulgences that don't appear bad or wrong, but often we feel the tug of the Holy Spirit to live without them. We may not realize why or even see the benefit, but obedience to the Lord will reveal it in His time. Do you desire more of Him in your life? Making more room for Him is our first priority so He can fill our lives more. Many of us have had people come to visit. We spend time getting ready for them to arrive. Maybe we have a guestroom for them that we prepare for their short stay. However, it is altogether a completely different situation to have someone come and "live" with you. Having someone come for a visit doesn't require as much preparation or commitment as the latter. Oh, that we might make room for Jesus to truly come in and live with us. Not as a visiting guest that we maintain formalities with and for, but may He have our welcome to make our heart His home.

2 Peter 1:3-4

His divine power has granted to us all things that pertain to life and godliness, through the knowledge of him who called us to his own glory and excellence, through these He has given us His precious and magnificent promises, so that through them you may become partakers of the divine nature, now that you have escaped the corruption in the world caused by evil desires.

Philippians 3:8 ♥ 1 Thessalonians 2:12 ♥ 1 Peter 5:10

Consistency

As I think about parenting, experts tell us that the most important and influential thing we can do for our children is to be consistent with them, in what we teach them, what we model to them, how we discipline and love them.
God is the most incredible parent of all.
He is our Heavenly Father and His ways are perfect.
I remember the title of an old TV sitcom
called, "Father Knows Best".
I never saw the show, it was a bit before my
time, but the title really says it all.

And today, the same is true, our Father knows best.
His love and discipline are consistent and He is calling us to be consistent in Him. Often we try to be consistent in ourselves and we will always fail unless we center our consistency in Him. It's so much like the plethora of New Year's resolutions that are made at the beginning of each New Year. They are made with the best of intentions, but most are short lived, and few are actually fulfilled.

We cannot live consistent lives for Christ on a whim, and we certainly cannot do it apart from Him. He is the essence of our consistency. There is blessing and intimacy in consistency and the enemy will do everything he can to keep us from it. That is why we need the power of the Holy Spirit to help us. We may falter and take three steps forward and one back from time to time, but may we realize that we don't have to. Christ desires that we grow from glory to glory consistently. May our consistency be centered on His greatness and be established in His strength and power.

Hebrews 6:17-18
In the same way God, desiring even more to show to the heirs of the promise the unchangeableness of His purpose, interposed with an oath, so that by two unchangeable things in which it is impossible for God to lie, we who have taken refuge would have strong encouragement to take hold of the hope set before us

Ephesians 4:1 ♥ Romans 8:28 ♥ Ephesians 2:20
1 Thessalonians 4:1

Life in Christ

As people age, a phenomenon seems to occur in which they desire to appear younger. And as the end of life approaches, there are often questions about how well we've lived. Most don't want to grow old, and we've heard it's not for the faint of heart. But we have hope in Christ when we belong to Him, which is a promise of eternal life. His word tells us that we hold eternity in our hearts, it means He made us to want to live forever, but not here. God's design for our salvation is so that we may have eternal life with Him. We shouldn't be afraid of age, but what is far worse, and that is of being eternally separated from the Lord. May we make the most of each day for His glory. Do we realize that once this life is lived, eternal life awaits, life is not over. Eternal life is for eternity, forever, it is ours always and evermore. May we hold loosely to this life on earth and firmly get a grip on the concept of eternal life and what that means for us. Our call is living our life in Christ, not in ourselves or the dictates of our circumstances.

Christ is there in them all, with us and we can choose to live in Him or in them. Can we see the difference and know that we have assurance.

When people are young, they have a plethora of opportunities to make the most of their life. When life is lived, those opportunities may seem to become fewer. However, that dear friend is a myth. We will continually have more than sufficient opportunities for our life to make a difference in Christ. Eternal life is ours when we live in Christ and surrender our sin, regret, and shame to Him, laying these things at His feet to be covered by the blood of Jesus. May we refuse to let those things be our life's significance. Eternity is in our hearts and we are in the heart of eternity in Christ.

May 19

Ecclesiastes 3:11
He has made everything beautiful in its time. Also, he has put eternity into man's heart, yet so that he cannot find out what God has done from the beginning to the end.
John 17:3 ♥ Psalm 16:11 ♥ 2 Corinthians 4:17
Psalm 21:4-6

139

King of kings

Royalty is very intriguing.
We sometimes imagine the palace of a royal family and
what it must be like to live in such a place. Thinking of
an earthly king gives us many different images.
Kings of the past were adored in robes of exquisite
fabrics and expensive embellishments. A crown filled
with precious jewels and gold on their head.
We might envision the place of their throne to be an awe-filled
room with elite furnishings of the highest quality and price.
Some bow in the presence of such a king and declare words of
honor by calling them, "your majesty". And while they may be
kings in their own right and heritage, they are temporary and
their kingdoms are not lasting. However, there is another who is
not an earthly king, but He is true Majesty, there is one King of
all kings, above the rest and His name is Jesus. The royal blood
of Jesus is what gives Him His eternal and unending reign.
Do you realize that we are His?
He welcomes us into His heart.
He set aside the splendor of His throne to live on earth.
Jesus didn't just come to earth because it's a wonderful place to live.
He had one purpose and that was to rescue, seek and save
us, who without Him, are lost. You are of more value to
Him that all the gems and treasures this world's resources
can hold. Jesus' reign and His love are unending.
No one will ever take His place.

1 Timothy 6:13-15

*I charge you in the presence of God, who gives life to all things,
and of Christ Jesus, who in his testimony before Pontius Pilate
made the good confession, to keep the commandment unstained
and free from reproach until the appearing of our Lord Jesus
Christ, which he will display at the proper time-he who is the
blessed and only Sovereign, the King of kings and Lord of lords.*

Revelation 17:14 ♥ Revelation 19:16 ♥ Psalm 136:3

Who's in Charge?

We have two horses, one of them is timid and old. The other horse is spunky and domineering. The other day, we heard a loud commotion in the barn. Going out, we found our old timid horse blocked in her stall by the sassy, "I'm in charge" mare. Gleefully she stood there as a horse-blockade, imprisoning the other horse and occasionally kicking her when she attempted to get out. All that was going on until, someone came out and took over. He was the one that was really in charge not just of the barn, but of the whole property. He said, "Hey! What do you think you're doing? Get out of there". Away she went bucking and carrying on. The hero pinned up the bully and she could only go as far as her small fence would allow. I saw this scenario as a picture of how the enemy attempts to pin us in. He tries to keep us from being free and often in our bondage, we feel his kicks and blows. But Jesus has come to our rescue. The Lord our God is in control, not the enemy! When He comes on the scene, everything changes. When Jesus was crucified, He paid the price for our freedom, but the enemy attempts to lead us into bondage in so many things and in so many ways. May we see it for what it is and realize that our hero has already come, and the enemy has been put in his place. We can come out now and live in the pastures of God's goodness, grace and mercy. He has given us abundant life through His love for us. So the next time, the enemy tries to pin you in, masquerading as the one in charge, don't go willingly! Instead take your stand because greater is He who is in you than he who is in the world. Put the enemy back in his rightful and appropriate place, he is the one to be confined, not you!

1 John 4:4
Little children, you are from God and have overcome them, for he who is in you is greater than he who is in the world.
Colossians 2:15 ♥ Revelation 12:11 ♥ 1 John 2:13-14
Colossians 1:13

He is Mighty

Most can remember a time when hearing children discuss the strength of their dads. "My dad's stronger than your dad" or "My dad is this or that". The implication is that our dad can "out-do" any other. There is something in knowing who your dad is. It equates with confidence and security.
Our heavenly Father is indeed, stronger, and mightier than any other force to be reckoned with in the universe. He cannot be out done by any other.
It's impossible and there's no questioning it.

May 22

When doubt tries to undermine our faith, instead of simply giving in, may we step back and say, "Wait a minute, I KNOW that my Father, my God, my Savior, my Deliverer is greater. I KNOW it, because I KNOW Him". You can't change my mind or my heart.
Who is there beside our mighty God? His power is able to save to utmost.
The enemy is no match for Him, for He has already conquered him. God's power is the strongest there is.
He alone is mighty because He is the mightiest and in His might He bequeaths to us His victory over fear, doubt, anxiety, insecurity and so much more.

Psalm 93:4
More than the sounds of many waters, than the mighty breakers of the sea, The LORD on high is mighty.
Psalm 135:6 ♥ Luke 1:37 ♥ Job 42:2
Revelation 1:8

Forever Changed

One single moment can forever change a person's life.
Such an instant happens when Jesus interrupts a
person's life to bring them wholeness and salvation.
We are forever changed by the sacrifice of Jesus.
A new beginning is initiated when we surrender what we think
life is, to what true life in Christ truly is. We may think we
can do both, have it partially our way and partially His, but
in that striving we continue to hold back pieces of our heart.
Jesus gave His whole-self for us, not pieces as we give pieces,
but He completely gave all. His whole heart pursues our
whole heart for our best so that we will know wholeness.
It can only be ours in Christ. We can work and try as hard
as we can to change, but we will never find contentment and
true fulfillment until the changes He has for us are known.
Have you ever gotten turned around or taken a wrong hiking path.
The further on the path you walked the deeper lost you were
becoming, maybe knowingly and maybe not. At this point you
may have found yourself lost and helpless, unable to discern the
right direction. The necessity was to turn around or to be shown
the right direction to go. Once you knew you were heading in
the right direction again, peace came. It is the same when we
give our life to Christ and choose His path for our life. There's no
greater feeling than knowing you are going in the right direction.
How gracious is God to help us find our way, gently guiding
and leading us if we will completely surrender to His ways.

May
23

Jeremiah 24:7
**I will give them a heart to know Me, for I am the LORD;
and they will be My people, and I will be their God, for
they will return to Me with their whole heart.**
Psalm 51:10 ♥ *Ezekiel 36:26*

Delight

As we have taken such delight in our own children, I can't help
but wonder about the delight God takes in us, His children.
When we see our children happy, pursuing Christ,
responsible and maturing, imagine the heart of God
as we walk with Him as He has called us to.
Typically, as parents, we won't allow anything to keep us from
being faithful to our children. And if we as earthly parents are
as devoted, how much more is our heavenly Father devoted?
Can we esteem God enough or thank Him
adequately for the depth of His love.

Sometimes we lavish on our children, and worry that we may be
overdoing it. How often are we so lavished upon by God, Himself?
We are so loved, so treasured, so blessed all because He is our
Father, and we walk with Him. He delights in us far more than
we delight in our children. Our delight is but a fraction of His.
Sometimes His delight brings correction
and discipline but it is for our best.
Know that you are delighted in today, simply because you are His.
You don't have to earn His delight or beg for it.
It's already sure and true for you.

John 1:12-13

But as many as received Him, to them He gave the right to become
children of God, even to those who believe in His name, who were born,
not of blood nor of the will of the flesh nor of the will of man, but of God.

Psalm 103:13 ♥ Matthew 7:11 ♥ Proverbs 3:12
Malachi 3:17

Disquieted

The great enemies of our faith and stability in Christ today are anxiety and worry. They often intrude into places in our life without an invitation from us. Panic and fear are their accomplices causing us to feel threatened and overwhelmed.
However, we know that Jesus is our Victor,
our Rescuer, and our High Priest.
His word promises that when the enemy comes in like a flood, He will raise up a standard around us. He promises that if we will submit to Him, resist the devil, he will flee. It's not an option, the enemy is under the dominion and authority of God, and we belong to God.
The enemy is not greater than the word of God or His power in us, but we forget that when moments of anxiety attempt to assail us and undermine our faith in the Truth. The real Truth is Christ and Him crucified. He defeated every piece and part of the enemy's arsenal, every one.
Jesus is our Defender and Protector.
When the enemy brings fear and anxiety, it is our God given right to have peace. May we hold on tight to Jesus and let Him battle those things for us, to bring us through and for them to be a thing of the past.

Psalm 94:19
When anxiety was great within me,
your consolation brought me joy.

Psalm 16:11
You make known to me the path of life;
you will fill me with joy in your presence,
with eternal pleasures at your right hand.

1 Timothy 6:6
But godliness with contentment is great gain.

Romans 12:12
Be joyful in hope, patient in affliction, faithful in prayer.

Unshakeable

If you've ever been in a major earthquake, you know the true meaning of being shaken. It's a helpless state where you find yourself doing all you can to hold on for dear life until the shaking stops. Issues in life can feel like an earthquake. Sometimes, they are merely tremors and others are life altering and bring devastation. Earth is all we know and when an earthquake happens, it affects our entire being. Spiritually speaking, we have been assured in God's word that His kingdom is unshakeable and regardless of the happenings of life, no matter how difficult or devastating, we have a sure foundation in Him. Not only is our foundation in Christ secure, but instead of just holding on, we are being held onto by the mighty hand of God, Himself. The writer of Hebrews tells us in chapter 12, that because of the unshakable kingdom of God, we should be brimming over with gratitude and thanksgiving. May we give our attention to our unshakable God and His ways, knowing that we are held and secure in His strength and power to stabilize our life no matter what we face.

Hebrews 12:28-29
Therefore let us be grateful for receiving a kingdom that cannot be shaken, and thus let us offer to God acceptable worship, with reverence and awe, for our God is a consuming fire.

1 Thessalonians 3:5
May the Lord direct your hearts to the love of God and to the steadfastness of Christ.

1 Corinthians 16:13
e watchful, stand firm in the faith, act like men, be strong.

Psalm 31:24
Be strong and let your heart take courage, All you who hope in the LORD.

Peace and Comfort

There are times in life that we must reassure our children that everything is okay and that they don't need to worry. We might tell them once and think that's enough, only to find out later that they need more assurance. Maybe it has been during a stormy night, we tell them, "I'm here with you, everything is going to be okay, don't worry!" Do you know that God doesn't mind reassuring us that He has us in His hands? In Hebrews the writer is the conduit for the heart of God when the word of God conveys His ever constant presence.

The message of the verse, "I will never leave you or forsake you" is actually an amazing verse. You see, in the original Greek, the verse contains 5 negatives. What that means to you and me, is that its true implication is more than just "one", I will never leave you or forsake you. There are FIVE! So, we might translate it this way: God speaking, "I will never, never, never, never, never leave you or abandon you". Or, "I will never, ever, no never, ever, never leave you or abandon you". Can we hear His loving reassurance in the stormy night, "I'm here, I'm here, I'm here, I'm here, I'm here! Have peace and comfort." It's remarkable that God doesn't just say it one time, He conveys it FIVE times! He knew we might face times of distress and that we would need His peace and comfort. In what we go through, He didn't want us to also worry or wonder about His faithfulness or Him being with us or being our Help. May this express to us just how near the Lord is to us in all things.

Hebrews 13:5b
God has said, "Never will I leave you; never will I forsake you."

Deuteronomy 4:31
For the LORD your God is a compassionate God; He will not fail you nor destroy you nor forget the covenant with your fathers which He swore to them.

Deuteronomy 31:6
Be strong and courageous, do not be afraid or tremble at them, for the LORD your God is the one who goes with you. He will not fail you or forsake you.

Deuteronomy 31:8 ♥ 1 Kings 8:57 ♥ Psalm 37:25

Tangible Treasure

Most may not consider themselves to be anything special. Some see only their weaknesses and personal insufficiencies. Ordinary or plain may describe the setting of our life. We know that we are strong in Christ Jesus, but find it sometimes hard to walk in the confidence of that. We don't see the treasure of Christ that we carry in our life for what He truly is. Let's not let the "average" of our life to undermine the treasure that is ours in Jesus. He shines when we least expect it as we are led by His spirit. Obedience is the avenue that allows the treasure in us to flow out to touch others. When the treasure of Jesus touches others and we give genuine help, hope, love and kindness, the heart of God is blessed. He didn't give us a treasure to be buried or keep for ourselves, but the treasure of Christ is His tangibleness. It catches others by surprise and it touches, not only them, but us as well, when we see it happen through our life.

The Lord, our God, never intended that we live in spiritual poverty. He said we have a treasure in our hearts. We carry the treasure of Him. His love, His grace, His mercy, His kindness, His long-suffering, His patience, His help, His hope, His peace, and His selflessness. It's all there, and the treasure of them is priceless, meaning we cannot put a price-tag on love, grace, mercy, kindness, long-suffering, patience, help, peace, hope, and selflessness. Do we recognize what we have been generously given. The word of God tells us plainly it is a treasure.

A treasure is something valuable. It conveys a sense of wealth and great fortune. We carry this as Christ lives in us and through us. Sometimes we dismiss His leading and forfeit the effect of what the treasure in us can accomplish. But as we are mindful of this great treasure, He does the magnificent and profound, the tangible!

May 28

2 Timothy 1:14
**Guard the good treasure entrusted to you, with the
help of the Holy Spirit who dwells in us.**
*Galatians 2:20 ♥ John 17:23 ♥ 2 Corinthians 13:5
2 Corinthians 4:7 ♥ Ephesians 3:17 NLT*

Gift of Repentance

The act of repentance is necessary in all of our lives. It is a necessity of every day. The message of repentance is sometimes shunned and avoided because we do not fully understand the gift that it is for us. There is no greater love and no greater gift than to have the opportunity to have peace in our soul with God our Father in heaven. Our centering on Jesus is often focused on His love and mercy, His kindness and peace. But may we come to cherish, truly cherish that His kingdom comes to our life through the gift of repentance. The gift of repentance is what brings us to freedom and reconciliation with God. It is the greatest longing of our being, as long as we live. Yet, we resist it and think that we're okay without repentance. Friends, His kingdom is so near and His call is to walk in, through the door of repentance. For greater understanding, more humility, a genuine obedience out of our heart of gratitude for His generosity to us. Repentance takes things out of the shadows of our heart and out of the places of grey, for His light to consume and His blood to cover. We want nothing more than all the Lord has for us. We want to know Him, live for Him, be obedient and consumed by Him. It is our faith to come to Jesus in humility, refusing our own spiritual pride, and to acknowledge that He is our everything. It conveys to Him that we care when we have offended His heart. It refuses to ignore when we've sinned, thinking that if we ignore it, it makes it okay and if we forget it, then the Lord does too. The psalmist, David, cried out, "Search me, O God, and know my heart! Try me and know my thoughts! And see if there be any hurtful way in me, And lead me in the everlasting way". The cry of the heart of God is not to condemn us, but to show us His love and grace more than we have ever experienced it before. May we believe, truly believe in His goodness for our life. May we not shrink back from sharing the message of repentance, for it is the message of His great love for those looking for hope.

May
29

"We must sit loose to the world; forsake everything that is against our duty to Christ, and that cannot be kept without hurt to our souls. There is much in the doctrine of Christ that is astonishing; and the more we hear it, the more cause we see to admire it." ~Matthew Henry

Mark 1:15
"The time is fulfilled, and the kingdom of God is at hand; repent and believe in the gospel."
Matthew 3:2 ♥ Titus 1:3 ♥ Acts 2:38
Matthew 4:17

Safe Guarding

We "safe-guard" many things in our lives every day. We lock our homes and cars to prevent or detour theft. We put our babies in car seats to protect them. We put our money in banks to keep it safe. We close our gates to safe-guard our animals and keep them from harm or becoming lost. We keep passwords secret to keep them private, and the list could go on and on. We understand the importance of such safe-guarding, but so often we underestimate the necessity of safe-guarding our families and our own hearts and minds. Sometimes procrastination, sometimes busyness, sometimes apathy keep us from safe-guarding our very souls and raising up a barrier against wrong influence and closing the gates we have left open for the enemy to take advantage of us through. The enemy downplays this importance and we often go along with it, without realizing the severity of neglect.

Jesus has given us victory and strength through the power of the cross to stand against the enemy of our soul. He has given us His authority and His name to ensure that are hearts and souls are well-kept. Our diligence is necessary and our attention is critical to the things that pertain to safe-guarding our hearts. The enemy's plan is to kill, steal and destroy and he attempts to accomplish it in any way he can. He looks for open doors and gates, neglected fences and preoccupation with responsibilities. He softens the significance and gets us to fall for the ever familiar, "it's no big deal" trap. The Lord, doesn't want us to be taken advantage of and so He cautions us, and gives us ample warnings against those attempts of the enemy. Safe-guarding is more a part of our life than we probably realize. The word of God encourages us in the area of safeguarding. Living careful and prudent lives in faith is our responsibility. Faith stands up and trusts the voice of Truth instead of giving into ignorance and being gullible. Safe-guarding keeps us from so much heartache but we must center on Jesus and the word of God, being ever sensitive to the leading of the Holy Spirit.

Proverbs 4:23
Keep your heart with all vigilance, for from it flow the springs of life.
Deuteronomy 4:9 ♥ Proverbs 23:19 ♥ Matthew 13:15
Ephesians 4:22

Flooded

When a flood occurs, the containment for the normal capacity of water is not sufficient to hold the quantity at hand. Flooding is an overflowing. It happens if a river overflows its banks, or if water is left running in a bathtub with a drain plug in place. Abundance is an overflowing that happens when we become so full of God's goodness and grace. It happens when our mind is renewed in who Christ is. His abundance floods our life and overflows into life around us. The abundance of Christ is not lacking in light of the evil in the world around us, though we may be tempted to have a misconception about that truth. Rather, He is more than sufficient, so much to the point that He desires to overflow in abundance. Flooding doesn't happen where there is no rain. It only happens when saturation occurs. The Lord calls us to be so saturated in Him that we cannot contain all that He pours out upon us. The Lord desires that we would be flooded by His presence, and that our minds would be flooded by His spirit and not dominated by our senses. As we seek to be in the presence of the Lord, He will flood all that we are with all that He is!

May
31

1 Timothy 1:14
And the grace of our Lord overflowed for me with the faith and love that are in Christ Jesus.

2 Corinthians 4:15
All this is for your benefit, so that the grace that is extending to more and more people may overflow in thanksgiving, to the glory of God.

2 Corinthians 9:8
And God is able to make all grace abound to you, so that having all sufficiency in all things at all times, you may abound in every good work.

2 Corinthians 8:7
But just as you excel in everything—in faith, in speech, in knowledge, in complete earnestness, and in the love we inspired in you—see that you also excel in this grace of giving.

Live

Daily people are faced with the questions of
life and what it means to truly live.
Many spend a lifetime trying to answer the
questions and to gain all they can.
We have been given the gift to live an amazing life in Jesus.
He is how we live, in Him, because of Him, with Him.
We are held when we live in Him. His ways lead us to live.
Often people attempt to "live" life apart from God, apart from what
brings life to their soul. Sadly, it causes a wandering and a searching,
day after day, year after year. All the while, the Holy Spirit calls
our souls to heed His leading and rest in His ways. Following His

June
1

leading is the path that leads us to truly live. Some have found
this to be true, but somehow they are constantly bombarded by
distractions that pull them elsewhere. Gladly, we can live in Christ,
and the truth is, that if we resist the devil, he must go away from
us. Our living is in His life. We don't have to wonder if it's the best
way because He is the only way for our soul to live. Repentance,
obedience, dependence, and reliance give us security to live in Jesus.
Emptiness becomes fullness when we live in Christ, trusting Him
completely. As He calls, we must listen. Have you ever heard people
talking, but you didn't know what they were saying because you
weren't really listening? Listening requires our attentiveness. Imagine
being turned around in an unfamiliar city. You find someone to ask
for directions. You can do one of two things, listen carefully, take
notes of what they are telling you so that you can find your way, or
you can nod and agree, without really listening, thinking that you
really know the way yourself. You half-way listen and go on, only to
find that you are still lost and are in need of help to find your way.
Sometimes that's how we are with the Lord. We listen partially and
we do not find all the life He has for us. O that we would hear Him
and know He is for our good and our best! He wants us to really live!

Isaiah 55:3
Incline your ear, and come to me; hear, that your soul may live;
and I will make with you an everlasting covenant,
my steadfast, sure love for David.
Isaiah 54:10 ♥ Leviticus 18:5 ♥ Romans 10:5
Psalm 119:175

Take Refuge

Refuge is described as a condition of being safe or sheltered from pursuit, danger, or trouble. In the Hebrew translation refuge also encompasses even more to include hope and trust. We are given instruction more than 40 times in the Word of God to "take refuge" in the Lord. It's not just instruction, but we are implored by the heart of God to find protection in who He is.

Why?

Because in life, alone, without the covering of God, we are out in the open as the enemy aims his weapons at us. Isn't it so amazing to know that we can be held and protected by God Almighty, Himself? Who can protect us above that, above Him? There is no place safer!

Interesting is the invitation of God. Come and take refuge. Relinquish your inadequate tactics and just come and take shelter in Me! How great is His love and provision for us individually? There is no lack in His refuge or protection. When we belong to the King of kings, we are not open game for the onslaught of the enemy. We have a refuge, a strong and mighty fortress that allows us to be obedient even in difficulty.

We have hope and we can trust in His greatness.

Why would we choose to live elsewhere?

Remind your soul of where your refuge is today!

Run there and abide there.

His presence is our refuge.

Psalm 31:19
How great is Your goodness,
Which You have stored up for those who fear You, Which You have
wrought for those who take refuge in You, Before the sons of men!
Psalm 25:12 ♥ Proverbs 1:33 ♥ Psalm 112:7

Upheld

Have you ever had to stand in one spot for a long period of time, perhaps in line waiting for your turn to make a purchase or acquire a ticket? It's not easy at all. We want to find something to sit on or lean on, and we wonder how much longer we will have to stand there. Standing can be wearisome and difficult at times. We shift from one foot to the other. If you've ever been to Buckingham Palace in London, you will see guards who must stand erect and at attention for their entire shift or watch. They cannot be deterred even to smile at those passersby who attempt to get their attention in all sorts of ways. I can't even imagine how difficult that must be. It's amazingly impressive to watch them and there is a certain admiration to see their discipline on public display. We walk away in awe of their determination to just stand. That's all they are doing and it grabs our attention and we admire it. What an example to us as in relation to when Christ asks us to diligently stand. We do okay for a while but get tired easily. We are not so strong and we often waver in our standing. Thankfully we are not standing alone. How wonderful to know that we stand in the power and presence of Jesus, our Strong Tower and we are upheld by His righteous right hand. We have someone greater than any other to lean on. When we get tired, we don't have to worry that we don't have what it takes, we already know that's true! But Jesus has what it takes and when we are in Him, our Lord, we are stronger than we will ever be alone. So when you feel your stance is getting weary and your weakness feels overwhelming, we must reposition, reset, and re-center our stance in the strength of Christ. In His word we find our anchor and in His presence our heart is renewed and reminded that He is able to uphold us.

Isaiah 41:10
Do not fear, for I am with you; Do not anxiously look about you, for I am your God I will strengthen you, surely I will help you, surely I will uphold you with My righteous right hand.
Psalm 18:5 ♥ Psalm 73:28 ♥ Psalm 17:7
Psalm 16:8 ♥ Psalm 138:7

Foundations

In Japan, and in various other places around the world, buildings are constructed to be able to withstand extremely severe earthquakes. Their structures, of course, need attention to special detail and specifications, but the most important part of the entire building is its foundation. In such places, it is not a matter of "if" an earthquake will occur, but "when" it will. A building can look gorgeous from the outside, its furnishings may be of the highest quality, but if the foundation is not properly built, then "when" the earthquake comes, devastation is the probable outcome. In the same way, our lives must be established on the foundation of Jesus, the One who is able to sustain us. Our attention to His ways is so instrumental for strengthening our foundation in Him. Sometimes we want to get on with the building and the fixtures, but we are not adequately tending the foundation to build on. Structures that are built on a foundation that can handle major earthquakes still face some damage, but they are easier to rebuild and repair. Have you ever watched someone walk through a devastating situation with an incredible amount of grace? It is an amazing and remarkable sight to behold. We expect people to fall apart when devastation happens but when they have a sound and strong foundation in Christ, though they are deeply shaken, they find their strength in the greater strength of God. They know they are held within the greater strength of Christ and He buffers the impact. They convey, "I don't know what I would have done without the Lord to help me." The enemy intends for "life-quakes" to halt life in their moment and prevent people from moving past their impact, but God, oh how generously strong He is to bring us through them. The word of God doesn't promise that life will bea "walk in the park", but, it does promise that the Lord, our God will be with us no matter what may come our way!

Psalm 16:8
I have set the LORD continually before me; Because
He is at my right hand, I will not be shaken.
Deuteronomy 32:4 ♥ Psalm 46:6-7 ♥ 2 Samuel 22:19
Psalm 23:4 ♥ Matthew 7:24 ♥ 1 Corinthians 3:11

Reconciliation

The healing of relationships is not an easy process.
It can take a very long time and sometimes,
it never happens because the wound is never addressed.
Injuries take on all shapes and forms, some
are severe and some minor.
The minor ones are often healed easily
without much effort or attention.
Then there are the deep ones that require a great deal of
intervention and help. If they are left unattended, they can
grow worse, cause immense infections and even death.
We may be working on various relationships in our life but
the most important one to consider is our relationship
with God. So many things try to interrupt its health
and well-being. Finding reconciliation through Jesus is
all we need for the healing of our relationship to God. It
happens by simply accepting His forgiveness and grace.
Often people struggle because they are looking in all the wrong
places to find their soul's healing. Jesus died on the cross for
our salvation and in His sacrifice we have healing for spirit,
mind, body and soul. There is nothing left out for us. He
has given all to us. When our relationship with God is right
through His Son, Jesus, then all of our other relationships
can be healed. Healing of relationships through the blood
and life of Christ is possible, even when it looks impossible.
Forgiveness is what we needed for our healing and it is what
is needed when relationships with others are broken.
A friend of mine said it this way, "Forgive & reconcile
with the one who has hurt you and let you down. They
are praying for you to do that more than you know".
Healing brings peace and rest!

2 Corinthians 5:18-19

Now all these things are from God, who reconciled us to Himself through Christ and gave us the ministry of reconciliation, namely, that God was in Christ reconciling the world to Himself, not counting their trespasses against them, and He has committed to us the word of reconciliation.

Romans 5:6-8 ♥ Romans 5:10 ♥ Colossians 1:20
Ephesians 4:32 ♥ Ephesians 1:79

Touchable

There is something of Sunday's communion service I cannot shake.
Something of significant relevance that matters deeply.
Grasping the simplicity of the cross and what Jesus truly intended
for us to hold as ours through His sacrifice, is not easy. We tend
to complicate it all, and when we do, our relationship and God's
place seems far removed from our day to day life. He begins to
appear and feel out of reach for us. That's something God never
intended for the Gospel to be. He came to touch and be touchable,
to be a part of everyday life and help people to see His place
in it, to live among the most common of men and women.
He gave His life so we can live.

He came not just to heal the big things we encounter, but to

be the answer for every little thing we face. He's not just the
antidotefor the impossible things, but His joy is doing those
things that catch us off guard and surprise us, just for the sheer
pleasure it brings to us. He loves loving us! He loves whispering
sweet nothings in our ear, things no one else hears, only us.
He is so individual and He is so very, very present in the life we
live every day. May we realize that we are treasured by our God,
the Almighty, and Creator of the universe! Walk in the intended
relationship He meant for you to know with Him. Centered on
sharing everything that matters to you with Him, and let Jesus
express to you the things that matter to Him. You'll be so surprised
by the nearness of Christ as you center on His closeness.

Jeremiah 31:3
The LORD appeared to us in the past, saying:
I have loved you with an everlasting love;
I have drawn you with loving-kindness.

Psalm 52:8b
I trust in God's unfailing love for ever and ever.
Ephesians 3:17-19 ♥ Psalm 136:2 ♥ Exodus 34:14 NLT

Cause for Celebration

I recently heard a precious testimony of a well-known Christian music artist, who at age 34, was desperate for the man of her dreams. Feeling as though God had forgotten her, she attempted to find the guy that the Lord had for her on her own. Sadly, her attempt left her broken hearted. Then, she surrendered her pursuit of a guy and began pursuing Jesus and just Him. It wasn't very long before the Lord brought the man of God, He had designed for her into her life. The difference was incomparable to what she thought it would be. She thought she had it all figured out, but God wanted something better for her. Her testimony was a wonderful cause for celebration!

How often are we the same way, wanting God's plan and His best for our life but instead of letting Him bring it, we go after what we think it is and all the while we should be waiting for Him to bring it. May we trust Him with all diligence and not be anxious, thinking that if we wait we will miss out. Fear is the most divisive tool of the enemy. It divides us from God, from His best and keeps us self-reliant.

Center your heart of Jesus, give your heart
to His keeping and trust Him.
He is God, alone! Amazing and Almighty!
Why do we think we must "help" Him do His will in our life.
Trust and rest in the grace of His peace.
He knows where you are and He wants to give
you His best more than you want it.

Psalm 107:8-9
Let them give thanks to the LORD for His lovingkindness,
And for His wonders to the sons of men
For He has satisfied the thirsty soul,
And the hungry soul He has filled with what is good.
Psalm 145:6-8 ♥ Psalm 100:5 ♥ 2 Chronicles 7:3
1 Timothy 4:4-5 ♥ Isaiah 63:7

Apart

For a vehicle to work, it must be connected to the battery. One gap in the connection incapacitates its ability to run. We know the engine won't start because it can't without this vital connection to the battery. Everything else can be right for the car. It can look great, it can have a full tank of gas, new oil, new belts, and new tires but without the battery, it won't run, it can't. The science of it isn't a difficult concept. The connection can be loose for a while and it might be increasingly difficult to start the car until the break down becomes severed completely. A car cannot run for one moment if it is apart from the battery. I don't know much about mechanics or vehicles and determining the problem for why it might not run would not be easy for me to figure out. I'd probably be puzzled by it all and wonder where to start looking for a solution. Sadly, we live this way sometimes, spiritually letting our connection with God become more and more loose. It happens gradually and we find it more and more difficult to sense His presence as we allow this part of our life to be in "coast" mode. Then it seems like suddenly we are completely disconnected from Him. Thankfully, even when we don't know the solution to what went array, we have Someone to call. The Mechanic has a name, He is called the Holy Spirit. He is able to fix our disconnection problem and correct the loose connection that has occurred. We cannot live life fully if we are apart from God, rather, He is vital and we must live joined and connected to Him. May we hold on tight, letting Christ be a part of this day and every day we live.

Galatians 2:20
I have been crucified with Christ; and it is no longer I who live, but Christ lives in me; and the life which I now live in the flesh I live by faith in the Son of God, who loved me and gave Himself up for me.
Ephesians 3:12 ♥ 1 John 2:28 ♥ 1 John 3:2

Honor of Love

The greatest honor we have been given is the honor of being loved by God. Honor means to regard with great respect. As some look at themselves they feel inferior in so many ways. Wishing they were better, stronger, or more of whatever it seems others are.

This can attempt to overtake us to the point that we begin attempting to be something that God never intended us to be. Granted, we can all learn and grow and we should, but constantly being tormented by thoughts of inferiority is not of God. Some think that God surely loves them to a certain measure but they are not sure about anything beyond that. Wondering if the Lord just "tolerates" them but in no wise imagining that they would be so honored to be lavished upon by true grace and love. May we resist the impositions of the enemy or our own thoughts. Instead let your heart be certain that you are so loved and it is evidenced with a most significant honor. The honor of God's love is far greater than any other blessing we could ever know or receive from Him. It's so important that we do not let the gifts of God become our focus, but instead realize how very honored we are to be loved by Him. It is with this honor that we have been loved and with the same honor we should give His love to each other.

June
9

1 Peter 4:8
*Above all, love one another deeply, because
love covers over a multitude of sins.*

Romans 12:10
*Be devoted to one another in brotherly love. Outdo
yourselves in honoring one another.*

1 Peter 2:17
Honor everyone. Love the brotherhood. Fear God. Honor the emperor.

1 Peter 1:22
*Since you have purified your souls by obedience to the
truth, so that you have a genuine love for your brothers,
love one another deeply, from a pure heart.*

Holding Onto & Letting Go Of

We accumulate so many things and sometimes our stuff can be overwhelming when we look around. We are then faced with the task of letting go and cleaning out. The same is true in our spiritual lives. As we allow the Lord to search our hearts, He will show us the things in our lives that we need to let go of and those things that we need to hold onto. The problem is that, often we want to hold onto things that we should let go of. So much that fills our time and lives distracts us from God and the fullness of the life He has for us to live. As we pray together, let's let Him show us. Let's open the door of our heart to allow the Lord to come in and help us. We must allow Him iInto every cluttered closet, every junk drawer, and even the attic of our heart. He longs to fill us with more of Himself, taking us to deeper places in the Holy Spirit and to bring us a higher height in Him. However, if we are so full of clutter, there's no place for Jesus. As often happens in our homes, we think we can fit more in. But the Bible tells us that the Lord, our God is a jealous God. He will not share the throne of our life with anything else. Not with another person, not with our own emotions, not with our stuff or our aspirations, desires and unholy pursuits. First, we need to take inventory of what's going on in our heart. Then, be willing to ask Him to help us weigh things by His scales to see if they belong or if we should let go of them so that He can fill those places. The Lord is so faithful and He will show us those things that clutter Him out of our life.

Hebrews 12:1
Therefore, since we are surrounded by such a huge crowd of witnesses to the life of faith, let us strip off every weight that slows us down, especially the sin that so easily trips us up. And let us run with endurance the race God has set before us.

John 6:20 ♥ *Psalm 73:24-26*

He Loves Me, He Loves Me Not

From flowers in a field, one is picked and the holder begins to systematically, pluck off the flower petals. One by one, and as they do, a question is repeated… "He/she loves me, he/she loves me not." The process continues until all of the petals have been pulled from the flower and it is with the last petal that the question ends… "He/she loves me" or "he/she loves me not". The ending petal is supposedly the final outcome, but we know that cannot possibly be so, because there is more to the definition of love, especially God's love. Somedays, we think, God couldn't possibly love me today, not after my yesterday. Surely I've run Him off and His patience has run out. We may feel more loved by God on somedays than on others, but the measure of His love doesn't change. We are never separated from His love, but our sin can cause us to feel separated from Him. That's why we need His mercy and grace. He made a way for us so that we can be restored when our sin separates us from Him. Jesus Christ is the same yesterday, today and forever. He does not change and neither does His love. Friends, we can pluck petals from every wild flower in every field, on every continent and every petal will ring from heaven, "He LOVES me!", "He LOVES me!!", "He LOVES me!!!". Endless is His love, great is His love, and constant is His love. His love is unconditional and it is the pattern for the love He calls us to share and give. You can rest assured today that you are loved with an everlasting love. You don't have to worry or wonder if it will change, it won't. Being centered in God's love allows us to accept it and grow in it and reciprocate by genuinely giving our love to Him. We will never know a greater love than the love God has for us, and we will never give a greater love than when we give His love to others.

John 3:16
For God so loved the world that He gave His only begotten Son that whosoever believeth in Him should not perish but have everlasting life.
1 John 3:11 ♥ 1 John 3:16 & 18 ♥ 1 Corinthians 13:4-8
1 John 3:19-23

Face to Face

Social media is a pretty big deal these days. Facebook, Twitter and Instagram dominate a large portion of our attention and time. Many who live far from family and friends have found social media to be a wonderful gift. However, there are countless people who are losing the connection with those around them. Instead of being more connected, we are running the risk of isolation. One thing that is amazing about social media is the constancy of it. This obsession can easily steal so much of our walk with Jesus if we are not careful. Some cannot let more than a few moments go by without checking status. Friends, that is how Jesus wants to interact with our life! He's constantly there, calling us and inviting us to see what He's up to? May we resist the constant influence of what's happening socially, and remember to focus on Jesus.

Instead of more Facebook, let us seek for more face to face with Him and with each other whenever possible.
He doesn't want to live in a "remote" place from you, but in a "present" and "now" life in and with you!
It's easy to let technology consume so much of our attention without realizing how much we give to it. And it will take far more than you ever intended to give it, but it cannot replace relationship! Do you know that Jesus wants to walk with us, and He wants to be involved with our every moment?
He desires us to be full of Him and not
left more empty and isolated.
The Spirit of the Lord is drawing us away from the many distractions to walk hand in hand and talk face to face with the King of kings, the Lover of our soul!

2 John 1:12
*Though I have much to write to you, I would
rather not use paper and ink.
Instead I hope to come to you and talk face to
face, so that our joy may be complete.*

3 John 1:14
Instead, I hope to see you soon and speak face to face. Peace to you.

Deuteronomy 4:29 ♥ Jeremiah 29:13 ♥ John 10:3

His Radiance

In thinking of our Heavenly Father, God of all, Beginning and End, First and Last, Creator and Almighty, His very being is radiant. The glory of God cannot adequately be described! He is so much brighter that even the sun! Imagine the sun on the brightest summer day or the brightness of the sun reflecting off a field of glistening snow! The radiance of God is brighter still.
One of the definitions of radiance means,
"Light reflected by something".
What could cause God to be so radiant? What is being reflected from His existence? Probability may surmise that His radiance is merely the reflection of His glory. Stunning and truly awesome! His glory is even as a thunder in power.
God's glory is near to us and He is reflected through and by His presence in us to show His love and grace. It not only can fill us, but radiates from Him in us to those around us. When people look at our life, my prayer is that they would see Jesus there. May our affinity for anything apart from His presence wane and the moments of our life be a reflection of His glory and grace.
Oh friends, He is so near!
He is so ready to be involved in the details of your life.
He is so able to navigate our decisions and direction.
When we realize who God truly is, we have nothing to fear, but our hearts can be filled with the greatest of confidence!
May we start distrusting what we can see and begin truly trusting, by faith, what we know but cannot see! We give far too much credence to what we can see, but God calls us to let His power override that impulse and realize His greatness.

Habakkuk 3:4
His radiance is like the sunlight; He has rays flashing from His hand, And there is the hiding of His power.
Ezekiel 1:26-28 ♥ Psalm 29:3 ♥ 2 Corinthians 4:6

Voice

Our voice is completely unique.
We each have a voice all our own and though sometimes two people
can have similar voices, no two are alike. The voices of our children
are unique and we would know them anywhere. When they need
help or we hear their laughter, something in our heart quickens.
The voice of God is specific and unique for each of us. In
His word, we hear His voice as we read, but there are times
when He merely whispers and we know it's Him. There are
other voices that try to mimic the voice of God to us, and
sometimes they fool us into thinking it's Him. Often, our
voice triesto be the voice of God in our heart, but we must be
careful that we are not led off course by our own thinking.
The Bible tells us that when we belong to Christ, we know
His voice. We can hear Him when He speaks. The Lord
wants to speak into our lives daily with His voice. He doesn't
try to keep or silence His voice from us. The Lord wants to
give us direction, to lead us by His voice and the Holy Spirit.
May we refuse the temptation of thinking
that God is too busy to lead us,
or not concerned and withholding Himself from us. He has
more to share with us than we can contain and more than we
can imagine He would want to reveal to us. May His voice speak
louder in your life than any other voice. May we tune into His
voice before all others and let His voice be the one that we follow.

Proverbs 2:1-5
*My son, if you receive my words and treasure up my commandments
with you, making your ear attentive to wisdom and inclining
your heart to understanding; yes, if you call out for insight and
raise your voice for understanding, if you seek it like silver and
search for it as for hidden treasures, then you will understand
the fear of the Lord and find the knowledge of God.*

John 10:27
My sheep hear my voice, and I know them, and they follow me.
1 Samuel 3:10 ♥ Psalm 32:8 ♥ John 10:4

Established

It's so interesting to visit different places and to understand their history. Most historical sites display placards that identify when they were built or established. It's hard to imagine what life was like during such times as the early 18 or 1900s, but we do our best to try to capture what it must have been like for those people to have lived in those days. Taking a moment now and then to recall the sacrifices of those who lived out their faith can help us re-center our own hearts and make determinations about what is important in life. Many gave all they had and all they were to the cause of the manuscripts of God's word, and the message of the Gospel, even laying down their life. Many refused to trust in the justification of men, but instead stood firm on the approval of God, it was more important to them than their own life. Today, life can seem extremely difficult. So much attempts to bombard our attention, our affections, and our attitude. But as we recall our history, what was it that caused our forefathers and mothers to be so established that they refused to be shaken, and refused to give in to popular mindsets of their day? They were rooted and established to the core of their spirit in Christ. It was what determined the passion of their life.

June 15

An excerpt from The Book of Martyrs written by John Foxe
An Account of the Life, Sufferings, and death of Mr. George Wishart, who was strangled and afterward burned, in Scotland, for professing the Truth of the Gospel.
This steadfast believer in Christ was eighty-two years of age, and exceedingly infirm; from whence it was supposed, that he could scarcely be heard. However, when he was taken to the place of execution, he expressed his religious sentiments with such courage, and at the same time composure of mind, as astonished even his enemies. As soon as he was fastened to the stake, and the fagots lighted, he addressed the spectators as follows: The cause why I suffer this day is not for any crime, (though I acknowledge myself a miserable sinner) but only for the defense of the truth as it is in Jesus Christ; and I praise God who hath called me, by his mercy, to seal the truth with my life; which, as I received it from him, so I willingly and joyfully offer it up to his glory. Therefore, as you would escape eternal death, be no longer seduced by the lies of the seat of Antichrist: but depend solely on Jesus Christ, and his mercy, that you may be delivered from condemnation. And then added, "That he trusted he should be the last who would suffer death in Scotland upon a religious account." Thus did this pious Christian cheerfully give up his life, in defense of the truth of Christ's gospel, not doubting but he should be made a partaker of his heavenly kingdom.
What causes someone to be so established? I believe it is a love and devotion deeper than what we can imagine in a physical sense. It comes from walking with and knowing Jesus more and more every day, refusing the distractions of self and thought, being established in our spirit to the spirit of God.

Colossians 2:6-8
Therefore, just as you have received Christ Jesus as Lord, continue to live in Him, rooted and built up in Him, established in the faith as you were taught, and overflowing with thankfulness. See to it that no one takes you captive through philosophy and empty deception, which are based on human tradition and the spiritual forces of the world rather than on Christ.
1 Corinthians 1:8 ♥ Ephesians 3:17 ♥ Colossians 1:23

Knowing Him

In life we know so many things and so many people. The word "know" is defined by: "being aware of, through observation, inquiry, or information", and "to have developed a relationship with (someone) through meeting and spending time with them; be familiar or friendly with". The way we know people differs based on our relationship to them. Knowing about someone does not constitute knowing them. Paul, the Apostle, shared his relationship with Jesus with us in many of the writings of the New Testament. He shared with us so much of what he knew of Christ and the beauty of his knowing was displayed in the way he served Jesus. Before he knew Christ, and had a relationship with Him, Paul was a person of affluence and means. He had power and authority by his position in life and upbringing. It's deeply intriguing to read his words after knowing Christ, when he tells us that everything is rubbish or garbage in comparison to this relationship. The exciting thing about God is that He does not hide from us, He is not exclusively removed from us regardless of our status in life. We have access to Him, to know Him! Get this… He wants us to know Him! He calls us to "get to know" Him. As we know Him more, our love for Him will increase. Our relationship with Jesus is like many relationships in our life. Interaction and pursuit of knowing Him causes us to be nearer in our relationship, but when we stop wanting to know Him, and we stop pursuing Him, we tend to drift backwards, and away. Have you ever been out in a fishing boat? As long as the engine or little motor was running and advancing the boat forward, you were continuing to cross the lake. But the moment the engine stops, depending on the direction of the wind or waves, your little boat would begin to drift in that direction. Maybe slowly, and ever so slowly, the drifting happened. May we be ever mindful and cautioned from the drifting that can happen in our relationship with Christ. To know Him! There is nothing greater, nothing sweeter, nothing more satisfying, regardless of situations and circumstances. Center on knowing Jesus again today.

June 16

Philippians 3:8
More than that, I count all things to be loss in view of the surpassing value of knowing Christ Jesus my Lord, for whom I have suffered the loss of all things, and count them but rubbish so that I may gain Christ.

1 John 5:20 ♥ 2 Peter 3:18 ♥ John 17:3

Mindset

Have you ever heard the phrase, "he's just set in his ways"? It's actually another way of describing a person's mindset that has become rigid and inflexible. Sometimes those mindsets can keep others and God at bay and prevent us from having close relationships. Our mindset can be critical or insensitive to the plight of others. It may keep us from hearing God's voice and being open to hear another person's view.

Our mind should be "set" on those things that the word of God calls us to, and the Holy Spirit should be the filter that our thoughts are set by. He calls us to think on those things that are true, honorable, just, pure, lovely, and commendable. Our own thoughts as well as the influences of others tend to condition the attitude of our life, and that is often referred to as our mindset.

June 17

Many things can influence our mindset, from a difficult and painful childhood to pride. Is our mind set on Jesus or those things above? Is it set on the insignificant and are we proactive and careful about the places our minds choose to be set?

Our mindset influences every decision of our life and so it makes it imperative that our mind is set on Christ. The word of God calls us to set our mind on things above and not things below. So many things will and do attempt to influence and cause our mind to be set on this life and not things that are eternal. However! There are drastic differences in the person who chooses to let his mindset be on Jesus and the love he has received in his life. Out of that mindset, the Lord can do mighty things. Healing can come to relationships, people will see the hope of Christ in us and we, ourselves, will have a greater peace. May we center or set our mind on Him today, letting Jesus change us and reset our mind if need be, through His grace and love.

Colossians 3:2
Set your minds on things that are above, not on things that are on earth.
1 Chronicles 22:19 ♥ Philippians 4:8 ♥ Luke 6:45

Inspiring

Inspiration is the application of something that we receive.
It can come in many forms and it motivates us to action.
By the inspiration of the Holy Spirit, men and women have
accomplished the unimaginable and overcome insurmountable
odds. There are countless times that we have been inspired,
but do we realize the moments of our life that inspire others?
Such moments happen in a split second, when we stand
up for truth and what is right, even if others don't.
There have been times that we didn't speak up for our faith, but
someone else did. Maybe we could've but fear and insecurity
held us back. When we see courage, it inspires courage.
When we live out our faith, it inspires others in their faith.
Inspiration is powerful and when we pursue Christ, it leads
others to Him. In the Book of Hebrews, the Apostle Paul
encouraged believers to follow him as he followed Christ. Yes,
that was a long time ago, but it is still an example for us.
Perhaps we don't feel very inspirational, but even
the smallest act of faith can touch and inspire
others in ways we may never see or realize.

1 Thessalonians 5:11
*Therefore encourage one another and build one
another up, just as you are doing.*

Ephesians 4:29
*Let no corrupting talk come out of your mouths, but
only such as is good for building up, as fits the occasion,
that it may give grace to those who hear.*

Hebrews 10:24-25
*And let us consider how to stir up one another to love and good works,
not neglecting to meet together, as is the habit of some, but encouraging
one another, and all the more as you see the Day drawing near.*

Proverbs 12:25
*Anxiety in a man's heart weighs him down,
but a good word makes him glad.*

Father

The Lord's prayer is our example.
It is the response to when the disciples
asked Jesus to teach them to pray.
I love the fact that it begins with these words, "Our Father".
The very first word is one of confidence and
strength. It is the ownership that tells us that God
is ours. He is my father and He is yours.
We serve a big God and He is so good.
What does that mean for us?
It means He is our covering, and it means
He knows what's best for our life.

It means that no matter what has or has not happened in
our relationship with our earthly father, we have a father in
heaven that we can always run to. When our children have
a big problem, they know that when they call their dad, he is
right there, ready and willing to help them. He will usually
drop whatever he is doing to be at their aid depending on
the urgency. They know where to go for help and today, I
want to remind you of where your help comes from!
May we be careful that we not let our problems become
bigger than who we know Our Father to be! He is
YOUR Father in heaven and He is your help.
As the song says, "He is your good, good father, it's who He is!"
He is great and so greatly to be praised
for His goodness to each of us.

Psalm 121:1-2
I lift up my eyes to the hills. From where does my help come?
My help comes from the LORD, who made heaven and earth.

2 Corinthians 1:3
Blessed be the God and Father of our Lord Jesus Christ,
the Father of mercies and God of all comfort.

Psalm 68:5
A father of the fatherless and a judge for the
widows, Is God in His holy habitation.

Protect Your Heart

Where is your heart today? What is stirring there?
The matters of our heart matter a great deal. Our heart is the
well-spring of our life, and it is imperative that we are prudent
in guarding it! In much the same way that treasures are guarded,
we must carefully keep our heart protected. We must guard the
gifts of God and vision of His purpose there. Many things will
attempt to steal the treasures of our heart, from fear and pride to
insecurities and apathy. Even more than these things are moments
of frustration, disappointment and circumstances that rob our
joy and peace, bringing a flood of fear and doubt. Treasures are
to be protected. They are not left out in the open for someone
to find easily or to steal easily. Within the interior of a bank
is the safe where valuable money is kept behind a massive
door that keeps it secure. This vault is fire and theft proof.
Much is invested in the security of what will need protection.
May I implore you to protect your heart! It is in our heart that God
begins to work and lead us. It is from here that He grows us and
brings our gifts and talents out for His glory. Our heart is constantly
the focus of the enemy. It is continually under his scrutiny and
assault. As we endeavor to guard our heart, let's realize that God has
not encouraged us to do something we are unable to do. May we
be careful not to expose our heart, leaving it open and vulnerable.
Our God is great and empowers us with His own strength. We are
empowered by Christ Jesus and the resurrection power that belongs
to Him alone. The Lord, our God is our Defender! As we boldly
stand to protect and guard our heart, may we realize that He is our
Mighty Commander in Chief, our Warrior, strong and mighty in
battle! Take a few moments to look inside, see if there are places
that you have left open. Are there exposed areas that we are leaving
unguarded? Protect that treasure under the covering of Christ!

Proverbs 4:23
Keep your heart with all vigilance, for from it flow the springs of life.
Psalm 24:8 ♥ Exodus 15:3 ♥ Exodus 15:6
Deuteronomy 4:9

Governing Authority
of God's Word

There are so many things and people that want to be our authority.
Of course, there are civil authorities and
laws that the Lord calls us to obey.
However, there are many other things that
should not have a say in our life.
For instance, our past should not govern our
future. Fear is not in charge of us!
The word of God is the governing authority for our life.
As entities like corporations, nations and organizations are established
there is a requirement for a governing authority to be the basis for
their existence. That governance usually comes in the form of a
constitution or articles of the corporation. It is what keeps that entity
from getting off track and away from the core values in and for which
they were created. In much the same way, are we to be personally
governed and anchored in the Word of God. So many other things
will attempt to get us off track and suddenly we will find ourselves far
from truth and far from the ways of the Lord. Diligence and careful
reflection in prayer, as the Word of God is our guide, will keep us from
the demise of self-governance that can be so adamant and stubborn.
May we completely be led by the Lord, letting His Word be our center
and the supreme governance within everything else must comply.

Joshua 1:8
This book of the law shall not depart from your mouth,
but you shall meditate on it day and night,
so that you may be careful to do according to all that is written in it;
for then you will make your way prosperous,
and then you will have success.

Joshua 23:6
Be very firm, then, to keep and do all that is written in
the book of the law of Moses, so that you may not turn
aside from it to the right hand or to the left.

Psalm 119:89
Forever, O LORD, Your word is settled in heaven.

Isaiah 40:8
The grass withers, the flower fades, But the
word of our God stands forever.

High Call

Have you ever been called out to do something special? Maybe your name was drawn in a drawing for the winning prize. Perhaps it was being honored for a job well done. Those are little instances and just dimly exemplify the meaning of a high calling. But the Lord, our God, sees us and He has called us to Himself, to walk in a place that is higher than where we've walked before. Imagine being the winning recipient of a very valuable prize and declining it. Imagine saying, "no, that's okay, I couldn't take that, I don't deserve it, surely it is intended for someone else". Sometimes we think that the blessings of God or His calling are for others and not us. We don't feel as though we are good enough and that they are for others who are more perfect than we are. There hasn't been a mistake made by our loving Heavenly Father. He has called us to walk in the high call of God in Christ Jesus. The key is to know that He has called us to walk in the high call of God, not in ourselves but in Jesus, the one and only Son of God. He is why we can walk there, and He is why we ever accomplish anything. As we walk in faith, we grow to know His sufficiency and His empowering. In those moments, we realize that it is not because we are anything in ourselves or because we are better than anyone else. The call of God is to live in freedom, out of a place that the enemy tries to imprison us within. May we see that to walk in the high call of God is to bring to others His great love and grace, extending and showing His peace and mercy. Know today, that He has divinely called you to walk in a calling that is higher than yourself, and greater than every insecurity, He is calling us to walk in His Son, Jesus.

2 Timothy 2:19
He has saved us and called us with a holy calling, not because of our own works, but by His own purpose and by the grace He granted us in Christ Jesus before time eternal.
Philippians 3:14 ♥ Romans 8:28 ♥ Romans 11:29
Hebrews 3:1

Fulfilled

To be fulfilled is, "to be satisfied or happy because of fully developing one's abilities or character". True and complete fulfillment has been given to us in the gift of the saving grace of Christ. The illusion of fulfillment is when we pursue what we think will bring us contentment and serenity, only to find that we are still lacking and still empty. For some it might be "status" or "wealth", for others it may be a rewarding career. All in all the deep longing of every heart is to have true fulfillment.

As we read in God's word, we find that Jesus came so that God's plan would be fulfilled or complete. So, the obvious is that without Jesus, the plan would have been incomplete or unfulfilled. Apart and removed from Jesus, our purpose and contentment will never be understood. Without realizing it, our pride or selfish ambition can be the irreconcilable conflict that contends for the place of rule in our hearts. How gracious and patient the Lord is with us and He lovingly draws us to Himself and away from ourselves.

Jesus is not only the means for the fulfillment of God's purposes for our life, He brings to each of us a fulfillment we will never find in ourselves.

Being centered in the fulfillment of Jesus will lead us to the fulfillment we long for day to day, and moment by moment.

Philippians 1:2
Grace to you and peace from God our Father and the Lord Jesus Christ.

Philippians 1:6
And I am sure of this, that he who began a good work in you will bring it to completion at the day of Jesus Christ.

Psalm 138:8
The LORD will accomplish what concerns me; Your lovingkindness, O LORD, is everlasting; Do not forsake the works of Your hands.

1 Corinthians 1:8
He will sustain you to the end, so that you will be blameless on the day of our Lord Jesus Christ.

Speak Life

The spoken word of God created the universe. He spoke the magnificence of creation into existence by just His voice. The Lord, Our Father, God of all, spoke and life began. It's an awesome thing to even try to understand that out of nothing, everything came into being just because God said so! His word is the authority of the universe. It is more powerful than we can imagine. He has generously given us His word to treasure in our hearts. Think of it! God, gave us His word so we would know Him, not just know about Him. I am overwhelmed by His love when I realize and remind myself that God didn't have to give His word to be written down for us. He did it out of love for us. Did you know that our words are very powerful as well? When we think about speech and our voice, the things we say, I think we often forget that we are made in the image of God. We do not speak as God and rule as His voice does, but our words carry powerful implications. He warns us to be careful about what we say. The Lord encourages us and wants us to know that we have the capacity to speak life by what we say. We have the Word of God to help us to be strong and courageous in our speech. It's exciting to realize that we can make a difference just by what we say and how we say it. However, sometimes self can get in the way, it brings pride and selfishness, and we tend to get focused on ourselves. Sometimes we forget that goodness can come into a situation by the way we handle it and what we say.

Turn the tide!

Instead of chiming in with a negative comment, may we speak life and hope!

Let's not think that because we feel a certain way that it would give us a right to speak foolishly. It's easy to get pulled into a negative mindset and let that become a pattern that can infect our own heart and the hearts of others around us. What we say really does matter and it can make a wonderful difference.

Proverbs 18:21
Death and life are in the power of the tongue,
and those who love it will eat its fruits.

Ephesians 4:29 ♥ Romans 14:19 ♥ Ecclesiastes 10:12
Romans 15:2 ♥ Ephesians 5:4 ♥ Colossians 3:8

God is for You

The enemy or the devil is described by the word of God as the accuser of the brethren. That means he is our accuser. He makes accusations and we often find we cannot defend ourselves. We may even wonder how he can haveour past down better than we do. He reminds us of every mistake and every disloyalty against the One who loves us most. We wonder if we will ever feel close to God… We are torn to our core, wondering how to divide the truth from the enemy's accusations between the truth of what God says about us. There comes a point when we must make a choice and it's not any easy one, no matter how easy is sounds like it would be. The choice is determining to live in the discipline of what is true about God's perspective. It's relinquishing and letting God have and cover our past by the blood of the gift of Jesus, His son so that we can go free. The sacrifice of His blood at Calvary decides what our future is, not our past and certainly not the enemy of our soul. Sometimes it takes more courage to stand up and refuse to believe the lies of the enemy than to just let them keep us imprisoned in defeat and under a shadow. Remember that the Word of God tells us, "Though I walk through the valley of the shadow of death, I will fear no evil for you are with me; Your rod and staff they comfort me." One scientific note is to remember that if there is a shadow, there is a Light! Believe what is true about God. He is for you, He really loves you and He's there, right there beside you. Each and every time we are bombarded by the enemy, we are faced with a quick decision of taking his side or God's. Let's resolve to side with God and not our enemy. Have you ever seen a team of 4 and 5 year olds playing soccer? It's so cute. They are all out there running after the ball, but they sometimes get turned around and don't realize they are running in the wrong direction. From the sidelines, parents are cheering and yelling, "run the other way!, your goal is that way!, turn around, that's the other team's goal!" Sometimes we forget to look at the goal of where we are running toward. Is it the goal of our enemy or the goal of the One who loves us and gave all He could give to make us winners through Christ Jesus?

June 25

Psalm 56:9
***Then my enemies will turn back in the day when
I call; This I know, that God is for me.***
*Romans 8:31-32 ♥ 2 Kings 6:16 ♥ Psalm 118:6
Isaiah 41:10*

His Will

When you consider the common everyday thought about a will, several things come to mind. We might think of a will that someone puts in place to communicate who will receive their possessions and money once their life is over on earth. The other thought regarding the word, will, is the internal desires of a person that causes them to do certain things. Then there is the issue of knowing and understanding the will of God and how it pertains to each of us personally. Sometimes we don't know which direction to go and we don't feel His presence. It causes us to wonder and contemplate how are we to proceed? What is His will for us? The answer is in His word and because we know that a will is the giving of an inheritance we can rest assured that His will can be known. Maybe not to the exact moment we want it because God's timing is part of His will. The principles of His goodness navigate for us the will He has for each of us. We hold in the Word of God the ultimateness of His inheritance because of the sacrifice of Christ.

In the moments of indecision and confusion that attempt to cloud our view of God's direction, we can refocus and re-center on Him and soon He becomes so clear in our situation and circumstance. We may not know exactly which way to proceed, but we hold in a depth of our heart, the assurance that we don't have to know right now because He does. We can rest in the timing of His will and stop striving inside. His peace is ours as we do.

Isaiah 55:12
For you will go out with joy And be led forth with peace; The mountains and the hills will break forth into shouts of joy before you, And all the trees of the field will clap their hands.

Jeremiah 29:11
For I know the plans I have for you, declares the LORD, plans for welfare and not for evil, to give you a future and a hope.

Psalm 40:5
Many, O LORD my God, are the wonders which You have done, And Your thoughts toward us; There is none to compare with You. If I would declare and speak of them, They would be too numerous to count.

Challenges

Our lives are filled with challenges every day. Some of those challenges are not just about the situations that we face, but they are often the ones that the Lord has allowed in our life for our good, or to make us stronger. Looking to our own abilities in dealing with challenges can be an automatic response, but the Lord calls us again and again to rely and depend on Him during those times.

The commonality of life is one of the reasons Jesus came to live on earth. He lived a life that was pleasing to God, the Father, so that we would know that as we live our life, there is nothing that we will face that He hasn't faced as well. He was sinless and we are not, however, in His sinless life, Jesus was tempted in every way just as we are.

The challenge is to automatically run and seek God's help in all that we face. We can know that Jesus knows exactly what we are going through and He has a plan to deal with it that is far better than our devised ideas and solutions.

In our relationships, in our family, in our finances, in our work, in ministry, in all we must do and everywhere we go. We have the Lord to help us, the Holy Spirit to guide us. We don't have to have all the answers, we just have to know where to go for the answers we need.

He is our ever present help in time of need!

Jesus calls us to give Him our cares because He cares for us.

1 Peter 5:7
Give all your worries and cares to God, for He cares for you.

Psalm 46:1-3
God is our refuge and strength, a very present help in trouble. Therefore we will not fear though the earth gives way, though the mountains be moved into the heart of the sea, though its waters roar and foam, though the mountains tremble at its swelling. Selah

1 Corinthians 1:9 ♥ Hebrews 10:23 ♥ 1 Corinthians 10:13

Lenses

Have you ever used a camera that does not automatically focus when you look through the lens? In order to use it effectively and get great pictures, the photographer must carefully hold the camera steady and adjust the lens until it's just perfect. It's only then that they will get the best pictures. We've all seen pictures that have been taken that are blurry and out of focus. We don't usually enjoy looking at photographs that are taken haphazardly, causing them to be severely out of focus.

Our natural desire is to see things clearly. We are naturally drawn to what we can see the easiest. While there are instances that we have to strain to see something or make out what it might be saying, by and large, we don't want to do that for a long length of time. We will either get our glasses or move closer so we can see well. Our hearts work much the same way. While the Lord continues to draw us closer to Himself through the Holy Spirit, our heart naturally desires to clearly see Him. We want to know and understand God more in our lives. As we look for Him, our view, and our focus gets steadily clearer. When Jesus lived on the earth, He would often touch the eyes of a blind person so they could see. This is what He does for us each day in the areas of our life where we are blinded and unable to see clearly. He's like our glasses, but there is one important element that is required. We must put our glasses on if they are going to help us at all. He wants to give us more and more clarity in knowing and walking with Him. It's a lot like putting our glasses on, except it comes in the form of asking and looking to Him for His view and perspective. You see, God's ways are not our ways and His ways can only been seen by looking to Him. Jesus is still opening the eyes of those that are spiritually blind. As we live for Him, we may no longer be blind but our lenses may have gotten out of focus. Out of His great love, the Lord wants to help us see Him more clearly, thus we will see our way through life more clearly.

Psalm 16:11
You will make known to me the path of life;
In Your presence is fullness of joy;
In Your right hand there are pleasures forever.
Jeremiah 29:13 ♥ Exodus 33:14 ♥ John 15:9

Nearness

Our daily need for the nearness of God is truly the most vital of all of our needs. Conversely, we don't always realize how very near He already is. Sometimes we say, "He's just a whisper away", but the other day, within this thought, I realized that He's never away. We just have to remember that Jesus is the friend that sticks closer than a brother to us. As we live each moment, we don't live alone. He is right beside us, waiting to share and have the sweetest of all relationships with us. What an incredible thought, that the God of this universe is with me right now as I write to you. He's right there as you are getting prepared for this day ahead, wondering about a loved one, and praying about a situation. He doesn't play hide 'n seek with us, the Lord our God is with us! He promises to never leave us or forsake us. It's important that we are wise to the tactics of the enemy who attempts to barricade us in a "feeling" mode or mentality. He will attempt to get us to base our faith on our feelings, but we must remember that Jesus is the way, the TRUTH and the life. Not our feelings and certainly not the advice of the enemy's doubts or the fear he attempts to capture us in.
We don't walk alone, we walk with Jesus, the
author and finisher of our faith!
We can talk with Him throughout our day
and not just in our "quiet" time.
He so wants to be a part of the details
and every moment
of our day.

Proverbs 18:24
*A man of many companions may come to ruin, but
there is a friend who sticks closer than a brother.*

Psalm 73:28
*But as for me, the nearness of God is my good; I have made the
Lord GOD my refuge, That I may tell of all Your works.*

Psalm 16:8 ♥ John 15:15 ♥ Psalm 145:18

Praise

The praise of our life carries a weight of who Christ is in our life.
It reflects much about our faith and trust in Him. The praise of
our day and the way we honor Jesus is so very precious. Likewise,
meeting others who carry praise as a part of who they are, conveys
the very greatness of God. The praise of our life, inside the deepest
part of our heart and soul, is a light to a wanderer, it is hope
to the desperate and it is a great comfort in bringing peace.
The Word of God reminds us that He inhabits the praise of
our life. As we magnify the Lord, our God, inside our own life,
we expand the welcome mat of our life to Him. Some make a
supposition that praise will be automatic because we have accepted
the gift of salvation, but it doesn't happen quite that way.
However, our praise is a determination to turn our heart,
our will, our desires, and our thoughts intentionally to
the greatness of the Lord our God. The Lord our God,
He is worthy! The Lord our God, He is wonderful!
The Lord our God, He is great! The Lord our God, He is faithful!
The Lord our God, He is supreme! The
Lord our God, He is above all!
He is the One and Only true and living God who is
more in love with us than we could ever imagine!
Our praise is our acknowledgement of all that He is.
As we love Jesus with our praise, we find Him nearer
and closer! He is made known by our praise.
May the praise of our life be centered on His majesty today!

Psalm 34:1
I will extol the LORD at all times; his praise will always be on my lips.
Exodus 15:2
The LORD is my strength and my defense; he has become my salvation.
He is my God, and I will praise him, my
father's God, and I will exalt him.
Deuteronomy 32:3 ♥ Psalm 44:8 ♥ 1 Chronicles 16:9
1 Chronicles 29:13

Friendship

Children can show us so much wisdom in regard to friendship. It's so precious to watch them. Maybe, like me, you can remember meeting a new friend when we were little and asking these 5 little words: "Want to be my friend"? And off we'd go, running and playing. I remember a moment several years ago when a co-worker I barely knew, sat down beside me at lunch one day and said, "let's be friends". Today, she's one of my dearest friends, but I don't know if that would have happened without the intentionality of deciding to be friends. I'm so very grateful for that day. Friendships in life take on many different faces. No two friendships are the same. Some friends are more knitted into our hearts and lives. Some we don't see for a length of time because of life, but we can pick up right where we left off and at that moment our hearts sense the gift that we hold. Others are sweet acquaintances that we treasure. Friendship is one of those things that grow more precious with time.

July 1

But the gift of friendship holds great value, and is so worth holding onto. It's worth investment and attentiveness. I've heard so many testimonies from people who needed a friend and when they asked God, He brought them that special friend. Friendship is a gift from God to our life to bring encouragement and joy to our days. Oh that we would see the treasure of our friends! In terms of our friendship with God, we must also cultivate and tend to it. It is the most amazing friendship of all. Independence is an enemy to our friendship with others and with God. When we find ourselves giving into the deception of isolation, it causes us to run the dangerous risk of thinking we don't need others and sadly that we don't need God. It's easy to do, especially if we've experienced pain in the past. Pride says, "I can do this alone" but there is joy in doing it together. May we be willing to be a friend, make new friends and invest in the lives of others. Sometimes our desire to control our life and the circumstances of our life keep us from allowing God to be the friend that He desires to be in our life. May we not shrink away from the friendship Jesus offers us. He comes to us each and every day, in simplicity and says, "let Me be your friend"!

Talk to Jesus about the little things in your heart. Share your dreams and bring Him your heartache. Appreciate Him for His goodness, wisdom and faithfulness.

Ecclesiastes 4:9-10

Two are better than one because they have a good return for their labor. For if either of them falls, the one will lift up his companion. ut woe to the one who falls when there is not another to lift him up.

John 15:12-15 ♥ Proverbs 27:9 ♥ Proverbs 17:17a

Stirring

Jesus is the King of ages. He stands as the Almighty and Everlasting Lord over all. In His presence we are invited to just be with Him. He stirs us out of our routine to know who He truly is. Sometimes we are content to just live in mediocrity. We get a bit lulled into going through the motions of faith. Jesus is far too wonderful to be worshipped with such an attitude. Paul encouraged Timothy to stir up the gift he held in his heart of Christ in him. He was saying, "Go out of your way, do something you've never done or something that you've let slip away from you". Something happens when we invite Jesus into our apathy. He wants to stir His love in us until our ho-humness is lost in His presence and purpose. We can fall into the enemy's trap of thinking we're fine and procrastinate our passion for Christ away until little of it remains. Or, instead, we can know and have complete trust that as the Lord stirs us, we can, by faith, take action and put our life once again in His hands. Stirring takes us out of the confines of our comfort and routine to the places that the Holy Spirit will lead us. May we refuse complacency and pursue with determination the heart of God and decide to make our passion for Christ be what fuels our lives.

Revelation 15:3-4

Great and marvelous are Your deeds, Lord God Almighty.
Just and true are Your ways, King of the ages. Who will
not fear You, O Lord, and bring glory to Your name?
For You alone are holy. All nations will come and worship
before You, for Your righteous acts have been revealed.

2 Timothy 1:6

For this reason I remind you to fan into flame the gift of God,
which is in you through the laying on of of my hands.

1 Timothy 4:14

Do not neglect the gift that is in you, which was given you through the
prophecy spoken over you at the laying on of the hands of the elders.

Romans 12:1-2 ♥ 2 Corinthians 4:7 ♥ Deuteronomy 6:45

Loved

You are so loved!
Just knowing we are loved by God, is an incredible gift that
is ours for every single day. Sometimes we confuse the gift
of God's love with a list of our limitations and insecurities.
But those things do not change His love for us. Living in the
security of God's love gives us a protection and shelter that
can help us to be stronger than we ever dreamed we could
be, and do much more than we ever imagined possible.
Living in His love gives us the ability to love others and in that, we
are displaying the love of God we have experienced for ourselves.
Every time we have a chance to love people, we have an opportunity
to love God. And the opposite is just as true. Every time we dismiss
or forgo opportunities to love others, we withhold a chance to
love God because loving others equates to loving God!
Oh that we not withhold love from the One who loves us
more than we could ever imagine. Oh that we would be eager
to do whatever we could, to take every opportunity and even look
to take advantage of every instance, big or small, and love Him
for all He has done for us! Oh friends, the love of our heavenly
Father is great and inconceivable in so many ways. We have
moments and instances each day to choose whether we will love
someone and when we do, the love we display is poured upon
our wonderful Savior and Lord. Love matters most and has the
greatest potential to heal and help brokenness, in us and in others.
In discord and issues of life, we can find resolution and hope
when we first lay down the barriers to love. May we realize that
when we love others, we love God. So it's not just us loving God
that shows Him our heart but our interaction in the gift of His
love, that's the evidence of what we hold in our heart for Him.

1 John 4:11
Beloved, if God so loved us, we also ought to love one another.
John 13:35 ♥ John 15:17 ♥ 1 John 4:7
1 John 3:14

Self-Evident Allegiance

Have you ever considered the allegiance of God? It has been conveyed to us since the beginning of time, since the first sin, to the cross and even today we can rest assured, without question, that it is and that it will not change. The undisputable truth of who God is has and will always be self-evident. Its essence is obvious; it requires no explanation or commentary. He stands strong on the merits of truth that remain plain and undeniable.

The allegiance of God to us is timeless and unchanging. God never changes and His truth never ceases. We never have to wonder if He cares about us, He just does. He always has and He always will. He is not far removed from us but is so very near. God's presence is all around us daily and continually. His truths cannot be explained away or reduced by the theology of men. He is divine, He is God and in those things, we will never have the capacity to fully grasp the magnificence of who the Lord, God truly is. But our inability to understand does not reduce His allegiance, His love or mercy.

As we consider what is self-evident about our God, may the magnitude and reality of Him be the essence of our very being and life. The Lord our God is Ever-lasting!

Psalm 102:27
But you are the same, and your years have no end.

Hebrews 13:8
Jesus Christ is the same yesterday and today and forever.

Psalm 12:6
The words of the LORD are pure words, like silver refined in a furnace on the ground, purified seven times.

Proverbs 30:5
Every word of God is tested; He is a shield to those who take refuge in Him.

Matthew 5:18
For truly, I say to you, until heaven and earth pass away, not an iota, not a dot, will pass from the Law until all is accomplished.

Growing

Growing, as we all know, doesn't happen overnight. Growth takes patience and attentiveness. No farmer plants corn seeds in a field and wakes up the next morning to a field of corn. A careful farmer, plants the seeds, and then diligently watches over the seed to be sure that it has all it needs to take root and grow. He protects it from birds and weeds to give it the chance it needs to develop to its full potential. The goal of every seed is be more than a seed. The seed is just the beginning. It takes times for seeds to germinate and then finally become something more. When God is working in our lives, it's not always easy to be patient. It's not always easy to wait on His timing and let the seeds He has planted germinate and grow in our lives. Often we want the spiritual seeds in our life to grow overnight into a mighty tree that produces an abundance of fruit. Growing in Christ is a beautiful process that we sometimes attempt to hurry along. A wise man put it this way, *"I've learned to stop rushing things that need to time to grow"*. Somethings need time to grow in us and in our life. God will use those things in His timing; we need simply to wait on Him. Don't rush it! When we harvest fruit before it is ripe, the fruit is generally hard and not very sweet. But when it is ready, then it's nourishment to us and to others. The timing of Christ's work in our life is beautiful and sweet as we take the time to grow in Him.

Matthew 13:32-33
He put another parable before them, saying, "The kingdom of heaven is like a grain of mustard seed that a man took and sowed in his field. 32 It is the smallest of all seeds, but when it has grown it is larger than all the garden plants and becomes a tree, so that the birds of the air come and make nests in its branches."

Hebrews 6:1
Therefore let us leave the elementary doctrine of Christ and go on to maturity, not laying again a foundation of repentance from dead works and of faith toward God,

Colossians 3:16 ♥ Philippians 3:13-14

Moments

A moment is a very short length of time.
Here then gone, and we move from one to the next. Our
moments become our days and our days become our lives.
From season to season, our moments march. Our moments
are a gift from God. He gives us simple joys to mark our days.
A gentle breeze, a smile from a friend, a sweet message out
of the blue or beautiful sunset. We sometimes worry that we
don't manage our moments as we should. We do our best
to be wise and remember those things in this life that really
matter the most. The moments we talk and share with Jesus.
The worth and time we give to others.
Living in and through the grace of God, and letting it mark
our moments, we will live each moment to the fullest in
simplicity. May we not become overwhelmed with the
moments of our life but realize that our moments are
treasures each day to have, to hold and to give to God
that He may use them for our good and His purpose.

*"That the greater perfection a soul aspires after, the
more dependent it is upon divine grace."*
~Brother Lawerence

Psalm 16:11
*You make known to me the path of life; in your presence there is
fullness of joy; at your right hand are pleasures forevermore.*

Proverbs 16:9
The heart of man plans his way, but the Lord establishes his steps.

Psalm 90:12
So teach us to number our days that we may get a heart of wisdom.

Colossians 3:23
Whatever you do, work heartily, as for the Lord and not for men.

Light

It's not easy to do things when it's dark if you don't have a light. When the electricity goes off at night, we scramble for flashlights and candles so we can see. We have a hard time navigating in the dark and as children; some of us were or still are, afraid of the dark. Darkness in the word of God is contrasted by the idea of light. Jesus gives believers a mandate to be light in the darkness. Jesus, Himself said, "I am the light of the world".

Sadly, though, in various situations in our day to day life, people don't always realize what the blessing of being a light can be, but being mindful of the contrast of light vs dark can help us to realize its goodness. One candle has the potential to light many other candles. It doesn't shorten the life of the candle and it doesn't diminish the brightness of it either. But what it does is multiply the light that one sole candle can have. Imagine an underground tunnel that is miles in length, completely dark as the path we walk. We have a lit candle and there are others in the tunnel with us but their candles are not lit. We can keep our light to ourselves and think that if we don't light the candles of others, ours will burn brighter. But what if we start lighting candles and then they begin lighting candles, then suddenly the whole tunnel is lit and the first candle is not any more diminished but the effect of its light has reached so far. May we go beyond just the mindset of being a light solely to ourselves and be delighted, with great joy to share our light with others.

*"There is a candle in every soul. Some brightly burning, some dark and cold.
There is a spirit who brings a fire. Ignites a candle
and makes His home. So carry your candle, run to the
darkness, seek out the hopeless, confused and torn.
Hold out your candle for all to see it, take your
candle and go light your world."*
-Kathy Troccoli, songwriter

As we center our life on Christ, and the incredible light
He has brought to our life, may His light in us make a
difference to others and bring them the light they need.

John 8:12
**Then Jesus again spoke to them, saying, "I am the
Light of the world; he who follows Me will not walk in
the darkness, but will have the Light of life."**
Matthew 5:14-16 ♥ Isaiah 60:1

Love for God

Love for God affects love for others. It's interesting
that the first 3 of the Ten Commandments are vertical,
meaning; they are between us and God.
So, before any horizontal interaction or talk about others, such
as father and mother and other people, the Lord calls us to
Himself. Furthermore, love for any person, when it is genuine,
affects how we regard all other persons. The love of God gives
us the ability to see them through the filterof love, through the
eyes of God. This happens because God IS love and when the
filter of love is the essence of the way we perceive and view others
and situations, we have an incredible opportunity to not see as
we would have but to see as God may view the situation.
When we ask God for His perspective, we are in reality asking Him
to show us how He sees things or people. This willingness takes
faith and trust in God. Then as everything changes and as we
engage in that way of life, we will find His love and grace start as a
trickle through our hearts. Then suddenly we find that the trickle
becomes a stream and it begins to flow a little stronger, and it will
continue to grow and become more impacting. If we're finding it
hard to love, it may be that we are attempting to function outside of
those first three mandates from the very heart of God. It's staggering
that these first three mandates are encapsulated by God's love. First,
He reminds us we have been rescued by Him and after those first
three commandments, God gives us a promise of His love that has
been lavished on us and will continue to be poured out into the lives
of our family. As much as we might like to think that the rescuing
of God and His loved lavished on us is solely for the purpose of
blessing us, God's purposes are bigger and much further-reaching.
They don't stop with us and thus the continuation of the rest of
the commandments. Now, it includes our life with others. Our
relationships are to be navigated by God's love in us. It is His love
living through us. May our love for God be the center of the outflow of
love in our lives. It is from here that everything else is or is not proven.
We are always welcome here and always loved.

July
8

1 John 4:19
We love because he first loved us.
Romans 5:8 ♥ John 13:34 ♥ Exodus 20:2-7

Reliance

The necessity of our reliance upon God
touches every part of our life.
It affects those who've been in a relationship with the Lord for
a long time and those who are newly walking with Christ. We
can easily forget to simply rely on Him. Someone has recently
been trying to teach me a whole new computer program. As
the process is going, I continually write notes and often refer
to them. I know that someday I won't need the notes anymore
because I will really know the system. However walking with
Christ is not at all like learning a computer system although
we can easily be tempted to look at it in the same sense.
It happens as we read the Word of God and we tend to go through
the motions or the pre-implanted thoughts that we have gained.

God gives us teachers and those that open His word and share
insights but to rely on God to speak into our hearts is what we
sometimes miss. Often we think we know what a certain passage
of scripture means because that's what we've been taught, but
we must be so sensitive to something new the Lord may want to
show us in His word. If we don't rely on Him as we study, we run
the risk of missing the heart of His word and only hearing with
our head. The Lord has so much to show and speak to us, each
of us, in individual ways and seasons of our lives. If we rush by
Him with only a glance in His direction, we'll miss the details of
who He truly is and the special things He has for us each day.
Reliance on Jesus is the essence of forgoing the temptation
to go through the motions or rely on ourselves. There is an
authenticity about Christ that He wants us to realize. He's
not a "cookie cutter" God, like a tract home in a crowded
suburb. He's unique, like a custom home or mansion. He's
intricate and special. While the Lord, our God, never changes,
He is matchless and personal to each of His children.

John 14:26
*But the Helper, the Holy Spirit, whom the Father will
send in my name, he will teach you all things and bring
to your remembrance all that I have said to you.*
John 10:27 ♥ Psalm 120:1 ♥ John 14:16
Psalm 127:1

Strong Arms

This week, precious friends have faced total losses.
The unexpected loss of a spouse, another, a devastating house fire,
and our nation tries to fathom the loss of multiple police officers.
These impacts have tremendous potential for
our lives to be completely swept away or cause us
to anchor our soul in the heart of God.
Getting through such events takes more than a moment.
In the season of total loss, our minds grasp for reasons and answers
that cannot be found. They are things that we may never
know this side of heaven. But, what we do know to be
true, is that our God is good and He is ever faithful, even
in times of total loss and things we don't understand.
The Lord, our God promises that when the trials
and hard issues of life try to overtake us, He will
be with us. We have a safe haven in Him.

We are secure in knowing that whatever the storms of life
bring, He is our sufficiency. He is, this moment, at the right
hand of God, our Father, interceding, (or negotiating, pleading,
and intervening) on our behalf. This moment, the Lord is
our safe haven and our portion for the troubles of life.
We can be completely centered on the strong arm of God today.
Let Him be the strength for the day we face
when total loss attempts to overtake us.

Hebrews 7:25
Consequently, he is able to save to the uttermost those who draw near to God through him, since he always lives to make intercession for them.
Isaiah 41:10 ♥ Psalm 89:13 ♥ Romans 8:34
Psalm 118:16 ♥ John 16:33

Ordinary

Most often, people feel they are just ordinary and that God somehow only uses those who are extra-ordinary. In our introductory remarks of someone, we often begin listing their most impressive accomplishments. While education and self-improvement are both worthy pursuits in life, it is so important to realize that the Lord cares more about our heart than those things. What's inside matters much to Him. When God sees a heart that is pursuing more and more of Him, we begin to be changed and in the change, He begins to open doors for us to be a blessing through.

I was reminded yesterday of David, a young shepherd boy that had a heart for God. He pursued the Lord, even though he was young and out in a field with sheep, alone, and very ordinary. Yet God, saw David's heart and called him to slay a giant that had completely oppressed the lives of a significant amount of people. And that was just the beginning.

Imagine what God has in store for you today! You may think that your imperfections are limiting God, but the truth is that our imperfection is what causes us to pursue Jesus. He will ultimately be the only perfection in our life.

There used to be a little chorus we sang at church some years ago that said, "if you can use anything Lord, you can use me". The essence of the song was that though we are ordinary, faith says, nonetheless, YOU, Lord can use me nd accomplish much because of who You are and not because of what I am. Without Him, it is no secret we lack so much, but that is exactly how the Lord wants us to come to Him. Oh that our prayer today would not be shrinking back in our insecurities, but may we realize that God wants us to be ordinary so that He can be extra-ordinary in and through us.

Acts 1:27

But God chose what is foolish in the world to shame the wise;
God chose what is weak in the world to shame the strong;

1 Corinthians 2:12 ♥ Acts 10:34-35 ♥ Romans 2:11
Deuteronomy 10:17 ♥ 1 Samuel 16:11-12

Water

When my family and I lived in Africa, we saw people who walked for miles just to get water. They would come to the river with empty buckets and fill them up. Next would be the task of putting them on their heads to walk back to their village. Most were women and children who had the responsibility for bringing the water home. This process was necessary for water to come to their homes. It might be hard to imagine the hardship that living without water can be. In many places, we have plumbing that allows us to have water in multiple places in our home. Once, we had the joy of helping to dig a water well in a remote location in the Sahara desert. When the clean water began being pumped out of the well in the middle of that ocean of sand, people came from out of nowhere to enjoy it. For miles we could see nothing but sand, and then suddenly people emerged and came. What is our water today? I believe we can agree that, yes there is the need for drinking water, but an even greater need is the living water of Christ. Many of us have the Gospel in our home just like our indoor plumbing. Sometimes it's left without being used or it is only a small trickle in our life when all the while, we could be the carrier of the living water we have so generously received. God is calling us to take the water to the places that do not have it or realize its goodness. The gospel of Christ and the hope we have in His love is a greater necessity than water is for our physical survival. Our spiritual survival depends on it. Jesus said that if people drink of Him, they will never thirst again. He is the ssence of being satisfied and content in the deepest places of our soul. It is what humanity longs and desires for above every other pursuit. Let's fill up some buckets from the water of the Gospel of Christ and be the carriers of sharing it with those that God has strategically placed in our life. There is a world of thirsty people around us! We don't have to go to Africa to find those that are in need of it, it may be the cashier at the grocery store or the young mom next door, the elderly person who needs a helping hand in the parking lot, or our own family that has become disconnected because of the demands of life. Jesus said He wants to become a fountain in us, springing up eternal life as we center on Him.

July 12

Isaiah 58:11

And the LORD will continually guide you, And satisfy your desire in scorched places, And give strength to your bones; And you will be like a watered garden, And like a spring of water whose waters do not fail.

John 4:14 Isaiah 55:1 John 4:10

Jeremiah 2:13

Bread of Life

The most important necessity for survival is water. But from there, we know that we cannot survive without something to eat. It is so interesting that Jesus, Himself, is not only our living water, but also the bread of life. In other words, He is the bread for our life, He sustains our life. Jesus cared so much about the felt needs of people, that He met them there. After He met their needs of thirst and hunger, He ministered to the very heart and greatest of their eternal needs. He is the bread that our soul needs to survive. Jesus isn't just the water our soul needs, He is the bread for our soul's hunger. In Him, there is nothing lacking that we need in the deepest recesses of our very being. He is completely and totally everything. We can search high and low, but all we need is in Jesus. Before the eyes of more than 5,000 people, Jesus brought the truth of who He was into a reality. The miracle of the five loaves and two fishes was more than the fact that they were all filled and there were 12 baskets left over. The deeper meaning of the miracle is that Jesus Himself could meet the need of each and every person and that no one was left out or left hungry. He is enough for us, each one of us, and all of us. Jesus was telling them through His compassion for their physical hunger that He was the answer for their soul's greatest needs. He remains our sufficiency. He remains enough, our fulfillment and contentment. To carry our miracle one step further, consider giving your "little" lunch to Jesus. What could He do with you? With whom you are? Maybe He will use you to meet the needs of a multitude? When we put our little, ordinary lunch in His hands, His blessing over it will compound its minimal potential into something greater than we could ever imagine. Opening our hand to receive all He wants to give us is the beginning and from there, opening our hand to give Him all we are is when our destiny begins to be realized.

July 13

John 4:10-13

Then Jesus took the loaves, gave thanks to God, and distributed them to the people. Afterward he did the same with the fish. And they all ate as much as they wanted. After everyone was full, Jesus told his disciples, "Now gather the leftovers, so that nothing is wasted." So they picked up the pieces and filled twelve baskets with scraps left by the people who had eaten from the five barley loaves.

John 6:35 ♥ John 6:51 ♥ John 7:37

Valleys

Difficulty and hardship happen in what we often refer to as "valleys" of our life. They are times when we feel overwhelmed and in a place that is the opposite of triumph. Valleys are inevitable and they will probably happen to most everyone during their life. No one generally wants to be in a valley, the exhilaration of the mountaintop is far more sought after. Valleys imply isolation and disparity.

But friends, may we always know that God never leaves us, but He is always right beside us, even in the valley and even when there isn't another person beside us. Sometimes we face personal valleys that only Jesus and we know about. In those times, we can be sure, that we are not alone. In spite of the whispers of the enemy, God is with us and He is our strength to bring us out of those difficult times.

In valley experiences, we will often discover that our greatest victories are won there. Take David for example, he was used mightily by God in many situations and places but in the valley, he won great victories and found that he was even stronger afterwards. The Lord is the One who goes with us, He is our deliverer and comfort for each and every valley. Valleys are a place that we can find His presence so near and so precious, when we can refocus and center our eyes on the Him. Sometimes all we can see are the circumstances of our valley and we forget to keep our eyes on Jesus through the valley. He never intended for us to stay in our valleys but to be with us through them. The key is to keep our eyes on Jesus as He leads us through. If we are not careful, valleys have the potential to swallow us up. But the Lord wants to pull us close to Him and lead us through victoriously!

Psalm 23:4
Even though I walk through the valley of the shadow of death, I fear no evil, for You are with me; Your rod and Your staff, they comfort me.
2 Samuel 8:13 ♥ Isaiah 41:8 ♥ John 18:1

Navigating

As many plan their summer family vacation and finally get into the car to drive to the destination, invariably from the backseat comes the infamous question, "are we there yet?". Generally, we can answer with certainty about how much longer the trip will take as we attempt to appease our little passengers. Often in life, though we have a different mentality. We just tend to coast without a goal other than our ultimate destination of heaven. But God has a lot for us to do and so many things along the journey of our life. He has a plan for the days and moments of our life. *There's an old story about a pilot who came over the intercom and said, "Good news, ladies and gentlemen: We've got a very strong tailwind and are making excellent time. The bad news is that our navigation equipment has gone down, so we have no idea where we are."* We are on the fast track, almost every day, running and doing, so very busy and I wonder if we really know where we are. I

love the story about a man named Paul who was overtaken by the love of God. His life was impacted in a dramatic way, he could never go back and ever be the same again. Paul was passionate about His calling. He knew what God had called him to do and he knew that it was about God's ability and not his. He had his marching orders and it was all his heart could contain to do what God had entrusted to him. The ways of God are vastly different from ours. There is a huge gap between the two. We really only have fragments and will never have the capacity to understand the depth of God's purposes. But we don't have to be consumed with just going through the motions and letting the days fly off our calendar without the navigation of God to lead us. The enemy would love nothing more than for us to waste our days, mindlessly consumed with the issues of life instead of rising above them. While it is true that the tasks of life must be tended, they are not the ultimate purpose of our life and yet they often become just that. We often want to be in control, but our navigation system is not the same as God's. May we flourish as Paul did. We must be sure that we walk hand in hand with the One who loves us beyond measure. He is the One who has a plan and direction for us every single day.

Isaiah 55:8-9
For my thoughts are not your thoughts, neither are your ways my ways, declares the LORD. For as the heavens are higher than the earth, so are my ways higher than your ways and my thoughts than your thoughts.

Proverbs 19:20 ♥ Philippians 3:7-9 ♥ Ephesians 3:2-11
1 Corinthians 13:12

Looking Forward

It's no secret that if we want to move forward, we will do it so much more easily if we are not looking backwards. Looking backwards while trying to move forward can prove to be a dangerous approach to just about every situation. Driving in reverse is much more difficult than driving forward. Even walking backwards is much harder than going forward and forget running backwards, that would prove extremely hazardous for most! Looking behind us and not realizing that God has so much for our future keeps us in a state of bondage when He wants to make us free from those things. Moving forward in Christ means that at some point we have to trust Him enough to let go.
It's a courageous move to let go. Some are holding onto pain while others are remaining in situations that they know the Lord wants to help them out of. The enemy wants us to believe that we can't let go or that it's easier to stay where we are than to do anything else.

Getting over a painful experience is much like crossing monkey bars. You have to let go at some point in order to move forward. —C.S. Lewis.

Letting go begins with looking forward and resisting the temptation to keep looking back. Let Jesus be your strength and guide. Rest in His peace and the security of His love. Let Him take the past and bring you freedom. He's the only One who can use your past to bring you blessing but it requires that we give it to Him.

Philippians 3:13-14
Brothers, I do not consider that I have made it my own. But one thing I do: forgetting what lies behind and straining forward to what lies ahead, I press on toward the goal to win the prize of God's heavenly calling in Christ Jesus.
Isaiah 26:3 ♥ Philippians 4:7 ♥ Psalm 119:165

Belonging

I was recently talking with a group of
friends about the word belonging.
We all agreed that it's a word that holds such a weighty meaning.
To belong is probably one of the greatest of all needs. We
interact with the idea of belonging multiple times throughout
each day. When we put things away, we put them where they
belong. We may ask, "Who does this or that belong to?" And
we've all been in places we had no business going, places where
we knew we shouldn't be, places where we didn't belong.
To belong is that there is a specific place that is solely for that
one thing, it has its place. When a baby is born, that baby
belongs to a specific mother, and it's unnatural for him to be
elsewhere. At work, or within families, in our churches, the
need to belong is so important. Belonging is being connected
with a sense of security which brings peace to us.
Since the foundations of the world there is a place for each
of us to belong in relationship with God, our Father. It comes
through accepting the gift of salvation in Jesus. It is the only
way we will ever feel a sense of belonging that will be sustaining.
Attempting life without being connected to God and knowing
where we belong, leaves us disheartened and unsettled.
Just as a new baby is melded into the heart of its mother,
we are so melded into the heart of God. There is no
place else we belong more than in that place.

John 1:12-13

**But to all who did receive him, who believed in his name, he
gave the right to become children of God, children born not of
blood, nor will of the flesh, nor will of man, but born of God.**

Romans 14:8 ♥ Colossians 2:9-10 ♥ 1 Corinthians 6:17
Luke 20:38

All the More

We've all had the joy of a delicious meal. Maybe we sat
down to eat one portion, but the deliciousness of it drew us
back for just a little more, or another whole "helping".
Our spiritual appetite and thirst are sometimes forgotten simply
because we listen to the demands of our physical body more.
But the Lord is calling us all the more to
find and seek Him and His ways.
All the more we are compelled by His heart to come near.
All the more to hear His voice.
All the more to be led by the Holy Spirit.
All the more means "on top of what we've done
before, or an additional portion".
All the more, may He be our substance.
Our surrender all the more, enveloped in His welcome,
will make a difference in the outcomes of each day.
All the more as you see the day approaching, take heart and
draw near to Him. May our love and encouragement to one
another to emulate and mirror this verse (Hebrews 10:25).
All the more may we love Him still deeper and
love each other as we have been loved.

Psalm 63:1-8

*O God, you are my God, earnestly I seek you; my soul thirsts for you, my
body longs for you, in a dry and weary land where there is no water. I
have seen you in the sanctuary and beheld your power and your glory.
Because your love is better than life, my lips will glorify you. I will praise
you as long as I live, and in your name I will lift up my hands. My soul
will be satisfied as with the richest of foods; with singing lips my mouth
will praise you. On my bed I remember you; I think of you through the
watches of the night. Because you are my help, I sing in the shadow
of your wings. My soul clings to you; your right hand upholds me.*

Psalm 108:1 ♥ Psalm 119:20, 8 ♥ Psalm 143:6

Worry

What worries your heart today?
For some, it's the unknown of tomorrow, how things will pan out.
For others, it's the regret of yesterday that they cannot undo or redo.
And for a many, it's simply your today. Worry seemingly
wants to have a "stand-off" with us every single day.
May we not doubt for a moment that the
Lord knew that this would happen.
We can rest assured that it is not His desire for us because
worry depletes our hope, faith and our peace. Notice I said
"our" hope, "our" faith, and "our" peace. These are gifts that
God has given us to live within for our good. Jesus doesn't want
us to worry about anything. In fact, He was very passionate
about it and He shared some very simple, easy to understand,
illustrations to communicate it to us. I believe He used these
simple illustrations so we could easily grasp them, especially
on those days that we find it difficult to not be overtaken
by worry. Worry can make it really hard to focus on truth.
The Lord tells us about our value to Him. He tells us that He cares
for us. May we never forget who Jesus is, and that this is what
makes His word to us of such worth. They are not just words on
a billboard or on a greeting card for our encouragement. These
are the words of Almighty God, the Creator of Heaven and
Earth, the One who holds the world in His hands, who placed
the stars in the sky. He is the One who says, "I've got this", He
says to us today, "let Me take your worry, and you take My gifts
of peace, hope and faith". Friend, His arms are stronger than
yours to carry the worry that overtakes our heart. Whisper a
prayer of surrender as you center your heart on Him today.

Philippians 4:6-7
**Do not be anxious about anything, but in everything by prayer and
supplication with thanksgiving let your requests be made known
to God. And the peace of God, which surpasses all understanding,
will guard your hearts and your minds in Christ Jesus.**
John 14:27 ♥ Isaiah 40:30-31 ♥ Matthew 6:26
Matthew 6:28 ♥ Matthew 6:34

Majesty

The majesty, magnificence, splendor, dignity,
grandeur, brilliance, glory, and radiance of God
are difficult to truly grasp and understand.
Our imagination cannot convey their immensity and these
characteristics can sometimes be blurred in light of the world's
filters and perspective. Sometimes we attempt to see God
from our own perception. But if we could truly see Him, we
would be completely undone by His awesomeness. If we truly
had a glimpse of His majesty, it would likely be as a cosmic
eclipse that would be blinding because of His eminence.
The Lord Jesus, in all His splendor and magnificence, is
truly the King of kings and Lord of lords for each and
every one our lives, for every and all situations.
As we attempt to grasp His greatness, let's
realize that He is our Savior.
Imagine… He not only allows us to cling to
Him but He welcomes us to do so.
Knowing that He controls the outside influences can bring us a
comfort regardless of the storm, for we are safe inside His loving
care and protection as we continually surrender our life to Him.
Why not take a moment to let the reality of His majesty pour
over your heart and be reminded of Who holds you today.
You are loved by the King.

Hebrews 1:3-4
And He is the radiance of His glory and the exact representation of
His nature, and upholds all things by the word of His power when
He had made purification of sins, He sat down at the right hand
of the Majesty on high, having become as much better than the
angels, as He has inherited a more excellent name than they.
Psalm 145:11-13 ♥ Psalm 96:3 ♥ Psalm 145:5
1 Chronicles 29:11

Wrinkles

Have you ever needed or wanted to wear a certain article of clothing that needed to be ironed? Perhaps a certain pair of pants or a shirt? Maybe you didn't have time to iron it or discounted just how wrinkled it really was. Or maybe you're the person who won't dare wear anything that has one wrinkle in it, but will take whatever time is needed to make sure it is well pressed before leaving the house. Back in the "June Cleaver" days that was the norm, no one left without mom making sure that everything was in order and ironed. But times have changed drastically and now permanent press is a huge relief to the pressure of having to iron everything. I can hear your "Hallelujahs!" Did you know that they used to even iron the kitchen towels and bed sheets? "What?", you might say! I know! I remember ironing my dad's handkerchiefs, along with his work shirts. So what about our walk with Jesus? Are we walking around all wrinkled or do we make sure that the wrinkles are taken care of each and every day. Did you know that He calls us to be clean and without wrinkles.

July 21

It's not something we can do on our own, but it's as if we must daily bring ourselves as His garment to be cleaned and ironed. You see, He lives in us, His glory fills our life. We display His goodness in a powerful way when we bring ourselves to Him. I've worn some things that really needed ironing or that had a "spot" on it, thinking to myself, "it doesn't matter that much" and it's true, it doesn't matter in regard to our clothes but it's funny when we leave the house that way, it's all we think others can see. We try to explain away our "spot" or the reason we are wrinkled. Jesus doesn't want us to go around with sense of undoneness because of a sin stained life or wrinkles. He's the One who wants to take care of our garments and give us a garment that is perfect and righteous. We'll really never be able to iron out our own wrinkles or get the stains of sin out without Jesus. As we bring ourselves to Christ, He takes care of all that. He wants us to walk out each day, knowing that He has covered us. Many keep trying, but the truth is, we'll never be able to make our rags look good. It's only through the blood of His sacrifice at the cross that we will have perfect garments.

Ephesians 5:26-28
Husbands, love your wives, just as Christ loved the church and gave Himself up for her to sanctify her, cleansing her by the washing with water through the word, so that he might present the church to himself in splendor, without spot or wrinkle or any such thing, that she might be holy and without blemish.

Ephesians 5:10 ♥ Colossians 1:22 ♥ Song of Solomon 4:7
2 Corinthians 5:18

More than Ever

Jesus wants us to walk with Him, more than ever.
His provision is sufficient for each and every day.
In discouragement the peace of God is still adequate.
Our joy is only complete in Christ.
We need Him in our life, more than ever.
For every moment, we have the grace of His sovereignty.
Day after day, His love remains passionate for you.
It's a "more than ever" love.
As we need Jesus more than ever,
He is there all the more.
Ever faithful, drawing us near.
He gives freely to those who call upon His name.
So don't delay or reason away your need for Him.
All the more and more than ever, Christ Jesus is our enough.

Psalm 63:1
O God, You are my God; I shall seek You earnestly;
My soul thirsts for You, my flesh yearns for You, In a
dry and weary land where there is no water.

John 6:27
But don't be so concerned about perishable things like food. Spend
your energy seeking the eternal life that the Son of Man can give
you. For God the Father has given me the seal of his approval."

Revelation 22:17
The Spirit and the bride say, "Come." Let anyone who
hears this say, "Come." Let anyone who is thirsty come. Let
anyone who desires drink freely from the water of life.

Psalm 73:25 ♥ Psalm 143:6 ♥ Revelation 21:6

All These Things

The priority of pursuing Jesus can easily lose its place in our life if we do not guard its place. In our busy life, time with Him can seem hard to find until we realize that it's here that we find our true joy, our ultimate peace and a strength that enables us to live abundantly. For some, it's in the morning that they find that time alone. Still others come at the end of their day to find a place of quiet to pray and read their Bible. These are special times that cultivate our relationship with Jesus. It gives Him the chance to speak into our hearts with other distractions put aside. Yes, it's true that we are also called to constant interaction with Him throughout our day, but there is a specialness that we may only find when we put everything else on hold to be with the Lover of our soul.

In Genesis, we read that after God created Adam and Eve, He came to walk with them in the cool of the day. The Psalmist, David, said, "early in the morning, I will seek Him". Jesus, Himself, often left His disciples and responsibilities of ministry, just to be alone with God.

Many may know a familiar verse found in Matthew 6:33. "Seek first the kingdom of God and His righteousness, and all these things will be added to you." But sometimes we have a different idea about "all these things". The things Jesus has for us are likely very different from the things we are pursuing. He is all we need. He alone is our sufficiency. He prioritizes our life when we seek Him first. Putting Jesus first is, in part, to be aware of His presence. To surrender our will to His and let go of the strife of self and life that attempt to take His place in our heart. Some, as in Hezekiah's day, wait to seek God, thinking that the timing isn't right, that we don't have things "together" enough, so we put it off for a later time. There's healing and grace now, and it's the best time to seek Him.

Deuteronomy 4:29
*But if from there you seek the Lord your God, you will find him
if you seek him with all your heart and with all your soul.*
2 Chronicles 30:18-20 ♥ Psalm 14:2 ♥ Isaiah 33:6

Submitting to His Strength

We've probably all seen someone struggle with
something that was too heavy for them to carry,
or too hard for them to do by themselves.
It's almost painful to watch, so we offer to help, but
sometimes help is refused and the struggle continues. We
wonder to ourselves, *"why won't they let me help them?"*
How strong is God in our life?
What allows us to see and experience His strength?
Could it be that we often refuse the power and
strength of God because our flesh and desires want
what they want more than we want God?
It's absurd to think that God's strength would somehow be
insufficient or inadequate to bring us to victory again and again.
We know in our mind that God is great and that His strength
is the greatest of all power, both in heaven and on earth.
So then, why do we not see its evidence?
Why don't we see it just plow over and plow through the
mountains in our life? Could it be that we hold Him at bay?
Do we continually attempt to work things out on our own?
When we submit to His strength, we see the apparentness of
God's faithfulness. There has to be a "letting go" of sorts so
that God can be God in our situations and in our life. When
we let Him be strong, we relinquish the inner striving of our
heart in a submission that allows Him access to be our strength.
Submitting to His strength is believing in practical terms, the
greatness of who God truly is and wants to be in our life.

Psalm 119:133
***Establish my footsteps in Your word, And do not
let any iniquity have dominion over me.***
1 Peter 5:6 ♥ Psalm 40:8 ♥ Hebrews 12:9
James 4:7

Understanding

The Gospels, Matthew, Mark, Luke and John, recount the life of Jesus, the period of time that He walked on the earth. There are variations of their stories, details and experiences because they were each different and their perspectives were their own. Inspired, they wrote about the friend and savior they had each found in Jesus. They wrote about the miracles that He did before their eyes. Each shared the things they didn't understand and the way that Jesus led them in patient love. Then, the unthinkable became their reality. Jesus gave His life and their hearts were filled with unanswered questions of why? Why didn't He just live forever? Why did He have to die, He was Jesus, God's son. They knew that He could have easily come down off the cross and yet He didn't. Now what? How could they recover? It seemed that everything they had lived for and declared by their life's song was gone. But, what the disciples didn't see was God's plan. What they couldn't understand was a heavenly perspective. Jesus died and gave His life for our good, it was God's plan. It was a plan that overrode their plans. It was beyond their understanding and sight. Sometimes things don't work out the way we had hoped or planned. We are left wondering why. Lord, why didn't you intervene? You could have but yet you didn't. At those moments, we can know that God is good. We can trust that He is our strong tower and strength. Secure in knowing we haven't been forgotten and that our life's song can still be sung. Heaven will someday reveal what earthly perspective cannot grasp. Until then we know that we are loved, we know that God is good and that regardless of the evil and devastation this life may bring, we have hope because we have Jesus. He is ours and we are His.

John 16:33
I have said these things to you, that in me you may have peace. In the world you will have tribulation. But take heart; I have overcome the world.

Psalm 147:5 ♥ Romans 5:8 ♥ John 6:51
1 John 4:10 ♥ Ephesians 2:13-14 ♥ Hebrews 2:17
1 John 2:2

The Author

When we read a book or a story, we are at a disadvantage because we do not know the end of the story. We do not fully know the characters and it is not until we read the book that we can even grasp the plot. The author is the only one who truly knows the whole story to a depth that even a reader who reads the story multiple times could not grasp. The author knows every twist and turn the story will take. He knows that the decisions of some of the characters will cause consequences that are hidden from the reader. The author is the one who gives meaning to the story, but it cannot be fully known until the story's end. God's word tells us that Jesus is the author and perfecter of our faith. We are not the author of our own life but it is in the hands of the ultimate Author. Sometimes, as the main character of the story of our life, we confuse our place with the place of God as the Author. He is the perfecter of our faith.

His call is for us to pursue Him and as we do, our faith will become more and more perfect. Could it be that the journey of our faith's perfection is the goal of the Author? Perhaps the main goal of our life's story is that our faith would be perfected in Christ. It is not in our resources, not in ourselves, not in our abilities or talents. Jesus is the Author and Perfecter of our faith and our faith is only made perfect in Him. We must submit to the His leading so that we will find our way to truly understand His goodness through our faith.

Hebrews 12:2

Therefore, since we are surrounded by such a great cloud of witnesses, let us throw off every encumbrance and the sin that so easily entangles, and let us run with endurance the race set out for us, looking to Jesus, the founder and perfecter of our faith, who for the joy that was set before him endured the cross, despising the shame, and is seated at the right hand of the throne of God.

Ephesians 1:4 ♥ Genesis 1:1 ♥ Jeremiah 1:5
Psalm 146:6

Finding Peace

There are few things more unsettling than when we lack peace in a certain area of our life. It seems as though it can overtake us and cause worry, fret, fear, doubt and anxiety to become our closest companions. However, beware, these are not the companions of God. He is the Prince of peace! When Jesus was born, a tiny infant, angels from heaven came to sing as an angelic host filling the sky, "Peace on Earth"! Then He said in John 14:27, I am leaving you with a gift—peace of mind and heart. And the peace I give is a gift the world cannot give. So don't be troubled or afraid. Jesus knew that the world and this life would continually attempt to rob us of peace. He knew we would need peace and He made a provision for us. His peace is perfect, not lacking in any way and the Lord, who loves us wants us to have peace inside. If we lack peace, it could be His caution and His shepherding that is attempting to move us from one place to another. When we are walking in peace with Jesus, our life is filled with a sweetness that nothing else can give. Confronting the underlying reasons for our lack of peace is the first step in submitting and hearing the voice of the Holy Spirit. We don't have to wonder if the Lord wants us to have peace because we know His word declares that He does, so we already know the answer to that question. Sustaining peace is only found in sustained and continual communication with God. It's a constant and ongoing relationship with the One who loves us and desires that we have peace with Him above everything else we gain in this life. May we be willing to let Him evaluate the condition of our heart and if we lack peace, He will lead us in reconciliation.

Colossians 3:15
And let the peace that comes from Christ rule in your hearts. For as members of one body you are called to live in peace. And always be thankful.

Psalm 46:1 ♥ Psalm 18:32-36 ♥ Numbers 6:26
Romans 8:6

Adoration

To adore God is to give Him our deepest
love and highest degree of respect;
It means to worship, to esteem and to revere Him for His holiness.
Sometimes we can lose sight of who God is and His greatness.
We get so used to the intense stimulation of our culture and the
influences of the demands of our life to the point that His greatness
isn't always in its proper place. Guarding the place in our life in
terms of adoring Him can be difficult, but we must be diligent.
The Lord our God is worthy of our adoration and praise. He is
above all and we must be careful not to reduce His greatness to
simplicity of our understanding, it must become what we live, in
our heart of hearts. Not just our love, but our deepest love to Him.
Not just our respect, but the highest degree of respect to Him.
The more we know Him and our relationship in Christ
deepens, we will find our adoration of His awesomeness will
be life changing and intimate. As we pray, "less of me, Lord
and more of You", we will find our hearts more and more filled
with a deeper sense of His greatness. A deeper and higher
praise will be the song of our heart. If you have lost your song
of adoration, just come to Him today and let the Lord renew
that in you once again. Be filled with awe at His awesomeness.
The Lord our God is great and greatly to be praised!

Psalm 33:8
Let all the earth fear the LORD; Let all the inhabitants
of the world stand in awe of Him.

Psalm 5:7
But as for me, by Your abundant lovingkindness I will enter Your house,
At Your holy temple I will bow in reverence for You.
Psalm 31:23 ♥ Isaiah 6:3 ♥ Psalm 99:5
Deuteronomy 10:12

Incredible

When Jesus lived and walked on the earth, His ways were incredulous to many. People had a very difficult time understanding many of the things He said and did. They were suspicious of so many of His miracles and teachings. Even His beloved disciples couldn't always grasp the things He taught them and they asked for many explanations. The ways of Christ are indeed, incredible not incredulous. His miracles of healing and deliverance did and still do cause people to be in awe of Him. Faith is the necessary component that gives us the ability to grasp the saving, redeeming, and healing power of Christ in our life and for our good. His incredible mercy and kindness stem from the incredible love of our Heavenly Father, who is not willing that any one of us should perish. He calls us again and again, over and over to repentance and life that refuses to entertain any other vision. Contempt for the incredible power of Christ is all around us, but with the instilled measure of faith, He is still doing miracles regardless of skeptics. Last week alone, I heard testimonies of a son who recently prayed for his dad, who had been pronounced dead for 45 minutes to come back to life. And another testimony of a young boy who'd been kidnapped and sang a song of worship, despite his captors' insistence that he stop until finally they let him go free.
Countless personal friends have been healed of cancer and addictions are being broken daily because of the power of Christ. He does not change; His mercies are new every morning. Great is His faithfulness.
He is the same, yesterday, today and forever… Still incredible!

Ephesians 1:18-20
I pray that the eyes of your heart may be enlightened, so that you will know what is the hope of His calling, what are the riches of the glory of His inheritance in the saints, and what is the surpassing greatness of His power toward us who believe. These are in accordance with the working of the strength of His might which He brought about in Christ, when He raised Him from the dead and seated Him at His right hand in the heavenly places.

Matthew 28:18 ♥ Isaiah 11:2 ♥ Ephesians 1:3
Colossians 1:16

Practicality

From time to time, it's easy to become a bit disconnected from the Gospel and the practicality of its message. Sometimes the loftiness of all that God is can seem a bit removed from our everyday, day in, and day out life. Finding practicality may not always be an easy thing. This mindset can become something that keeps us from experiencing the reality of God's presence in the situations and moments of our day if we are not careful. In the Gospels, we read of Jesus' life on earth. We see that while He ministered to so many, that wasn't the entire reason for His life. But the ministry of His life was walking with the disciples as well. He gave them and others, who didn't always understand Him, practical insights and examples that we find today in the form of the parables He taught. Jesus wanted them and us to experience the practicality of the Gospel message for ourselves so that we would know that we are individually loved and that the details of our lives matter to God. So, what does that really look like?

How does it apply to us today? It means that Jesus wants to teach us about who He is every day. He wants to show us and reveal more of His kingdom treasures are all about as we walk through this life. It requires an invitation on our part to welcome Him into the day to day moments we often try to navigate on our own. It doesn't take long before we begin to hear His voice and sense His direction. Making time to pray and read His word is paramount to help us. Those two things are like having the speakers that allow us a greater ability of hearing His voice. Imagine your stereo or radio with no speakers. You turn it on and you can hear only a tiny bit until you plug the speakers in. Then there's the volume knob and that's where the Holy Spirit comes in. Prayer and accountability to His word amplify the voice of the Lord. And when we roll out the welcome mat of our heart to the Holy Spirit, suddenly the volume goes even higher, making it easier to hear the voice of God. He's there friend, to lead you in so many practical ways as you welcome Him in.

John 10:4

When he has brought out all who are his own, he goes on ahead of them, and his sheep follow him because they know his voice.

Micah 6:8 ♥ John 10:27 ♥ Genesis 6:9
Genesis 17:1 ♥ Genesis 48:15

Make Him Known

We all have influences in our life. Some influences
are good and some not so good. What we do with
the calling of our influence is no small thing.
We carry influence and the potential of making Jesus known more
than we probably realize. Sometimes we think it's all about the big
and dramatic things we accomplish for the Lord, but in reality it's
the cumulative of our faithfulness that is magnified and reaches far.
Making Him known deepens with the
small and little things of our life.
It's in our attitude, by our smile, a prayer given or listening
ear, and our helping hands. We make Him known by
our words, by our song, and by our pursuits.
As we consider influence, think for a moment of how you
are affected by the little things that others do. Maybe
it's by a kind or not so kind word or gesture?
We have all felt the cutting of a sharp word or negative gesture,
something considered to be small but the weightiness of its
impact is great. Big things do matter, but often it's just the little
things that bring sweet joy and assurance that Jesus is near.
Making Jesus known happens as we live life with the people
He has placed in our life. Making Him known is to incite
hope and encouragement. It is bringing peace to the unrest
of this world by the power of His spirit living in us.

Deuteronomy 4:9-10
*Only give heed to yourself and keep your soul diligently, so that you do
not forget the things which your eyes have seen and they do not depart
from your heart all the days of your life; but make them known to your
sons and your grandsons. Remember the day you stood before the LORD
your God at Horeb, when the LORD said to me, 'Assemble the people to
Me, that I may let them hear My words so they may learn to fear Me all
the days they live on the earth, and that they may teach their children.'*

Deuteronomy 6:7 ♥ Psalm 78:4 ♥ Psalm 78:6
Proverbs 22:6 ♥ Isaiah 38:19

God is Able

What have you given to the Lord for His keeping?
Likely they are things of your heart that have never been revealed
to another human being. For most, we have committed dreams
and desires to the keeping of the Lord. However, we can sometimes
forget those things, thinking that time has passed us by. Or that
perhaps they weren't really dreams or visions from God. But as
we are sustained in His word, we are called to trust and have faith
in His ability to keep those things we have committed to Him.
For some, it's a wayward child that we have committed to the
Lord. Whatever the deep things of your heart, be reminded and
encouraged today that the Lord our God, is faithful to keep those
things. He remains able. We must remind our own heart and be
convinced in His ability to be faithful. Our position doesn't change
God in the least, but it does affect our faith. Being convinced
means that we cannot be talked out of the faithfulness of God. We
cannot be discouraged out of it, but as we are convinced to greater
depth, we will experience the depth of His faithfulness. Some
underestimate the depth of God's goodness and faithfulness.
We must guard His perspective and our perception.

Oh! That we might somehow grasp how deep His goodness is for
each of us today. It's like comparing a mud puddle to the Atlantic
Ocean. There's no comparison, but sometimes, because we cannot
see what He is doing and because we cannot understand His ways,
we become discouraged, thinking that He is limited to a small
puddle of water when all the while, the vastness of the entirety of
Christ is more than the oceans of the world could ever contain.
He is God! He is able to keep all that you have committed to Him,
my friend. He is with you, may your faith be so encouraged today.
Refuse to believe that He is limited. The faithfulness of God is
limitless and in Him we can have great confidence that He is able
to keep us and keep those things that we have committed to Him.

Ephesians 3:20
*Now to Him who is able to do exceedingly abundantly all that we ask
or think, according to the power that works in us, to Him be glory
in the church by Christ Jesus to all generations, forever and ever.*
Luke 1:3 ♥ Matthew 17:20 ♥ Hebrews 11:6
Romans 8:37-39 ♥ 2 Timothy 2:14

Caution

In a training symposium, the statement was made that, "A person's culture is the most influential factor in determining their behavior, values and beliefs." When I heard that, it stopped me and I thought what danger might be contained in those words. Perhaps the writer was just stating a fact as they see it, but could that be true? Whether we agree or disagree, the reality of its potential is very real. The probability is dangerously likely as we see the demise of our world. The caution for us is to be on our guard. To be aware of the influences we allow to impact our thoughts and attitudes. What do we give credence to in our day to day life? Are we filtering our culture's influence through the word of God and asking the Holy Spirit to give us His discernment? Some may or may not remember the Christian artists called "Out of the Gray".

They were popular in the mid-1990's. But it's their name that I thought of in relationship to this thought of being so influenced by our culture. God is calling us out of the gray, refusing to let our culture be the guiding influence of our life. Jesus calls us to be alert, knowing that the enemy of our soul prowls around like a lion looking for those who have been lulled away from godly influence. Things that may appear insignificant or innocent could be the very thing that leads us further away spiritually. We must be so careful to guard our hearts and to let our light shine in the darkness of our culture. We must be wise and diligent to avoid being overtaken by the influences that are contrary to the word of God. The Lord doesn't want us to be deceived or taken advantage of, but to be led by the Holy Spirit as we live in this culture. He has appointed us to this generation to be His voice and influence. May we realize the powerful potential of His glory in us.

1 Thessalonians 5:21
But test everything; hold fast what is good.
Matthew 10:16 ♥ Romans 16:29 ♥ 2 Timothy 2:15
Ephesians 4:15-16

Capacity

The meaning of capacity is, "a maximum amount that something can hold". It's a volume. When long haul semi-trucks travel the roadways, there are regulations that limit the capacity or weight they can carry. Along their route, they encounter weigh stations that they are required to stop at. At the weigh stations, their load is weighed and the capacity is measured by the scale. If they go over the amount mandated in the regulations, the driver must pay penalties. In some places there are no regulations and the word "over-capacity" is an understatement. I wish I could show you a picture of an African truck piled so high that as it drives down a primitively paved road, you wonder if it will sustain its balance because it is so top-heavy from its load. It really is an amazing sight to behold. I remember marveling that the poor vehicle could even move, and it wasn't uncommon to see them broken down part way to their destination.

As we live our lives, we need to take time to stop by the "weigh station" or to "take an inventory". Are we attempting to carry more than we should, are we at capacity or have we even exceeded our capacity? What are the things that encroach or crowd Jesus out of our life? What is crowding our thoughts and feelings? If we are "at capacity" with life, and have no room for Christ, we are overcapacity. When this happens we will

be unable to sustain life's demands. It is imperative that we avoid living this way. However, some have a difficult time regulating their capacity, and often find that they are living in "overcapacity" mode on a continual basis. The Lord doesn't want us to be so maxed out that we don't have room for Him in our life. We know Jesus is our anchor and that our relationship with Him is paramount, but life encroaches and we can easily reach the limits of capacity far too quickly, leaving Him little room and little of us if we are not careful. Take some time to think about the level of capacity you are functioning at. Perhaps you are under-capacity, underestimating all that the Lord wants to accomplish through your life, and you feel Him leading you to reach out beyond yourself. But you may be the one overextended and at maximum capacity. If so, He will help you as you open and surrender all that you are carrying and doing to Him today. Live in His abundance and be unburdened today.

Matthew 11:28-30

Come to me, all you who are weary and burdened, and I will give you rest. Take My yoke upon you and learn from Me; for I am gentle and humble in heart, and you will find rest for your souls. For my yoke is easy, and my burden is light.

1 John 5:3 ♥ Mark 6:31 ♥ Jeremiah 31:25
Psalm 127:2 ♥ Proverbs 17:1 ♥ Psalm 4:8

Dedication

One of the most precious joys to watch is when parents bring
their children to be dedicated to the Lord. At various ages,
some newborn babies and others as toddlers or school age, it is
still impacting and deeply meaningful. In dedication, parents
bring back to God, the priceless gift He has given to them.
As He has entrusted them, they return to the Lord to entrust
Him. They come to acknowledge that their greatest necessity
in raising a child is not money, or things, but it is God alone.
The sweetness is their humility to say, "Lord, we want You to
have full reign in our little one's life, may your will be done
in and through them, we are giving this child back to you for
your purpose". As that little life is placed again in the Father's
hands, they know that they are placing him in the safest place
possible. They acknowledge the gift God has given, and with
gratitude recognize that the greatest gift they can give to their
child is to raise them in the ways of the Lord. As they put him

again in God's hands, in dedication, they are placing him
or her in a place of provision. They realize that they will fail
but God will not. Dedication is seeking God's covering.
Dedication is a beautiful demonstration of our need for God. It
doesn't just happen when we bring our little ones to Him, but
it is also a daily place of surrender of our own lives to Jesus. It's
acknowledging that we desperately need the Lord to lead us.
We need His grace, mercy, strength and wisdom.
He calls us daily into a place of childlike faith, to simply trust Him.
The expression of such childlike faith is the demonstration
of dedication to His supremacy in our life.

1 Samuel 2:27-28

*"For this child I have prayed, and the Lord has granted me my petition
which I asked of Him. Therefore I also have lent him to the Lord;
as long as he lives he shall be lent to the Lord."
So they worshipped the Lord there.*

*Genesis 33:5 ♥ Psalm 127:3 ♥ Colossians 3:17
1 Peter 1:13 ♥ Psalm 32:8 ♥ Matthew 18:3
Matthew 19:14*

Counsel

There is a genuine need and importance in asking God to help us and give us His counsel. His input is the wisest counsel of all counseling. It is found by seeking Him in prayer and reading His word, but it is also found in Godly counselors. It is found in seeking the Godly counsel of those that we know hear His voice and walk closely in obedience to His instruction. We walk dangerously when we are isolated or when we accept ungodly counsel in our life. Walking without Godly counsel can lead us into places that are away from His will and His best for us. We can ask God for wisdom and partner closer to Him when we listen first and then take His counsel. It is so important that we are open and willing to hear wise and Godly counsel from others and from the Lord Himself. It's not uncommon, though, to attempt to work things out on our own, without looking for His direction and instruction. Fear is a tool of the enemy that can be a reason that people are unwilling to ask God for His direction, or His answer to their needs. What if His ways don't line up with our wants or desires? Some would rather not ask than to feel as though they are being disobedient to His leading. The only problem with this approach is that we forfeit our own peace when we refuse to ask the Lord for His wisdom. How many of us just want to do things without instructions? Instructions can sometimes seem as though they are a barrier to getting things done. They somehow seem to slow us down and pride says we can surely figure things out. We've all heard of the guy on Christmas Eve who attempts to put together a swing set for this children without reading the instructions. It doesn't look that hard but half way into it, he finds himself in a bigger mess than if he'd just taken the time to read the directions. Imagine getting in the car to find a friend's home without the address and without a GPS or her directions. Chances are we will get lost in attempting to find the house, when we could have saved so much energy and frustration if we'd just asked. The same is true for our life, His instruction and wisdom are the safest and for our benefit. Look to Him for the instructions you need for today. Take the time to ask for His wisdom. Refuse being impulsive and hasty with your decisions, take time inquire of those around you who have Godly character. Rest assured today, that the Lord's plan is for our best. We can trust His counsel and wisdom.

Proverbs 8:32-35
Listen to my instruction and be wise; do not ignore it. Blessed is the man who listens to me, watching daily at my doors, waiting at my doorway. For whoever finds me finds life and receives favor from the Lord.
Proverbs 7:12 ♥ Proverbs 1:5 ♥ Psalm 1:1-2

Hands

Since becoming a nurse, I have been preoccupied with looking at people's hands. We can learn so much about people just by looking at their hands.

The type of work a person does is often reflected by their hands. A mechanic's hands often contain the residue of black grease, that no matter how hard they try, they are unable to completely remove. If a person works hard outdoors, we can usually tell just by looking at their hands. I've cared for people whose hands reflect an internal autoimmune disorder that cause their hands to become twisted. And regardless of cosmetic facial enhancements to attempt to hide a person's age, their hands can rarely keep the secret. For the most part, these people never say a word but their hands tell us a story about them. What do our hands say about our life? Not the appearance of our hands, but the life our hands give?

There are examples we can learn from in God's word…

The man we know as the Good Samaritan,

who saw someone that needed help.

He had hands of compassion. His hands and the compassion they gave were very likely a way of life for him. The story of the day he stopped to help a man that everyone else passed by, was just one day of his life we got to see. These hands reflect the hands of Christ. Hands of mercy are the hands of people who are willing to show mercy to others regardless of personal expense. Notice I didn't say financial expense. Mercy often requires personal expense and being willing to extend it generously. There is such an overwhelming relief to the recipient of mercy. These hands reflect the hands of Christ. Hands of hospitality are the hands of those that always welcome others. Being welcomed somewhere extends a sense of belonging that the hands of hospitality extend. Open arms and an open heart to welcome, out of our love has lasting implications. These hands reflect the hands of Christ. We could go on and on, but you get the thought. Ideally, our hands should reflect the hands of Christ. Willingness to tend to the needs of others with generosity. Not only do our hands reflect so much about our life, but the hands of Christ reflect a gracious and loving God. His hands hold and help us daily. His hands and every example of His life tell us so much about who He is. The example of His hands is a meaningful pattern for our own life.

Psalm 63:4
So I will bless You as long as I live; I will lift up my hands in Your name.
Ecclesiastes 9:10 ♥ Exodus 15:6 ♥ Matthew 14:31
Psalm 28:2 ♥ 1 Timothy 2:8 ♥ Genesis 14:20

Equipped

Have you ever attempted to do a project only to find that you didn't have all the tools or supplies you needed? It's frustrating when you're in the middle of something to have to stop to find or go get what you forgot. It's much easier and goes much smoother when we're prepared. Did you know that the Lord has given us everything we need. We have been faithfully equipped by Him. There isn't anything that Jesus left out, absolutely nothing. His provision for us has been established thoroughly and completely, all we have to do is use all that He has given and made available to us. All He has given is for our good and for His glory. May we truly realize that Jesus is the King of kings. A king doesn't lack for anything and because we were adopted into the family of God, we have been given, by virtue of our place in Christ, everything that is His. Our job is to develop and utilize what Christ has given and extended to us. Imagine you are a carpenter that builds houses. You have your tools, you have the plans, you are begin putting your supplies together. However on the day you begin, you discount your need for 5 out of 8 tools that you know from your past experiences that you will need. Imagine leaving behind your saw, your hammer, the nails, your tape measure, and level. It would be sheer foolishness to think that you could build a house without these things, but we often think we can do life without implementing the strategies and weapons that the Lord has given us. There will be trials in life; the Bible clearly tells us that in this life we will have tribulation. But we don't have to be taken out by them, because Jesus has overcome and will bring us to victory. However, we have a part to play as we refuse to be mowed over by the enemy and stand up strong in the name and authority of Jesus, utilizing the provisions He has given us. They're all there, waiting, and ready, but we might need to dust them off, polish them up, and remind ourselves of just how powerful they are. We can try to do things on our own, but why would we ever think that we can be as effective as we would be without making the most of all that the Lord has given us to be victorious. Our calculations can be easily misguided and skewed by an apathetic spirit that attempts to impose spiritual laziness upon us. But let's shake that off in the name of Jesus and stand tall and strong in the power of His might and the glory of His word.

2 Peter 1:3-8

His divine power has granted to us all things that pertain to life and godliness, through the knowledge of him who called us to his own glory and excellence, by which he has granted to us his precious and very great promises, so that through them you may become partakers of the divine nature, having escaped from the corruption that is in the world because of sinful desire. For this very reason, make every effort to supplement your faith with virtue, and virtue with knowledge, and knowledge with self-control, and self-control with steadfastness, and steadfastness with godliness, and godliness with brotherly affection, and brotherly affection with love. For if these qualities are yours and are increasing, they keep you from being ineffective or unfruitful.

Ephesians 6:10-11 ♥ Romans 8:17 ♥ 1 Thessalonians 4:13
1 Thessalonians 5:6

A Lion

It is a well-known fact that lions are referred to as the king of the jungle. When we think of a lion, we picture a fierce and majestic animal that is powerful in many ways. They are far superior to the other animals of the jungle and they can easily overtake their prey. They are fierce protectors of their families and no predator can subdue them. The lion is a renowned symbol of royal authority and power. If you talk about somebody being "lion-hearted" you're talking about somebody who is courageous. They're bold and fearless. The dictionary tells us the term "lion" or "lion-hearted" can refer to a person of great importance, a person of great influence." He's a lion of a man. There is a picture of what John describes when he refers to Jesus as the "lion" in the throne room of heaven. God will be as a lion to His people chastening them until they repent and return to Him. The Lord our God, loves us to the point that He will pursue us and protect us from the enemy that tries to overtake us.

It's interesting that the Bible refers to the devil as a roaring lion. He is not a true lion, he may have the ability to inflict fear, but he is no match for the true Lion of the tribe of Judah. Sadly, we can be deceived into thinking that somehow the roar of the devil carries authority, but it does not, and it cannot because the authority it tries to implicate belongs to God alone. As we think about the tribe of Judah, we know that Biblical history defines this as God's people, those He loves and has done everything possible through every means necessary to rescue them from destruction. When we forget about God, He doesn't forget about us. He is faithful to pursue us because of His immense love for us. He rescued His people and He rescues us again and again, from ourselves and from the enemy of our soul who wants to destroy us. May we be reminded of who Christ truly is today.

Isaiah 31:4-5

For thus the Lord said to me, As a lion or a young lion growls over his prey, and when a band of shepherds is called out against him he is not terrified by their shouting or daunted at their noise, so the Lord of hosts will come down to fight on Mount Zion and on its hill. Like birds hovering, so the Lord of hosts will protect Jerusalem; he will protect and deliver it; he will spare and rescue it.

Hosea 13:4-7 ♥ Revelation 5:5 ♥ I Peter 5:8

Absolutes

There are absolutes in life that cannot be changed regardless
of our opinion. Consider that when you plant apple seeds,
if they successfully take root, you will grow an apple tree.
There is the law of gravity that is a defined scientific absolute.
We must have water to survive. Air is not an option if we
want to breathe. Truth is an absolute regardless of how
many philosophers attempt to redefine it as relative.
The greatest and most supreme absolute of life is God.
His love is absolutely infinite. His grace is absolutely amazing.
His mercy is absolutely the richest treasure we can ever know.
His hope is absolutely alive and His promises are absolutely sure.
He is absolutely the One and Only, True and Living
God. And He is absolutely crazy about you with a
love that is deeper than the deepest ocean.
We can have peace in the absoluteness of God that is never overcome
with evil, His love is never dependent on anything else. He is absolute
love. He is absolute healing. He is absolute freedom. He is absolute
peace. He is absolute sufficiency for every need and nothing replaces
our necessity for God. He is absolute authority and sovereignty.

Colossians 1:15-23

*He is the image of the invisible God, the firstborn over all creation, for all
things in heaven and on earth were created in him—all things, whether
visible or invisible, whether thrones or dominions, whether principalities
or powers—all things were created through him and for him. He himself is
before all things and all things are held together in him. He is the head of
the body, the church, as well as the beginning, the firstborn from the dead,
so that he himself may become first in all things. For God was pleased
to have all his fullness dwell in the Son and through him to reconcile all
things to himself by making peace through the blood of his cross—through
him, whether things on earth or things in heaven. And you were at one
time strangers and enemies in your minds as expressed through your evil
deeds, but now he has reconciled you by his physical body through death
to present you holy, without blemish, and blameless before him—if indeed
you remain in the faith, established and firm, without shifting from the
hope of the gospel that you heard. This gospel has also been preached
in all creation under heaven, and I, Paul, have become its servant.*

Psalm 47:2 ♥ Hebrews 13:8 ♥ Ephesians 2:4-5
Genesis 21:33 ♥ Jude 1:23-25 ♥ 1 Peter 1:3
1 Timothy 1:17

The Answer is on the Way

We all face personal struggles. They can easily attempt to overtake our thoughts and focus. In a sense they attempt to rise above the truth of God's word. When we are faced with these struggles, it's important that we remember to keep our anchor set in Christ. In 1 Kings there is a story of a man named Elijah who prayed that it would rain after a 3 ½ year drought. When he began praying, there wasn't a cloud in the sky but he kept praying. As he prayed, he sent his servant out 7 times to look for clouds. On the seventh time, the servant reported seeing a cloud the size of a man's hand. At that moment, Elijah told the servant to pack up everything, it was about to rain. The Bible says that the sky filled with black storm clouds and a huge storm came. There was so much water that it filled all the rivers, streams and tributaries. Sometimes, we pray, asking God for a miracle and we reserve our faith for the moment we see the miracle take place. But I wonder what would happen if we truly believed God to do exceedingly, abundantly, above ALL that we thought He could do. There are prayers and then there are fervent prayers. In other words, prayers prayed with heartfelt passion, sincere zeal and serious intention. At the littlest sign of the miracle, let's begin declaring, "He's doing it! He's doing it! God is working! The downpour is on the way!"

Good prayers are not always determined prayers. In Romans 4, Paul tells us about the promise God made to Abraham. The Bible says that the promise of God happened in Abraham's life because of his faith. God made a promise, but if Abraham and chosen not to believe, the promise would not have come to pass. This recounting of Abraham's faith was recorded not just to honor Abraham's faith but for us to see and understand how much God is calling us to believe Him with our whole hearted confidence. Don't forget what you are entitled to in Christ. Your inheritance is rich my friend, stand up to the enemy and defend your family, your life and your destiny.

Luke 11:9-10 Amplified

So I say to you, Ask and keep on asking and it shall be given you; seek and keep on seeking and you shall find; knock and keep on knocking and the door shall be opened to you. For everyone who asks and keeps on asking receives; and he who seeks and keeps on seeking finds; and to him who knocks and keeps on knocking, the door will be opened.

1 Kings 18:42-45 ♥ James 5:17-18 ♥ Luke 18:1-8

Powerful Bond

We are mindfully aware of the incredibleness of who God is.
His sovereignty is unsurpassed and in our knowledge base
we know this to be true. The challenge can sometimes be
within our hearts. It is simple faith that we are established
in, as His power has been set before us. But as amazing as
it is, it is necessary to guard it from being diminished.
The essence of His power is the expression that assures us of His
unparalleled supremacy, as the One who holds and covers us in
every way. Regardless of the trial or situation, suffering or tragedy,
He alone is ultimately all-powerful.
And in that, there is the treasure of knowing we belong to God.
He calls us His very own!
This reality becomes easier to grasp when
I relate it to my own children.
They are mine. There is an attachment that no one else
shares with them, a bond that cannot be fabricated. The
bond with our Heavenly Father is even more substantial
than the depth of the bond we have with our children.

When God, our Heavenly Father, calls us His own, there is a
security and provisional dimension to this bond He has with us.
It is a bond that cannot be duplicated though many attempt to
fulfill it in a variety of different ways. He never ever wants us to
walk outside of what this bond holds. As we embrace our place
in Christ, we will know this bond more divinely, and the beauty
of what that truly means will become more and more evident.

Colossians 1:16-17

*For by Him all things were created, both in the heavens and on
earth, visible and invisible, whether thrones or dominions or rulers
or authorities—all things have been created through Him and for
Him. He is before all things, and in Him all things hold together.*
Hebrews 1:3 ♥ Hebrews 7:25 ♥ John 1:3

Blindness

Blindness is the inability to see. Whether from birth or due to a devastating event, blindness is never a chosen situation. Often, blindness is gradual and happens slowly until one day, all light is blocked and only darkness remains. Physical blindness, as we know, is not the only type of blindness there is. In reading the Gospels, the blindness of the religious rulers is almost mind-boggling. Something in our hearts wants to scream out, "don't you know what you are doing?", "don't you know that, that's JESUS!" Why couldn't they see Him for who He was? Sadly, their hearts were in utter darkness, even with Jesus so near to them. Somehow they were blind and could not see who He was. It's unimaginable that they could literally be so blind as to crucify the Son of God. And while it's understood that it was God's plan and necessary for our redemption, still, their blindness should not be overlooked. Jesus was right there with them, they saw the miracles He did. May it serve to warn our own hearts to be on guard against the gradual blindness that can occur to our own spirits. You may say, "Jesus isn't here today, we don't see Him walking around and talking to us". Yes, that's true, however, evidence of His presence is daily continually with us. He has shown us His glory and even creation is evidence of His reality.

We choose every day, whether or not to walk toward a place of more blindness or more of His light in our life. It takes diligence and work to walk against the cultural imposition of relativity. Swimming upstream, so to speak, requires the strength of a provision only God can give us. And He gives it when we call on His name and our hearts cry out to Him to keep us from being spiritually blinded. Did the things of God once look clearer to you than they do today? Has your vision become blurred in some areas? If so, run to the Light of God's word and let the Holy Spirit show you the way back. The enemy wants us to feel as though it's impossible but, my friend, it's as easy as whispering a prayer… "Jesus, I need You, flood my heart with Your light and don't let me walk into blindness. Please lead me out of the places I've wandered into or even intentionally pursued that are not where I need to be."

Ephesians 1:18
I pray that the eyes of your heart may be enlightened,
so that you will know what is the hope of His calling,
what are the riches of the glory of His inheritance in the saints,

Psalm 146:8 ♥ Ephesians 5:8 ♥ Isaiah 42:16
John 12:35

One Thing

I was lovingly reminded of the "one thing" so needed, and so necessary. How often it gets tangled up in the responsibilities of our life and while we know its place, somehow we can easily become so misfocused. We have a front row seat as we get to glimpse into the lives of two sisters in the Bible. Their names you may know and maybe you identify with one or the other of them. They are Mary and Martha. They both loved Jesus very much.

Their differences, Mary just wanted to be with Jesus in the moment unfolded to us. However, Martha had made a special event out of Jesus' visit and in doing so, caused herself great distress to the point that she could not even enjoy His presence. Suddenly for Martha, it became all about her and not about Jesus at all. She fell into a place of deception as her intentions were to do something of a gift for Him. But in the process, she lost sight of Jesus and became entirely consumed by the event. She still loved Him so much and she thought she was doing something to please Him. All the while Jesus just wanted her to come and sit near. Not to worry about the things that would distract her from His presence.

Whoa, does that ever happen to us? Yes, it so can and it so does! Distraction brings a disconnection from being able to see what is really important. Jesus told Martha that day, "Martha, Martha, you are worried and troubled about many things, but *one thing* is needed. Mary has chosen the best part;" The things Martha was doing weren't bad but they weren't the "best". Jesus calls us to the better things when life tries to take over. And like Martha, sometimes we are easily engulfed to the point that we cry out to Him to help us. That was the best thing that Martha could have done, however, she didn't get the answer she had hoped for. Martha had it all figured out. She told Jesus her problem and how He should fix it. Are you smiling? We do that same thing, don't we? But Jesus probably is quite possibly saying, that's not the best for you. Come and just be with me, that's the best thing. Stop worrying about all those other things and be here with Me. *Don't let the noise of the world keep you from hearing the voice of the Lord.*

Hebrews 12:2

Let us fix our eyes on Jesus, the pioneer and perfecter of our faith, who for the joy set before Him, endured the cross, scorning its shame, and sat down at the right hand of the throne of God.

Luke 10:38-42 ♥ 1 Corinthians 1:18 ♥ Isaiah 45:22
Micah 7:7

Unforsaken

The words of Jesus as He prayed just before he went to the cross
were words of anguish. They were words of feelings reflecting
a hopelessness to face what lie ahead of Him, seemingly, alone.
Jesus, prayed, "My God, my God, why have you forsaken Me?"
Imagine Jesus, the Son of God, King of kings, Lord of lords, laying
His feelings bare in a way that caused them to be recorded for the
ages to know and read about. Jesus, God's one and only Son, left
abandoned by His father? It is absolutely how Jesus felt as His father
had to turn His face away because of the sin of the world that Jesus
bore. However, in the place of Jesus so feeling abandoned, He was
never more in the center of God's will than at that very moment.
He felt very abandoned, very alone, and very forsaken. Perhaps
Jesus let us see His humanity so that we would know He has
experienced what feeling abandoned is like. We know that
God's word promises, He will never, never, no never leave us
or forsake us, even on days when we "feel" alone. Sometimes
the Lord takes us to a place that is "lonely" to show us the
power that His presence alone can bring in our life.
When our lives are full of so many things, there is little room
for Him at times. God moved so powerfully in Jesus' life as
He empowered Him to face the cross, and not call a legion of
angels to rescue Him. Then God the Father, completely takes
over when Jesus' body lie lifeless in the tomb. He empowered
Him from heaven as His resurrection power flooded Jesus' body
and eternal life was on display. When Jesus felt abandoned, He
is was in the center of God's will. Circumstances and feelings
can sometimes take center stage in our life, but they are just
"setting" the stage for God's power to show up to resurrect
what the enemy thinks he has squelched in our life.

August
14

Deuteronomy 31:6
**Be strong and courageous. Do not fear or be in dread of them, for it is the
LORD your God who goes with you. He will not leave you or forsake you.**
Genesis 28:15 ♥ Deuteronomy 11:8 ♥ Hebrews 13:5
John 11:25 ♥ John 14:6

Power of the Gospel

There is a message in the Gospel of Christ. The message of the Gospel has always been to impact change in the lives of many. This was foretold even before Jesus' birth. The plan of the Gospel is the fulfillment of God's great love for us. The message of the Gospel that John preached was to turn the hearts of the people. The influence of Christ was a message that was carried by others to proclaim God's love. It was not only a message that Jesus shared, but as it was received, it was then shared by those whose life it touched. Jesus' very presence brings healing and hope. The very essence of the message of His love impacted and brought restoration, just as it does today. The Gospel message is to turn the hearts of fathers to their children, and for the disobedient to walk in wisdom. We carry the message of the Gospel with us everywhere we go and we have so many opportunities to convey hope and healing to those who have gone astray and lost their bearings in Christ. People can often find themselves in a place of being disoriented, feeling as though life has taken its toll. Searching within their hearts for stability, the Gospel message can renew their hope and re-establish their stance in Christ. For each and all of us, the message of the Gospel is for every new day. It is not just a "one time" working that happens when we accept Christ, but it works in us daily. Its power is to re-align our hearts to His. We were never created to live life without Jesus to help us. So many need to know that and realize that He is the key to their turmoil. We have the message of the Gospel to share as He shepherds us. Within the message of the Gospel there is so much power to bring redemption to the hopeless and lost. It is for all of us every day. The message of the Gospel holds more than our salvation but it is what sustains our daily lives in Christ Jesus.

August
15

1 Peter 1:3-5
Blessed be the God and Father of our Lord Jesus Christ, who according to His great mercy has caused us to be born again to a living hope through the resurrection of Jesus Christ from the dead, to obtain an inheritance which is imperishable and undefiled and will not fade away, reserved in heaven for you, who are protected by the power of God through faith for a salvation ready to be revealed in the last time.

Luke 1:17 ♥ Romans 1:16 ♥ 1 Thessalonians 1:5
1 Corinthians 6:14

Magnified

A magnifying glass helps us see more clearly something we cannot see on our own. Our vision can be limited and often magnification is necessary for clarity. Without magnification, some of the simplest tasks become really difficult. Things like threading a needle, reading small print or getting a tiny splinter out. Even though these things seem simple, they can become relatively impossible without a means of magnification. Another word for magnify is to enlarge, to expand, and to amplify. When we magnify the Lord's goodness by making the wonders of our heart public, we are enlarging Him before those who are looking for Him. In searching for reality for life, the value of our magnification of Christ gives others the ability to see Him more clearly. People know He's near, but there is a certain measure of clarity that becomes apparent when He is magnified in someone's life. Just as attempting certain tasks without a magnifying glass, many are struggling to see and find Jesus. As His presence fills us, and we magnify Him with our praise and adoration, then He is more easily seen through our life. People have the ability to realize what they are looking and longing for when they see Him magnified through our life. Jesus said in John 12:32, "And I, when I am lifted up from the earth, will draw all people to myself." We are part of the plans of God to draw people to Himself. He needs us and He calls us to magnify what we know to be true of God's goodness and faithfulness. As we magnify Jesus, we will find that not only is He magnified to others, but it reaffirms our faith as well. Watch and see what He does as you magnify Him.

Psalm 96:3-9

Tell of His glory among the nations, His wonderful deeds among all the peoples. For great is the LORD and greatly to be praised; He is to be feared above all gods. For all the gods of the peoples are idols, But the LORD made the heavens. Splendor and majesty are before Him, Strength and beauty are in His sanctuary. Ascribe to the LORD, O families of the peoples, Ascribe to the LORD glory and strength. Ascribe to the LORD the glory of His name; bring an offering and come into His courts. Worship the LORD in holy attire; Tremble before Him, all the earth.

Psalm 34:1-3 ♥ Psalm 117:1-2 ♥ Psalm 104:1
Psalm 106:1-2

Seasons

Summer will soon be coming to a close and on its heels is the wonderful season of fall when the leaves change color and the air becomes brisk. Seasons and time are measured in two ways: Chronos— "chronological", meaning days, weeks, months and years. Kairos—"a period of time"; example: "in the days of Noah or King David". It's important that we do not miss God's seasons or His opportune time for us. Missing a certain season that we are in can happen when we are distracted and just waiting for it to be over. Sometimes we miss seasons because we are looking forward to a better season and sometimes we are simply distracted. For instance, on Monday, we say, "oh Monday... a few days until Wednesday, yay, it's the middle of the week and then we're making plans for the weekend ahead. We can become so focused on the weekend that we miss those next few days in-between. Sadly, this pattern can cause us to miss so much of what God has for each new and special day. Special days are not just holidays but each day is a gift from God. What we do with each day is our gift to Him. When we lived in Africa, we learned that the days are measured much differently than they are in the Western world. Here, if we have an appointment, that appointment becomes important and everything else must be structured around that commitment. In Africa, we may have an appointment but if on the way to the appointment, we meet a friend or see someone in need, they become the priority. Our friends there realize the joy of the journey and are not so focused on the destination though it is very important. It's important to realize that seasons are not always pure joy, they are sometimes difficult. In the hard and difficult days of our seasons, the Lord is still in control and He is still good and faithful. He works in each and every season. As we rejoice in our days, we will find that the seasons of our life hold greater meaning and purpose. Embrace the new day you hold today with anticipation of God's purpose for this day. Ask for His perspective and for a heart that is sensitive to the Holy Spirit's work around you.

August 17

Hosea 6:3
Let us know; let us press on to know the LORD; his going out is sure as the dawn; he will come to us as the showers, as the spring rains that water the earth.
Psalm 118:24 Psalm 31:7-8 James 4:13-15
2 Corinthians 6:2

Just As I Am

I'll never forget the day that, as an 8 year old little girl, I walked down the aisle to give my heart to Jesus at a little church in Mississippi. To this day, I am overwhelmed by the love of Jesus in my life. I don't think I will ever truly be able to grasp the depth of it. The inspiring truth about our testimony and the reality of Jesus' love for each of us, is His specific and deliberate pursuit of each one of us.

It's as if He looks at each of our lives, He knows and sees what no one else can, and He begins calculating and planning a specially designed plan of salvation to reach us. It's no accident that we find Him. If the truth be known, it is probable that Jesus has, orchestrated a plethora of ways to put Himself in various places throughout the journey of our life. Often people don't recognize Him, they walk on by, too busy to see, listen or hear. They pursue other venues for fulfillment and resist His call to their souls. He doesn't relent though. Jesus will be just a bit further down the path, attempting again to be seen for who He truly is for every heart as they search.

The love of the Father is to save us from our sin, for each and every person to know Jesus as our savior, to know His joy and abundance for today. In that, His desire is to have fellowship or more specifically a relationship with us that exceeds the life we live on earth. It's a relationship that transcends all time and space and continues throughout eternity. That is amazing love. Jesus has been and continues to be incredibly patient and kind. He does not just give us love. He is love and therefore, it is in His very nature to be all the things that love is. In His character those attributes are displayed to us each and every day. It is why He calls us to live within Him so that this unconditional love can also be seen in us, because we are His.

"Just as I am" was the song that was playing as this little girl walked down the aisle to receive Jesus. Today is the anniversary of that day in my life. So much has happened since then and as it is with most all of us, there have been some days of wandering, but He has remained overwhelmingly faithful to His promises. I hope you will take a moment with me to reflect on the pivotal day that Jesus came into your life, and you surrendered your heart to Him just as you were.

August
18

2 Peter 3:9
***The Lord is not slow in keeping his promise,
as some understand slowness.
Instead he is patient with you, not wanting anyone to
perish, but everyone to come to repentance.***

Acts 4:12 ♥ 2 Timothy 1:9 ♥ Psalm 62:1
Acts 2:21

Significance

Details in our day to day life are important in ways we may not realize.
Often we do so many things as a part of our daily routine.
We get up, get ready for the day, have breakfast, feed the dog
and on our list goes. However, in those moments and menial
tasks, let us realize that Jesus is right there with us.
He is the friend that sticks closer than a brother. He
literally wants us to know that He is walking in each
and every moment of every day with us.
The sweetness is that we can understand
His call for us to walk with Him.
When Jesus called the disciples, he said to them, "Come, follow me".
Often we go through a good portion of our
day without really "following Jesus"
because the demands of our life do not seem "spiritual"
in a sense. But Jesus said Himself, that He came so
we might have life and life more abundantly.
Our relationship with Him is not on hold
until we reach heaven's gates.

He will help us with the priorities of life when we make
our commitment to follow Him first. Those menial
tasks will suddenly take on new joy because
we are fellowshipping with Him in them.
Washing the dishes or mucking
the stalls become precious times of fellowship that stir our hearts to
love Jesus more. His presence brings significance to our life.
Pursuing worldly significance will always prove to be a
deflating endeavor. It's one that leaves us empty and depleted.
But living in the presence of Jesus will be the significance of our life.
The key to true contentment, true joy, true peace is to walk with Him
and let His presence flood more and more of the moments of our day.

Revelation 21:3
And I heard a loud voice from the throne saying,
"Behold, the dwelling place of God is with man.
He will dwell with them, and they will be his people,
and God himself will be with them as their God.

Exodus 33:14 ♥ 1 John 4:16 ♥ Genesis 28:15
Psalm 16:11

Faith

Faith is a necessity for our life. The graciousness of the Lord is that He has given us each the "measure" of faith. When we take that faith and let it be engaged in our life, that's the open door for God to move. Faith is where we give more credence to the Father than to our fear. Faith is where we acknowledge the greatness of God rather than our weakness. Faith is believing God's promises and refusing to own the world's perspective. Faith has seen many a miracle that would have never happened without it. Why? Because God is God, all the time, He never changes and neither does His goodness. But men and women can sometimes allow circumstances and feelings to dictate believability. Not so with God. He never ever changes. Every day He is amazing and awesome! Imagine having a beautiful car, you can sit in it all day long and admire it to your heart's content. You can even start the engine and adjust the radio to your favorite station. But if you never put the car in gear, you will never go anywhere. Faith is putting your life in Christ in gear, believing Him for His best in your life, even if it's not the plan you had. Faith is trusting in the God who loves you more and knows you better than anyone else ever could. It's refusing to let others override His place in your heart and life.

Every move towards Christ is faith. Every word of thanksgiving for His goodness is faith. There's a story in the Bible, the book of Luke chapter 7 when a woman who had nothing and whose life was absolutely bankrupt, found Jesus and poured out her heart to him through a bottle of expensive perfume. She was ridiculed for her act of worship, but she didn't care. She gave out of love and it was an expression of the faith she had found in Christ. Jesus told her, "Your faith has saved you; go in peace." Faith was letting go of the past and refusing to keep going back to it. Faith allowed Jesus to break her free from the bondage of the chains of shame. Peace comes when we stop trusting and looking to everything else to be our source. She finally got to that place, she stopped all her searching and fell at Jesus' feet. This faith in the only One who was the lover of her soul was the door that welcomed her in. Her search was over. Where is your faith today in Jesus? He is all we need but sometimes we can't quite grasp that reality. But as we ask Him, he will help our little faith to be strong…

"Ladies and gentlemen, start your engines."

But don't stop there!

Luke 7:50 NLT
And Jesus said to the woman, "Your faith has saved you; go in peace."
Galatians 2:20 ♥ Romans 3:22 ♥ Ephesians 3:16-17
2 Corinthians 5:7 ♥ Romans 12:3

Forward

It's a proven fact that people are at a higher risk of having an accident when they are driving backwards than when they are driving forward. Reverse was never an intended gear for people to travel in. It is intended backing up for a short distance. If you've ever had to back up for a long distance, you have experienced the awkwardness of how that feels. You are more inclined to waver. Driving backwards is very hazardous and so is living backwards. Sometimes it's really hard to let go of past pain, past relationships that are unhealthy and even regret. We go back to them again and again, as if there were some way to undo or redo those moments. Some re-visit the pain in their hearts every day and it has become their identity. Changing our mindset means letting go and surrendering those things. It's not easy and often we've held on pretty tightly to such things. But as we open our hands and our hearts, Jesus will take the past and replace it with His grace and the fullness that only He can give. It takes courage and trust in Him. God calls us forward, not backwards. Keep your eyes on Jesus, and as you do, your focus will be on Him. What you are looking to is what you are focused on. We are called to keep our eyes on Jesus, the author and finisher of our faith. It's tough, though, not to look backward and sometimes the pull in that direction is great. But as we let go and let God, He will bring us into so much more than we ever imagined possible. The plans of God for you are to bless you, giving you hope and a future in His grace and sufficiency.

Job 17:9
**The righteous keep moving forward, and those with
clean hands become stronger and stronger.**

Isaiah 43:18
**Forget what happened in the past, and do not
dwell on events from long ago.**

Philippians 3:13-14 ♥ *Hebrews 6:1* ♥ *Romans 8:1*

Ownership

Ownership requires that we take a certain
responsibility for what belongs to us.
What if we were to wholeheartedly take ownership of our
spiritual life and guard it for the treasure that it truly is. In
looking at our life in Christ, wouldn't it take on more significance
to view the aspects of walking with Jesus in a way that says,
"this is *my* prayer life", or "this is my relationship" with Him.
What if we started looking at our relationships
with others with the same view?
"This is *my* marriage" or "this is my relationship with *my* children".
Something happens when we realize that true value of
what we hold in our hands. Looking down into your hands
and evaluating what you are truly holding can bring an
overwhelming sense of wealth and responsibility.
Those things are yours alone, they do not belong to anyone else.
In that ownership, our hearts can take on a greater sense
of guarding, protecting, nurturing and developing that
sometimes go un-regarded for what they truly are.
Inattentiveness can cause us to be lax, but something happens
in our heart of hearts when we look head-on into a need, a
relationship, or a situation and courageously stand to our feet
and say, "this is *my* responsibility". Taking ownership through
the power and strength of the Holy Spirit to be led by the word
of God and not our feelings will be some of the greatest steps
of faith we begin to take in seeing miracles happen. If we've
just been going through the motions or have been feeling
"out of control" in a sense, may we look to Jesus, the author
and finisher of our faith as we step into the place in Christ,
already established for us long ago through His resurrection.

2 Peter 1:10
***Therefore, brothers, be all the more diligent to make your calling and
election sure, for if you practice these qualities you will never fall.***
1 Corinthians 13:11 ♥ *Colossians 3:23* ♥ *Philippians 1:6*
Ezra 10:4 ♥ *Philippians 2:12*

Sheepish

In our day to day lives, we are much more like
sheep than we probably care to admit. Sheep
really do need a shepherd and so do we.
Many attempt to live as if they don't need a shepherd,
but sadly those sheep are easily lost and
trapped by the enemy's schemes.
As our shepherd, we can follow the leading
and voice of the Lord in our lives.
He is near and lovingly guiding each of us, His sheep.
Charles Spurgeon said,

*"Some Christians try to go to heaven alone, in solitude. But believers
are not compared to bears or lions or other animals that wander
alone. Those who belong to Christ are sheep, in this respect, that they
love to get together. Sheep go in flocks, and so do God's people."*

Sheep need a protector from predators, a guide from danger
and an escort to lead them to green pastures and good water.
Without these things, they would become
scattered and easily disbanded.
Jesus holds us together for our good and His glory.
Jesus longs to lead us but, are we willing
to be led or are we stubborn?
May we be "sheepish" in our ways, acknowledging
our need for Jesus to be our shepherd.

Mark 6:34
*Jesus saw the huge crowd as he stepped from the boat, and he
had compassion on them because they were like sheep without
a shepherd. So he began teaching them many things.*

Isaiah 40:10-11
*Yes, the Sovereign Lord is coming in power.
He will rule with a powerful arm.
See, he brings his reward with him as he comes.
11 He will feed his flock like a shepherd.
He will carry the lambs in his arms,
holding them close to his heart.
He will gently lead the mother sheep with their young.*

Psalm 100:3 ♥ Psalm 79:13 ♥ Hebrews 13:20-21

Shield of Rest

There is nothing that brings solace to our souls except the spirit
of God in His grace. Even as a new day begins, if we are not
careful, our minds are continually filled up with so many, many
things. The daily routine of life can be burdensome. Even the
weighing of what our priorities for each day should be can be
weighty to the point that we are not resting in the peace of God.
While it is true that there is much to be done and much that
we can and should accomplish to make the most of our days,
we can still know His rest even there. The Lord, our God, knew
that we would need His covering for rest, and in His divine
goodness gave words to the psalmist for our reassurance.
I wonder if we can really grasp how very much the Lord desires to
strengthen and protect us from unrest when we are overwhelmed.
His rest is a shelter, it is a refuge, it is a place of protection from
all the things of this life that attempt to rob us of our peace.
Inner turmoil is one of the greatest weapons of the enemy and
many struggle to find victory in this area of their lives.
But God is our strength, and His rest is
our victory. His rest is our shield.

*"When the heart is softened with grief, and burdened with guilt; when
all human refuge fails; when no rest can be found to the troubled
mind, then it is that God applies the healing balm by his Spirit."*
-Matthew Henry

Psalm 32:7
*You are a hiding place for me; you preserve me from trouble;
you surround me with shouts of deliverance. Selah*
Psalm 9:9 ♥ Psalm 91:1 ♥ Psalm 31:20
Psalm 5:12

Dependence

Our culture often fosters an "independent" mindset. There are many who function well alone to a certain degree. However, the whole of our existence is dependent on God. For our well-being we need to rely on Him and seek His direction. There is also an aspect to our life that can leave us forlorn. It happens when we mistake independence and doing thingson our own for the deception of isolation. We need each other. The body of Christ is a gift to us for life and in that fellowship we enjoy and experience more fullness. No World Series or soccer tournament has ever been won by just one person. The value of each other has been so torn down and diminished that many people have the opinion that they don't need anyone else…that they can make it alone. Friendship is giving and loving, it's being a part of something greater than yourself. Purpose is multiplied and joys are increased exponentially when we live life with each other. Even more than that, we will know greater joy and grace as we rest and depend on our Heavenly Father, in the measure He intended. We must be careful not to take on what He has already assured us is His responsibility. He loves us and has our best in His heart and plans. He is glorified when we depend on Him and our faith is displayed and even fostered in the lives of others.

August 25

Ecclesiastes 4:9-12

Two are better than one, because they have a good reward for their toil. For if they fall, one will lift up his fellow. But woe to him who is alone when he falls and has not another to lift him up! Again, if two lie together, they keep warm, but how can one keep warm alone? And though a man might prevail against one who is alone, two will withstand him—a threefold cord is not quickly broken.

Psalm 5:3 ♥ Psalms 27:13-14 ♥ Philippians 4:6

Foolish

Most people that seem wise have a confidence about their wisdom.
However, those that are foolish don't
usually see themselves as foolish.
No one wants to appear foolish and yet the
Bible teaches us that sometimes,
those who see themselves as wise are really foolish. This is a
truth that we all must be on guard in our own hearts about. We
can so easily think we are wise in the choices and decisions of
our life, but if we are not careful to consider wise and Godly
counsel or seek the word of God, we can easily be led astray.
I know of a precious Christian couple, who when they were
young, heard of a "get rich quick" idea from another Christian
couple. It all sounded great and without seeking more counsel
or investigating the idea further, the couple invested a hefty
amount of their meager savings in the venture. As you may
have guessed it, they lost all that they invested in the scheme.

August 26

What may seem wise in the world's eyes may be very foolishness.
The Bible clearly teaches us that what is seemingly foolish
in the world's eyes, the Lord will use to confound the wise.
This approach that God takes is to help us see Him for who
He truly is, much greater and more able than men will ever
be. We can hardly understand the idea of God's wisdom, but it
exceeds our own and is the means for us to see His greatness.
He may ask us to do things that seem ridiculous in the eyes of
others, but in our hearts, we know that we are following His
instruction. When we walk in obedience, then we will see His
goodness and experience miracles that only He could have done.
Believing God for the impossible is our joy as His children.

1 Corinthians 1:27
But God chose what is foolish in the world to shame the wise;
God chose what is weak in the world to shame the strong;
1 Corinthians 2:12 ♥ Proverbs 1:5-7 ♥ Proverbs 12:15

Constant Fathomless

It is who Jesus is…
He is constant and He is utterly fathomless.
He is more wonderful than our minds can comprehend.
He is more wonderful than our hearts could ever begin to contain.
His power surpasses the attempts of the
enemy against us in every aspect.
As the reality of who Jesus is and all He has planned for us
on purpose for His purpose settles deep in our hearts again
today, let's begin to try again to really grasp what that means.
As we do, barriers that the enemy has tried to impose in
our way will be overtaken by the greatness of our God.
The innermost place of our heart and soul has
the capacity to experience Jesus continually. It is
why we are called to pray without ceasing.
May we thank Him as much as we can, constantly,
remembering His greatness throughout our day.
In John 7:38, Jesus promises that whoever believes
in Him, that rivers of living water will flow
from them. This promise is for us today.
The blessings of God are yes and amen to them that believe.

*If any man desires to be truly and forever happy, let him apply
to Christ, and be ruled by him. This thirst means strong desires
after spiritual blessings, which nothing else can satisfy;*
—Matthew Henry

Through our lives, we share the unsearchable riches of Christ.
As we do, they become more and more a part of who we are.
His unsearchable riches change us, they
shelter us and they sustain us.

Romans 11:33
***Oh, the depth of the riches and wisdom and knowledge of God! How
unsearchable are his judgments and how inscrutable his ways!***
Psalm 145:3 ♥ Psalm 92:5 ♥ Job 5:9

Celebrating Little

*"It is not how much we have, but how much
we enjoy, that makes happiness."*
~Charles Spurgeon

Jesus said that He came that we might have life and have it more abundantly. I truly believe that He desires that we would be happy. But often our focus is not on where true happiness comes from. We get side-tracked with material things and ambition, believing that somehow these are the things that will bring us happiness. But the salvation of our hearts is where true happiness lies, its where it begins and ends. From there we must refocus and re-center, enjoying the blessings of our salvation and all that the Lord has blessed our life with. We choose to enjoy or not, all that we have received of the Lord. Many stay in the "gotta get more" mode, while others live blindly, not seeing all that they are holding in their hands and their lives.

God is gracious and kind. He has blessed us with so much. When we lived in Mali, I watched the poorest of the world's poor, find Jesus and find true happiness and joy. They had so little in the world's eyes, but were rich in their hearts because they had found the treasure of Christ and His love for them. Besides the richness of their salvation, their possessions were meager. But they taught me the value of celebrating little. Celebrating little brought huge enjoyment to them and I learned so much from experiencing such a culture. It's not how much we do or do not have that will bring us happiness, it is realizing how amazing the love of the Father is for us personally and individually. Celebrate and enjoy Jesus and His love in your life today.

Jeremiah 17:7-8

But blessed is the one who trusts in the Lord, whose confidence is in him. They will be like a tree planted by the water that sends out its roots by the stream. It does not fear when heat comes; its leaves are always green. It has no worries in a year of drought and never fails to bear fruit.

Deuteronomy 30:16 ♥ Psalm 34:8 ♥ Philippians 4:9
James 1:17

Struggles

There are few who never face a difficulty or struggle in life.
Sometimes we face issues that are not that hard to navigate.
However, there are times that the struggles of
life seem too overwhelming for us.
We need to remember that no matter what, Jesus is our
strength and that we are not alone in the struggles that we
face. In the middle of loneliness and despair, there is a friend
that sticks closer than a brother. His name is Jesus and He
has overcome all that the enemy can use against us.
The issue comes in when we can't feel His presence
and when we seemingly lose our bearings in
Christ. Remember today, that you are His.
You are precious in the sight of your
Heavenly Father and He loves you.
We have a shelter from every storm in His covering.
Victory is ahead.
Renewed mercy and grace are His measure for each day.
For every struggle, Jesus is there, right beside us. You can
lean on Him and hold onto His strong and steady
hand as He leads you through.

August
29

Psalm 34:17-18

*"The righteous cry out, and the Lord hears them; he delivers
them from all their troubles. The Lord is close to the
brokenhearted and saves those who are crushed in spirit."*

Philippians 4:12-13 ♥ *Isaiah 54:17* ♥ *2 Corinthians 4:8-9*

One Thing

If there were one thing we could ask of the Lord I wonder
if it would be what the Psalmist asked of Him in his prayer
one day. He recognized that though there are many things
in our life, there is one thing that is paramount. It was
one thing that was more important than all the rest.
Mary found the "one thing" as she worshipped at Jesus' feet.

Psalm 27:4
One thing I have asked from the LORD, that I shall seek:
That I may dwell in the house of the LORD all the days of my life,
To behold the beauty of the LORD And to meditate in His temple.

So many things each day can attempt to take our attention.
We can easily become focused on all the other things and lose
sight of the "one" thing. Jesus and His presence is so near.
Is there one thing that has attempted to take His place in your days?
It may not be the same thing every day, but every day it seems
like there is something that wants to take the place of prominence
above Jesus. Being mindful that His place is His alone can help
us keep other things from invading that space in our hearts.
What one thing is it that wants to have our focus? There is
one thing that brings everything into perspective and it
is to truly seek being in the presence of God as we walk
through each day. Do we realize how very much the Lord,
our God, who loves us so much, desires to continually
be with us? He never wants us to be without Him.
We can come Him on this new day and every new
day, and ask for that one thing, that we would truly
seek Him to be a part of all we do and all we are.

Psalm 63:1
O God, You are my God; I shall seek You earnestly; My
soul thirsts for You, my flesh yearns for You,
In a dry and weary land where there is no water.
Psalm 42:1-2 ♥ Psalm 26:8 ♥ Psalm 27:4
Psalm 90:17

Without A Doubt

There isn't much in life that gives us the
assurance of never having to doubt it.
We are hopeful for and about many things. But the only
security of assurance is our foundation in Jesus, our Savior.
He is the foundation and the only surety we can truly stand
on. Without a doubt, He is faithful. Without a doubt, His
mercies are new every morning. Without a doubt, He loves
us. Without a doubt, He has a plan for our future. Without
a doubt, His grace is sufficient for everything we will face.
Without a doubt, He wants us to walk with Him.
When fear tries to steal away your confidence and your assurance
that God is working, refuse its imposition on your heart. Take those
things that attempt to set themselves up against the knowledge of
God in your mind, and know that without a doubt, God is able.
Lately there's been a lot of painful discussion about the devastation
that "bullying" causes. It is not a new concept for since the garden,
that spirit has been around, bullying and harassing the people
that God loves. It can easily come in when we least expect us
and torment, imposing so many things that will cause us to
doubt God. Even in the garden, the devil came to Eve and asked
her to doubt God with his question: "Did God really say?"
Well today, we can know that, yes, God really did say He is all
we need. He really did say that He will be faithful because He
is faithfulness. He really did say that He loves you, because He
alone is love. He really did say that He came to give us life and life
more abundantly because He is life! We can rest assured, without
a doubt that Jesus is our portion and our deliverer forever.

August 31

Mark 11:22-23
*Then Jesus said to the disciples, "Have faith in God. I tell you
the truth, you can say to this mountain, 'May you be lifted up
and thrown into the sea,' and it will happen. But you must really
believe it will happen and have no doubt in your heart.*

2 Timothy 1:14 ♥ Psalm 33:4-6 ♥ James 1:6

Widow's Mite

Last year a dear friend found a rare a "widow's mite" and gave it to me for Christmas. It's a tiny coin that represents so much more than its appearance. While other people gave large offerings from their means, Jesus took notice of the smaller gift because it was given with a more generous heart His the other offerings. How could a smaller or lesser gift, given to Jesus, hold more significance than a large, impressive amount? It's a matter of heart that Jesus saw. He looked beyond the display to the heart behind it. It's something He wanted us to realize and it still matters today. Yes, giving our offering with our whole heart matters to Him very much. However, in addition to that, we have the great joy of giving generously in many ways. Giving our love with our whole heart when it's hard, being gracious when our flesh wants to retaliate are just two examples of giving generously from our heart. When this woman brought her offering that day, I don't think she came hoping anyone would even notice her. She probably hoped no one would see her because of her seemingly small offering. But to Christ, she was seen above the rest. He saw her heart that day, not what men would have seen. Jesus was so touched by her gift that the Bible says He called His disciples to Him and told them how significant it was. What gifts can we bring to Jesus that will reflect the heart that blesses Him. Perhaps we are like those who had large gifts, who gave with only the selfish ambition of being seen by others. If so, we can ask the Lord to change what is in our hearts, that we would have an honest heart of generosity and love. The widow's gift was given because of her love. She gave because she could do no less. She gave because she was driven to respond to God's love within her and that response required an action. Most might have thought that if that was all they could give, why bother? Why give at all? What difference could such a small contribution make? Well, we know from scripture that it made a big impact and it is still impacting us today if we will take a moment to reflect on the heart behind it all. Jesus' heart is so impacted when we let our love for Him be displayed in the little ways of our life. Those little instances when we resist being offended and let His grace reign in love. All day long, the tiny offerings of our love have great potential to touch the heart of Jesus, and in return we are more blessed by His presence than we could have imagined possible.

September 1

Mark 12:42-43

A poor widow came and put in two small copper coins, which amount to a cent. Jesus called His disciples to Him and said, "Truly I tell you, this poor widow has put more than all the others into the treasury."

Psalm 51:10 ♥ Jeremiah 24:7 ♥ Ezekiel 36:26

Cling

Dryer sheets and fabric softeners are used to keep clothes from sticking together or being full of static. It's disappointing to realize as you are walking out the door to an appointment that you must have forgotten that little item as your clothing is sticking to everything. It's pretty amazing that such a tiny item can be such a blessing but today I am thinking that we use other things that replicate dryer sheets in our life that keep us from clinging to Jesus. Most of us long to cling to Jesus with more and more of our hearts but are blinded to the need of clinging to Him. An old favorite hymn of my dad and grandmother is the "Old Rugged Cross". Maybe you remember it? It is one of my favorite now and I wonder if it isn't because of how they loved it which caused me to really hear its words. The chorus rings out, "I will cling to the old rugged cross and exchange it someday for a crown". What is it about the cross? What is it about clinging that really matters for us? What we cling to makes huge impacts in our life. Do we cling to traditions or things, people or comforts that can become closer to us than Jesus? Maybe it's our, one of many, mobile devices or our TV show that doesn't glorify and enrich our life in Christ? It can be our schedule or self-indulgence. We can take inventory today and ask Jesus to show us what we are honestly clinging to and then give Him permission to pull us away from it. As He does, it's important that we don't resist the detachment. He longs for us to cling to Him. To really hold on as though our very life depended on it, because it truly and honestly does. As long as we cling and hold onto ourselves and our hands are full of many things, we cannot hold onto Him. Let your heart cling to His today in a new way. Let Him detach you from the familiar and bring you closer to His amazing presence. Cling close enough to hear His voice and His heart.

Deuteronomy 10:20
"You shall fear the LORD your God; you shall serve Him and cling to Him, and you shall swear by His name.
Joshua 23:8 ♥ Deuteronomy 11:22 ♥ 2 Kings 18:6
Psalm 63:8

Given

Today I have the joy of visiting my sweet daughter. I love her so much and my heart is full as we are just being together. I am imagining the heart of God as I think about how much He loved Jesus and how much He loves us. We are getting ready to go to a wedding and are making a special wedding gift.

As it is coming together, we are getting more excited as we anticipate the reaction of the bride when she opens it. It's so fun to make something special for a friend on such a precious occasion of her life. How much more is my heart even fuller at the reality that God gave the most precious gift of His son, Jesus for and to us. I wonder if He anticipates our joy to open the gift He has given, each new day, getting to know and understand Him more and more. Not only that! But the gift goes beyond the gift of the Father to being a gift given by Jesus, Himself. The word of God tells us that Jesus literally gave His life for us. The Word of God tells us that when Jesus hung dying on the cross, He GAVE up His spirit. He gave it, was not taken from Him. It was amazing because He had the power to come down and slay them all, but instead of hating even those who were killing Him, His heart was full of loving compassion. The gift we have been given is not a once in a lifetime gift but a gift FOR a lifetime! May we experience the gift we have in Jesus In a new way. Might the treasure of what He has truly given enthrall our hearts again today. The most wonderful gift we have ever known or received is from the very heart of God.

Galatians 2:20
I have been crucified with Christ. It is no longer I who live, but Christ who lives in me. And the life I now live in the flesh I live by faith in the Son of God, who loved me and gave himself for me.
John 3:16-17 ♥ Make 15:37 ♥ Matthew 27:50
John 9:30

Tapestry

In the day to day and moment by moment part of life, it's not always easy to see the tapestry that God is weaving. Typically we just see the immediate and what is right before us within a certain span of nearness. We try to see what God is doing, but sometimes it's not that easy and we may wonder where He is. Dear friend, He is near, in the middle of where you are. He can take the mishaps of our life and weave them into something beautiful. It takes time, His time to tie up all those frays and loose ends, but with our surrender, He is able to show us more and more of His beauty. We want to live as perfect before the Lord, and to serve Him wholeheartedly without the failures of life. Failing usually causes us to "feel" like we are a failure. And yes, we cannot deny our weakness because it is here we find the strong arm of God working to hold us up.

Throughout God's word there are many characters who experienced failures in their lives. Yet that did not keep them from the greatness that God intended to do through them. It can be very difficult to allow yourself out of the past failures of your life and to live in all that the Lord has for you. We can somehow think only of our failure, but friend, Jesus forgives and helps as we surrender them to Him. Just as He called Lazarus out of the tomb, He calls us out of the place of past failure that can bring death to us in a way that He has already conquered for us. Who would want to live in a cemetery or a tomb? That's a place for the dead, not the living. Live today! Know you have been called out from that place into the new dawning of the beauty that God has established over your life through Jesus His son. It's okay to let go of the past failure to grasp what is ahead. His life in you is His glory being revealed. As it is displayed, it will not only be known and seen by you but by those around you. He is still weaving. He has not left the weaving undone without His attentiveness. It has not been laid aside, and He never has intended that it be left unfinished.

Ephesians 2:10
You are His handiwork For we are his workmanship, created in Christ Jesus for good works, which God prepared beforehand, that we should walk in them.

Another translation says we are His masterpiece. Perhaps you don't feel like a masterpiece today but it doesn't mean that God is wrong. Live today and speak life over your life by faith. Step out as His glory dawns upon you.

Psalm 37:23
"If the Lord delights in a man's way, he makes his steps firm; though he stumbles, he will not fall, for the Lord upholds him with his hand."

1 John 5:4 ♥ Lamentations 3:22 ♥ Psalm 60:12
Romans 8:31 ♥ 2 Corinthians 2:14

Every Praise

Recently when a little boy was abducted, it was reported that as he rode in the backseat of his kidnapper's vehicle, he began singing these words of praise: Every praise is to our God. Every word of worship with one accord. *Every praise every praise is to our God. Sing hallelujah to our God. Glory hallelujah is due our God. Every praise every praise is to our God.*

As the little boy sang, the kidnapper became increasing irritated and annoyed. He ranted, telling the little boy to stop singing. The boy's response was to sing on and sing on he did. He kept singing the song his mom had sung often and taught him to the point that his heart was filled and the outflow was, "Every praise is to our God, sing hallelujah to our God..." Over and over the driver told him to stop singing but he sang on, refusing to be intimidated by the captor or his situation. You may have heard the true story, that the kidnapper became so annoyed with the little boy's song that after 3 hours, he could stand it no more and he finally freed the little guy. Some things to consider in this heartwarming story are the facts that our praise is a great annoyance to the enemy, and it is often why he tries to silence our praise to God. We probably seldom realize how powerful our praise is against the enemy, but it matters so much. When we praise God, His power is released and He does miracles. Our praise is an incredible weapon against the enemy who constantly tries to intimidate us. It's our song and the enemy wants to take it from us because if he can, he can strip away from us one of our most important weapons. May we see our praise for all that it truly is. It is a powerful weapon against the enemy and every attack he attempts to threaten us with. It is the means that we can glorify God and it deepens the more we sing and worship Him with our whole heart. Turn your focus in every praise to our God. May it annoy the enemy to such a degree that he lets go and we find freedom from his grip.

2 Chronicles 20:2
Praise the Lord, for His mercy endureth forever!" And the scripture says, "...when they began to sing and to praise, the LORD set ambushments against the children of Ammon, Moab, and mount Seir, which were come against Judah; and they were smitten.
Deuteronomy 10:21 ♥ Psalm 22:3 ♥ Acts 16:23-26

Going Public

Before we say a word, a work happens in our hearts. It can be for good or it can tear down. Deep within us is the place where the Lord works and as we allow Him to cultivate and work in that place, the good seeds planted there are tended and guarded. As Jesus works in the depths of our heart, we may begin to notice the things of God begin coming out from that place. Our life begins to exemplify and glorify Him more and more. Our actions and our speech begin taking on a role of worship and our very lives declare the goodness of God. Going public with our private love for Jesus is just the beginning. As we declare Him more and more, we must carefully guard all He is doing in us, in the deep places of our heart. The entrusting is an intimate relationship that is ours alone with Jesus, the One who loves us so deeply. May we not be frivolous with His love and the deep things He has done and is doing in our heart? Relationship with Jesus is formed in this secret place, hidden away for you and He to share and delight in. However, letting our love for Jesus show to others creates a bond with Him that cannot be underestimated.

Maybe it has been a while since you have sensed such a depth of His working in you. From this place of honesty, we can come and lay before Him our openness.

Deuteronomy 4:9
Only give heed to yourself and keep your soul diligently, so that you do not forget the things which your eyes have seen and they do not depart from your heart all the days of your life; but make them known to your sons and your grandsons.

Proverbs 23:19
My child, listen and be wise:
Keep your heart on the right course.
Luke 6:45 ♥ Proverbs 4:23 ♥ 2 Kings 10:31

Searching

The Lord calls us to search for Him.
Isaiah 55:6
"Search for Me while I may be found".
Searching is looking intensely, it's a focused effort of looking for something specific. When something is missing, something of importance, or something of great value to us, our search becomes very focused. We're not thinking about looking for anything else, we look and look, often going back to the same places we've looked before just in case we've overlooked what is lost.
The searching and pursuit of Jesus is a necessity
for each and every one of us.
Misplacing our keys and not realizing it until we're ready to leave for work is one thing, but what about when our child has wandered off inside a busy market or mall without our knowing it. An urgency sets in and our hearts are gripped. Suddenly, nothing else on the planet matters until our lost love is found again. This is the urgency that God searches for us with. But with what urgency do we search for Jesus with? Our hearts are often distracted and we don't even realize our distance from Him. He is drawing us to His heart and He daily calls us to search for Him. The searching for Him is faith. It is our surrender. It is our dependency on Him. It is our lifeline.
I love the first words of 1 Chronicles 22:19 that say,
"Now set your heart and your soul to seek the Lord your God..."
We see the urgency... Now! Then there is an action of faith... set your heart and soul. Focus on your search of Him. To seek the Lord your God acknowledging His lordship over you and your life, your family, your job, your home, your influence, your purpose and your motives. The most wonderful part of searching is knowing that He is findable! He wants us to find Him! Please never think that He is hiding from you. Daily you will find Him but it takes looking. Search and look for Jesus today.

Acts 17:27
That they would seek God, if perhaps they might grope for Him
and find Him, though He is not far from each one of us;
1 Chronicles 22:19 ♥ 1 Chronicles 16:

Presently Present

Have you ever felt a little preoccupied during your prayers? Maybe your mind tends to wander and you have to work to settle your heart for even a few moments. It seems our mind can run in a million directions when we are just trying to have some time alone with Jesus. In those times and others, we can focus on the present and be presently present there. It's not always easy, but it is always far more fulfilling if we will take the time and reign in those thoughts and lasso our heart for a few quiet moments in the presence of the King of kings. He longs to just share with us and fellowship together, but if we attempt to be there without being presently present, chances are we will get up feeling as though the time was not all it could have been. Letting our rampant thoughts dictate over our prayer life and fellowship with the Lord, will undermine our ability to hear His voice and be renewed as we wait there. Somehow we must stop and see what is truly happening and distinguish the wrestling that attempts to demand our focus. In a moment's whisper, they can all be silenced as if in the presence of a ruling king or judge. Imagine the word from heaven, "SILENCE"! to our restless thoughts? May we really and truly see where our strength lies. It is in the present of His presence. His authority is ours to exercise over those things that attempt to take charge that are not of God. As we bow, as we wait, as we walk, and as we live, presently in His presence, may His glory flood our thoughts and heart, replacing turmoil with tranquility and confusion with contentment.

Isaiah 57:15
For thus says the high and exalted One Who lives forever, whose name is Holy, "I dwell on a high and holy place, And also with the contrite and lowly of spirit In order to revive the spirit of the lowly And to revive the heart of the contrite.

Psalm 16:11 ♥ Jeremiah 29:13 ♥ 2 Chronicles 6:18
Psalm 139:7-12

Demonstrate

Thinking about the countless ways that you have seen God work in your life can spur us on to love others more. In a world that is full of violence and adversity, the impact of love can be so great. Yesterday, Steven Dunn, received Fire Fighter of the Year Award, for heroically going into a burning building where propane bottles were exploding. Why did he go in? It was what he was trained to do, He went in to save someone who was trapped inside, someone who couldn't save themselves. What a demonstration of selflessness. He suffered burns, was treated and was ready to go back on-duty when his next shift started. Love demonstrated happens every day by countless people. In 2009, a trained sky-diver instructor, Dave Hartsock, did a tandem jump with a "first-time" grandma. When he pulled for the parachutes, neither would open all the way, instead they became tangled. As they free fell, Dave knew he had to save his jumper and so he maneuvered his body to cushion her fall. It worked and she only sustained minor injuries. Dave, though was left paralyzed from the neck down. When asked if he would do it again, he said, "Absolutely". We may not be called upon to do the heroic to such depth, but the little things we do are given to do can be so incredibly impacting. Yes, we get to choose to demonstrate God's love, but did you know that we are called to demonstrate it. What kind of love is that? It's heroic love. It's selfless. It's "God-kind" of love. It's loving when it's hard. It's loving when we don't "feel" like it. It's putting someone else's well-being before our own. The more we are in His presence, the more His love will pour out of us. It will take over, without our even thinking that we need to make it happen. I am reminded of a dear friend, a police officer, who did just that when his tow truck driver friend was suffering a massive heart attack. As he began CPR on the man lying on the side of a road, out loud he prayed, "Live in Jesus' name!" Over and over with each compression, "Live in Jesus' name" he commanded and prayed. The friend did live and made an miraculous recovery. We have the chance to do CPR every day in the lives of those around us, to speak life and demonstrate God's love. Resist frustration, anger and the necessity to "be right". Let Jesus' love pour through you!

september 9

Isaiah 63:7

I shall make mention of the loving-kindnesses of the LORD, the praises of the LORD, According to all that the LORD has granted us, And the great goodness toward the house of Israel, Which He has granted them according to His compassion And according to the abundance of His loving-kindnesses.

Psalm 86:15 ♥ Exodus 34:6 ♥ Psalm 86:5
Psalm 103:8 Psalm 111:4

A Diligent Heart

How do we get to the place that we long to
be in the dreams God has given us?
Perhaps it is a place in your marriage, a closer walk with Jesus,
or being a person of His word? It takes having a diligent heart.
Diligence is the same as being careful, attentive, persistent, and
meticulous about what you are doing. Having a diligent heart takes
faith and action. It requires a determination of refusing to just coast
through life without direction or purpose. Diligence has its place
in many arenas of our life but perhaps the most important is its
place in our relationship with Jesus. Applying our diligence with
faith, carries our faith to another level in Him. It pushes through
the barriers of the enemy that attempt to distract, discourage and
distance us from seeing our God-dreams fulfilled. Steadiness in
diligence is to continue to leave your situation and your perspective
in God's hands as you walk with Him. Careful diligence then
added to discernment given by the Holy Spirit carries us to be
more rooted and anchored in His ways instead of our own. God
values a diligent heart that won't be swayed and tossed around. But,
diligence doesn't just happen overnight, it's a process of getting
stronger and stronger every day. The first step is seeing where
you are and then looking at where you're not. From there, what is
God leading you to and where have you been negligent to pursue?
Has He been calling you to speak to your neighbor or coworker
about His love? Perhaps He's simply asking you to spend more
concentrated time, being still in His presence? Could it be time
to have courage and serve in a ministry capacity? Maybe it's the
great treasures He has been waiting for you to find in His word
that you have felt drawn to? Is there a dream that has grown cold
that you know is from Him? Diligence is the place of being, in your
heart first. Spend time there and see what He will do from there.

Proverbs 13:4
**The soul of the sluggard craves and gets nothing, while
the soul of the diligent is richly supplied.**
Colossians 3:2 ♥ 2 Peter 1:10 ♥ Galatians 6:9

Heart of a Hero

Most every person who was alive on what is referred to as "9/11", knows exactly where they were and what they were doing when they heard the tragic news. By far, the most devastating event in U.S. history took place on this day. Two thousand nine hundred and ninety six people lost their lives that day. In writing and thinking about heroes and courage earlier in this week in our devotions, today could not go by without remembering the champions of that day. Fifty police officers and 343 firefighters died on 9/11 as living heroes, helping those that needed rescuing. When they heard the news and received the call, their hearts raced as they knew that they had to go. They had to help, it wasn't negotiable. That was their job, that is what they lived to do. Rescue and save people. Recently, I visited with a former New York UPS driver who lived and worked in New York City on that tragic day. As he shared, it was almost too much to bear just to listen to him recount his story and experience. He told me about the day and then the days that followed. He shared that people gave so much and in his line of work, he delivered whatever people could send to help. From socks to portable eye wash stations to be used at ground zero and shelters, people wanted to help those that were hurting. Packages came from around the world...they came and came and came. The heart of a hero was seen in so many forms and so many ways. As we saw it unfold, we have to stop and ask where did such a spirit originate from? Is it solely from the human heart? I dare say, no. I believe that the heart of a hero is but a mere reflection of the heart of God. As He created Adam and Eve, and watched them become entangled by the grips of sin and their greatest enemy, but God made a way for them and He, Himself rescued them. Approximately 107 billion people have lived since creation and their rescue was made possible by the One true and living God who loves us more than we can imagine. When we are in trouble, for those who are lost and away from Him, something deep in His heart runs because He can do no less. He dispatches angels on our behalf and the Holy Spirit is ever near calling and calling and calling us to surrender to His love. The heart of a hero is the heart of God. It is the heart that loves and has made a way for us through the gift of Jesus, the son of God. God has made a way out of the devastation of your life. He is not far, no matter how far you think you have strayed. The gospel message of the cross is for you today, Jesus saves. He always has and He always can. Our sin and choices are not greater than His love for us. The heart of a hero is the heart of God for you.

Luke 19:10
"For the Son of Man has come to seek and to save that which was lost."
Matthew 18:12-13 ♥ Ezekiel 34:11 ♥ Genesis 3:8-9

Bantering

When is the last time you had the joy of waiting your turn in a check-out line, while a parent/grandparent bantered with a child about all the goodies within the reach? "No" is not a child's favorite word, especially when their eyes are filled with so many temptations. Those temptations are usually not at all good for them, but they cannot understand that aspect at all. I remember the same kind of moments with my own little darlings. If we are onlookers at such an event, we might be quick to come to a variety of inward conclusions about handling such a situation. Some of us try not to stare, some of us try to help by getting the little person's attention with a wave, or we look at that mom with empathy, having been there ourselves. For the child and parent, just getting out of the store and past it, can seem like a major event. Throughout God's word we see the heart of God displayed for such moments with us, His children. He calls us to deny ourselves again and again, for our own good and His glory. It sounds all so easy, but living that call can be more difficult than we expect. It is the reason that many find themselves caught in a place of unhealthy habits. They can be physical or emotional, from unedifying television shows to the foods we eat. May we realize that Jesus is calling us by His spirit to follow Him out of those things without having a spiritual temper-tantrum. Often we are just like that little 2-3 year old in the check-out lane, we want what we want. Again and again, the Lord is trying to get us past those things, for our good. The candy bars in the check-out lane would completely spoil the lunch that lies at the next stop. God has so much more for us than what our flesh screams for and it's not easy to surrender and trust Him. But when we do, our spirit grows stronger, and the flesh that demands its way becomes weaker. If we never start saying no to our flesh, we will always be bantering with the Lord. We will continually try to wiggle our way to have what we want. We will only partially obey Him and live a life of compromise, because those moments of compromise become days of compromise then, weeks of such, turning into months…thus becoming what we are living. God is calling us out of that as we grow in Him. Is there something your flesh just doesn't want to let go of? Today's the day of surrender. When we release those things to Him, we can finally move on to greater things ahead. How long do we want to hang out in the checkout lane? Hasn't it been long enough?

1 Corinthians 13:11
When I was a child, I spoke and thought and reasoned as a child. But when I grew up, I put away childish things.
Luke 9:23-24 ♥ *Titus 2:11-13* ♥ *1 Peter 2:11*
Romans 12:1

He Remains

We sometimes like to think of ourselves in terms that are a bit above where we should, and we view God for far less than He is. It can happen without even realizing it and subtly without intention. He is before all things and in Him all things hold together. There isn't anything that was before God. What we can see is sometimes what we focus on, and we do based on the measure of our understanding. What can we grasp of God's faithfulness? Is it based on what we can comprehend or see? Do we know that God is faithful to a place that is further than just beyond what we know faithfulness to be? It's not uncommon to think of the limitations of humanity and then to put God just a little further than that in His attributes. However, God is, for lack of a better term, "galaxies" beyond even that. God is faithful when we feel as though the bottom has fallen out of our world. When we have made mistakes or been the cause of our situations by wrong choices. God is still faithfully there to love and see us through. His desire is to still want to lead us and help us beyond that place of crisis. He can take what the world would throw away and make it new again. He can take left over pieces and remnants to fashion something beautiful from the scraps. He can take the rubble of our lives and restore it to more than what we can imagine, all we have to do is put it in His hands and stand on His word. He is faithful and He remains able to do more than we can imagine with what little might remain.

2 Timothy 2:13
If we are unfaithful, he remains faithful, for he cannot deny who he is.

Romans 3:3
What if some did not have faith? Will their lack of faith nullify God's faithfulness?

1 Corinthians 1:9 ♥ 1 John 4:16

Named

There are 10 billion galaxies, according to
scientists. There is an average of one billion stars
per galaxy. Calculated that is approximately
one billion trillion stars in the universe. It's a pretty big
number 1,000,000,000,000,000,000,000. Every single
star has a name according to the recorded word of God.
In Psalm 147:4, God's word tells us, "He determines the
number of the stars and calls them each by name."
It's pretty magnificent to imagine what that means and its vastness,
but what is even more profound is to know that we are known by
God. He knows our names and even has the number of hairs on
our head calculated. The other day as I was walking into work,
I came across a little sparrow on the sidewalk that had died.
The moment I saw it, in my heart, the thought came to me that
God sees that little bird! How amazing is it that in the mass of
humanity and the chaos of life, God knows us and He sees us.
Even greater is the realization that He LOVES us and CARES
about each and every one of us specifically and individually.
He knows your name today, my friend. You are not alone.
He is right there with you. When we struggle
and when we are rejoicing!
His love is not dependent on circumstances.
Your name is known by God!
And, may we not discount that if He knows us and our names,
that He also knows and is so concerned for those that we love
and need Him today, even though they may not realize it.

Matthew 10:29-30
*Are not two sparrows sold for a penny? And not one of
them will fall to the ground apart from your Father. And
even the very hairs of your head are all numbered.*
Jeremiah 1:5 ♥ John 10:3 ♥ John 10:14-15
Isaiah 43:1

Not Absent

What a joy it is to know that our God is never absent from our life.
He never goes on vacation…at least not
without taking His kids with Him!
He promises that we are never left alone, never forsaken, and
never forgotten by Him. *The presence of hardships and struggles
are not the absence of God's goodness and faithfulness.*
As issues rise up in our life, struggles and difficulties, we may
be tempted to wonder where God is. But, no matter what the
issues are, we are can know that we are not alone. Could it be
that the struggles or difficulty of our life can prove to be the
thing that brings us to the place God has designed for us?
One of the hardest parts of working through the difficult
places in our life is relying on God. Instead of focusing on
the situation, the key to our growth will be focusing on the
One who sustains us, our God who promised to be
We read and have heard 2 Corinthians 12:9 many times.
It says, "My grace is sufficient for you, for my power is made
perfect in weakness." The New Living Translation says it just
a little differently and it a sweet reminder for us today. *"My
grace is all you need. My power works best in weakness".*
Don't be afraid to let Jesus have your weakness and let His
grace flood in as you place your questions and problems in His
loving care today. Temptation may try to get us to doubt God's
faithfulness and His presence, but He is strongest when we let
Him have control and we stop fighting against His strength.
We gain more and more strength when He is in control.
He is more than able and will be all that we need for each day.
God is not absent, but very, very present!

Hebrews 13:5
**Keep your life free from love of money,
and be content with what you have, for he has said,
"I will never leave you nor forsake you."**
Deuteronomy 31:8 ♥ Luke 11:5-13 ♥ 2 Corinthians 12:9

Accustomed to the Dark

I don't know if you're like me or not, but when it's dark in the mornings, I don't want to turn on any lights for a little while. I'm very happy with dim lighting when it's still dark in the morning. It's because my eyes are accustomed to the dark of the night and a bright light seems so abrupt. But if, by chance, someone else gets up and turns on a bright light, I may shield my eyes for a moment or two as my eyes adjust and then all is well. If left up to me, though, I prolong the process as long as I possibly can. God created our eyes to do amazing things. They focus on objects at various distances within milliseconds and we never even have to think about it. When we enter a darkened place, our eyes automatically adjust for us so that we can see after only a few minutes. However, we cannot see as well as we do when we are in a fully lit room or place. It is interesting that this can also happen spiritually. There are times when we enter into a place that we should not be, and it's darkened from the light of where Jesus has called us to live. We enter there and initially the darkness is very apparent to our spirit, but the longer we stay there, resisting the Holy Spirit's wooing, the more our spiritual eyes adjust to the dim lighting. It doesn't take long before we begin to become accustomed to living in such hues. We may even forget that we are in a dark place because we have shut the Light of Christ out, little by little, for an extended period of time. May we be ever so aware of where we are truly living? Let us not pretend to live in the Light but refuse to come out of the dark places? We only deceive our own hearts when this happens. It's interesting that when we choose to leave a dark place, our eyes must adjust again. It can even cause us to want to turn back into the dark but if we will but wait, our eyes will adjust to the light and we will see so much clearer. Sometimes, though, we are prolonging the process that we know Jesus is calling us to. Allowing the light of His presence and the light of His love to penetrate the dark places of our heart and life is vital to our spiritual well-being. What have your spiritual eyes adjusted to? Will we be willing to let Jesus' light search our hearts today? It will take courage and the outcome may cause us not to want to open our eyes completely, but if we will, His loving grace and the flood of the light of who Christ is will bring us to incredible freedom and direction. His light not only searches our heart but it leads us to places we do not yet see. Let Him be your source and your guide for each new day.

September 16

Colossians 1:13

For He rescued us from the domain of darkness, and transferred us to the kingdom of His beloved Son,

John 1:5 ♥ John 8:12 ♥ Ephesians 5:8
1 Peter 2:9 ♥ 1 Thessalonians 5:4-5

His Honor

Recently, I attended a special ceremony to honor those of our military that had been captured as prisoners of war or were still missing in action. It was tearfully sobering to remember the courage of those men and women. There was such a sense of emotion as we honored those heroes. So within the event, the sense of "honor" has left me yet unsettled. I wonder what it truly means to honor God and honor His name. Honor means, "to regard with high respect, esteem", "to fulfill (an obligation) or keep (a promise)". It would be easy at this point to feel shame or guilt for the many times we have failed to honor God, maybe we have broken many of our promises to Him or not esteemed Him as He is worthy of. However, that is not the goal of my message to your heart. Today, just like that day, what if we just simply begin to take the time to remember Him and the great sacrifice of His love, just as we remembered those POWs and the MIAs for their sacrifice.

Several hours after the ceremony, as I was walking, a vehicle of a marine slowly passed by. It had a decal that read, "Death before Dishonor". It felt blatant and I wanted to turn away from the thought. Its expectation carries a heavy weight. Reading it was what brought me to the unsettledness in my heart. That was exactly what Christ portrayed for us. He would not be dishonored and furthermore, He would not allow us to be dishonored. He died and rose again so that we would have honor and now we live to honor Him. Honoring Jesus is loving Him, it's living a life of remembering and helping others to remember too, what an extravagant sacrifice He made for our honor. We have been given such an incredible place of honor in Christ. We are chosen by Him. We are loved by Him. We belong to Him. We are His! We have been given the title of belonging to Christ, the greatest honor we could ever receive. This life is about honoring the place that the blood of Jesus purchased for us at the cross. It is our honor to honor Jesus and portray His honor. May we never be ashamed but stand proudly to help others remember Him!

Isaiah 25:1
O LORD, You are my God; I will exalt You, I will give thanks to Your name; For You have worked wonders, Plans formed long ago, with perfect faithfulness.
1 Corinthians 10:31 ♥ 1 Samuel 2:20 ♥ Psalm 29:2
1 Corinthians 6:20

Closeness

One of the most comforting verses in the Bible is Proverbs 18:24. It reminds us that we have a friend that sticks closer than a brother. We can be at home, in a quiet place of being still in God's presence and know that He is so near, but we can also be in a crowd of people and He is just as close. When I think of the nearness of God, I picture attending a large event with my husband or a close friend. There are times in the evening when we may lean over to each other and whisper something that only they can hear. No one else in the room can hear, no one else could know except them. That's how close Jesus is to us. We can whisper to Him anytime, anyplace. And, He can whisper to us as well, in a crowded baseball stadium or at an altar where we bow before Him. His nearness is a comfort from the storms of life. It is a refuge from all the demands. For every question, He is the answer. There is not a season we go through that He does not go too. His nearness is an amazing reality when we consider that He is God. He is not only the Creator and Lord of all but He is our friend. Knowing that strengthens our faith like nothing else can and gives us a confidence that we are never alone.

1 Chronicles 28:20
David also said to Solomon his son, "Be strong and courageous, and do the work. "Do not be afraid or discouraged, for the LORD God, my God, is with you. He will not fail you or forsake you until all the work for the service of the temple of the LORD is finished."

Deuteronomy 31:8
Do not be afraid or discouraged, for the Lord will personally go ahead of you. He will be with you; he will neither fail you nor abandon you."

Proverbs 18:24 ♥ Psalm 145:8 ♥ Psalm 37:28
Psalm 94:14

Before the King

Remember the story of Queen Esther? She had been called by God to stand before the King on behalf of her people who were in a life-threatening and desperate situation. She had been placed in a position of influence that had been completely orchestrated by God Himself. When the moment came for Esther to weigh her options and whether she would "chicken out" or completely depend on God's sovereignty, she choose to live out her God given destiny, even if it meant the end of her life. Suddenly, everything came into focus and she began to prepare herself to meet the king, who had the power to order her death for coming into his presence without being summoned. As we know, Esther found great favor in the king's sight and her people were saved by His grace and her obedience.

Any person, anywhere, when preparing to meet a king, would go to extreme measures to be sure they were prepared to come into his presence. Humbly they would come and find it difficult to form the words for the moment. Everything would have to be just right. Their clothes, hair, nothing could be out of place if coming before a king, right? Well for earthly kings, I suppose that is true. However, when we come before the King of kings, Jesus, there is nothing at all we can do to make ourselves presentable, but we still try and think that somehow it is in our own ability to do so. It is actually when we leave His presence, that we are presentable, because in His presence we are changed. We are given priestly garments of sanctification and righteousness that we can never gain on our own. Imagine going into meet an earthly king in only our rags? But as we come just as we are into the presence of Jesus, He adorns us with His robes of righteousness and we walk away with garments more beautiful than ours could ever be.
We leave our rags for the robes of a king.

In His generosity, we are also lavished on by His immeasurable love and forgiveness, as mercy and grace are extended to us beyond what we could ever deserve. You can come in today, into the presence of the King of kings. Not only that, but you are welcome, the doors are open wide into His throne room for you. Don't try to fix yourself up first, just go there and He will do the fixing and make you more beautiful than you ever could on your own.

eptember 19

Hebrews 4:16
et us then with confidence draw near to the throne of grace, that we may receive mercy and find grace to help in time of need.
Isaiah 64:6 ♥ Isaiah 6:5 ♥ Ephesians 3:12
Romans 1:17 ♥ Romans 3:22-23

Apart

In the beginning, God created…the heavens and the earth, the oceans and dry land. He created the animals and birds, plants and trees. He created life. Then He created man and woman in His image. We know and believe in the truth that the story of creation holds. God is the source of life. There is no life apart from life in Him. We know that this is true, but often we let the reality of our source for our very life be "us" focused instead of "God" focused. In other words, we can go through our days without being connected to Christ. We know and expect Him to be there, standing in the shadows of our life in case we need Him, but how much do we include Jesus in the moments that make up our day? The Bible tells us that Jesus Himself, said, He is the Vine and we are His branches, a part of Him we can do nothing. You may say, "I do a lot of things without Him, I don't think I even need Jesus like this, I'm doing okay on my own." But living without being connected to Jesus is not sustainable. When a branch is cut off from the vine, it is only a matter of time until it will start to wither and die from lack of nourishment. Branches cannot survive or live without the Vine. The same is true for us. We, as branches, must be connected and stay connected to the Vine, Jesus. Our life is in Him. Our substance is in Him. Our strength is in Him. We can try to do life on our own, without Jesus but we will most likely find that we will flounder more than thrive without Jesus. But with Him, we will find the opposite to become the reality we live in, we will flourish more than we will flounder. Apart from Him, we can do nothing of lasting or fulfilling purpose. He began life and He continues to give life to us, each and every day. And in that life, there is abundance and purpos that we can only know as we are connected to Him.

September 20

John 15:5
I am the vine; you are the branches. The one abiding in Me and I in him, he bears much fruit. For apart from Me you are able to do nothing.
Philippians 4:6-7 ♥ 1 Peter 5:6-7 ♥ Isaiah 40:31
John 14:27

Mindful of His Kindness

Again and again I am overwhelmed by the kindnesses of God.
In my prayers it has surfaced over and over, especially lately.
Lord, make me more mindful of your kindness. I believe
the Lord our God is so kind and as we are mindful of His
kindness in our lives, it allows kindness to be more a part
of our life. If we are not mindful of God's kindnesses, then
kindness is less important to us. Don't misunderstand, it's
there in a measure, but not in the measure that it could be.
The kindness of God is very much, always around us, but if we
are not mindful of it, its presence is less impacting. But what if
we started looking for it? I believe we will see it more than we
ever realized it was there. There have been times that I have
been the recipient of a random act of kindness. Has someone
you don't know done something for you? It has a ripple effect
that can continue as we give what we have been given.
I was shopping in a store one day and when I went up to pay
for my items, someone had left money at the counter to cover
my purchases. Not only that, but they told the cashier to give
me the change as well. Their only request was that I continue
the kindness as I could. There is great joy in knowing
kindness and giving kindness. It's a joy that God experiences
continually by His kindnesses in our life. It's a joy that I believe
He wants us to experience as well. Kindness is fulfilling joy.
We have received more kindness from God than we
could ever repay no matter how hard we try. In simple
mindfulness, looking all around, we will find His kindness
and have plenty to give and share with others. May we never
withhold kindness when we have it to give! As we have been
given to so generously, may we also give generously.

Proverbs 3:3
**Do not let kindness and truth leave you; Bind them around
your neck, Write them on the tablet of your heart.**
*Luke 6:35 ♥ Ephesians 4:32 ♥ Colossians 3:12
Hebrews 6:10*

Hopefulness

Most of us live day to day filled with hope, but what kind of hope is your hope? Our hope is most generally for future things and dreams. We live in hopefulness by faith, but if we are not careful we can easily let hopefulness be a distraction from today. Living life each moment is fulfilling our hopefulness of yesterday. The two go hand in hand, it's not one or the other. However, from here, it's important to realize the difference between human hope and Biblical hope. Human hopes can otherwise be described as "wishfulness" or "wishful thinking". "I hope it doesn't rain", or "I hope my team wins the Super bowl". This may help us see where Biblical hope is part of our faith, it's concrete and based on the assurance of God's steadfastness in our life. *"Instead of wishing or hoping for something to happen, a believer knows that their hope is solid, concrete evidence because it is grounded in the Word of God and we know that God cannot lie."* If we're not careful, we can spend our days wishing and wish our life away, waiting for those things that we wish for without placing our faith and hope in Jesus who holds our life's purpose. In Him we can have true hope and know that we don't live in the uncertainty of wishfulness, but in the certainty of hope in Christ. In God's word, Paul wrote often about having hope and being firmly established in our salvation. That is the only place we will know true hope. Let your hope be anchored, let it be strong, let it be established and founded in Christ alone.

Romans 15:13
May the God of hope fill you with all joy and peace in believing, so that by the power of the Holy Spirit you may abound in hope.
2 Corinthians 4:16-18 ♥ Romans 15:4 ♥ Romans 12:12
Romans 8:18-25

Recognize Him

Today is the best day to tell you…
I have never known the kind of mercy that I have known
in Christ anywhere else. I have never known the kind of
love that I have known in Christ anywhere else. I have
never known the kind of grace that I have known in Christ
anywhere else. He is so precious and generous to us!
How much do we recognize Him?

John 1:10-12 NLT
"He came into the very world He created, but
the world didn't recognize Him.
He came into His own people and even they rejected
Him. But to all who believed Him and accepted Him,
He gave the right to become children of God."

The mercy, love and grace of God may take on many different
forms. It can be seen by us and in us. When we love, His love is
seen. When we show mercy, His mercy is seen. When we give
grace, His grace is seen. May we show Jesus so that others
recognize Him in us. May we watch and be mindful of how
the Lord is working around us so that we may see Him. If we
really could see, if we really knew the script of heaven, we would
be completely undone by the volume of God's mercy, His grace
and the enormity of the love He has extended and poured out on
each of us. May our hearts be so full today again by the incredible
goodness and from there may it overflow from us to others! Many
people say that you can't "out-give" God. I think that that is so true.
It's is often said in the context of money and financial giving, but I
believe it is also true when we give out of His goodness in our life.

Ephesians 3:16-19
Therefore, prepare your minds for action, keep sober
in spirit, fix your hope completely on the grace to be
brought to you at the revelation of Jesus Christ.
1 John 3:1 ♥ Colossians 1:9 ♥ John 17:3

Leaving Things Behind

I had been anticipating a conference recently and I had everything together that I needed but somehow, I still managed to forget my ticket and had to go back home to get it. Sometimes it's easy to forget things, but there are other times that it is almost impossible to do so. There are times in God's word that we are actually encouraged to "forget it", to leave things in the past and let them have their place there. Reliving the past or hanging onto the painful actually undermines what God wants for us. We want the blessings of God and He so desires to give them to us, but when we are unwilling to lay down those things of the past down, we make ourselves unable to receive all that God has just waiting for us. I want to tell you today that it's okay to let go, lay them down, to give them to the One who said He is more than able to carry the burdens of our heart. There are things we hold onto and carry that we were never intended to carry. If God has given us permission, then we ought to give ourselves permission. Refuse the words, "I can't". Let Him have the injustice of your pain and disappointments. In their place, He will replace them with joy and the peace we long for. When we lay them down, the turmoil of their presences dissipates because of His presence. It's much different than leaving behind our lunch or a ticket for a conference. Letting go is sometimes so very hard and it takes faith and intention. But it is possible and there is a sweet peace in doing so.

*"Leave the broken, irreversible past in God's hands,
and step out into the invincible future with Him."*
~ Oswald Chambers

This is the work of grace.

Philippians 3:13-14
**Brothers, I do not consider that I have made it my own. But
one thing I do: forgetting what lies behind and straining
forward to what lies ahead, I press on toward the goal for
the prize of the upward call of God in Christ Jesus.**
Romans 5:1-2 ♥ Psalm 147:3 ♥ Psalm 73:26
Revelation 21:3-4

Without Words

Have you ever looked at a loved one and known without a word what they needed or what they were thinking? When we get closer and closer in relationship, this is something that often happens. It's almost as if your heart hears and understands without words. It's a sweet and intimate feeling that is not only assuring, but honestly very profound. There have been so many times that I have experienced such moments in prayer. As I come into the presence of the Lord, it's as if words would spoil the closeness that just His presence brings. Basking in it is precious but there is also something so special to engaging in such moments with our heart. Without words we can meet with Jesus. Listen to His heart. Be led to even unexpected direction. He extends beyond words into a language that only our soul understands as we are quiet. In the presence of the Lord there is joy beyond measure. Sometimes we talk a little too much and all we need is His presence. There are times that I do all the talking in my prayer time and never let Jesus get a word in at all. It may be the awkward silence that we think we need to fill up, but it's not true. Being still and quiet, without words, allows the Lord to speak what He wants to say. Take some time, just to be with Him, without words and experience His presence.

Psalm 16:11
You make known to me the path of life;
in your presence there is fullness of joy;
at your right hand are pleasures forevermore.

Psalm 36:7
How precious is your unfailing love, O God!
All humanity finds shelter
in the shadow of your wings.

Psalm 46:10 ♥ Psalm 46:4

Where We Want to Be

I have been enjoying riding my horse so much lately. It's a sweet
joy that I am so glad I have taken the time to do. It definitely has
its challenges as I am not a very experienced rider. One of the
best pieces of advice came from my nephew, who has reminded
me again and again to look ahead to where I want my horse to
go. He would say, don't look down at the horse, but keep your
head up and look out to where you want her to go and she will
respond much better. It has taken while, but I'm finally doing
that more and more. It has occurred to me that I can be a bit
of a deterrent to the direction of the Holy Spirit if I cannot
let Him lead me. He wants to lift our head and help us to see
where He intends to take us. It is a place of freedom, a place of
purpose and a place of restoration. It was amazing how much
frustration I caused my sweet Callie when I first started riding
because I didn't understand how important it was to simply
look up. Typically, she responds to my slight nudges and strife
is dissipating from our relationship. I wonder how often I cause
strife to my own soul when I refuse to let the Lord be in control.
He can see so much further than I can, but sometimes I want to
lead like I'm the one with the greatest vantage point. You see, the
Lord's ways are much higher than our ways and He can see things
that we cannot see. He sees ahead of us the dangers as well as the
path most that will bless us most. His plan is not to frustrate us but
to help us find abundance and immense joy in the life we live.
We may be still stuck in the mode of trying to do things our way
but today, what if we started loosening our grip and allowing Him
the control that will lead our path in His ways. As we do,
He will lead us to the places we really want to be.
Ultimately that place is where He wants us to be!

Septemb
26

Isaiah 30:21
**And your ears shall hear a word behind you, saying, "This is the way,
walk in it," when you turn to the right or when you turn to the left.**
Psalm 16:11 ♥ John 8:12 ♥ Psalm 119:105
John 10:3-4 ♥ Romans 8:14

Perish

The word perish is an older word that we
seldom use in our daily vocabulary.
It's a word that means, "to suffer death, or complete ruin". It
is the perfect word for God our loving Father to use when He
says again and again, it is His will that none should "perish"!
He calls things like silver and gold "perishable" and that these
things cannot save us. Only the precious blood of Jesus can
save us from our sin. He patiently waits for our repentance and
acceptance of the greatest gift of our life. It's interesting that He
is so generous and patient with the gift of salvation. How many
of us would be so gracious? Extending ourselves and being
rejected is not an enjoyable experience. But again and again, the
Lord generously extends the gift of Himself to those who are
perishing with hopes that they will see His lovingkindness.
Praise God that He is longsuffering and patient, willing to take
any and every opportunity to keep us from perishing for eternity
without Him. God, Himself, knows that the message of the cross
can easily be missed if we rationalize it and try to understand it
in our humanity. The complexity of the cross simply requires
trust and faith, it is just believing that the work of Jesus there
is all we need. It allows us to stop the striving we naturally
engage in as we attempt to stop the perishing. Perhaps the most
known verse in all of scripture is John 3:16: "For God so loved
the world that He gave His only begotten son, that whosoever
believeth in Him would perish not but have everlasting life."
Perishing becomes now our choice, do we perish or do we
surrender to the love of the cross? Who would choose to suffer
death or suffer complete ruin or destruction, if they could
have abundant life? God our loving heavenly Father has made
a way through every imaginable detour of our life, to bring
us His life; all we have to do is receive it from His heart.

1 Corinthians 1:18
**For the word of the cross is folly to those who are perishing,
but to us who are being saved it is the power of God.**
*1 Peter 1:18-19 ♥ 2 Peter 3:9 ♥ Isaiah 30:18
1 Corinthians 1:21*

How Does Love Love?

I've been thinking about love and how it is displayed in my life. How do I show it from a genuine place of the Father's love? I realize that this place is only source that the love I ever attempt to show can come from. His love is not arrogant or prideful. He doesn't love to be noticed or applauded. He doesn't love with an altered motive. He just simply loves. His love is unconditional, but how often is my love conditional? His love is faultless and constant. Our love on the other hand can sometimes change from day to day. But God's love is the pattern we must follow after. May the river of our love not become filled with things that resemble beaver dams. If it has happened, we must get busy and get rid of those things that clog the river of the love of God that He wants to flood our lives with. The truth is that sometimes we have the idea that love can just trickle through life's obstacles, but God wants His love to overflow the banks of our hearts, and encompass far more than the direction of the river barriers that hold it inside a predetermined destination. Oh if we could see that our love grows when His love floods outside of ourselves. He is the source of our love. There is no greater way for love to happen from our heart to others. It's not an option to find it and give it, we must find it and we must give it. Often we think it's much harder than it truly is. In simplicity and faith, we can look at Jesus and find it in His loving grace and mercy that has been so generously given to us. From there, we can begin to see it all around us and know that there is more than enough to share.

Here is a little more inspiration from some kids for you…

"Love is when your puppy licks your face even after you left him alone all day." Mary Ann—age 4; "Love is what's in the room with you at Christmas if you stop opening presents and listen." Bobby—age 7 (Wow!); Author and lecturer Leo Buscaglia once talked about a contest he was asked to judge. The purpose of the contest was to find the most caring child. The winner was a four year old child whose next door neighbor was an elderly gentleman who had recently lost his wife. Upon seeing the man cry, the little boy went into the old gentleman's yard, climbed onto his lap, and just sat there. When his Mother asked what he had said to the neighbor, the little boy said, "Nothing, I just helped him cry." The next time you're not sure how to love, just ask the Father, "how does love love?" He will show you.

1 John 3:18
Little children, let us not love in word or talk but in deed and in truth.
Philippians 2:1-3 ♥ Galatians 5:13 ♥ 1 Peter 1:22
1 John 4:7

Inclinations

We all have our inclinations, meaning,
things we are easily drawn to do.
Some of those things are good and some, not so much.
Often it's in our character to be drawn in
one direction more than others.
We've all known a friend that is always optimistic about everything
and we've all known the opposite kind of friend, one that is
inclined to be the pessimist in almost every situation. No matter
what, if we are honest with ourselves, we will realize that the best
inclinations are those of the word of God. In practical terms,
what do we need to change in our life that will bring us closer
to Him? Are there inclinations that we have allowed into our
lives that are causing us to be less attentive to the Holy Spirit?
It's not an easy thing to change inclinations that the Holy Spirit
is calling us out of, but it is so rewarding to win those victories
in our life through the power of Jesus strength working in us.
Maybe it's sarcasm that the Holy Spirit has been speaking to
you about, gossip or selfish ambition, maybe it's being too quick
with correction when grace is needed in your child's life.

There is a richness that we have not yet known that is found in
the inclinations that the Lord is calling each of us to. He is patiently
waiting with goodness in those areas for you. We grow in Christ as
we yield to Him in faith. *"Emunah"* is the Hebrew word for faith.
Surprisingly it doesn't mean an intellectual decision. It literally
means "to take firm action". It is not what we know, it's what
we do. Inclinations may not be an area that you ever thought
about letting God work in, but as the Holy Spirit nudges us,
may we be quick to respond with willing action to "do".

Psalm 119:36
Incline my heart to Your testimonies and not to dishonest gain.
Psalm 141:4 ♥ Joshua 24:23

Inclined

So yesterday we talked about "Inclinations" and today we can take that thought a step further and look at being "inclined". As I went away from writing yesterday, I felt the Holy Spirit say, "tell them to lean into Me". Isn't that the sweetest thought, that God, Almighty, Himself, longs and wants us to come closer to Him? My heart was so touched at that thought and I hope that yours will be too. May our prayer be to come as close to Him as we possibly can. Yesterday's look was about our inclinations and what that means. A further reiteration is to know that the Greek word is *"strateuo"*, which means to make war, hence to serve as a soldier, to content with carnal inclinations. Today, we can realize that as we work on pursuing the inclinations of the heart of God, it carries an idea of "pressing into the ways of God." To incline our ear to His voice means to come close and listen carefully. What is He speaking to your spirit and your heart? As a nurse, one of the questions I ask my patients before their surgery is whether or not they wear hearing aids. I am not exaggerating to say that, hands down, 40% of them say, "what did you say?" or their spouse will answer, "no, but I wish they did"! While it could be the low tone of my voice, I always smile to myself and go on with my questions. But thoughtfully, I know that if people cannot hear, they are at a considerable disadvantage. I make a note in my charting that the patient is hard of hearing, so that others that care for them will be mindful of their needs. There is significant confusion and questions that people do not understand if they cannot hear. Sometimes, they are too embarrassed that they cannot hear to even ask for clarification. The same is true for us spiritually. If we cannot hear the voice of God, we may need some spiritual hearing aids. When we cannot hear His voice, there will be confusion and questions that will attempt to overwhelm us. Recognizing that we cannot hear God without the help of the Holy Spirit takes humility and dethrones our pride. The word of God and fellowship with Him and other believers helps us hear His voice. Being inclined carries the attitude of reliance. We have to quiet our own voice to hear His. And, I believe that when we are attentive and ready to hear, the Lord has so much to tell us. That's relationship! That's inclining to know and hear Him.

Isaiah 55:3
Incline your ear, and come to me; hear, that your soul may live; and I will make with you an everlasting covenant, my steadfast, sure love for David.
Proverbs 22:17-18 ♥ Proverbs 5:1

Starry Splendor

Have you ever done something for someone
and they didn't really notice it?
Were you just waiting to be acknowledged, not that you needed
a big parade or fanfare about it, but just hoped the gesture would
be seen because what you did, you did for someone's good and
to bless them? Is God like us in that way? No moon this dark
early morning. Stepping outside, the sky is filled with what
looks like glistening diamonds. It was bright and full of the
reflection of God's splendor. I stood for a long time, just looking
at them, all of them, too many to count. Bright against the dark
morning sky…wow Lord, my heart marveled inside me.
Wow!
It was splendor and beauty beyond my ability to truly grasp it. And
the reality is that it is always there, He is always there. When I see
Him, when I notice, when I take the time to look, and all the times in
between. The splendor of our majestic God is immensely more than
we can fathom, just as this multitude of the glistening stars that filled
this morning's dark sky. The same response overwhelms our hearts
as we realize how awesome God truly is. Another… Wow! And the
most profound thought is that He loves us. He loves you. He loves me.
I know there are days that I don't even notice
the enormity of His splendor.
Today, the thought makes me wonder what
I miss that He has done or is doing.
I can't help but think that He does things like the dark sparkling
diamond filled starry morning sky just for us to see and He
hopes in His heart that we will notice His splendor. He is
God and so worthy of our praise, but often we miss the starry
splendors of life. Our limited view of His splendor is like looking
at the dark star filled sky. We can't see all that is truly there,
it's like seeing just a glimpse of Him. May we see Him more,
and as we simply acknowledge His splendor, His presence
and nearness will fill us with assurance that He is so near.

October
1

Psalm 96:6
**Splendor and majesty are before him; strength
and beauty are in his sanctuary.**
1 Chronicles 29:11 ♥ Psalm 104:1-2 ♥ Psalm 145:5
Psalm 111:3

Treasure of Salvation

The greatest treasure we can ever know is the
treasure we have in our salvation.
It is why the enemy tries so hard to get us off-
track and distance us from Jesus.
In that we will question if we are truly saved and our stability
may begin to waver. The longer the enemy can keep us in this
state, the longer we will be kept from our destiny in Christ Jesus.
The Bible says that we have a treasure in us that we can know
is unchanging and sure. We can know that greater is He that is
in us than he who is in the world. We can have confidence that
He who started a good work in us will complete it. Our stability
cannot rest in the number of our failures or in our feelings, it
must lie in knowing who Jesus is and how great a salvation He has
given to us. He calls us out of mediocrity into a life that realizes
that we have a treasure in us. Friends, a treasure is something
of value, it is something that is highly prized and cherished.
We have something worth cherishing in our life today. Our
treasure is Jesus and knowing that we are His. Many miss this
reality because they keep thinking that they, themselves are the
treasure. And while we are fearfully and wonderfully made, the
treasure of Christ outweighs our abilities, and He always will.
We cannot live life thinking that we have to make ourselves
better or stronger to be valued. My pride will try to get me to
think that I can better myself to be great. The enemy will let
you stay in this mode and strive and strive your life away. But
Jesus wants you to know that the treasure of your salvation is in
Him and He is sufficient for you to have contentment and rest.
The treasure of who He is outweighs our capacity to even
realize. Know that you are treasured today and that in your
salvation you carry the greatest treasure of life in you!

Isaiah 33:6
*And He will be the stability of your times, A wealth of salvation,
wisdom and knowledge; The fear of the LORD is his treasure.*
2 Corinthians 4:7 ♥ Isaiah 45:3 ♥ Isaiah 43:1

Rest

Beginning a new week can sometimes feel
overwhelming and a bit intimidating. How do the
days go by so fast? We question our purpose.
We wonder about the quality of our days.
Are we being effective with what God has placed in our hands?
It's easy to get all tied up in knots before
Monday even gets underway.
While we definitely need to be aware of what
is happening in and around us,
remember, there is yet a firm Rock in Christ, beneath us for our
feet to be firmly planted on. There is an anchor that holds us
steady as we allow God to lead us in each and every new week.
As our weeks are lived out, may we live Him out to a world that
is looking for hope. May our soul find its rest in His rest and the
tranquility of knowing we are loved and led. Joy comes from resting
in Jesus. It allows us to live Him out and let Him live through us
in whatever fills each of our days. We must release worry and
allow His rest to come into that place of our heart and mind.
So, it's a new week, and this is the day the Lord has made...
so may we say, "rejoice, o my soul and all that is within
me, bless His amazing and holy name". Rest is one of the
most important things we do for our life and our very
soul. No one can survive for very long if they don't
rest, we were never designed to live that way.
We actually find strength when we allow our soul to find rest,
and it can happen even as we head out
the door to another busy week.
Rest in the peace of Jesus' provision for you today,
know that you are so loved and held by Him.

October
3

Psalm 62:5
"Yes, my soul, find rest in God: my hope comes from him."
Hebrews 4:9 ♥ Psalm 127:1-2 ♥ 1 Peter 5:7
Matthew 11:28

Measure of Faith

What is faith?

Many immediately remember Hebrews 11:1, a verse in God's word that tells us it is the measure of things hoped for and the evidence of things not seen. We can describe it as simply trusting God. The evidence of our faith is trusting God and not worrying. We have all been given a measure of faith and I wonder if we truly understand what that means for us. It means we have "enough" faith. We have all we need. You might wonder why your faith seems too small.

Could it be that our faith is lying in a semi-dormant state? Is it "just there"?

The measure of faith given to us by God is an amount that He, Himself, has said, "This is the right amount; this will carry my son and daughter to Me". In His gift of this measure of faith, we must realize that He is the rest of what we need. If your faith feels a little atrophied, then begin to exercise that faith and as you do, it will grow and become healthier and stronger. Recently my husband had to have surgery on his arm. It wasn't a major surgery but it did require that he wear a sling for 6 weeks afterward. During that time, because he wasn't using his arm, the muscles became very weak and now he is in the process of rebuilding them. The muscles are still there, but they aren't as strong as they once were or should be for a healthy guy.

It's going to take work and some pain to increase their strength again.

Faith is much the same way, we have a measure of faith but we need to exercise it so that it can be as strong as it has the potential to be in our life. So much goes unbelieved for in our lives and the circumstances we face simply because we do not extend our faith. May you know today that you have been given a God measurement of faith by His love. You may not see yet what the activation of your faith is doing but it is making a difference. Hold steady, trust Him today.

Psalm 9:10
And those who know your name put their trust in you, for you, O LORD, have not forsaken those who seek you.
Romans 12:3 ♥ 1 Chronicles 5:20 ♥ Psalm 34:4

Going the Distance

Sometimes the distance to the destination we need to go to is longer than at other times. In our day to day life, we can often only see the immediate and daily routine of what we are doing. Have you ever had to drive a long distance to get to where you needed to be? It requires that you just keep going. Maybe hours and hours are needed for travel. Along the way are plenty of temptations to stop and get out of the car for food and fun. But if we keep stopping, it will take us far longer to reach the destination. As we travel, there are signs along the way to tell us if we are going the right direction. Have you ever thought you were headed in the right direction, only to realize that somehow you'd made a wrong turn? At that point, turning around is not an option if you want to reach your original destination. During the trip you will see plenty of different options for changing your mind. You can decide you want to take another road or highway, but doing so will only delay or change your destination point all together. Weariness comes when we travel long distances. It is especially difficult if we are traveling alone. In the beginning, it may seem exciting to be off all on our own, but before long we can become overwhelmed, wondering how we will ever make it. Jesus gives us a direction to pursue, it's Him alone. Many other things and ideas can become lengthy detours if we are not careful. It's so important that once we realize we need re-evaluate our direction that we make whatever changes the Holy Spirit is leading us to. Often we just keep going and somehow think that magically we'll somehow get back on track. Sadly we will only stray further and further away from all that God has for us. Sweetly though is the assurance that He will make a way for us to get back on the right path if we simply seek for His help and we obey the leading of His heart. We all know when God is urging and directing us when we stray. Sometimes we obey quickly and sometimes we don't.

I pray this prayer for you today: *"May He grant you out of the rich treasury of His glory to be strengthened and reinforced with mighty power in the inner man by the Holy Spirit, (Himself indwelling your innermost being)".*

Ephesians 3:16 Amplified.
If we're going to go the distance, we must stay the course!

Philippians 1:6
And I am sure of this, that he who began a good work in you will bring it to completion at the day of Jesus Christ.

Hebrews 12:1-2 ♥ 1 Chronicles 16:11 ♥ Isaiah 48:17

Go Back

I love the story of Moses and all that God did in and through His life. He was someone rescued by God at a young age, literally out of the hand of death. He was divinely protected by God. He was given a place of honor in the eyes of men. Then he lost that place and fled from all that he knew because of shame and guilt. He found himself alone, he found himself isolated and he found himself convinced that his life and destiny were over because he could not undo the past. Many live in similar circumstances. Once they walked with God in their younger years but something, somewhere along the journey of their life, happened and now they feel isolated and alone, certain that what they have done or where they have ended up has nullified the destiny of God in their life. But, God has not decided what we sometime perceive. Sometimes we attempt to measure by our understanding, but God's ways are higher. Redemption and reconciliation are gifts that extend beyond our weakest moments. God is greater and when we come to Him, He waits with open arms. We often think that judgement is our destiny now when Jesus says, My grace is bigger than that. Come to Me all you who are heavy laden and I will give rest to you and to your soul, to all that rages inside of you. He wants you to know that He longs to take the regret of your past, every mistake and painful occurrence. Our past can become a grave if we don't realize that Jesus conquered it. He is our victor, He came to give us life in Him, we will never know true abundance without letting Him take our past. Jesus is our victory and He stands able to take our pain and our past to draw us closer to Him. In the parables, the people who drew close to Jesus were the tax collectors and sinners. Why? They needed Him. The Pharisees stood afar off, they attempted to justify themselves by their religious ways. We need Jesus and as we draw close to Him, we will be welcomed into His gracious love. He is our future. He calls us out of the past into a place of wholeness. Moses thought his past had consumed him, just like the natural fire of the desert that caught bushes on fire. But the bush that the angel of the Lord spoke out of was not consumed and neither was Moses. The desert for Moses was dry and isolated but it wasn't too far away from God. The Lord saw Moses there and He sees everywhere we are, near or far. We are no distance from Him. What is distance to God? Is it the same as distance to us? I think we measure things in our natural understanding. He is close and He will bring us out of the desert places. We might think we should stay there, others might think we should stay there, but God has other plans for you. Plans of destiny and purpose. God was calling Moses out of the desert, to go back and live. Go back because He had a purpose and a destiny that only Moses could live out.

October 6

2 Corinthians 5:17
Therefore if anyone is in Christ, he is a new creature; the old things passed away; behold, new things have come.

John 10:10 ♥ Exodus 3:2 ♥ Galatians 2:20

The Final Word

From the beginning of time, God spoke what is, out of what was not. When there was literally nothing, God spoke and from just His words, all that we know to be, came into being. From things like our seasons, animals, trees and flowers, life itself came from the Word of God when He spoke them into existence. Then God sent His word to us in the form of Jesus. He came to seek and to save what was lost. With His word, the wind and waves obeyed Him and people marveled at His insight. Healing happened when Jesus spoke. His word holds such amazing power, but sometimes we let the totality of it remain in the days that Jesus walked on the earth, instead of believing all that is within it for our personal life and situation. Now, we have the written word of God. We carry it with us wherever we go on our mobile device or even have a hard copy in multiple places in our home or office. Is His word in our hand changing us? It has the power to create in us newness and destroy the weapons of the enemy over our lives and our family. The word of God tells us that life and death are in the power of the tongue, in other terms, the spoken word. God is so amazing and He spoke over the face of the earth and created our world in such a short amount of time, but in unspoken thoughts we think that He's stopped speaking. If we allow His word to be in that sort of context, we miss His invitation to hear His voice. The world is filled with so much in terms of media, news, and it is at a pace that is consuming all that our ears can hear. We often look to other people to hear from God instead of thinking that He might whisper to us directly. Our reminder today is that He has the final say. He has something to tell us each and every day, through His word, through praise and prayer. He cares for you and wants to show Himself more and more clearly, no matter what is going on in your life. Framing your life in the context of what God has to say, will give you a greater strength and testimony through it. I am certain that I miss His voice in various ways every day. I long to hear from the Lord more and more. It's not a reprimand, but an encouragement that we can hear Him! We can because He has not stopped speaking His word over us. He is still speaking! He still wants to create things in our life out of nothing and speak healing to brokenness and pain. He had the first word and He has the final word. May we stop believing the words of our own mind and begin to ask God what He has to say about it all. "What, God, do You want to do in this part of my life or relationship?" The things He has to say may seem impossible but that's God! He simply asks us to listen, believe and obey. The Word of God was and is life!

October 7

Exodus 19:5
Now then, if you will indeed obey My voice and keep My covenant, then you shall be My own possession among all the peoples, for all the earth is Mine;

James 1:21 ♥ Exodus 23:21 ♥ 2 Corinthians 10:5
1 Peter 1:14 ♥ James 1:22

First Things First

Before you can do certain things, there are
other things that must be done first.

Before you can bake cookies, you need cookie dough. Before you
can take a road trip, you need a vehicle of some sort. Before you
can eat, food must be prepared. Our list might get quite long but
you get the idea. The preparation of the first things is important
in order for other things to take place. Preparation isn't usually the
fun part of life but with preparation, anticipation heightens and
awareness of the details that surround an event begin to become
more apparent. When it comes to life, God calls us to put Him first.
To look to Him before we look to other things. The instruction of
God is an instruction of His love and provision. He knows that all
we need is found in Him alone. When we waste our resources and
energy on the fleeting things of life, we are only left disappointed.

As our day begins, what if, instead of looking at the morning
news, we looked to the good news of the Gospel first. What if
we let the Holy Spirit send our heart His notifications before
we look at our Facebook notifications? Our life would be so
impacted by His power and grace. It is why He calls us to Him
first, because nothing else will satisfy the hunger of our hearts.
As we make Jesus our priority and let all the other pursuits of our
lives come after Him, our contentment in Him will be our stability.
Our passion for Him will grow into what propels us into His plans.

Here's a very practical example: I spoke with a young woman
of God who shared with me that she knows that Jesus has
her future in His hands. She knows she doesn't have to worry
and keep praying over and over about it. She has a healthy
faith and assurance that allows her to pursue Jesus' heart and
not her own. She knows that He has that all taken care of.

The Lord has spiritual riches and wealth that are
eternally enduring beyond our earthly life. As we put
Him first, we will find the treasure of Him.

Proverbs 8:17-19

I love those who love me; And those who diligently seek me will find me.
Riches and honor are with me, Enduring wealth and righteousness.
My fruit is better than gold, even pure gold, And
my yield better than choicest silver.

Psalm 112:3 ♥ Matthew 6:33 ♥ Philippians 4:19
Isaiah 33:6

Rejoicing

We were made to rejoice! Think of it, have you ever gone to a basketball game where people didn't cheer? Have you ever gone to a concert where people didn't cheer? Events of life are to be celebrated and some people are indeed more celebratory in their personalities than others, but we are all made and created by God with the inherency to celebrate. When we celebrate the joys and blessings of life that God has given and lavished on us, I believe it touches the heart of God. Rejoicing always is a mandate found in scripture for us, for today. You may think you don't have much of anything in your life to celebrate or rejoice over. Take some time and ask the Lord to show you, begin to take notice of all that surrounds you and you will find your list is much longer than you realized.

You see, while we were created to celebrate and rejoice, the enemy wants to discourage and tear us down with negative thinking and pessimism. May we reject that influence and embrace the hope that is ours in Christ Jesus, the One who came to seek and save us, to give us an incredible fullness of joy as we allow His ways in our life above our ways. The Bible tells us that God, Himself rejoices and He calls us to rejoice as well.

The instruction is given to help us and to keep us close to the place of stability in Jesus. As we rejoice for the goodness of God, we find our hearts even more full for the blessings that are a part of our life. There are many influences that will attempt to undermine the grace and goodness of God, but He is great and His love for us unsurpassed because of who He is!

Philippians 4:4
Rejoice in the Lord always; again I will say, rejoice!

Deuteronomy 12:7
There also you and your households shall eat before the LORD your God, and rejoice in all your undertakings in which the LORD your God has blessed you.

Psalm 5:11
But let all who take refuge in You be glad, Let them ever sing for joy; And may You shelter them, That those who love Your name may exult in You.

1 Thessalonians 5:16
Rejoice always.

Discovery

There is so much to discover about Jesus that we don't know yet.
God has a depth that cannot be completely
known, even in a lifetime.

Today is a day of remembering a man named Christopher
Columbus, the man renowned for discovering America. When he
reached the shores of America, many thought he had arrived and
indeed he did, but it was truly only the beginning of discovering.
While it is historically recorded that Columbus was not
the first to reach America, it is nonetheless, attributed to
his accomplishments. Many today, find Christ, but they
don't discover Him. May we refuse to settle for just our
reaching Christ and go onto pursue discovering Him.
Digging deeper into His word, spending more and
more time with Him and launching out into obedience
are all ways we can discover Him more.

Just as the first step onto American soil could not communicate
the wealth and joy of the place Columbus had landed,
the same is true in our walk with Jesus. Finding Him is
just the beginning but discovering Him requires time and
exploration. If you've settled down after reaching Christ,
if you've stopped discovering Him, launch out again after
Him today and discover more of all He has for you.

October
10

1 Corinthians 2:9
*But, as it is written, "What no eye has seen, nor ear heard, nor the heart
of man imagined, what God has prepared for those who love him.*

Isaiah 64:4
*For from days of old they have not heard or perceived
by ear, Nor has the eye seen a God besides You, Who
acts in behalf of the one who waits for Him.*

Psalm 63:1
*You, God, are my God, earnestly I seek you; I thirst
for you, my whole being longs for you,
in a dry and parched land, where there is no water.*

Jeremiah 29:13
You will seek me and find me when you seek me with all your heart.

Less Is More

Have you ever looked around your home, perhaps in your closet and become overwhelmed by all that you have accumulated? It's amazing how quickly we can gain so many things. The influence of materialism can easily infect. We don't always see what it can erode away in our life, but ever so slyly our sense of want turns into a sense of being overwhelmed by all that we have collected. Suddenly we wonder where it all came from. We wonder how to manage it all.

The pursuit and drive to obtain more is a silent ambition that we think will bring us satisfaction. The truth is that we often find fewer fulfillments in the more we have gained. It's not only things that can have this impact on our life but it can be other things as well. Maybe it's knowing all the gossip that is going on. Maybe it's having more Facebook friends than others. Maybe it's gaining significance in our workplace or family. We may not even realize how it is happening in our hearts and it usually starts in a small way. It begins to feel difficult to be organized and we may begin to feel like life is out of control. The enemy uses what we think will be contentment, to be so overwhelmed us, that we forget how to ask Jesus to help us bring perspective. The truth is that less is really more for us. We honestly need far less than we have and we have the capacity to flourish when we begin to rid our lives of the clutter. When there is too much for us to manage, fear and anxiety can begin to take over. We aren't sure how to juggle it all and we aren't sure we even can.

Imagine a garden in beautifully manicured rows. It's beauty and purpose can easily be choked out by weeds left unattended or if too many seeds are planted in the soil. As the seeds grow, they become a tangled mass of plants that produce little fruit.

October 11

Jesus called us to be servants of others. He said that the first will ultimately be last. He calls us to let Him increase in our life and let our "self" decrease. It is the only antidote to the "get more" mentality of humanity. As we let the Lord declutter our lives, we can carry that even further into our minds and hearts. May we give Him permission to come in and helps us clean things out so that there is more room for Him in the less of our life.

Philippians 3:13-14
Brethren, I do not regard myself as having laid hold of it yet; but one thing I do: forgetting what lies behind and reaching forward to what lies ahead, I press on toward the goal for the prize of the upward call of God in Christ Jesus.

Ephesians 2:10 ♥ Romans 12:1-2 ♥ John 3:30
Matthew 6:19-20 ♥ Proverbs 23:4

Perfect Strength

We all want to be strong, it's something that
is inherently a part of our make-up.
Some strive for strength in their lives more than others
do. But what is strength? Have you ever wondered how it's
defined? The Hebrew word is "taqeph" and it is interpreted
"all or full authority". The word also means, "power" but
its first and higher definition is "full-authority".
We often quote 2 Corinthians 12:9 where the Lord tells Paul,
"My grace is sufficient for you". But that verse goes on. *And he
said unto me, My grace is sufficient for thee: for my strength is
made perfect in weakness. Most gladly therefore will I rather glory
in my infirmities, that the power of Christ may rest upon me.*
God's strength or full authority is made perfect in our weakness.
When we stop trying to be strong in ourselves and let God be the
strength in our life, then His authority takes is rightful place in
our life, our job, our family, our relationships and our purpose.
God is strong and we know that, but how often do we recognize
that there is an authority for us that He wants to cover our life
with. As we strive in our own strength and do not recognize that
it is weakness, at best, then we will continue to spin our wheels
and make little progress in those things we feel that God is calling
us to. In our culture and society, admitting weakness is looked
down upon but in the culture of heaven it is mandatory! It is
only then that we will truly know the strength and authority of
God's love, His grace, and His presence in and through our life.
His strength is the authority that our soul longs for and
He is calling us to let His full authority reign as Lord in
our life. We are not our own lord but sometimes we live
as though we are. He is Lord and His authority will be
made perfect as we surrender our weakness to it.

Daniel 10:29
*He said, "O man of high esteem, do not be afraid. Peace be with you; take
courage and be courageous!" Now as soon as he spoke to me, I received
strength and said, "May my lord speak, for you have strengthened me."*
1 Corinthians 2:5 ♥ 2 Corinthians 12:9 ♥ Ephesians 3:16

Generously

Have you ever received a gift of generous proportion?
There have been times in my life that I have.
I remember an occasion before leaving for our mission assignment
when a precious group of people lavished gifts on our family.
The gifts were items that we did not need, but they were items
that would prove to be an incredible blessing as we left for a land
far from home. We were overwhelmed, they gave so generously
out of hearts that loved, more than we felt we deserved.
Today, I feel the same sense of being
overwhelmed, but in a deeper way.
My heart is overwhelmed by the generosity of God's goodness.
He has dealt so generously with us. When we consider
the grace that we have known, may we give as
generously as we have received from His hand.
When we reflect on the kindness of His gentleness, may we be more
ready to be gentle and refuse the temptation of being abrasive.
As I think about who God is, I mean His power and
authority over us and over our lives, over all creation, I
know that He, above everyone else has more "right" to be
stern or abrasive with us and yet He chooses to be gracious
and deal generously with each of us in patient love.
How wonderful are the gifts He has given and lavished
on us. May our hearts be filled with gratitude and faith
to know that if He has already been so kind, that He has
our best in mind, and He is so aware of all we need.

Exodus 34:6
**Then the LORD passed by in front of him and proclaimed, "The
LORD, the LORD God, compassionate and gracious, slow to anger,
and abounding in lovingkindness and truth; who keeps lovingkindness
for thousands, who forgives iniquity, transgression and sin;**
*Matthew 7:11 ♥ Ephesians 1:7-9 ♥ Jeremiah 33:6-9
Psalm 33:5*

Live out Light

On many occasions, living in a third world country, our lights would go off without warning. It was no surprise that our power wasn't consistently reliable. No matter where you live, chances are you have experienced the loss of power and lights. We scramble around looking for a flashlight or candle so we can see. Once we find that light, we feel we have our "bearings" and can maneuver until the power comes back on. Lights are needed, of course, to illuminate darkness. That's the very reason that God created "light". Imagine the darkness of the earth when God spoke in that darkness, and light lit up that darkness for the very first time. The Bible tells us that God created light and saw that it was good. Light was made by God and His purpose was to separate light from darkness. He put lights in the sky, sun, moon and stars. These are lights that are so intriguing to us as we look up at their vastness and realize that only God could have placed them there. That was in the very beginning of Genesis. Then much later, Jesus arrives in the form of a man to become, *"the light of the world"* in John 8:12. Once again, God gave us light to separate us from darkness, only this time, it's a light that illuminates our hearts and shines on the path of our life. In Psalms, the Lord reminds us that His word is a light for us. Darkness can be very overwhelming. It can be heavy and it can bring fear. When there is darkness all around us, there is no way we can know which direction we should go. So many wander around, thinking that they will somehow figure life out, without Christ. They have high hopes that they will manage to make strides, only to discover they've been walking around in circles, bumping into things in the dark that have caused more setbacks than progress. In a dark night, we know that we will surely stumble without a light. Who would attempt to go this route with a light in hand without turning it on? Few, I would imagine, especially if they were surrounded by danger. May we realize how very much we need the light of Jesus to show us the way in the darkness that encroaches upon our life and the path that we are walking each day. As the world becomes increasingly darker, His light is our only hope for clarity. As His light shines for us, we will know which way He is leading. The light of Christ doesn't just stop with us because He has designed light to do so many things and He declares that we are the light of the world and that we should let our light shine bright before all men. As His light shines through us, we will reflect Him for those around us. What an amazing and awesome thing that God would use us to bring light to darkness, just as He began creation! Separating light from dark is what He does best and we have the joy of living out light each day.

Matthew 5:14-16
"You are the light of the world. A city set on a hill cannot be hidden. Nor do people light a lamp and put it under a basket, but on a stand, and it gives light to all in the house. In the same way, let your light shine before others, so that they may see your good works and give glory to your Father who is in heaven."

Genesis 1:1-5 ♥ John 8:12

With You

Sometimes life brings battles that we don't necessarily want to face.
Sometimes we aren't given that choice and we don't understand
what the Lord is doing. Is He idly watching from afar? We may
wonder for a moment but then as we reflect on His goodness, we
can know that He is so very near to us. The issues that life brings
are no surprise to God. He is closer than we can truly even fathom.
His word assures us again and again that He is so near. He sees
every sparrow that falls to the ground and He literally numbers
the hairs on our head. He has to be really close by to know
such a thing and He is. But, the enemy would like us to believe
that God is a bit removed from the battle we may be facing.
The nearness of His presence is our strength. The weight
of an ongoing battle can wear us down and we may
be overwhelmed. But He is not overwhelmed!
There's a place that we can have peace and it is in realizing
that we are held in the cleft of His hand, and that He is
fighting this battle. All He calls us to do is trust Him,
listen to His leading and obey His direction.
That we can do.
He is with you. You are so loved! You are
more protected than you realize.

His strength is perfect in your weakness so don't attempt
to fight the armies of the enemy on your own.
Don't try to be Superman or Wonder woman.
God is our super Hero.
Let His super power be all that you need for the battle.
Give Him your worry and heavy heart.
That we can do.
He is with you!

Exodus 14:14
The LORD will fight for you; you need only to be still.
2 Chronicles 20:15 ♥ Deuteronomy 20:1 ♥ Exodus 14:13
Deuteronomy 3:22

Necessity of Him

God is the necessity of our life, before and
above even our physical needs.
We don't often realize the depth of how very much we need God.
We sometimes let our focus falter and our
view of Him can become very hazy.
There are moments when some find that their
heart feels distant from God's presence.
When those times come, there is an uneasy, unsettledness that
lets us know that we need Him. His influence in our lives matters
more than we can understand. Imagine a person who is in survival
mode, say, on a desert island without much food or water. Maybe
they are surviving on very, very little, but not flourishing.
People live life this way, and they become so accustomed to this
"survival mode" that they think all is just fine. The necessity of
Jesus in our life is like our necessity of nutrients. If all we ever fill
our bodies with are empty calories, we will become sickly and
weak. The same is true of our minds, if all we engage in is negative
and detrimental thinking, all that stirs in us can become toxic.
God has so much more for us!
He has made a way for us to live and flourish if we will only see that
He is the key. He is our necessity. Make time for Him today, and ask
the Lord to show you where you might need to refocus or make
some changes in how you are living. The Holy Spirit will show us
when we look to Him as our vital necessity. When we search for
Him like a man or woman in desperate search of water or food.

Isaiah 61:10

*I delight greatly in the Lord; my soul rejoices in my God. For he has
clothed me with garments of salvation and arrayed me in a robe of
his righteousness, as a bridegroom adorns his head like a priest,
and as a bride adorns herself with her jewels.*
Isaiah 25:1 ♥ Psalm 34:19 ♥ Psalm 18:1-2

Faith

How many mountains do we leave unconquered
because they look too big?
How many battles do we just surrender to
because the enemy looks too mean?
How many times do we simply walk away when God is calling
us to believe Him to be all that He is? Or maybe, like me, there
are times when we've tried once or twice and given up too soon.
Faith is action, but sometimes it's being tenacious and stubborn
as we stand strong. Sometimes answers are not immediate and
it is in those moments that we must keep our eyes on Jesus,
and not on the circumstances that will undermine our faith.
Have you ever watched water evaporate? You can, of course,
but more often than not, it happens so slowly that we don't
even notice it until the water is all gone from the container
it started in. The vapor carries away the liquid and the same
thing can happen to our faith. I wonder if God sometimes is
asking us to not give in so quickly when answers don't come
as immediately as we would want them to. I wonder if He is
saying," don't worry, just wait a little longer, be patient, I'm
working and I hear you." Maybe He's saying, "Trust Me, I know
you don't understand but My ways are higher than yours".

October 17

Don't give up or give in.
Fear causes worry and it causes our faith to evaporate just like
heat causes water to evaporate. What if we refuse worry, what if
we forbid fear in our hearts and thoughts? Then what? Then our
faith can have room to become stronger and then we can walk
confidently, knowing that even though we may not see what God
is doing, we know that He is working and we are not forgotten.
Don't stop believing just short of your miracle!

Mark 10:52
*And Jesus said to him, "Go; your faith has made you well." Immediately
he regained his sight and {began} following Him on the road.*
*Mark 4:40 ♥ Mark 11:22 ♥ Matthew 21:21
Matthew 9:29 ♥ Matthew 9:22*

Led by His Direction

The leading of God is for us today. It has not been left in the pages of the Bible, held only for the Biblical characters that we read about. The Holy Spirit is the gift of the Father to us that came after Jesus ascended into heaven. He is our Comforter and He leads us in many ways. Often it is through the Word of God. Other times, the still small voice of God knocks on the door of our heart, when we stray away. Nothing gets past His eyes in our lives or in our hearts and thoughts. The Lord cares about the details of what we are navigating through and He helps us by giving us His direction. Peace comes when we are walking as He is leading. He leads us to walk uprightly when the world attempts to influence us to do otherwise. He leads us in our prayers, when we don't know what to pray. He leads us to walk in His principles and keep His word. He leads us into all truth, not just some truth. He leads us from the very heart of God, our Father. He leads us to share the love of the message of the Gospel. He leads us because we are His sons and daughters. May we listen attentively and carefully to His voice and not our own. I was reading today about Noah and when the flood waters began to recede. There was a process to Noah and His family coming out of the ark and the Bible tells us in Genesis 8, that God told Noah when it was time to leave the ark. Then God spoke to Noah, saying, *"Go out of the ark, you and your wife, and your sons and your sons' wives with you. Bring out with you every living thing of all flesh that is with you: birds and cattle and every creeping thing that creeps on the earth, so that they may abound on the earth, and be fruitful and multiply on the earth."* When I read that passage, I was so impacted to realize that God didn't just expect Noah to decide or figure out when he should leave the ark. Maybe he was tempted to decide on his own but nonetheless, when it was time, God let Noah know. His timing has our best and provision as we are led by Him.

Psalm 143:10
"Teach me to do Your will, for You are my God; Your Spirit is good. Lead me in the land of uprightness."
Romans 8:26-27 ♥ Ezekiel 36:27 ♥ John 16:13
Luke 4:18 ♥ Romans 8:14

Daily Life

When we ask someone how they are doing, they usually say, "I'm fine" or "doing well". It conveys that the day to day of our lives isn't always full of excitement. Most often it's ordinary and familiar. We usually have the same routine for most days and look forward to the weekend or a special event. In between we go to work, care for our families, and take care of the daily chores that must be done. On these days, the word that best describes the mandate of God's call in our life is, "faithfulness". He calls us to just be faithful to live as He guides us. We must also be careful to give attention to the things that will otherwise get swallowed up in the mundane.

Moments with Him, moments with those we love,
moments with friends that need our love and concern,
a stranger that needs someone to notice
them and say a prayer with them.

The moments of our day to day life may not be filled with fireworks and celebration, but they can and are filled with "God moments" if we will watch for them and look to see what He is doing. Paul encourages us in 2 Corinthians 13:11 to be joyful, to grow in maturity, to encourage each other, to live in harmony and peace, then the love and peace of God will be with us.

That sounds like a happy life!

October 19

If your life has gotten out of control and has become chaotic, take a step back and let His presence come in to be the anchor and solace of your days. The routine and day to day will be uplifting in ways that we didn't imagine as we celebrate God's goodness in the life of joy He gives.

2 Corinthians 13:11
Finally, brothers, rejoice. Aim for restoration, comfort one another, agree with one another, live in peace; and the God of love and peace will be with you.
Romans 12:16 ♥ Proverbs 21:21 ♥ 1 Peter 3:10-11
Ephesians 5:15-16

Sober-Minded

Almost daily we hear of people driving under
the influence of drugs or alcohol.
Often the results are devastating. When a person is not sober, they
are impaired; they cannot function as they normally should. Their
responses are delayed and their judgement is compromised, even
when they don't know it. As a nurse, I have people tell me that they
feel perfectly fine after having anesthesia. They want to drive home
or go to work, but they don't realize how dangerous it would be to
allow them to do that. Without notice they can drift off to sleep.
Throughout God's word we are cautioned to live soberly. We are to be
mindful of the days we are living in and the evil around us. We are to
live soberly or seriously, not with our heads in the clouds, oblivious
to the plight of the lost or the evil that surrounds us. We are to stand
for truth and refuse to be lulled to sleep by the enemy's tactics.
Prudence is important, even if it's ridiculed by others. Living soberly
is not the option that we may think it is. Without sobriety, we live
impaired and Godly judgement is diminished in our hearts. We must
be careful to seek His face and to know that it matters so very much.
Each day is a gift and we are given a treasure in each one
to walk with God and to live by His principles. So many
things can intoxicate us, like the pursuit of our self or our
desires. Material possessions, social status, our profession,
food, gossip, pride, and the list could go on and on.
We must see these things for what they truly are. If left unchecked,
these distractions and intoxications will impair us spiritually and
we will be unable to live as Christ has called us to live. May we live
with His grace, His discernment and His joy, but not in the world's
folly, thinking that we can mix the two. It takes being intentional...

*Simply, be prepared for action, set your hope fully on the grace that will
be brought to you at the revelation of Jesus Christ. Then, put on the
breastplate of faith and love, and the helmet of our hope of salvation.
Let us not sleep as the others do, but let us remain awake and sober.*

1 Peter 1:13
**Therefore, preparing your minds for action, and being sober-minded,
set your hope fully on the grace that will be brought
to you at the revelation of Jesus Christ.**
*Luke 12:35 ♥ 2 Timothy 4:5 ♥ 1 Thessalonians 5:6
1 Thessalonians 5:8 ♥ Ephesians 6:14*

Moderation

The Grand Canyon and the ocean are two of my favorite places to visit. At both of these places of beauty, our internal common sense keeps us from danger. For the Grand Canyon, it's not getting too close to the edge. At the ocean, it's not going out too far. There is an internal restraint in us that is an invisible boundary. Our spiritual boundaries are similar and the Bible calls it "self-control". The word "moderation" is used to convey the necessity of having self-control in our lives. However, while moderation is important, somethings must never even be allowed to be a part of our life. We live in such a world and culture of self-indulgence that it takes determination to exercise self-control. We need to remember that there is a wealth of benefit for us in moderation. Literally, anything and everything can easily become an obsession in our personal life. We can easily fall into sin if we do not practice moderation, so the caution is for our good and not to be considered a forbiddance. It is such a good thing that we should welcome it into our life. The wisdom of Proverbs tells us that a person without self-control is like a city whose walls are broken through. We can use our imagination to see this word picture from the Lord. It conveys that the city's security is in jeopardy and that it is very vulnerable to the enemy coming in to harm it in various ways.

Today, maybe you've ignored the whisper of the Holy Spirit regarding moderation in your life. Listen to His calling to come away from the edge of the place of danger, and know that you do not have to be a slave to self-indulgence. Perhaps you find that you've gotten out to a place too deep, let God's grace be your lifeline today as He leads you back to safety. Remember His strength is made perfect in our weaknesses.

Proverbs 25:26-28
Like a muddied spring or a polluted well are the righteous who give way to the wicked. It is not good to eat too much honey, nor is it honorable to search out matters that are too deep. Like a city whose walls are broken through is a person who lacks self-control.

2 Corinthians 12:9 ♥ Galatians 6:8-9 ♥ Galatians 5:22-23
Proverbs 23:2-3 ♥ Galatians 5:16-17

Gratitude

Nothing is more discouraging than ingratitude.
To witness a situation in which so much is done but the one thing
that wasn't done becomes the focus. I'm sure that's happened
to all of us at one time or another. But I wonder how often
we do that in light of all that God has done in our lives?
Pursuing Jesus is to pursue the heart of gratitude in your life.
Maybe you've been lacking a bit, focusing
on what isn't instead of what is.
Is there an area in your life that is clearly a gift but
instead of being grateful, you've been a bit cynical,
voicing the minor negativities whenever possible.
It's easy to make a mountain out of a mole hill in such instances,
but how often do we take a mole hill of positive and make it into
a mountain of faith? That's a completely foreign concept for us.
One glimmer of hope is better focused on
than getting stuck in the negative.
Letting the negative take its place in the background allows
us to give God praise out of a heart of thankfulness. That's
when God is pleased, that's when He can work, and we might
just find that there is something that the Lord is working
for our good, in the place that we've not been grateful.
Challenge:

Start blessing instead of cursing the situation.
Focus on all the good instead of the little bad.
Praise out of gratitude for God's provision.
This turn around will help us see how God
is working in our life to bless us.

1 Thessalonians 5:16-18
Rejoice always, pray continually, give thanks in all
circumstances; for this is God's will for you in Christ Jesus.
1 Corinthians 15:57 ♥ 1 Chronicles 16:34 ♥ Colossians 3:15
Romans 11:36

Blessible

When we ask God to bless something in our lives,
we are asking Him to give His approval. Sometimes
we expect it just because we ask Him for it.
God wants to bless us and answer our prayers but there are often
issues that we are asking God to bless that are not "blessible".
We continue, thinking that if we pray for blessing, it
will automatically come in time, but I wonder if God
withholds blessing from those areas in an attempt
to help us see what is not His plan for us.
I recently heard a mom share about her 10 year old son, who
asked her if he could have a soda at 10 o'clock at night.
She loves her son dearly and would give her
life for his good and protection.
But she stopped and looked at him and said, "no way!"
She said, "I love you, but that's "dumb, no, you can't have a coke,
that's not good for you, it's bedtime!".
How often do we ask God to bless our unblessibles?
As we pray, may we be willing to allow the Holy Spirit to
speak to us when we pray "amiss". May we not be hardened
in our hearts and bent toward what is not His plan for us.
Oh friends, He has so much for us, for our good.
Not to bring us down, but to lift us up to
a place of strength and stability.

October
23

Ephesians 1:3-5
*All praise to God, the Father of our Lord Jesus Christ, who has blessed us
with every spiritual blessing in the heavenly realms because we are united
with Christ. Even before he made the world, God loved us and chose us
in Christ to be holy and without fault in his eyes. God decided in advance
to adopt us into his own family by bringing us to himself through Jesus
Christ. This is what he wanted to do, and it gave him great pleasure.*

James 1:12 ♥ Luke 11:28 ♥ James 1:25
Deuteronomy 7:13

Where is the Answer?

There are times when we are faced with a situation or circumstance and we simply are not sure the best way to handle it. We may begin to pray about it but before we know it, we are looking inwardly for a solution or reasonable decision to make. Anxiety may begin to increase as the inner tension rises and the longer it remains unsettled. We just want to know what to do, what is the best path to take?
In those many instances, we can know that
God is with us and He will lead us.
Fear can come in easily and begin to take our thoughts far from focusing on Jesus. But as we go to the Lord in honest surrender with our heartache, we must refuse to let the tide turn back inward, but remain sure that He is able to show us the way to go. The enemy of our soul loves to bring turmoil into our heart and mind, but the Bible tells us that God is the God of all peace. He is the One who frees us from fear that attempts to set in when we are unsure of what to do. God cares about the issues we face and He longs to help us as we simply turn to Him. When we do, things may even look a little worse before they get better, but our heart of faith can be sure that God is our Father and He loves us. He will make a way because He promises to do so.
His heart of love is from everlasting to
everlasting, and that's a really long time!
You are the object of His affection, my friend.
He has you in the palm of His loving hand and as you look to Him, and ask for His help, He will be there as you simply place your hope and trust in Him.

Philippians 4:7
Be anxious for nothing, but in everything, by prayer and petition, with thanksgiving, present your requests to God. And the peace of God, which surpasses all understanding, will guard your hearts and your minds in Christ Jesus.
Isaiah 30:21 ♥ Isaiah 26:3 ♥ Matthew 14:30
Matthew 21:21 ♥ Psalm 143:7-9 ♥ 1 John 4:18
Isaiah 48:7

Safe Inside

There is no greater feeling than to be inside, in a safe place during a storm. When the rain pours down and thunder rumbles and booms across the sky, sometimes the sound and shaking can feel tremendously threatening. There is an awesome sense of God's power when there's a powerful storm outside. Being safe inside brings a sense of comfort and security like nothing else can. Not long ago, we went camping up in Northern Arizona. The day was gorgeous and we enjoyed it immensely, but as nightfall came, dark clouds formed overhead and thunder began rumbling across the sky. We put everything away and headed to our tiny camper. There inside, as the rain poured and the thunder roared, we felt safe and protected. There were other people that were camping that night in the surrounding area. I must say my heart went out to the "tent" camping people. I wondered how their tents would fair in the tempest as the wind blew harder and harder. Where do we attempt to bunker down when the storms of life rage around us? Do we do our best to make it through as the tent campers did or are we safe and secure inside, where it's warm and dry nestled in the arms of Jesus? There's room in His arms for all of us. He desires that we would let Him hold us and protect us from any and every threat that life brings across our path. He is so willing to lead and even carry us, if need be, through those moments and trials. Once Jesus, Himself was caught in a pretty bad storm. It was out on a big lake where he and His friends had been fishing. Jesus had fallen asleep and the storm didn't wake Him up. Even though they had Jesus in the boat, His friends began to panic and they allowed fear to come in, even though they knew that Jesus was there. As they called Him, He came, half asleep and He spoke to the wind and waves. He commanded them to stop and be still. The friends in the boat thought they were going to die and sometimes we think we are going to die too because life is not always a walk in the park. Storms will come and go but Jesus will never go, He will always be there. He promises us that He will never leave us or forsake us. He promises He is our anchor.

Isaiah 25:4

For You have been a defense for the helpless, A defense for the needy in his distress, A refuge from the storm, a shade from the heat; For the breath of the ruthless is like a rain storm against a wall.

Isaiah 32:2 ♥ Matthew 7:24-26 ♥ Psalm 55:8

Endorsed

What is endorsed by God? What might it look like in our life today?
The word defined means, "to declare one's
public approval or support of".
For today, the endorsements of God in His
word are important for us to know.
While there are many in the Word of God, there is one that is
first and foremost. Found throughout the passages of scriptures
is a call for us to love the Lord with our whole heart and to
pursue His ways. The Lord, our Creator and King desires
that we would know Him for who He is. As we do, the love
that we long to have for Him will take precedence in our life.
It will grow and flourish as we set our hearts on Him.
The Bible calls loving God the greatest
commandment out of all the others.
It is the premise for everything else in our life, but sometimes
we just expect God to love us and we forget about loving Him.
There is an endorsement of God calling us to Himself!
Above everything else, we are to be His first.
You might think it an odd commandment, "to love God".
But it really happens so beautifully as we begin
to look to what matters to Him.
We consult Him in our prayers before making
decisions, to really know what He would have us to
do, not just to seek for the blessing of His hand.
God's love for us just is.
We never have to question it and as we decidedly pursue Jesus,
we will find ourselves enveloped in a love for Him that exceeds
the expectations or our human limitations. We are called to
love Him so that we can experience all the love He has for us.

October
26

Deuteronomy 10:12
*Now, Israel, what does the LORD your God require from you, but to
fear the LORD your God, to walk in all His ways and love Him, and to
serve the LORD your God with all your heart and with all your soul.*
Matthew 22:37 ♥ Deuteronomy 6:5 ♥ Mark 12:30
Luke 10:27

Don't Forget

A new day to begin is here.
May you stand strong and not in fear.
Lift your heart in praise,
For God's goodness is your stay.
Let no doubt be entertained,
in Him alone you are sustained!
Believe and don't forget
He is greater than any regret.
His love is for you is the real deal,
it doesn't stop though it may seem surreal.
His mercy cannot compare to any other,
He is the friend who is closer than a brother.
You are His daughter, His son
The covering of grace has already been won.
Don't forget, God loves you today.
He is by your side, to protect & help,
whatever comes your way.

October
27

Psalm 77:11
I shall remember the deeds of the LORD;
Surely I will remember Your wonders of old.

Psalm 103:2-3
Praise the Lord, my soul,
and forget not all his benefits—
who forgives all your sins
and heals all your diseases,
1 Chronicles 16:12 ♥ Psalm 105:5-6

Walking in Purpose

Leisure walks are so nice…down a tree shaded path on a fall day or on the beach on a summer day. We all appreciate the time in such settings, but they are not always found so frequently. In our day to day life, we are busy and generally walk purposefully to accomplish a certain lists of tasks. Our stride is quick and efficient. There are times that we don't have to walk fast, but we find ourselves doing so anyway, just because we do it so often. It isn't always just a quick pace, but it can also be the step of our heart and attitude. Today, let's take time to slow the stride of our heart and enjoy walking with God. It's in the walking with Him that we hear His voice and find rest in His presence. May we slow our pace, and let the tasks that demand our attention fall into perspective in the light of who Christ is in our life. Some will remember the old song, "In the Garden", written by a man named C. Austin Miles one day in March, 1912. It's a very old hymn that says, "and He walks with me and He talks with me and He tells me I am His own and the joy we share as we tarry there, none other have ever known. Miles had a profound spiritual experience in which he saw an incredible vision of Mary Magdalene visiting the empty tomb. He saw her leave the tomb and walk into a garden where she met the Master and heard Him speak her name. Walking with purpose means more than a quick step of accomplishment. It is taking the time to hear the voice of the heart of God. It is slowing our pace to purposefully hear Him in our walking through each day.

When we walk with someone, we obviously don't walk in different directions. We stay together, sometimes even our stride is exactly the same. Walking with God is a precious lifestyle He desires for us to have with Him.

Philippians 1:6
Being confident of this very thing, that he which hath begun a good work in you will perform it until the day of Jesus Christ.
1 John 1:6-7 ♥ Galatians 5:16 ♥ Luke 10:40-42
Hebrews 10:22 ♥ Hebrews 12:2

Clutter

Sometimes clutter takes over so gradually
that we don't even realize it.
It seems that when we're not looking, things have
accumulated in our homes, our cars and our life. We can
easily be overwhelmed by all the stuff that crowds our life.
It can take us away from each other and from the Lord.
We can decide when it's time to "clean house" and
make the changes we need to in our lives.
Thankfully, there is strength for the weary.
Help for those that are overwhelmed.
The psalmist David, wrote, "when my heart is overwhelmed,
lead me to the Rock that is higher than I am".
We all need to run to the Rock that is our
hope and strength for each day.
While we can't run away from the "stuff" in our life, we
can deal with it as God helps us. Clearing our heart of
encroachments that shouldn't have priority is the beginning.
As long as we think we can manage it all on our own,
the longer we will just feel the weight of the burden.
Life without letting God help will never be easy.
But He is here with us right now, for today, and every day.

Deuteronomy 31:8
*It is the Lord who goes before you. He will be with you; he will
not fail you or forsake you. Do not fear or be dismayed.*

Psalm 34:17
*When the righteous cry for help, the Lord hears,
and rescues them from all their troubles.*

1 Peter 5:7
Cast all your anxiety on Him because He cares for you.

Psalm 32:7-8
*You are my hiding place; you will protect me from trouble
and surround me with songs of deliverance.*

Anchored

Don't you love that the Lord uses so many practical
applications in His word to convey the principles
and the truths that matter in our life?
There are so many ways that the Lord gives us the
assurance of His strength in our lives and situations.
He tells us that we can be anchored in Him.
When we consider that, we can picture
an anchor held by a large rock.
Boats often go adrift when their anchor is not secured.
Sometimes we let our anchor down but instead of making
sure it is secure on the rock of Christ and in our salvation
in Him, we carry on adrift as the anchor drags along
depending on how the wind and waves direct.
When we place our hope and trust in Christ, we
can know that no matter the storm's impact, we
will be safe because our anchor is secure.
There are times we receive a warning that a storm is coming.
We may even search for calmer waters in an attempt
to avoid it, but that isn't always possible. Sometimes
storms come upon us without much warning.
Storms of life can come in many forms.
They can leave us shipwrecked and at a loss in many ways.
But even as the Apostle Paul chose to rise above 3
shipwrecks and carry on, we can too. He knew that
God was in control. He chose to allow prayer to lock the
door of the past and unlock the door of the future.
God is our anchor for the storms that life brings our way.
As you look to Him, He will be your security.

Hebrews 6:19
*This hope we have as an anchor of the soul,
a hope both sure and steadfast and one which enters within the veil,*

Psalm 39:7
**But now, Lord, what do I look for?
My hope is in you.**

Acts 27:40 ♥ Romans 5:2-5

Surrender & Acceptance

Accepting generosity is often easier said than done. It doesn't seem like it would be that way and we don't often even realize the barriers that keep us from it, but it happens subtly. Receiving the gift of God is not like receiving just any gift. It requires us to allow Jesus to help us surrender other things to Him, so that we can fully accept His gift of salvation. As Christians, the gift of salvation is both simple and yet very complex. In both the Hebrew and Greek, the word salvation means: "Deliverance or Rescue". Who would need a gift of deliverance or rescuing? Isn't salvation just receiving the Jesus as our Savior and His love demonstrated on the cross of Calvary, accepting that He has washed us of our sins? Yes it is, but it is so much more than that. Receiving Jesus as our Savoir is just the beginning of what salvation really is. It is absolutely the freedom from the weight of our sin but it is also deliverance from a life of sin that leads to death. Once we are saved, deliverance continues as we grow in the image and identity of Christ. The Bible tells us in 2 Corinthians, that "today is the day of salvation". We often think this means that there is no better day for people to give their life to Christ than today. In other words, don't put it off until tomorrow. While this is extremely true in every sense, I wonder if it could also bethat Christ is compelling us that today is another day of allowing Him to rescue us and bring us closer and closer to Him.

Acceptance of the grace of God in our lives requires our surrender daily. Paul, the great apostle, spoke and shares with us such a nugget of pursuing Jesus when he said, "I die every day"; meaning that every single day, our will must be submitted and surrendered to the will of Christ. Otherwise we are controlling and occupying the place that belongs to Jesus in our life. From the depth of our being, we must seek Him first and refuse to let self be the thing we seek. That's continual and lifelong, but as we do, we will find Him waiting to embrace us. There is so much more to the gift of our salvation. It will take a lifetime to unwrap!

2 Corinthians 6:2

*For he says, "In a favorable time I listened to you,
and in a day of salvation I have helped you."
Behold, now is the favorable time; behold, now is the day of salvation.*

1 Corinthians 15:31 ♥ Psalm 69:13 ♥ Isaiah 49:8
Ephesians 1:7

Named

Names are important. As the birth of a new baby nears, the choice of a name is important. Some choose a name that they love, while others choose names with specific meanings. Family names are likely part of the combination when making the decision. What we are called matters a lot to each of us. As life goes on, our name spoken of in a positive way vs. a negative way has a profound impact. We see the damage that happens when shame is spoken over someone for an extended period of time. It is important to know today, that our name matters to God. He is fully aware of who and where you are in this life. Why? Because He is the One who gives each of us life. We were all born into this life we are now living, of course, but God is the giver of our life. We matter more to God than we even matter to our earthly parents. The joy that fills the heart of God is when we realize that we are His ultimately and we begin hearing Him call our name. When we seek Him and His kingdom first, everything else will begin to take on a new perspective. If it feels that life has been a long series of the enemy berating our name, then today, let's begin to see that when we come to God, in surrender, everything changes. Because we are His, He takes our name and adds His to it. It is no match for the lies of the enemy. When we have the name of Christ over our life, suddenly we are no longer attempting to live within the meaning of our own name, but now we can live in the context of His. The strength of His name is ours. The covering of His name is ours. We are no longer victims but overcomers. We are no longer destitute, but we are heirs of the King of kings and Lord of lords. However, if we don't choose to walk in what He has given us in His name, we will remain under the falsely imposed disposition of the enemy. We have a name from our parents but Jesus has ultimately named us His, from before we were ever formed and before we were ever named on this earth. The Bible says that when we become His, He give us the right to be called His children. Don't easily give up your rights today! Stand for the right of His name in your life, because if we don't, the enemy will keep taking it as long as we will let him.

John 1:12-13
But to all who did receive him, who believed in his name,
he gave the right to become children of God,
children born not of blood, nor of the will of the flesh,
nor of the will of man, but born of God.
Galatians 3:26 ♥ 1 John 3:1 ♥ Romans 8:14
Romans 8:16

His Credit

In life, every day, as things are accomplished, someone or some group take credit for them. We have a sense of fulfillment when we are able to complete a project well. From mowing the grass to an important business transaction, even finding a great sale, there is a certain unspoken sense that can be so gratifying for us. There is nothing more wonderful than knowing that we did a good job but as we do, may we remember to give credit or to give honor to whom honor is due.

Often it may be tempting to take credit or partial credit for those things, but as those moments come, may we give the honor and credit to God for all that He has done to allow and help us with each of those tasks and responsibilities.

Sometimes the Lord is left to be blessed and honored only on Sunday, when we are at church. He may be acknowledged in our prayer closet as we begin our day, but how important it is to see how He is blessing us throughout each day.

As we bless our children for a job well done, may we encourage them to see God at work in their lives. How He is blessing their gifts and talents. When He blesses them, they can be multiplied so much further than if they or we take all the credit.

Self has a pretty big ego and pride wants as much of the credit as we can muster and it even demands inflation on many occasions, but humility comes and blessing is even more precious when self takes its place and God is exalted instead.

Let's remember that without Him, we can do nothing. We are only the branches and He is the Vine of our life.

John 5:4-5

Remain in Me, and I will remain in you. Just as no branch can bear fruit by itself unless it remains in the vine, neither can you bear fruit unless you remain in Me. I am the vine; you are the branches. Whoever abides in me and I in him, he it is that bears much fruit, for apart from me you can do nothing.

John 15:16 ♥ Psalm 126:3 ♥ Psalm 71:19
Luke 1:49 ♥ Isaiah 25:9

Adored

Recently, I was standing with a mom and her brand new baby.
Only a few weeks old, we oohhed and
ahhhed over the precious bundle.
He was sleeping soundly as we chatted around him,
completely unaware of the small gathering about him.
Amid our admirations, this new mom said,
"I just can't stop looking at him, sometimes, that's all I do."
Another mom, who has school aged children,
smiled and spoke up saying,
*"when I was a new mom, my neck hurt almost all the time
because my head was bent over all the time because I could
hardly take my eyes off of my babies!"* Most every mom knows
this is true and it doesn't stop when they grow out of infancy.
We love watching our children, just looking at them.
Our children are grown and I still love to just look at them.
In that instant, my heart caught a glimpse of what God thinks of us!
I saw in their exchange over this precious new life, a small
reflection of how God feels about us. Imagine it, the God of the
universe, the stars, all creation, cares for us. We are loved by Him!
I could see it in that moment but there
are times when we can't see it.
There are times when it is really hard to grasp.
The measure of God's great love! We wonder how it could be.
In our wonder, we can dismiss it too quickly
and forget to work at grasping it.
But today, may you realize how deeply you are loved and
how cherished you are by the God who made you.

Isaiah 63:7
*I shall make mention of the loving kindnesses of the LORD, the
praises of the LORD, According to all that the LORD has granted
us, And the great goodness toward the house of Israel,
Which He has granted them according to His compassion And
according to the abundance of His loving kindnesses.*
1 John 3:1 ♥ John 3:16 ♥ Romans 8:16
Ephesians 2:4-5

Pardoned

Having served a prison sentence and receiving an official pardon more than 20 years ago, she applied for a yet another position. Things looked hopeful, until the very end when her application was rejected because of her past.

Again! Rejected!

Another piercing arrow to her heart forced her to relive the past. Though she desperately wanted to forget the regret of it, the present circumstances prohibited her such a luxury. To be pardoned means, "the action of forgiving or being forgiven for an error or offense".

The story is true and as I heard it, gratitude welled up in my heart as I thought about the pardon that Christ has extended to each of us. Our past no longer rules our future. Thank God that we are no longer defined by what we have done, but by the gift of grace of God and who we are in Christ. Grace is something that only God can fully extend. Even in our story, men attempted to give mercy and grace but it was limited in her life. The most important pardon we will ever need is the pardon of Christ. It is His pardon to cover the eternity of our life. Maybe we've never had to serve a prison sentence on this earth, but we were destined to live life in a prison of sin except for the grace of God in our life.

Pardon is another word for forgiveness.
It is something that God not only does for us but
He calls us to give it to others just as freely.

"If we really want to love, we must learn to forgive."
~Mother Teresa.

Micah 7:18
Who is a God like you, pardoning iniquity and passing over transgression for the remnant of his inheritance?
He does not retain his anger forever,
because he delights in steadfast love.

Micah 7:18
For I will forgive their iniquities, and remember their sins no more.
Isaiah 43:25 ♥ 2 Chronicles 30:9 ♥ Exodus 34:9
Jeremiah 38:20

Miracles

Miracles are moments when we are in need of God's intervention. We are sometimes overwhelmed to find ourselves in such a state, but if we are never there, we will never know the goodness of God working in a miraculous way on our behalf. The need of a miracles defines our limitations and unleashes God's ability to do something greater than we are. Realizing the miracle of salvation is our beginning and from there, the hand of God is so divinely evident when we continue to look to Him again and again. When we are thrust into the need of a miracle, the heart of God is touched by compassion. His love initiates a response to our need. However, the need does not dictate the need for a miracle. The need is already known before we ever experience it. Our good is held in God's hand and His provision is already established. It is interesting to note that the very first miracle that Jesus performed was at a wedding. The miracle that day carries a great significance that was more than saving face and deflecting embarrassment because the wedding host ran out of wine. Jesus was telling us that marriage is holy. It is important and precious to Him. Perhaps Him doing His first miracle there was God's way of saying, marriage may be hard from time to time and you may not have all the answers, but I show up in marriages and I do miracles in the moments of despair when you need Me most. We know that God loves the covenant of marriage and His miracle working provision for doing miracles within marriage was set in motion on the wedding day, as the bride and groom entered a covenant with Him. Perhaps it is His way of reminding us that He is the strongest part of the covenant we make in marriage. He was perhaps saying, "when you need a miracle, it's already been provided for."

Ecclesiastes 4:9
"Two are better than one, because they have a good return for their labor:
If either of them falls down, one can help the other up.
But pity anyone who falls and has no one to help them up.
Also, if two lie down together, they will keep warm.
But how can one keep warm alone?"

John 2:1-11 ♥ Ephesians 4:2-3 ♥ Colossians 3:14

Our Heart

When centering our life, the very first and most crucial part is centering our heart. Have you ever felt like a little rubber duck, meant for a bathtub but felt as though you are out on the high seas? That little rubber duck is no match for the massive waves and swells that the sea naturally invokes. In the same way, it is mere foolishness to think that somehow, in ourselves, we can stand in combat without Jesus.

There must come a moment in our life in Christ when we realize that we are no match for the schemes of the enemy without Jesus. He is our anchor. He is the One that God provided to fight for us. He is not only a viable opponent for the enemy of our soul but He is a VICTORIOUS warrior. When we stop trying in our "rubber duck" ability to weather the waves, and take refuge in Him, we will find victory.

Of course we are not a rubber duck are we?

No! We are children of the Most High God, who He has made more than conquerors in Christ Jesus, our Lord.

We've been made victorious through the blood of Jesus Christ. Faith is the necessity to letting God be God, in centering our heart. Faith agrees with the Word of God, as we walk in obedience, letting God fight the battle that we can never win without Him. It is submitting to His authority.

Centering our heart on Jesus is paramount to living in victory.

November
6

2 Chronicles 20:15
And he said,
"Listen, all Judah and inhabitants of Jerusalem and King Jehoshaphat:
Thus says the LORD to you, 'Do not be afraid and do not be dismayed
at this great horde, for the battle is not yours but God's.
Ephesians 1:15-23 ♥ Ephesians 6:12 ♥ Psalm 61:2-4

Too Little

There is nothing, there is no one that compares to the Lord our God. He is faithful to 1,000 generations and stands on our behalf as we call on Him. As we pray and seek His face, He fights our battles and does the impossible. How much of God would you say you have in your life today? Are you growing in Him and in your relationship with Him? These are reflective question that will help us to take inventory of our soul, and to think about where we are? More importantly, where is God? God has so much for us as we look to and seek after Him. However, sometimes we stop just short of the miracle we have trusted Him for. Often we settle for far less of Him when His abundance far exceeds our capacity. I believe if we had any idea of just how much God wants to flood our lives with His Spirit, we would be blown away by it. There may be a shallow portion of God's presence in us simply because life is so crazy! Our interaction with Jesus may be minimal at best. We think, we're okay and we're getting by, but He has so much more for us. He wants us to experience Him in a greater way and measure. We are far too content with little and we are satisfied with far less than we should be. We are called to contend for Him, to look for Him, to search for Him as a treasure. In his book, "The Practice of the Presence of God", Brother Lawrence challenges readers, "God, has infinite treasure to bestow, and we take up a little sensible devotion, which passes in a moment. Blind as we are, we hinder God and stop the current of His graces. But when He finds a soul penetrated with a lively faith, He pours into it His graces and favors plentifully; there they flow like a torrent which, after being forcibly stopped against its ordinary course, when it has found a passage, spreads itself with impetuosity (done quickly, and without thought or care, torrentially, powerfully forceful) and abundant." Imagine being at the edge of a massive river. Its sparkling water is so inviting. Thirsty, you stand there and instead of jumping in and drinking, for whatever reason, you bend down at the edge and drink only a tiny amount. Jesus is calling us in, to have our fill of Him and more so that we have His abundance in our life to share and give to others that are looking for hope. If we are empty, we will have little to give. Jesus wants to fill us on the inside but also to live in the wealth of His presence. Be encouraged to stop settling for so little and listen to the thirst of our souls. Isaiah 55:1 says, *"Come, everyone who thirsts, come to the waters; and he who has no money, come, buy and eat! Come, buy wine and milk without money and without price."* Everyone! That's you and that's me! We are invited to come and have more of God. May we refuse the other things that attempt to fill us up, that He may have His place, and let Him fill us with His abundance!

Isaiah 35:6
Then the lame will leap like a deer and the mute tongue will shout for joy. For waters will gush forth in the wilderness, and streams in the desert.

John 14:12 ♥ Ephesians 3:20 ♥ Isaiah 26:9
Psalm 63:1 ♥ Revelation 21:6

Diligent Election

As the eyes of the world look to an election, may we defer
our focus from men to God? He is the One who can never
be voted in and He can never be voted out. He remains
divinely God and Lord over all. Though men in their
limited intelligence choose to disregard God's supremacy, it
remains unshaken and unshakeable. To comprehend that
God is, means looking to the Holy Spirit for wisdom
beyond ourselves. The word of God encourages
us today to make our election sure.

May what we choose to personally and spiritually endorse, be
the Kingdom of God and His nature. While there may not be
a Godly candidate, it doesn't change who God is. It causes us
to look beyond people to the supremacy of God. This is the
focus that God has been calling people to since time began.
The Lord has never wanted us to look to men before we look
to Him for wisdom or security. As the coming of the Lord
approaches, sadly, depravity will continue to spiral downward.
But, as the Bible tells us, "be of good cheer anyway".
God is God alone and beside Him, there is no other.
Our refuge is here. As we make our election sure, in Christ,
we can have peace in Him. We can breathe a sigh of relief
to know that we don't have to expect a man to be in control,
because God is! He is able to handle what men cannot.
He is our strength and portion forever.

November
8

Jude 1:24
*Now to Him who is able to keep you from stumbling and to present
you unblemished in His glorious presence, with great joy.*
Romans 11:2 ♥ 2 Peter 3:14 ♥ 2 Peter 1:3-11

Never Lose Sight

God hears and answers our prayers.
When we pray, it matters, but when we pray
together, it matters even more.
Our prayers touch heaven and as we look to Him alone, we
will find that the Lord our God is who He said He would be.
Ever faithful.
The moment we are living in, like every other, is evidence
that God is calling each and every soul to Himself. The day
we live in reveals His loving grace and call to repentance for
the nations of the world. As we acknowledge God's Lordship
in our lives, we untie His hands to work on our behalf.
Let's we never lose sight of Christ and the
ultimate victory He has won for us.
When we experience a divine victory in our lives,
sometimes it is easy to go back to "life as usual", but may
this call we have heard from heaven, keep us on our
knees and diligently seeking God like never before.
History continues to be changed because we are
praying for His kingdom to come, and His will
to be done on earth as it is in heaven.
Oh, friends, God is so good!
Let's never lose sight of Him as He continually
pours out His goodness and blessing.
May it draw us closer still and may we remain assembled
to fight the good fight of faith in our generation.
El Hanne'eman is the Hebrew name of God
that means, The Faithful God.

1 Corinthians 1:9
*God, who has called you into fellowship with His
Son Jesus Christ our Lord, is faithful.*

Deuteronomy 7:9
*Know therefore that the LORD your God is God, the faithful God
who keeps covenant and steadfast love with those who love him
and keep his commandments, to a thousand generations.*

*1 Thessalonians 5:24 ♥ 2 Timothy 2:13 ♥ Genesis 28:15
Proverbs 3:1*

Management

Management is a big term that is a part of our life every day. From the management of major corporations to the management of a family and home, daily, management happens in our lives. Some manage well and others struggle. Then there's God, Almighty, who manages the entire universe. God is the ultimate manager, managing with excellence. As we think of our life, and the way we manage, every day we are given opportunity to manage with the ultimate manager, whose name is Jesus.

There are many ways of managing and sadly some manage their life separate from God's counsel. But if we only had a glimpse of the difference that His input would make in our life, it would change everything. He stands ready and able to help us manage each and every day. In the days we are blessed with, we can live inwardly consumed or we can live generously outward. It is all in the management of our life. May our prayer be, "Lord, help me to manage my life in a way that pleases You." And from there, break down the areas of our life. "Lord, please show me how to manage my home in a way that pleases You." "Lord, give me wisdom to manage my relationships in a way that pleases You." "Lord, help me manage my career in a way that pleases You." On and on it goes down to the details of your life in regard to finances, time, resources, etc. Our lives, of course, are made up of years, and our years are made up of months. Our months are made up of weeks and our weeks are made up of days. Our days are made up of hours and our hours are made up of minutes.

May we not be too quick to pray generic prayers, lumping it all together without allowing God to be a part of the details of our moments. He wants to help us manage the moments of our lives that become hours, and the hours that become our days, and days that become our weeks, and our weeks that become our months, and our months that become our years, and our years that become our lives. We can have confidence and assurance in knowing that we have the greatest resource in all the universe that stands ready to help us when we whisper His name. May we invite Him in, to give us better insight to the management of our lives. His word is the wealth of His wisdom, we'll find so much direction there. He calls us to manage well and the Lord, who loves us, gives us all that we need to make it possible. Call on Him today, He is just waiting for your invitation to come in and lead you in it all.

Amos 4:13
For behold, He who forms mountains and creates the wind And declares to man what are His thoughts, He who makes dawn into darkness And treads on the high places of the earth, The LORD God of hosts is His name.

James 1:5 ♥ Proverbs 2:6 ♥ Hebrews 1:10
1 Kings 3:9 ♥ Matthew 7:7 ♥ James 3:17

Valor

As we remember the gifts of our lives, let's pause today to remember those who have gone before us. In so many ways, there are many pioneers that have given so much and paved a way for those that would come behind them. Giving honor to these in remembrance is a way that helps us to realize what gifts have been given. Gifts that we sometimes take for granted. Those gifts pass us every day in the lives of those around us. The magnitude of the accumulation of them is powerful and magnificent. The greatest gift is the gift of our salvation and it is found when Jesus comes into our life. He is the greatest of all gifts and through Him, we have received gifts that are priceless and costly. Men and women who have served for freedom followed His example of selflessness. They set their lives aside for a calling that cost them great sacrifices. "All gave some and some gave all". Throughout the word of God, we can find so many instances of courage and valor. It is the essence of faith and it is the essence of being driven by hope. The greatest example of faith is the example of Christ Jesus when He said, "not my will but Thine be done". It was well said of Publius Cornelius Tacitus when he said, "In valor there is hope". Valor defined is "great courage in the face of danger, especially in battle." We are the recipients of Christ's great valor and of those who, today, have great courage, standing for what we hold so dear and precious in freedoms. The call to courage and valor is not in the past, it is our present as well. It continues to be a gift given by those we may never know but it doesn't change their gift to us. We can be encouraged to live a life of courage and valor as we live for Christ and stand for truth. Even in the smallest ways, we can honor the gift of Christ and the gift of those who have given.

Judges 6:12
And the angel of the LORD appeared to him and said to him, "The LORD is with you, O mighty man of valor."

Ruth 2:4 ♥ 1 Samuel 10:7 ♥ Joshua 1:7
Joshua 1:9 ♥ Deuteronomy 1:21

Whatcha Got?

When people have something, other people
naturally want to know what it is.
Sometimes it's something in a box or a sack.
Sometimes it's wondering about a text message or letter
that comes in the mail. We are curious creatures.
We often say or hear, "Hey, whatcha got there?"
We hold a heart full of God's goodness and whether others say
it or not, they are wondering what it's all about. Sometimes
we forget that there are people that God places around us
that are just looking for someone to point them in a different
and better direction. Their actions may not convey that,
but there is a desire in their soul to know what God has to say
about them and their life. Silently, they are asking, "Hey, whatcha
got?" They wonder, "is there hope for me?" and "can God really
love me". We know He does but helping people know that it is
really true is a process that requires our intentional interaction
with them. As we live each day, may we first, allow our own heart
to be certain of the love that God has for us. May we continue
to live with an intention of sharing what we've got. As we share
even in small ways, God can use it to make a huge difference
to those around us. May we not believe the enemy who would
intimidate us to keep what we have a secret at the expense of
someone else. May we refuse to believe the lie that our treasure
might offend, but as the Holy Spirit leads us, let's reach beyond
our limitations and share what we have be given to give.
There is hope and love for a quiet heart that is wondering if
God cares about them and their life. We are His voice that says,
"Come and see! I have plenty to share and I'm happy to let you
know what God has done in my life. He has great things for you."

November
12

Luke 6:38
*Give, and it will be given to you. Good measure, pressed down,
shaken together, running over, will be put into your lap. For
with the measure you use it will be measured back to you.*
Proverbs 19:17 ♥ Deuteronomy 16:7 ♥ 1 Chronicles 29:9
Proverbs 21:26

Touching Heaven

There used to be an old saying about prayer.
It was an action that created a sense of
persistence called "praying through".
What it means is to pray until you know you have touched
heaven, until you know that you have engaged and that your soul
has the assurance that your prayer has been heard by God.
Sometimes we find ourselves praying
superficial prayers that lack depth.
We forget the importance of praying specifically and being willing
to pour our heart out to God. Perseverance is a discipline of prayer
to carry us past our shallow splashing of the beach of our faith to
go out into the deep places of God of being immersed in Him.
The Lord our God calls us to boldly enter His throne room of grace
and let Him into every part of our life. Our generic and general
prayers are usually a more shallow sort of prayer. But when we
get serious, that is a whole other story. Being specific with our
prayer opens the door for God to work. Our faith deepens in the
promises of God as we declare it before Him in perseverance.

Psalm 116:2
*Because He has inclined His ear to me, Therefore
I shall call upon Him as long as I live.*

1 Chronicles 16:11
Seek the LORD and His strength; Seek His face continually.

1 Thessalonians 5:17
Pray without ceasing;

Psalm 119:147-149
*I rise before dawn and cry for help; I wait for Your words.
My eyes anticipate the night watches, hat I may meditate on
Your word. Hear my voice according to Your lovingkindness;
Revive me, O LORD, according to Your ordinances.*

Well-Lit

Have you ever noticed how different things look in a well-lit room or area than they do in a dimly lit place? Have you ever tried to find something without turning on a light only to become exasperated? When you finally turn the light on, what you've been looking for is easily found. Jesus said of Himself, I am the Light of the world. He leads us to live for Him and to let His light shine through us. Have you ever noticed that when a light is turned inward against something, it is diminished but when we turn it outward, then it has the potential to shine the brightest. Darkness does not have the capability, nor the capacity to overtake light. Light will always win!

Sometimes God is calling us to let His light shine in the deep places of our heart to expose what is hidden so that He can redeem that in us. He also leads us to turn the light that we may have turned inward for a long period of time, outward. As we do, the brightness of His goodness causes the light of Christ in us to shine so brightly. The moon has the amazing capacity to shine brightly, but it doesn't always. It reflects the light of the sun but sometimes it is covered by clouds and sometimes it's only a sliver of light. But we have seen that it shines the brightest when it is the closes to us. The word assures us that as we come close to God, He will come close to us.

He is as close as the whisper of His name and His light has the capacity to shine brightly in and through our lives. Jesus' light in us brings hope in a way that nothing else can. Today, He remains the Light of the world. He is our hope and the hope of those that see His light in us. May we carry it well, may refuse to walk in darkness. Jesus is the way and His light will help us each day in the path of our life. There is abundant sufficiency in the light of Christ for you.

John 8:12
Again Jesus spoke to them, saying, "I am the light of the world. Whoever follows me will not walk in darkness, but will have the light of life."
John 12:46 ♥ John 1:4 ♥ John 12:36

Following

When we travel in two different vehicles, I am generally more comfortable following my husband. He's a great leader and is always watching to make sure I'm right behind him. However, there are times when we are in a lot of traffic and other cars cut in front of me or I get stuck at a traffic light. When those instances happen, I have to work to catch up or make sure I keep my eye on his truck. There are times when I lose sight of him, but I always know he is there. Often in our day to day life, we have set out following Jesus, but things and people can get in between us and we can easily lose sight of Christ. Sometimes those moments are brief, and other times they last a little longer. When we are navigating our life, we must be so careful to keep our eyes on Jesus. He is the One who sees what we cannot see ahead and He knows which turns are best for us. If we are not diligent to follow as closely as we can, we can get off course and lose our way. There are times when we may be following Jesus, but someone comes between us. We begin following that person because we think they are following Christ. Deception can creep in and take our focus in a completely different direction. We are cautioned in the word of God to keep our focus on Christ, and we must be diligent to make sure we do not let Him out of our sight. It's critical to our spiritual well-being, that we not fall behind and let other things between us and Him. Perhaps you have lost sight of following Jesus. Maybe at one time, you could see Him easily but you have allowed other things to come between you and now you are trying to catch a glimpse of Him ahead but you can't see Him. There are times that I am following in my car and I lose sight of my husband. Too much distance comes between us and I know that I cannot just "catch up". There comes a time when I have to call him to find out where he is. So many times, he pulls off to the side and waits for me to find him. The Lord is so gracious and waits patiently for us to call Him. He is eager to help us find our way back to Him so that we can follow His leading in our lives. God is so faithful and He never ever calls us to lead our life without Him. He is our shepherd and we are the sheep of His pasture. He calls us to follow Him but we can't follow Him if we are in front of Him or if we don't know where He is. It may be time to stop and call Him in prayer, and to acknowledge the need of your life and heart. He is well acquainted with the traps and detours the enemy puts along the road for us. They are strategically placed but Jesus will always lead us through them if we will keep our eyes on Him.

November 15

Psalm 143:6

I stretch out my hands to you; my soul thirsts for you like a parched land. Selah

Hosea 6:3 ♥ Psalm 63:8 ♥ Psalm 5:8
Psalm 16:7-8 ♥ Psalm 27:11 ♥ Psalm 73:23-24

Cultivate

To cultivate means to "prepare and use"; "try to acquire or develop"; "to foster growth". Psalm 37:3-5 is a verse in God's word that gives us such clear direction. In it we find the means for following Christ and His ways. In it He gives us the promise of the desires of our heart being fulfilled. He knows better than we do that those desires are only fulfilled when He is our focus, and not the desires that we so desperately want or feel we need.

Could it be that we can easily get things backwards? Do we focus on the desires of our heart first instead of trusting in God? He calls us to cultivate faithfulness first and foremost. Then He calls us to delight ourselves in the Lord and commit our ways to Him and trust Him. Take pleasure in Him!

Trusting Him isn't always easy because it requires that we give control to God instead of hanging on to it ourselves. It can be a little scary to let go of something that is so dear to you? Maybe we are reluctant because we wonder about the outcome, what if God doesn't give us the answer we were hoping for? Sometimes we need to remind ourselves of how trustworthy and faithful God is and has been. He has so much more for us than we could ever imagine and His desire is to bless us with His goodness.

Won't you give Him your trust today!

Cultivate faithfulness to Him in your life. Let it be the goal of this season in all you do, and watch to see the seeds begin to grow.

November
16

Psalm 37:4
Trust in the LORD and do good; Dwell in the land and cultivate faithfulness. Delight yourself in the Lord; And He will give you the desires of your heart. Commit your way to the LORD, Trust also in Him, and He will do it.

Psalm 16:11
You will make known to me the path of life; In Your presence is fullness of joy; In Your right hand there are pleasures forever.

Psalm 145:19 ♥ Psalm 94:19 ♥ Psalm 43:3-5

Matthew 7:7-8

Enough to Go Around

As we get ready for Thanksgiving and are thinking about the meal we will arrange or the meal we will attend, our concern is usually what we will prepare and how much. How many people will be there? We want to make sure there is enough to go around, meaning that there will be enough food for everyone. One day, Jesus was teaching a large group of people, the Bible tells us that it was over 5,000. They had been listening all day and Jesus realized that they were getting hungry. Well, even though they were outside, they were really at "His house" in a sense. He took on the responsibility of the meal that needed to be prepared for them and their families. We are most familiar with the story of the loaves and the fishes in the Bible. It's a story about a little boy's lunch that Jesus blessed and it fed everyone that day. Interestingly enough, the little boy's lunch was enough for just one person. It was in no way enough for 5,000 plus people! Sometimes we look at our life and we contemplate what we have and we attempt to manage it. But what if we did what the little boy did that day? Remember that the disciples overlooked the potential of the little lunch, but Jesus said, "this is enough to go around!" What if we put what we have in Jesus' hands as He asks us to and let Him use it for His glory. Jesus did a miracle that day and He is still doing miracles! As we put our "little" in His hands, He can do so much more with it than we ever could. The little boy gladly gave his lunch to Jesus that day. I wonder why he even offered it. Why didn't he just hide it and keep it for himself? I believe that he had been sitting there with a hungry heart and perhaps he just wanted to bless Jesus because something in his heart was touched by the words he heard that day. Today, my friends, nothing is impossible with God. He is able to do more than we can imagine possible as we trust His provision. You see, the Bible tells us that Jesus sits at the right hand of God, ever making intercession for us. Just as He lifted the little boy's lunch to our Heavenly Father that day, He is lifting us up as we place ourselves and all we are in His hands. It may not seem like much to you, even as the little boy's lunch could never have been enough without the blessing of God. But when Jesus lifts us and all we are to God, He takes what was just enough for one, what was just enough for ourselves and He multiplies to be a blessing beyond what we could ever imagine for His glory. As we take our eyes off our "little" and put them on Jesus, we will see Him do wonderful things that otherwise could never be possible. He makes our impossible, possible; because that is the kind of God we serve. He loves to bless His people and show us His love and faithfulness! Go ahead, let Jesus have the little that you hold today.

Matthew 19:26
But Jesus looked at them and said, "With man this is impossible, but with God all things are possible."
Genesis 18:14 ♥ Matthew 14:13-21 ♥ Luke 1:37
Mark 10:27 ♥ Jeremiah 32:17

Gratitude

When children are asked what they are thankful for, their answers can be so precious. They will often say things like, "I'm thankful for my grandma, my dog, pizza, or my family". So many tiny instances can fill our heart with gratitude but at the same time, our gratitude can be stolen away when ingratitude becomes our focus. May be begin to look at all God has done and refuse to buy into the enemy's perspective. Gratitude andthanksgiving are action words for us to live out. Thanksgiving preparations are a big part of the day we celebrate gratitude.
And just as we prepare for the holiday, preparations are important to maintain a heart of gratitude. It comes when we begin to look at who God is and His generous goodness. He is the anchor from which gratitude is birthed in our heart. When we simply acknowledge Him, we will see our perspective change and become unselfish. Thankfulness and thanksgiving will become a part of our life, in what we say, how we act and what we do. It is a wonderful testimony of life, to live in gratitude. May Thanksgiving not just be a holiday that we celebrate, but may it be a lifestyle we live for His glory.'

As we express our gratitude, we must never forget that the highestappreciation is not to utter words, but to live by them.
—John Fitzgerald Kennedy

Psalm 136:1-3
Give thanks to the LORD, for He is good, For His lovingkindness is everlasting. Give thanks to the God of gods, For His lovingkindness is everlasting. Give thanks to the Lord of lords, For His lovingkindness is everlasting.
Hebrews 13:15 ♥ Romans 1:8

Secure in your Stand

There's something liberating about making a decision you know that God has led you too. In the process, you have realized the importance of yielding and deep inside we know that He is right. Once you take that stand, the reality of what it means begins to take shape and form in your life. When situations and temptations come along, we know we've left the matter to follow Christ and His ways. No longer are we entangled, imprisoned, or powerless against what may have ruled us for a very long time. Entanglements are cautioned for our lives in the word of God. Sometimes it happens without our realizing the depth of it, and at other times we are fully aware of the disobedience that leads us deeper still. Thank God we have a Rescuer and His name is Jesus. He is ready, willing and more than able to bring freedom to our lives. It's no small thing to take on the enemy and make that stand. But as we do, Jesus steps right in front of us in the battle and the enemy is no contest for Him. The problem is that we sometimes try to take the devil on in ourselves, and think that we have to get it all together and then we'll come to Jesus, when our life is put in order. But that mentality is a little skewed, because we will never be able to win the war of the spirit without the Holy and Supreme Spirit. He is the one and only one that has authority to break those chains and bring freedom. Every attempt to let Jesus lead and bring you out is a step of faith and He sees it. The word of God tells us that our faith pleases God and touches His heart. Sometimes if failure has been our mantra, we think, "what's the use to try again?". But if it didn't matter we wouldn't keep hearing His voice call us and say…"this is the way, walk ye in it". He has not given up on you so why do we so easily give up on Him and the work He is doing in us?

Our place of comfort is often the cycle that God wants to break to bring us through. We know deep inside that He is able and we must walk forward instead of so easily giving in. The truth is that even though we know we could be stronger if we call out to Jesus, our flesh simply doesn't want to. But His grace can lead us out of that cycle of deception if we will just let Him. Greater is He who is IN you, my friend, than he who is in the world!! Today's your day, go ahead and let His hand take yours…it's a good thing!

2 Timothy 2:4
No soldier gets entangled in civilian pursuits, since his aim is to please the one who enlisted him.
Galatians 5:1 ♥ John 8:36 ♥ Galatians 5:13
Romans 8:15 ♥ 1 Corinthians 16:13

The Joy of Being His

Being found in Christ is to come to the end of self,
to be defined together and alive in Him. What a joy to
realize that we are not doomed to an end without Jesus in
our sin, but we have a new life because of His life in us.
He is alive and His resurrection takes over our life as we
yield ourselves to His plan and relinquish our own. As we
accept the invitation of salvation, we often say that we are
inviting Jesus into our heart because the Bible says that we
are His dwelling place, thus we invite Him in. As much as
this is the Word of God, it is also true that we become alive in
Christ Jesus when we accept Him as our Lord and Savior.
Coming to the end of ourselves means that we end the struggle
between what we want and what God wants for us. We can have
peace and know that our worth in Christ Jesus is precious.
Without such a gift we will ever flounder, and
contentment will be an ever elusive mirage for us.
Some, however, do not hold a correct understanding of the
gracious kindness of God, our Father. He is not calling us to
a life of bondage but to a life free from bondage. His love is
a liberating love that never disappoints us. Disappointment
comes when we put our hope and trust elsewhere.
We are fulfilled in being His.
That is where joy is truly known.

November
20

Philippians 3:8-9

More than that, I count all things as loss compared to the surpassing
excellence of knowing Christ Jesus my Lord, for whom I have lost all
things. I consider them rubbish, that I may gain Christ and be found in
Him, not having my own righteousness from the Law, but that which is
through faith in Christ, the righteousness from God on the basis of faith.

1 Corinthians 3:16

Don't you know that you yourselves are God's temple
and that God's Spirit dwells in your midst?

1 Corinthians 6:19 ♥ 1 Corinthians 1:30

Fear Not

Nothing brings more fear than hopelessness. Hopelessness happens when we don't see a means for change or freedom. Darkness can loom over us and we do not have the ability to see God for who He truly is. When we cannot see, fear can take up residence but that place belongs to faith. If fear has set up camp in your heart where faith should be, today is the day to give fear an eviction notice. We may not have all the answers, and we may not be able to see how things will work out, BUT we do know Jesus, our Savior. In knowing Him, we can rest assured in the faith He has given us to simply trust Him. Fear and hopelessness are not from God. If that's what seems to be surrounding you and closing in on you, take this moment to let faith be stirred up again in your heart. Refuse to let those feelings dominate yoursituation. As we stand on the truth of God's word, our feelings have to surrender to His spirit. It might take work, a lot of hard work at first, but once things are put in order, our perspective will change. Instead of hopelessness, we will have a secure hope in Jesus. We don't have to fear because God has our best in His plan. He is all we need. He wants to lead us out of fear into greater faith. He is more than trustworthy and He doesn't want us to live in fear! He has so much better for us. We are His children and He is God Almighty! Let your heart grasp that truth again today for whatever you are facing! You are not alone dear friend. You are held, and you are loved. Doom and gloom are not your destiny! Remind your heart that life in Christ is yours. Fear is defeated as you let the Lover of your soul take charge and take care! This provision was made especially for you at the cross a very long time ago.

Psalm 56:3
When I am afraid, I put my trust in you.
Psalm 94:19
When anxiety was great within me, your consolation brought joy to my soul.
John 14:27 ♥ 2 Timothy 1:7 ♥ 1 John 4:18

Surrendered to His Grace

The Lord, our God, is full of grace and His love calls us to
be surrendered to that grace as it is extended into our life.
So if surrendering to His grace is His plan for us, how is that
accomplished to the fullest potential in us? Understanding
what grace means gives us a glimpse of the answer. In the New
Testament, grace is defined as "God's love in action towards men
who merited the opposite of love." In the Old Testament, grace
is described through the Greek word, "chesed" which speaks of
"deliverance from enemies, affliction and adversity. It also denotes
enablement, daily guidance, forgiveness and preservation."
Being surrendered to grace is our willingness to simply accept
the fullness of what it means. It has been given to us freely, but it
means so much more than accepting salvation in a partial way.
There is a fullness of surrendering our life to the grace of God
that is the difference between standing in a babbling brook and
swimming in the ocean of who Christ is and wants to be in our life.
Surrendering to grace is letting go of our own understanding and
our ways to let His rule and reign in us. It is not allowing our pride
to be in control, but letting Jesus be in control of our life. It is living
selflessly and preferring one another. It is accepting the fullness
of what salvation bring to our life, instead of still thinking that
there is a price we must suffer for our sin. It is accepting that even
when we were sinners, Jesus loved us and gave Himself a ransom
for our freedom. Sometimes we think that's for everyone else.
Surrendering to grace is having confidence in the
price of salvation that Jesus paid at the cross for
us. It is trusting and believing, completely, in the work
of redemption put in place by the God who loves us.

Romans 5:1-2
*Therefore, since we have been justified by faith, we have
peace with God through our Lord Jesus Christ. Through him
we have also obtained access by faith into this grace in which
we stand, and we rejoice in hope of the glory of God.*

Psalm 32:8 ♥ Hebrews 11:6 ♥ Hebrews 4:16
Romans 8:7-8 ♥ Isaiah 64:8

Family & Friends

Families and friends come in many different shapes and sizes. No two relationships are alike, even though we don't always think of our relationships as being unique. Because there are no two people that are alike, there are no two relationships that are alike. We have incredible gifts in the friends and family God has blessed us with. Sometimes, when there is tension, we tend to think that the people involved are the issue. The reality is that we must diligently guard and care for the relationships of our life. There are so many things that the enemy can and will gladly use to ruin the precious relationships of our life. As we think about the gift of relationships, may we be more and more willing to lay pride aside for the sake of those that matter so much to us. May we realize the root of turmoil and the destructive ways the devil uses to try to destroy. Sometimes we give in and don't see situations for what they really are. We can often only see our side instead of looking deeper to the root of the inflicted issues that are not of God. Let us be willing to stand up for those we love, refusing to let go so easily of these dear gifts in our life.

I believe we bless the heart of God when we love each other as He has called us to. We can all ask the Lord to show us if we've allowed a division in a relationship that was once very dear to us? What can we do to reach out and change that today? The Lord is the God of reconciliation. It is why Jesus came to earth. Without reconciliation, we would never be able to know God and for us to have a relationship with Him. Our tendency can be to let pride keep us from making the first move or maybe the second and third move. But as we try again, being led by the Holy Spirit, He can do a work beyond every pain of the past. The greatest miracle happens when a person receives Christ and is reconciled to God. But incredible miracles also happen when relationships are mended and healed. Let God work and restore hope where there has been hopelessness. Loving God is the first commandment. Loving each other is the second!

John 15:12-13
This is my commandment, that you love one another as I have loved you. Greater love has no one than this, that someone lay down his life for his friends.
1 Corinthians 13:4-13 ♥ Galatians 6:10 ♥ Proverbs 27:10
Galatians 6:2 ♥ Psalm 133:1

Temperance

Today is a day when temperance is not the highest goal of observance. In meaning, temperance is conveyed as "self-control", "self-restraint", and finally, "one's mastery of self". There is great value and honor in temperance. It's a principle of God's word that brings balance in our lives and boundaries to restrain indulgence that leads astray. Whether we are contending for a bridled tongue, rampant thoughts, or restrained eyes, we must be diligent and refuse to allow our lives to go unchecked. As we remain inside the perimeters of Godly mandates, we have more freedom than we could ever truly understand. You see, unrestraint ultimately leads to bondage and oppression. It can be so subtle and somehow justified by the ever elusive tactics of the enemy of our soul. Constraint brings contentment. Self-restraint through Christ leads us to a victory that we will never find apart from Him. It's interesting that one of the fruit of the Spirit would be "temperance or self-control", but we can never attain it without the Spirit to empower us and help us. When we look at the word, we think it's doing something ourselves. But truly it's only found with the help and strength of the Lord. The lifelong pursuit of temperance is one that we will grow in continually, as Christ perfects His purpose in us for His glory. Whether there is an addiction, overcoming sin, obeying God's direction or refusing to indulge in gluttony, the need for discipline is more profound than we realize. Putting it off for another time is a sly deception that is not from God. The Word of God tells us that "today is the day of salvation". In other words, today is the day to make things right with God. Today is the day to let His rule be the guide that leads us to abundance in Him. The Lord our God is so faithful and His good is for us to partake of each day. Our temperance is contagious just as indulgence can be. It affects not only our lives, but it conveys something to those around us. The blessing of it is fruit for our spirit. It is not legalism, it is finding wholeness in the goodness of Jesus, and in the salvation He has so generously and freely given. What a gift to be celebrated!

2 Peter 1:5-6
And beside this, giving all diligence, add to your faith virtue; and to virtue knowledge; And to knowledge temperance; and to temperance patience; and to patience godliness;

Galatians 5:22-24 ♥ Proverbs 25:28 ♥ 1 Corinthians 9:27
Philippians 4:5

Blessed

Our hearts are full at the blessings we have.
Gratitude is a precious way to live and in it may we take time to be
more thankful. It becomes magnified and multiplied over and over
as a stream that becomes unclogged from debris. Of course, we have
been blessed and today, as I sat still with the Lord, I didn't want to
ask Him to bless anything or anyone as I sometimes pray. Today, I
felt challenged as I wondered how my life has blessed His heart.
I pray that every part of our life would bless Him…
that our thoughts would bless Him,
that our actions and attitude would bless Him,
that our words would bless Him,
that our life would bless Him every day.
May we be mindful of all we do
and how it affects the heart of God.
That we would love more,
That we would be kinder,
That we would live with generosity!
We have been so blessed!
There is no higher love than His,
no greater goodness,
no kinder kindness,
no more merciful
mercy than His mercy.

John 15:13
*Greater love has no one than this, that someone
lay down his life for his friends.*

Genesis 12:2
*And I will make of you a great nation,
and I will bless you and make your name great,
so that you will be a blessing.*

1 John 3:16 ♥ Proverbs 10:22 ♥ Deuteronomy 8:18

Measurements

Throughout the lives of my children, when they were younger, they would often have a hard time grasping the actions of others. For example if another child was given permission to do a certain thing but they could not, it was hard for them to understand why. From the smallest of issues, there was usually a discrepancy. For example, growing up, our children weren't allowed to "brag" and there were certain words we didn't say. They would wonder and compare what they could do to what others were allowed to. In those moments, I would tell them, "they are not the measuring stick for what we do, Jesus is." They probably didn't fully understand what that meant at the time. And the saying even got shortened to, "they're not the stick!" I believe it is so important that we do not move away from the accuracy of measuring our lives against the truth of who Christ is and what He came to save us from and for. There are so many ways we can compare ourselves to others and think that we're not doing too well, or we're not doing so badly, but how does that measure up against the life of Jesus has called us to live? May we not dismiss the measurement of Christ and think that He is asking us for too much, or giving us a task that is too hard to accomplish. It isn't and yes we may stumble, but Jesus said that He came to give us abundant life and to do even greater things than He did. He has called us to live simply and walk humbly before Him and to weigh the intentions of our heart. That dear friends is not too hard, and it is where we must begin and it is where we must remain. It is foundational to the depth of where we will walk with Jesus. People attempt to manage their spiritual life in many ways that can easily lead them far from Christ. May we be ever diligent to stay as close as we can to Him! Ask Jesus to help you to allow Him to be the measure of your life, instead of trying to measure Him according to the ever changing and inaccurate weights of life.

John 13:15
For I have given you an example, that you also should do just as I have done to you.
Micah 6:8 ♥ 1 John 2:6 ♥ Jeremiah 17:101
Thessalonians 4:10b-12 ♥ Deuteronomy 10:12

Delighted in His Day

Each and every new day is a gift from God. He gives so generously and we have the joy of living for His glory. His day is the day we live today. Our life matters and when we have the light of Christ in our life, each day is His day. Some may think that the Lord's Day is on Sunday and yes we absolutely honor Him on this day, but truly each and every day is His day. May we be careful not to limit our acknowledgement of Him only on Sunday but each and every day. When our flesh fights our spirit in regards to the idea of honoring Jesus, then we must see this for the warning sign that it truly is. The Bible tells us again and again to "Delight ourselves in the Lord". We can't wait to be delighted in the Lord by a song or a person or even a sermon. Delighting in the Lord begins with acknowledging the God given knowingness that has been given to each and every one of us in the depth of our soul. Each day is His day, and as we delight ourselves in the Lord we will find that our delighting in Him exceeds what we imagine this might even mean from His heart. At His right side are pleasures and blessings forevermore. Stop for a moment and consider what forevermore" truly means. It is an attempt to describe in a word the endlessness of the blessings of God, and the vastness of who He is and what He wants to be in our life. From Genesis to Revelation His word is filled with examples of His attempts to interrupt and bring grace and mercy into the hardest of hearts to restore people in relationship to Himself. If we could only see that display of our own life… the many times He has attempted to get our attention, but we chose not to see or acknowledge. Again and again, He attempts to show us His love. As He calls us to delight ourselves in Him, it becomes so clear that we are the delight of His heart, and He welcomes us again and again to come in. What delights you today? It may not be bad but it may not be God. If we put Him first, He will help us organize the rest. They will take their place after Him and there may even be some things that we find we don't delight in anymore. But don't be afraid of that transition because it is for our good and out of His heart of love. If He calls us out of something, it is to take us into something better!

Psalm 181:19
He brought me out into a broad place; he rescued me, because he delighted in me.
Psalm 1:2 ♥ Psalm 119:92-93 ♥ Isaiah 58:13-14
Psalm 37:10 ♥ Psalm 37:4

Remain Calm

In a crisis, one of the most important things to do is to remain calm. The moment we allow emotions to take over, the more difficult it is to manage the situation. We face daily situations that can demand that we respond with our emotions, but God is calling us to respond in faith. Panic may attempt to bring fear when we realize the intensity of a situation or matter. We can stand strong and refuse to allow that feeling to lead us to fear, but let it be the means to draw us closer to God in prayer. He is the answer we need. God can see what we cannot see and that is why we must trust Him in faith. If all we can do when we face a problem is to look at our own ability to fix it or our own plans to work it out, we miss the joy of letting our faith grow and letting God work. I recently heard a story of a couple who felt challenged by the Lord to begin tithing. Though they wanted to tithe, they also had student loans that they were trying to manage and pay. They rationalized that the money owed was not truly theirs and that it would be best for them to wait to pay tithes until after the loans were paid off. The Holy Spirit nudged their hearts again about tithing. Their plan was not God's plan. They began to see that while their plan sounded good to them, they were leaving God completely out of the issue. They weren't allowing Him in. But surrender came and they began to give as God had been leading them to. Within a very short time, God provided a miracle and they were debt free from those loans. Corrie Ten Boom said it well when she said,

*"Worry does not empty tomorrow of sorrow.
It empties today of its strength."*

God is our hope, and our faith in Him
is our answer, no matter what we are facing.

Psalm 121:1-2
I lift up my eyes to the hills. From where does my help come? My help comes from the LORD, who made heaven and earth.
*Hebrews 13:6 ♥ Colossians 3:15 ♥ Romans 8:31
Proverbs 12:25*

Confidence

Did you know that the Lord wants you to be confident?
As we look to Him, He gives us His strength to
do more than we can do on our own.
There are moments when each of us is faced with situations
that cause us wonder how we will manage. But we must
remember that the Lord our God is so faithful. The strength of
God is made perfect when we realize our need in light of the
limitations of our inability. I can remember moments and times
of accomplishment in things that were so hard and things that I
felt so inapt for. It was in those times that the confidence of Christ
helped me to do what I could have never have accomplished
without Him. Displaying confidence in Christ is an expression
of our security in Him. It's trusting in His love by faith.
In our heart, we may be crying out, "this is too much Lord"
or "this is too hard for me". But as we follow His leading, He
will help us each and every step of the way. There were times
in the challenges of life's processes that I have wanted to quit
and take an easier road, but as I trusted in His strength, I
found myself accomplishing what I never dreamed I could.
There in so much more potential in us than we can see, but it's not
beyond the vision of God. He accomplishes things in and through
us as a means of a testimony to others that point to His glory and
grace. He is faithful and He is your strength today as you place
your confidence in the One who holds your hand and leads you.

November
29

Hebrews 10:35
Therefore do not throw away your confidence, which has a great reward.

Philippians 4:13
I can do all things through Him who strengthens me.

Deuteronomy 3:16
*e strong and courageous, do not be afraid or tremble
at them, for the LORD your God is the one who goes
with you He will not fail you or forsake you.*

Proverbs 3:26 ♥ Philippians 1:6

O How I Love You!

As songwriters and even the beloved Psalmist of God's word have written over the centuries of their love for God, we have a song that is all our own. We can never truly know the love of another person's heart like we know the love that floods our own heart and life for God. As His love fills us to overflowing, His presence takes over and causes a desire in us to know Him more than we ever have before.

As we lift our heart in surrender to His love, we will find our heart seeking a deeper understanding of who God is. When we do, we allow our relationship with Jesus to come to the front of all the others of our life. Letting our heart truly focus on Christ and resisting the influences that attempt to bombard our mind gives us the ability to sing the song our heart holds for Him.

He is the One who has rescued us. He is the One who holds our life and causes our losses to be redeemed through the plan He set in place for our life alone. Our song and our life are ours alone and that is the song that we can sing from the depths of our soul to the One who loves us beyond our understanding.

The amazingness of Christ is an incredible truth that will transform every situation and circumstance. It will lead us to not let anything stand in the way of finding Him and knowing Him more and more. O how we love Him!

May we remind our heart and soul today of how amazingly we are loved by Him and as we do, may the song of our love be poured out as we lavish our love upon the One who loves us more than we can imagine.

Exodus 15:2
The LORD is my strength and song, And He has become my salvation; This is my God, and I will praise Him; My father's God, and I will extol Him.

Psalm 59:17
O my strength, I will sing praises to You; For God is my stronghold, the God who shows me lovingkindness.

Psalm 116:1 ♥ Psalm 43:2 ♥ Psalm 18:1

Insight

May we never believe or think for a moment that God does not want to show us His ways. From the beginning of the creation of man, He has deeply desired fellowship and a relationship with us. As we realize the intensity of His desire to have us know Him, we will gain a greater understanding of His love and desire to move us from being focused elsewhere. Insight is given by God but if we continue to look inwardly or to other sources, we will only remain frustrated and limited in our pursuit of it. The desire for insight is a natural part of every human heart. We can attempt to find it in people who are more educated than we are, thinking that they have some hidden way of reasoning. We can read every newly published author, believing that their insight will change us. But it is only when we look to the most pure form of insightfulness that we will know true understanding. There is spiritual insight that the human heart will never be able to grasp without the Spirit of God to help us. Resources are wonderful but they cannot or should not take the premier place of God's word and the necessary time of waiting in His presence to hear His voice. The Lord our God loves us and desires to show us insight into the way we should live every day. Insight must be sought. We are deceived if we just expect that it will magically fall out of the sky into our heart. The lack of insight is a difficult experience that is much like blindness, but as we seek the ways of God, He will unveil our eyes to see the direction He has for us. He is our wisdom. He is our understanding. He is our insight. He is our confidence. Paul prayed this prayer over his friends in Philippi in Philippians 1:9-10:

> *"And it is my prayer that your love may abound more and more, with knowledge and all discernment, so that you may approve what is excellent, and so be pure and blameless for the day of Christ, filled with the fruit of righteousness that comes through Jesus Christ, to the glory and praise of God."*

The point of his prayer and the point of our desire for insight is that we would be filled with the fruit of righteousness or in other words that we would live blamelessly before God. This is the place we will know true joy and a fullness that cannot be fabricated or substituted.

2 Timothy 2:7
Consider what I say, for the Lord will give
you understanding in everything.
Isaiah 64:4 ♥ Psalm 119:34 ♥ Proverbs 2:6

Hope & Joy in the Air

As Christmas approaches ever so quickly, there seems to be something in the air this time of year. Something of celebration that we sense and it's as if all creation begins to anticipate it. The joy of the season of Christmas is all around us as we sense the gift that Jesus' birth truly is. However, sometimes life attempts to bring many to despair this time of year because of loss or regret. Sadness can rob joy from so many and people find it difficult to face the holidays. There is a day recorded in the pages of God's word that dramatically changed the life of a woman who had been completely shredded by the life she had led. She's often called the "woman at the well". Jesus saw her. He spoke to her and in a way, held her life in His hands that day only to give it back to her healed. She'd been restored, she had been reconciled when she was in a place of hopelessness. During their conversation, Jesus said this to her: "If you only knew the gift of God and who it is that asks you for a drink". What was He saying? He was saying if you could realize who I am! Today He is still speaking those words to us, "if you only knew...who I truly AM!" That is the joy we sense in this season of celebration. If we could grasp a glimpse of whom He is and who it is that desires our surrender. The more we see, moment by moment, encounter by encounter, the awesomeness of Him, our life will overflow more and more. In Him, there is great joy, therefore, there is no containment of our praise.

December
2

John 4:10
Jesus answered her, "If you knew the gift of God and who it is that asks you for a drink, you would have asked him and he would have given you living water."

Psalms 8:1
O LORD, our Lord, how majestic is your name in all the earth! You have set your glory above the heavens.

Psalms 29:2 ♥ Psalms 95:6 ♥ Psalms 99:5

Whole-Hearted

We all know of things we have seen done half-heartedly. Most think that it won't matter, but in the end, it's so obvious because of the end result.

There are times when we can feel pretty scattered in terms of the day to day issues of our life. The Lord our God wants us to be whole and He desires that our hearts would be whole in Him as well. We can easily fall into the half-hearted approach with God, and think that any attempt at relationship with Him is better than none. This my dear friends is a deception of the enemy that doesn't work, in fact it will likely lead you urther from Him than you ever dreamed you'd be.

The half-hearted approach is one of procrastination. It is an attitude that if honestly examined would reveal spiritual apathy. From there, we will begin to adopt an attitude that serving or knowing God is a lot of effort and work, burdensome to an already over-full life. The opposite is the real truth. Knowing God intimately, giving Him our whole heart instead of pieces of our heart, leads and brings a wholeness to our life that is forever elusive otherwise.

Consider it this way:

You have a puzzle but it's not put together.

You carry it around in the box.

Inside the box are, of course, all the pieces that are necessary for the puzzle to be put together completely. Do we sometimes carry our life around like pieces of a puzzle, not put together? When all the time, God wants to take the pieces and fit them together as the Designer of the incredible picture that the puzzle of our life was made to be. Jesus calls us to have an undivided heart. Surrender and submission to His ways with all of our heart is joy and freedom to be whole!

Psalm 86:11
***Teach me your way, O LORD, that I may walk in
your truth; unite my heart to fear your name.***
*1 Samuel 7:3 ♥ Isaiah 29:13 ♥ James 1:8
Job 28:28 ♥ 2 Chronicles 19:9 ♥ Matthew 22:37*

He is Near

I woke up thinking of an old song that says,
"I serve a risen Savior; He's in the world today,
I know that He is with me whatever men may say.
I see His hand of mercy, I hear His voice of cheer
and just the time I need Him, He's always near.
He Lives! He Lives!
Christ Jesus lives today.
He walks with me and talks with me along life's narrow way.
He Lives! He Lives! Salvation to impart…
You ask me how I know He lives? He lives within my heart."
The words of this song reflect the heartfelt
assurance that is found in the
Word of God. He is ever near as we draw near to Him and
call on His name. Men will attempt to dismiss the nearness of
God due to circumstances that are difficult, but circumstances
of life do not deter God or His presence from our lives.
Always near.
He lives *always* near, never far.
Always close, always faithful. *Always.*
It's not up for controversial discussion, my friend. God is near.
We can know it because we experience
Him, but even more we can know
it because His word is true. And it declares
that God is not a man that
He should lie to us. We can take Him at His word
and believe to trust in faith, regardless of hardship
or trial. We serve a risen savior today,
He is not dead but alive and well, the One who is always near!

Psalm 119:151
You are near, O LORD,
And all Your commandments are truth.
Psalm 16:8 ♥ Psalm 145:8 ♥ Psalm 34:8
Psalm 119:151 ♥ Jeremiah 23:23

Tune In

In the city, finding a radio station isn't too difficult.
There are usually a good number of choices that suit every preference.
That's because the radio towers are most generally located within
a short distance of the city, and some are located in the heart
of the city limits. However, the further away from the city you
travel, the more difficult it is to maintain the radio signal.
Most of us have traveled and experienced,
first hand, a waning radio signal.
We work carefully, attempting to tune in by adjusting the tuning dial.
Tuning into the sound of the Lord requires that we remain
in close proximity to the signal of the Holy Spirit. As we
quietly and carefully begin to tune our hearts closer to
His, we will begin to hear His voice more clearly.
Let's think of it as traveling toward the signal and not away from it.
We can extend our antennae, sometimes referred to as raising our hands
up in worship. We can reduce the distractions of life by turning them off.
In our attentiveness, we will begin to hear more and more
clearly. There's nothing quite like trying to listen to static
filled music. The more static, the harder it is to hear, and the
words of our favorite song become harder to understand.
Our struggle in tuning into God, can be in many ways, the same. It can
lead to frustration and hopelessness. But as we tune in closely to the
signal of God's heart, those things fade, and static diminishes into clarity.
Being tuned into Christ is life, it is breath, it is necessity, it is vital. If
the signal of God's presence has faded and it seems that you're having a
hard time hearing Him, take the time, as Christmas approaches to reset
the dial of your heart toward Him. Emmanuel is the name of Jesus that
means "God with us". Come closer to the signal until its sound is crisp
and clear. Peace comes when we are in a place of being close to Christ.
When we have drifted too far away, there is an internal signal in us
that is unsettled. Jesus came to earth, born a baby, to be with us.
He came so that we could be reunited in relationship to God.
His nearness is for us today and every day.

December
5

Matthew 1:23
*Behold, the virgin shall conceive and bear a son, and they shall
call His name Emmanuel (which means, God with us).*

Isaiah 7:14
*Therefore the Lord Himself will give you a sign: Behold, a virgin
will be with child and bear a son, and she will call His name Emmanuel.*

*Psalm 46:7 ♥ Psalm 20:1 ♥ Psalm 46:11
Psalm 50:14-15*

Signs of Christmas

Imagine the excitement that stirred in heaven on the day that God, the Father, gathered the angels around and began to share with them their assignment of announcing the birth of Jesus. As He told them that they would be the ones that got to go, I can only imagine what they felt. "Us, Lord? We get to go? We get to tell of the birth of Jesus?" I'm sure they were filled with an excitement that was hard to contain. Imagine them assembling, waiting for the moment to be discharged for the assignment of a lifetime! For this one moment, they would be gathered like never before, filling the sky with a song of praise like no other time before or since. Have you ever considered that God could have filled the heavens with His booming thunderous voice and told of the birth of Jesus, but He chose to allow the angels to make the proclamation? Today, as the celebration of that day nears, we are given a similar, joyful assignment of sharing the news that Jesus was not only born but He lives! He is the Savior who came to the earth because God so loved His creation, and couldn't bear the thought of eternity without us. The angels told the shepherds who were tending their sheep about the birth of Jesus. They told them that there would be a sign of Him and when they found it, it brought confirmation to their hearts. What signs do our lives show that confirm He is the reason for Christmas? At Christmastime, so many things, little and big, that we do and say reveal the confirmation that our hearts hold. As we refocus on the joy of Christmas and the reality of what Jesus' birth really brings to us, on a personal level, then others will see it. I believe the sign of our life can point them to the manger this Christmas season. May we be so careful not to let the true meaning of Christmas be lost in the season, but may the season take on its true purpose by the signs of Christ's love in us. He is the gift, but if we are not careful, we can easily miss the treasure of it amid the festivities of celebration. How we celebrate Christmas reflects so much about what is in our hearts. May we be so careful to handle carefully this joyous and precious sign of Christmas? We remember and His love is stirred up in us. We sense a depth when we stop and consider not the materialness of Christmas, but the gift of who God truly is and what Jesus' birth means for us and those around us. Our testimony is a sign. Our life is a sign. Our words and attitude are signs, that Jesus is Christmas to us and for the world!

December 6

Luke 2:12-14

And this will be a sign for you: you will find a baby wrapped in swaddling clothes and lying in a manger. And suddenly there was with the angel a multitude of the heavenly host praising God and saying, Glory to God in the highest, and on earth peace to men on whom His favor rests!

Atonement

Christmas fills our hearts with special warmth as we sense the depth of the gift of Jesus' life from our heavenly Father. The reason that Jesus was even born was about a word that some have never heard called, "Atonement". The English word actually means, "to be one with". For us, we know that through the life and cross of Christ, He made a way for us to be one with God or reconciled to Him.

From there we can look at the Hebrew word for atonement called, "kipur". As a verb, "kaphar" means "to cover, purge, and make reconciliation" and "to cover with or coat with pitch". It is actually the very form of the word that God used when He told Noah to cover the ark with pitch, when He was about to send flood waters in judgement because of the sinfulness of the people. The pitch covered the outside of the ark and it kept the family of Noah with all the animals safe inside. Safe from the judgement of God. The atonement of Christ is the means for God protecting us from His own judgement. The interesting thing about the pitch that God told Noah to use is that Noah had to apply it to the ark. It didn't just "happen". It required an action on Noah's part and living in the atonement of Christ is the same for us. We must apply it to our lives. The provision is made. Meaning, it's available for us and we are given access to the atonement of Christ, but it requires our taking action and letting His atonement cover every part of our life. May we carefully and prayerfully not let any part of our life be left uncovered? As we think of atonement, may this Christmas fill our hearts even fuller to know that the love of God is the provision He made for our spiritual safety. The purpose of the pitch for Noah and his ark was not only to keep it water-tight, but it was to keep it together. The pitch actually held the ark together on the high seas of the flood. Imagine the tossing to and fro, back and forth of the large vessel through the storm of the flood. We know that God has promised never to flood the earth again and cause such a literal flood, but there are storms that we face every day in our life. Let the assurance of the atonement of Christ serve to remind us of the strength of the keeping power of Christ. Let it serve to remind us also that He is our only covering.

December 7

1 John 4:10
***And love consists in this: not that we loved God,
but that He loved us and sent His Son as an atoning sacrifice for our sins.***

Hebrews 2:17 ♥ Romans 3:25 ♥ 1 John 2:2

Genesis 6:14

Preparations

As Christmas approaches, the details and
preparations can be endless.

With the joy of the season, we all have our lists of plans. They
may be our Christmas gift list or our Christmas card list,
our Christmas dinner shopping list or our Christmas party
detail list. Whatever your list, there is no doubt a degree of
preparation that is required. Preparations bring anticipation for
the celebration that awaits the date of its presentation. For some,
this preparation is simple and seemingly effortless. For others,
it's weighty and even overwhelming as the time gets closer.
The preparation of Christmas is heard in a wonderful hymn that
we sing again and again in the song, "Joy to the World". These are
words that the angels brought to the shepherds as they announced
the birth of Jesus. The song goes on with lyrics written by Isaac
Watts in 1719, to encourage all of us to prepare a place in our
hearts for Him. Though the birth of Jesus is one of celebration
and joyfulness, none of us can forget the one sad note of the story
when Joseph and Mary arrived in Bethlehem. The Bible tells us that
there was no place for them in the inn. Another way of stating this
would be to say that there was no room for them in the "interior"
place of the house. They were left to manage outside, in a stable.
Our lives can be the illustration of being so full, especially at
Christmastime that there is no room for Him. We must make
preparation for Him in the interior of our heart and life. May we
not make accommodations for Jesus in an exterior place of our
life. But with joy, welcome Him into the interior of our life.
Just as we would make preparations for our guests
this Christmas season, let's first and foremost make
preparations for the Guest of Honor. May Jesus be the
center and not left as a part of our Christmas celebration.

"Let every heart prepare Him room."

Luke 2:10
**And the angel said to them, "Fear not, for behold, I bring you
good news of great joy that will be for all the people.**
Luke 2:7 ♥ Psalm 51:10 ♥ Psalm 78:8

Christmas Exchanging

Christmas is filled with the joy and the fun of giving gifts. However, invariably the following happens…wrong size, wrong color, and wrong style. How many times have we given a gift only to realize later it's the wrong one, the wrong size, or the wrong color? So then, the infamous return and exchange process ensues to find a more suitable replacement. If we let Christmas become more about what gifts we give and receive, we do Christ an injustice. We may not even realize that we can place greater importance on the gifts of Christmas than the Giver of Christmas, and the wonderful gift of salvation we have been given. Whenever we attempt to exchange the perfection of God's gift of Jesus with material things, we will always be disappointed. The purpose of gifts is to convey love and appreciation. It is a way of telling those in our lives that they are important to us. What is so beautiful is that the greatest gift we will give or receive is found in Christ Jesus and Him alone. It is God's way of saying to each and every one of us, I love you more than you will ever know". The question may be, how do we keep from letting His significance lose its place in our Christmas? Well, it's not something that we can just check off our list, but it's the ongoing continual acknowledgement of our heart of gratitude for Him and the gift He is. All that He has blessed us with and through is more gift than we could ever truly contain if we could actually see all that it holds. It's just simply remembering His goodness and sharing that goodness with others. God was the first giver of gifts on the very first Christmas, and what a wonderful gift He gave!

Romans 5:8
But God shows His love for us in that while we were still sinners, Christ died for us.
Romans 8:32 ♥ John 3:16 ♥ Galatians 2:2
Ephesians 5:2

Variables

Life is full of variables.
No two people are exactly identical and neither are our lives.
We are intricately different and when we attempt to be the
same, we limit the glorious creation of who God made us
to be. When our intellect or appearance seems less, in our
opinion, than that of someone else, we naturally feel belittled.
But we must remember that we are who God made us to be,
and they are a completely different creation of His hands.
The variables in our life are the things that change,
however, they cannot ever change who God is.
He doesn't ever call us to be the anchor.
He is our anchor. He is our constant.
Because the Lord, our God, knows what we face daily, that we
are so limited in ourselves, He takes on the role of constant
and tells us that He can handle the variables of our life. He
is capable and He is eternally faithful when we are not. He
holds the things that are unknown. He sees what we cannot
see and He calls us to trust in Him to be who He is.
We will always feel inadequate if we attempt to carry the
role of God in our lives. Take a look inside your life. Are you
trying to handle it all on your own? If you are, the Lord is
near to help you and handle the things that are overwhelming
you today, right now. Don't put it off. Let Him be God. Your
invitation for His involvement in your life, is what opens
the door for His love and provision to be poured out.

December
10

Jude 1:24-25
*Now to Him who is able to keep you from stumbling and to present
you unblemished in His glorious presence, with great joy—to the only
God, our Savior, through Jesus Christ our Lord, be glory, majesty,
dominion, and authority, before all time and now and forever. Amen.*

Romans 11:36 ♥ 2 Corinthians 1:20 ♥ John 5:44
Exodus 3:14 ♥ Hebrews 13:8

Jesus Came

Jesus came, He left heaven. He came to people, rich and poor.
He was born, as we know, in Bethlehem to Mary and Joseph,
as the Son of God. In a manger, not a palace as some might
think more suitable for the King of kings. Jesus came into our
world in order to give us life and rescue us from the power of
sin. It was the most honorable thing that God could have done
for us. Not that we could ever deserve such a gift, but in it He
was declaring our worth in spite of the depravity of sin.
He came and that is, by far the most remarkable part of Christmas.
He came for us. He didn't come with the intent of being crowned on
the earth, but to be crowned in our hearts and lives. What continues
to be so impacting is that Jesus not only came in His birth, but He
continued to "come" to places where people needed His love. He
wasn't just born, remaining in a place where people would have to
come to find Him, but He went and He kept going to places that
were inconvenient, and where He knew He would even be rejected.
It didn't deter Jesus, He went regardless of the response
of those He came to save. In His heart, He knew that
the will of the Father was that He go anyway.
He came!
And He continues to come, knocking on the door
of our hearts that we might not just allow Him
in, but that we would welcome Him there.
He keeps coming because He loves you dear friend.
He keeps coming by the Holy Spirit now,
because He knows your best can only be found in Him.

1 Timothy 1:15
*The saying is trustworthy and deserving of full acceptance, that Christ
Jesus came into the world to save sinners, of whom I am the foremost.*
Matthew 1:18 ♥ Galatians 3:24 ♥ John 1:171
John 5:6 ♥ Matthew 16:13

Ponderings

God spoke to Mary through Gabriel about the birth of Jesus.
When He did, she undoubtedly did not completely understand,
but nonetheless, she chose to trust Him. From there the plan of
God began to unfold before her very eyes. It was His doing, and
His plan to save the world. When it all began to happen, Mary
treasured all that was happening, the Bible tells us, pondering
them in her heart. I love the example of her life. She could have
allowed fear or doubt to undermine the work of God and the
miracle that He was doing, but instead she choose to trust and
be confident that God was well equipped to do all that He had
spoken to her and Joseph. Ponderings are those things that we
think about again and again. They are things that dominate our
thinking. It is so important that the words of God are allowed
to be paramount in our heart and mind. Pondering can give
us such perspective, some good and some not so spiritually
healthy. In her pondering, Mary knew that God's ways were
beyond her and beyond who she was. The plan was a God sized,
God implemented, God ordained plan and not one that she had
control over. Mary recognized the honor of God in her life and
she pondered it. She recognized the gift of Jesus and she pondered
it. She recognized the miracle of Joseph's love and she pondered
it. She remembered the visit of Gabriel and she pondered it.
So these things and so many more were seen by Mary. Not
completely understood, but what she did know, was that what
God was doing, was *His* doing. We have the same joy today.
We know that God loves us and He will be with us in all that
our life brings. Mary had to surrender her heart in order to
ponder the things of God. It's the same for us today, we must
surrender what we may not understand and definitely what
we cannot see with a deeper faith that God is with us. What
will you ponder today? It really matters. Mary knew that God
was with her and it was the greatest of all her ponderings.

Luke 2:19
But Mary treasured up all these things, pondering them in her heart.
Psalm 139:23 ♥ Psalm 119:11 ♥ 1 Thessalonians 2:4
Philippians 4:8

Righteousness

There is little mentioned in God's word about the man that He would entrust Jesus to. One man alone would be Jesus' dad. A man by the name of Joseph was called to be the earthly father of God's one and only son. As we imagine it, we can easily see that the entrustment of God to Joseph was huge. But who was Joseph and what do we know about him? The one thing that we know of him is that Joseph lived a life devoted to God. Because of what we know of Mary and God's choosing of her, we can easily see Joseph's heart in choosing her to be his wife, before God's presence overshadowed her and she became pregnant. Joseph sought God's direction for a Godly wife. When he found out that she was pregnant, his heart must have been crushed for an instant. Imagine the thought, the disappointment, until the angel came to set the record straight. Nonetheless, Joseph had devised a plan to protect Mary, even in his pain and his personal disappointment. He was a gracious man but one that also worked hard as a carpenter. Imagine rugged hands and a wise but gentle heart. Joseph was a man of God, who was called upon to carry the responsibility of being a father on earth to the Son of God. Imagine the weight of the calling that God honored him with. At the time that Jesus was to be born God took His time in looking for a man and woman that He could use. He had undoubtedly prepared them, but at the same time, they had prepared themselves simply out of their devotion and love of God. Their preparation and devotion to God wasn't so that they would be chosen by Him for such an incredible assignment. The example of Joseph is a reminder to us that he prepared himself to be righteous and when God needed him, he was ready. We don't know all that God has in store for us, and many put off their pursuit of right living before God, when all the while it may be the very key that opens the door to our destiny in God's plan and purpose. As we continue to pursue the righteousness of Christ, though we may stumble, He is amazingly merciful and faithful to be the strength we need to live as overcomers, no longer bound by sin but free to be used by Him for the glory of His grace.

Matthew 1:19-20

Because Joseph her husband, a righteous man, was unwilling to disgrace her publicly, he resolved to divorce her quietly. But after he had pondered these things, an angel of the Lord appeared to him in a dream and said, "Joseph, son of David, do not be afraid to take Mary as your wife, for the One conceived in her is from the Holy Spirit.

1 Peter 2:24 ♥ Deuteronomy 6:25 ♥ 1 John 3:7
Matthew 6:33

Glory to God

The purpose of God is to continually reveal His glory to us. Every day, in so many instances, we can see His hand at work. When Jesus was born in Bethlehem, God sent angels to sing of His glory. Of course, angels don't fill the sky every day, even so, His glory is all around us. But why? Why does God want His glory to be known? Perhaps it is His divine means for displaying His love. His love is displayed in His glory. His glory contains His provision and peace for us today, just as it did that starry Christmas night when Jesus was born.

We must realize that God's objective has always been to display His love. His greatest display of love was seen in the birth of Jesus and that night He sent angels to proclaim it. Imagine as the incarnate Son of God was born, angels that normally sang in the throne room of God, took a field trip from heaven to earth. His glory was no longer just in heaven but it was on earth when Jesus was born. John wrote in his gospel that, "The Word became flesh and dwelt among us, and we have seen his glory, glory as of the only Son from the Father, full of grace and truth". (John 1:14).

The declaration of God in His glory is His sufficiency for each and every one of us, both individually and collectively as humanity. When Jesus was born, it was the beginning of God's plan of grace. It was the unveiling of His love demonstrated through what had only been prophesied up until this moment. The proclaimed glory of God was the pronouncement that Christ is the center of everything. Let Him be your center today and as the season of Christmas unfolds. Let His great glory fill your heart and be the anchor of hope you hold tightly to.

December 14

Luke 2:14
Glory to God in the highest, and on earth peace among those with whom he is pleased!

Philippians 2:13
For it is God who works in you to will and to act on behalf of His good pleasure.

Psalm 85:9 ♥ John 17:22

Time

Busyness fills our life, especially this time of year. We
do our best to happily enjoy the Christmas season.
However, frantic can easily fill our feelings if we are not
careful to guard what the joy of Christmas means.
The joy is the hope we have in Christ because He came to
earth to bring us salvation. A dear friend wrote me a line
yesterday in a message, "thank God for the blessed hope
we have". It was a precious reminder of something we
know to be so true, that this world is only temporary.
The life we live is short and time is in God's hands.
He has a place prepared for us.
Sometimes it's hard to imagine being anywhere
but here in the life we have,
but because of our salvation, we have eternity
in heaven when this life closes.
Heaven is the destination of our life here on earth!
To live well and make the most of the
time God gives us for His glory.
Our hearts are full as we realize the extent of love that He has so
generously poured out on us. Christmas is the door that leads
us to heaven's gates by the grace and salvation that can only
come through Jesus, the precious baby born in a manger.
Peace on Earth, goodwill toward men is the song
the angels sang that holy night. We have salvation
as we accept Him as the gift of Christmas.
His peace is ours for today and for eternity.

Psalm 62:5
For God alone, O my soul, wait in silence, for my hope is from him.
Psalm 130:5
I wait for the LORD, my soul does wait, And in His word do I hope.
Titus 2:11-14 ♥ Romans 8:18 ♥ Hebrews 9:27-28
Jude 1:20-21

Making Declaration of Him

I spent part of my childhood growing up in a small southern town in Mississippi. My grandmother lived nearby and I remember a little saying she would make often. It was about making a statement, and she would say, "I do declare..." Then she would go on to give her stance on whatever topic was at hand. I remember well her firmness and even when my grandpa tried to talk her out of something, there was no changing her mind. A declaration is a pronouncement of a conviction of depth. There are all kinds of declarations. We know the famous historical document of the United States called the "Declaration of Independence". It was a proclamation of liberation for a group of people who felt so passionately about a conviction, that they dedicated their lives to its cause, even if it meant death. The wise men and the shepherds made a declaration of what they saw when Jesus was born. When they experienced Him, everything changed. They would never be the same again. Experiencing Jesus causes us to make a declaration, and we will never be the same again! What do we declare today by our life and the words we speak? Do we declare the glory of God or the discouragement or worry of the world? We are invited by the Spirit of the Lord to join the hosts of heaven in declaring the glory and the goodness of God. We have the greatest of hope and the most powerful of declaration because of who Jesus truly is. He was born Majesty in a manger for us! Making a declaration of our life to Christ, and taking our place in Him is a conviction worth our entire life and our determined pursuit.

Psalm 19:1
*The heavens declare the glory of God, and the
sky above proclaims his handiwork.*

Romans 1:19-20
*For what may be known about God is plain to them, because
God has made it plain to them. For since the creation of
the world God's invisible qualities, His eternal power and
divine nature, have been clearly seen, being understood from
His workmanship, so that men are without excuse.*

Psalm 50:6 ♥ Psalm 97:6 ♥ Psalm 145:10

Peace

We know that when angels filled the sky the night of Jesus' birth, that they sang a song given to them by God. It was a song declaring peace on earth. That was then and this is now, you might say. In life, in our day to day peace is sometimes hard to find. So many things attempt to steal our peace or keep it hidden, just out of reach for many. But as we remember that blessed night when Jesus was born, life was still happening. People were living on earth and doing what people do every day. They worked and played, they had things to do and Jesus came in the middle of it all. So in the middle of life, Peace was born for us all. Receiving His peace as the beautiful gift that it is requires that we let go of things that are barriers to peace.

F.B. Meyer, born in 1847, an pastor and evangelist in England during a time of tremendous difficulty, said these words, *"As we pour out our bitterness, God pours in His peace"*. Could it be that what we are holding onto is hindering what we long for most? The Lord's love for us contends for our peace every moment of every day. As we feel the tension in our heart, this is the Lord continually trying to steer us to Him by the Holy Spirit. He longs to give us peace, more than we long for it ourselves. Loss and disappointment may have robbed every ounce of peace from your heart today, but Jesus wants to pour His peace into those places of pain. He can give your heart rest and peace really can be ours, in spite of what life has been. The peace is already there, we just have to accept it and let Him handle what we cannot. He is Peace and the song the angels sang that night is the song that is still ours today. The gift of Christmas is Jesus and the peace His birth brought for us. Peace on Earth!

John 14:27
Peace I leave with you, My peace I give to you; not as the world gives do I give to you. Let not your heart be troubled, neither let it be afraid.
Luke 2:14 ♥ Isaiah 26:3 ♥ John 16:33
Philippians 4:6-7

Contagious Love Revealed

Recently I met an older woman who was so feisty and full of life. It was her 80th birthday. I sat next to her and she shared with me her recent struggles. She had be bombarded by crippling panic attacks and had all she could take. For several nights, at the end of her rope, she prayed that God would let her die. However, God did not answer her prayers, and after waking up to new mornings having prayed her life would end, she said, "well, Lord, you must have a reason for me to be here". She said, at that moment, she began looking at life differently and joy has come to her. In her neighborhood, her friends remember how down she has been for so long. But not anymore, she is full and I mean full of joyful life and laughter.

Her 80th birthday was not just a birthday that her family celebrated, but it was one that she was celebrating with true gratitude for the life that God has blessed her with. He has replaced anxiety and panic with a greater love for Himself and for those that surround her. Her joy and love were a contagious expression of God's goodness. She told me of how she has had so many opportunities to share Jesus with her neighbors, and how glad she is that God did not answer her prayer! Precious!

As I walked away, I was so blessed by her story of the contagious love of God that filled her life. 1 John 4:9 tells us that God's love was revealed among us, and I believe it is still being revealed as we realize that He sent Jesus so that we might truly live! It's for you today! Let Jesus' love be contagiously revealed in your life.

1 John 4:9
***This is how God's love was revealed among us: God sent His one
and only Son into the world, so that we might live through Him.***
1 John 5:11-13 ♥ 1 John 1:2 ♥ 1 John 2:25

Highest Name of All

There is no other name above the name of the Lord our God. He is above all other authorities that there are, above all that ever were and above all that will ever be. His name is greater and in the authority of His name, He holds the entirety of all power. Beside Him, there are no others, there is no comparison to the greatness of who God is. This, of course, is an understatement of the obvious, but sometimes, we can become so easily distracted from its truth. In the distractions, we forget that in Christ, we have all hope. He is the God who supplies and redeems. He is the Only One who holds all that we cannot see. When we begin to grasp this truth and it becomes a part of our daily reality, our faith changes. Our hope changes from hopelessness, and our strength becomes renewed by the awe of Christ that fills our hearts. After the angels came to the shepherds on the night of Jesus' birth, they said to each other, let's go to Bethlehem and see what the Lord has made known to us. The greatness of God has been made known to us again and again, but sometimes we dismiss the invitation to come and see Him in all His glory. Jesus longs and desires that we might have a relationship with Him that is personal and close. He wants us to live in the confidence of who He is and realize the fullness that is ours in the authority of His name. He is our strength and hope.

December 19

Luke 2:14
Glory to God in the highest, and on earth peace among those with whom he is pleased!

Philippians 2:9-11
Therefore God has highly exalted him and bestowed on him the name that is above every name, so that at the name of Jesus every knee should bow, in heaven and on earth and under the earth, and every tongue confess that Jesus Christ is Lord, to the glory of God the Father.

Ephesians 1:16-21 ♥ John 17:11 ♥ 2 Thessalonians 1:11-12

Seeking Him

"Wise men still seek Him" is a saying we often
see and hear this time of year.

When Jesus was born in Bethlehem, there was a star that appeared and caused the Magi to begin looking for Him. The light of the star, even from far away, was so impacting. It was unusually bright and the display of its presence caused them to travel an incredible distance to find Jesus. They knew that there was to be a Savior born and the star brought them to where He was. Often there are signs in our lives that point us to Jesus. They can be usual blessings and at other times, they are painful and difficult circumstances. But in the depth of our hearts, we know that He can be found in it all. What we must ask ourselves is whether or not we will be wise. Will we lay aside everything else, and allow the pursuit of Jesus to take over and become our navigator as the wise men did. The Magi knew well the word of God and the prophecies about the coming Messiah. Their wisdom is perhaps derived from their knowledge of God's word. Nothing could deter them and as they found their way, we know they were led by the Holy Spirit. What an example the wise men are for us today. To diligently search for Jesus until we find Him. The wise men did not give up as their journey undoubtedly became difficult and long. How many of us give us too soon because of the roadblocks the enemy tries to deter us with? As was the case of the wise men, it is still the case today, that there was a great treasure in finding Jesus. How did they know it and how can we know it? Our soul bears witness with the heart of God and the drawing of the Holy Spirit compels us to come to Him. As we come, as the wise men did, so long ago, may we present first the gift of just our coming and ourselves? Following their coming and worship, they began to offer Jesus the gifts that their lives afforded them to bring. They brought gifts of their lives to be a blessing to Him. May we see that what our lives are to Christ are gifts. It is only when brought to Him and unwrapped by Him that their full potential can be developed. When the wise men found Jesus, the Bible says, "And when they were come into the house, they saw the young child with Mary, His mother, and fell down and worshipped Him:" Before we can bring any gifts of our life to Christ, we must first bring Him ourselves in surrender and worship as the Magi did. As we do, we will realize, as the wise men did, that Jesus is what we've been searching for all along.

December 20

Matthew 2:11

*And going into the house, they saw the child with Mary his mother,
and they fell down and worshiped him. Then, opening their treasures,
they offered him gifts, gold and frankincense and myrrh.*

Jeremiah 7:23 ♥ Joshua 1:8 ♥ James 1:22
Jeremiah 38:20

The Wonder of Jesus

Have you ever wondered what it is about Christmas? What fills our hearts this time of year that is so impacting? So often we talk about the wonder of Christmas. There are feelings felt at Christmastime that are undeniably different than most other times of the year. They cause us to feel the effects of love so deeply. As we consider why, I believe there is a definite and divine reason found in the wonder of Jesus. We may not think of it in those terms, we only know that gratitude is most overwhelming to us. But why? It is because of who Jesus is and all that His birth means for all mankind, not just us. We hope that somehow, as even those who do not know Him, experience the true wonder of Christmas, which is embedded in the wonder of Jesus, that they will realize Him. Could it be that the wonder of Jesus is a gift that God gives every single Christmas, to draw us closer and closer to Him and to each other? I've heard it said that everyday should be like Christmas Day. Not in terms of receiving gifts but of the experience of our hearts. The gratitude and love that we cannot be credited with. The experience is far beyond ourselves and even feels a bit supernatural. Its basis is not the wonder of Christmas, but the wonder of Jesus and we feel it at Christmas time, more than any other time of the year. Embracing the wonder of Jesus brings us nearer to knowing Him. Some reject the attraction of this wonder because of circumstances, but it is powerful and can change even the hardest heart as we allow Him to. As you sense the gift of Christmas, realize it is the wonder of Jesus that brings us together. In the wonder of Jesus, we all experience the love of heaven.

December 21

Psalm 36:5
Your steadfast love, O LORD, extends to the heavens, your faithfulness to the clouds.
Psalm 103:11 ♥ Psalm 57:10 ♥ Psalm 3:5
Psalm 117:2 ♥ Isaiah 55:9

A Manger

In a manger, found in a stable within the town of Bethlehem, in the City of David, the Son of God was born. The significance of the "manger" is quite amazing as we realize the purpose of it. The Christmas story relays to us a picture that we can hardly imagine possible, that the one and only Son of God, Jesus was born a birth of poverty and laid in a manger. A manger was common, and everyday people put hay in them to feed their animals. Jesus came to earth, to be the provision for all we need. There comes a time that we must fully grasp that He is the substance for our existence and we are sustained in Him. We may have been distracted from this truth and even blinded to it for a good portion of our life, but Jesus said in John 6:35, "I am the bread of life". He came to the commonness of our lives so intentionally.
In Matthew 6:11, we are taught to pray, "Give us this day our daily bread". May we be so careful not to think we can be sustained without Him, and the nourishment that He alone can bring to our soul? It's a proven fact that our physical health deteriorates when we eat poorly, attempting to survive on empty calories and non-nutritious food. The same is true of our soul. When we attempt to survive on our own, without Jesus to bring true nourishment to our starving souls, our spiritual vitality is extremely compromised. We may be able to look as though we have it all together, and play the part well, but inside we all know when we are starving for Him.
Sadly, we can let day after day go by without realizing that the culmination of these days are seriously impacting our life. Jesus came so that we would be filled with all that He is. He is our sufficiency and our portion. We are sustained and secure as we know Him more. Animals ate their food from the manger on a regular basis, but if animals did not come to eat from where their food was placed, they would starve. The same is true for us today, we must come to the manger to find His word and the amazing life He has for us there. The manger was the divine and carefully chosen place where God orchestrated that Jesus would lay. It was no accident and not an afterthought of Mary and Joseph. It was God's way of telling us that throughout life, He will always care for our needs, those that are physical and spiritual through the life and salvation of Christ.

December 22

Lamentations 3:24
"The Lord is my portion", says my soul, "therefore I will hope in Him".
John 6:35 ♥ Matthew 6:11 ♥ Psalm 73:26
2 Corinthians 3:5

Haste

Songs are a very integral part of Christmas in cultures around the world. There's something about those Christmas carols that fill our hearts. One of the most beloved Christmas carols is called, "What Child is This" and its lyrics tell of Jesus' birth and all that surrounded it. In the chorus, we find that there is a call for us to enter into the story. "Haste, Haste to bring Him laud, The Babe, the Son of Mary." What is laud you may wonder as I did? It is defined in the dictionary as, "highest praise, especially in a public context." From there we must ask what does it mean to haste, and it is defined as, "excessive speed or urgency of movement or action; hurry". William Chatterton Dix (1837-1898) was an insurance salesman. At the age of 29, 1865, in England, he was bedridden for many months due to depression and a near fatal illness. This brought about a spiritual renewal in him while he was recovering. During this trying time, William began to write hymns and from his poem, entitled, "The Manger Throne", this beloved Christmas carol came. As we wonder about the crisis of Mr. Dix's life, knowing that he undoubtedly had an encounter with Christ touches us deeply. Through every situation and trial, we can know that God is with us and from its tragedy; God can bring a miraculous triumph of victory. I wonder if Mr. Dix would have ever penned these words or more importantly encountered such a spiritual renewal had he not had been faced with the necessity of crying out to God for His strength and help. When we find ourselves in such a place, may we remember that God is with us. May we realize His great love and that it is in His birth that we can have life, for in His life, our salvation is found. He is our strength and victory for Christmas. His love breaks the grip of depression and the devastation of every crisis we face. The Bible tells us the story of when the shepherds were visited by the angels as they tended their sheep. The shepherds were the lowliest of men, uneducated, and usually lived with very meager means. They more often than not, tended sheep that belonged to someone else of wealth. But as they heard the news the angels brought to them, the Bible tells us that they went with haste to find Jesus. May we do the very same this Christmas. We must find Him, we must hurry to find Him. For in Jesus, we will find all hope and all life. We don't have to have all the answers to where we are or where we are going, that's His tending.

This, this is Christ the King,
Whom shepherds guard and angels sing.
Haste, Haste to bring Him laud!

Luke 2:16
**And they went with haste and found Mary and
Joseph, and the baby lying in a manger.**

Shhhh! Listen, He is God

The birth of Jesus is, of course, the true meaning of Christmas.
Just reading the Christmas story from the Bible causes our hearts
to settle as we imagine the scene again. What it must have been
like for Mary and Joseph to travel Bethlehem…to wander from
place to place searching for a place to stay in the clamor of the
busy little town. The greatest gift to all of mankind was about
to be presented the world. The Bible says that Mary gave birth
while they were there. She wrapped Him snugly and laid Jesus
in a manger because there was no room for them in the inn.

I imagine the setting with you today, and in it I imagine
that a precious hush settled over the stable that Joseph had
found for Mary. Instead of a fanfare of celebration, I imagine
that it was quiet and that Mary and Joseph remembered
the visit of Gabriel. I'm quite certain that they stared in
awe at baby Jesus as they held Him for the first time.

It can be such a crazy busy time for us,
just as it was in the town of Bethlehem that
surrounded Mary and Joseph.

But let's take some time to just be still and know that
Christmas is all about God's love. Throughout all of our
lives, Jesus continues to call us to a place of stillness so
that we can know Him and realize that He is God.
He is our Salvation from the manger to the cross. His
love transcends and in the stillness of Christmas, this
love of God wants to deeply touch our hearts.

December
24

Psalm 46:10
"*Be still, and know that I am God. I will be exalted*
among the nations; I will be exalted in the earth!"

Luke 2:7
And she gave birth to her firstborn son and wrapped
him in swaddling cloths and laid him in a manger,
because there was no place for them in the inn.

Isaiah 9:6-7
For to us a child is born, to us a son is given; and the government
shall be upon his shoulder, and his name shall be called Wonderful
Counselor, Mighty God, Everlasting Father, Prince of Peace.

Jesus our Savior

Jesus, name above all names.
Messiah
Savior
Lord
The Son of God
Christ
Immanuel
Wonderful
Counselor
Mighty God
Everlasting Father
The Prince of Peace
Christmas Day is here!
The birth of Jesus celebrated by time shared with family and family.
Gifts given to show our love reminds me of
something a friend recently said.
We should change the "i" in "holiday" to a
"y" because Christmas is truly holy.
I loved it!
And waking up to a beautiful snow covered Christmas
morning reminds us of just how beautiful our lives are in
Christ when His precious blood washes us whiter than snow.
This is why Jesus came. It is why He was born in a manger!
My heart is full at the gift of Christmas and I pray yours is as well.

December
25

Isaiah 9:6
For to us a child is born, to us a son is given; and the government
shall be upon his shoulder, and his name shall be called Wonderful
Counselor, Mighty God, Everlasting Father, Prince of Peace.
Ephesians 1:16-21 ♥ 2 Thessalonians 2:14 ♥ Psalm 51:7-8
Philippians 2:9

Emmanuel, God with us

The other day, I was chatting with a friend who shared her sadness as she'd been Christmas shopping a few weeks before Christmas and down the aisle, out of the corner of her eye, she caught a glimpse of a Valentine's Day display. She thought, "it couldn't be!" She'd been happily enjoying the day, knowing that it was Christmastime, but at that moment, something seemed to rob a bit of Christmas spirit from her. The moment made her heart say, "Wait! It's Christmas, don't rush us through this wonderful time." The celebration of the birth of Jesus may have ended for another year. Life resumes as the festivities conclude. But the experience of what Jesus came to earth to bring does not end because the "holiday" is over. It continues and the same blessing of Christmas should be held in our hearts every day of the year. Let the hope of what Jesus' birth truly means be reflected in our hearts like never before. As we understand the depth of His grace and merciful love, life can be forever changed. The gift God gave is the gift He is for each of us individually. As we experience Him for ourselves, personally knowing Him more and more, the greater His impact in and through our lives will be. But we can never know this depth if we let the sweetness of Christmas end because a holiday concludes. Pursuing Jesus is to rise above the norm and the routine of our life. He is with us, it is not just His name, it is our reality. He is Immanuel. Not just to be in the world but to be with us. There is something so very powerful about knowing that God is with you. No matter what we face or what touches our life, we are not alone. He is with us. As the day to day resumes, it doesn't mean that Jesus is no longer celebrated, but it means that all the more we must remind others that He is with them even though Christmas is over for this year. He is with you! Immanuel, our Savior for every day, Christ the Lord.

Isaiah 7:14
Therefore the Lord Himself will give you a sign: Behold, a virgin will be with child and bear a son, and she will call His name Immanuel.
Matthew 1:22-23 ♥ Exodus 33:14 ♥ Psalm 46:7
Leviticus 26:11-12

Surrounded

One of the wonders of my heart is the
surrounding presence of the Lord.
Sometimes, when I see it happening for me or to those I
love, it almost takes my breath away and I marvel a bit at
God. Being surrounded is often one of those lines we hear
in a movie where the good guys surround the bad guys and
say, "You're surrounded, come out with your hands up".
As a people so in need of God's intervention and help,
I wonder if sometimes He doesn't surround us with
His love and say the very same thing to us.
"Stop your struggling and just let down your guard, surrender to Me".
We are so surrounded by God, iIn so many
ways, in levels high and deep.
If we only knew the extent of God's amazing compassion in our life,
I believe it would change us more than it already has.
God is surrounding us always. He is so near,
much nearer than we realize,
even when are thoughts are far from Him. May we begin to see Him
more and as we do, may our acknowledgement of His presence
cause our hearts to marvel in awe of His constant surrounding.
He divinely and miraculously surrounds us inside and out. As
we surrender our inner thoughts to His direction, they will be
the cause for our life to realize His presence more and more.
God surrounds us, each and every one,
where we are.

Psalm 139:7-12

*Where shall I go from your Spirit? Or where
shall I flee from your presence?
If I ascend to heaven, you are there! If I make
my bed in Sheol, you are there!
If I take the wings of the morning and dwell
in the uttermost parts of the sea,
even there your hand shall lead me, and your right hand shall hold me.
If I say, "Surely the darkness shall cover me,
and the light about me be night,"
even the darkness is not dark to you; the night is bright
as the day, for darkness is as light with you.*

Psalm 125:2 ♥ Psalm 139:5 ♥ Psalm 121:8
Psalm 32:7 ♥ Psalm 5:12

My Soul Knows

What our soul knows, we often disregard and allow our self to overrule. For instance, without our knowledge, God made us. What do I mean? You were made apart, of course, from yourself. We were not a part of the creation of who we are, but sometimes we think we are the creator of me. And so we live that way, forgoing the influence of the Holy Spirit in a significant percentage of our day. But, the Bible says, our soul knows some things, because our soul was made to know and love God. It was created in us to be one with the Father who made us. His greatest longing is our greatest need. To live in harmony with the One who created us. If you are an artist who writes music or paints a masterpiece, no matter how much other people admire the work, they can never fully grasp what the artist is communicating. It will always be limited because they are not the creator of the art. The artist is the only one who fully knows the piece of art that he or she put on canvas or joins as notes on a keyboard. The observer cannot understand it fully and it is in this same context, that we must realize that there is so much more to what we know of God and the purpose of our life He is orchestrating. But joyfully, as we surrender our soul back to Him, He will begin to show us the expression of the love He has graciously established in our life, and the salvation of rescuing us from ourselves and the grip of sin. The Bible tells us in Psalms that the works of God are wonderful and our soul knows it very well. When we relinquish our soul to Christ, it begins to identify more and more, closer and closer to Him until we can say, "my soul knows it very well". Not just well, but very well! How amazing it is to know that we have a standing invitation to know Him very well! That should excite every part of our life! Jesus desires, and came so that we could know Him…very well! How well do you know Him today? If we find ourselves thinking that we don't know Him very well at all, then praise Him for seeing honestly where we stand and know that He is calling us to come closer. Don't stay at a distance, thinking that someday you'll know Him more. Today is the day to take a step from where you are towards, "very well". As we surrender our soul to Him, and walk in obedience, we will find that we are knowing Him better and better, more and more. It won't be long until we find "very well".

Psalm 139:14
I will give thanks to You, for I am fearfully and wonderfully made; Wonderful are Your works, And my soul knows it very well.
Psalm 40:5 ♥ Psalm 40:17 ♥ Psalm 119:73
Psalm 36:7 ♥ Psalm 71:15

His Will

There are many instances that we are not ready to accept the way God may be leading us. Often we wonder if this is the direction of His will. It may seem so completely contrary to where our heart is. If we have so entrenched our thinking to our own perspective, it may take God leading us through a different route to see His work. May we be, willing to respond to His will, even though it may not make sense? At some point, we must release our bent to His leading. If we truly trust and truly believe that He holds our best, we can have rest and assurance that we are cared for by His plans and goodness. What if, instead of demanding our own way, we change our prayer to reliance on Him and with humility say, "God, I'm depending on You"! It isn't just relinquishing control, it acknowledging His lordship over us and those things that are most dear to us. I am reminded of the story of Abraham. God had given him a son, the most precious to his heart of all that he knew. And then God asked him to bring this same son, Isaac, in sacrifice to Him. Amazingly, Abraham did not hesitate but immediately, he made preparations and brought his son to the Lord. Only then could God show Abraham His faithfulness. God posed a question to Abraham that day, "will you trust Me? or will you not trust Me?" Abraham had a very difficult decision to make that day. But what helped Abraham was that he knew God and he knew that God loved and cared for him and his family. He remembered in an instant, the faithfulness of God. There are times when we pray, as Jesus did, and we search out the will of the Father. Sometimes we need to stand when we've done all else in trust and faith. As we do, I believe we will see the goodness of His faithfulness in our lives as Abraham did that day. He will provide a way for us and for our families that perhaps we cannot see, because He is God and He is good. Sometimes our attitude and actions hold out on God attempting to figure things out and find understanding. Instead, may we say, "Lord, I trust You even though I don't understand". May our hearts sing out as Abraham's did, "I know Him".

December 29

Psalm 40:5
Many, O LORD my God, are the wonders which You have done, And Your thoughts toward us; There is none to compare with You. If I would declare and speak of them, they would be too numerous to count.

Jeremiah 29:11
For I know the plans I have for you," declares the Lord, "plans to prosper you and not to harm you, plans to give you hope and a future.

1 Thessalonians 5:16-18 ♥ Hebrews 13:20-21
Philippians 2:12-13 ♥ Genesis 22:7-8

Greatness

What does it mean to be great? In the opinion of men, there are various dimensions to greatness, but none hold a candle to the divine greatness of God. The greatness of our God is beyond our understanding. His name is above all other names and within Him is the greatest greatness we could ever know. Why mention the greatness of God today and why not let the understood be just that, without reiterating it here? Because when we begin to acknowledge the greatness of God, first, in our hearts, and then allow it to be demonstrated through the praise of our words, not only is God glorified, but we intentionally re-center on Him. As this year of "Centered on Majesty" nears its end, my hope is that you will take the greatness of our God to heart in determination, not allowing it to just be an unstated truth, but taking it on as the center of your faith. Keep it there; guard it well against distraction and circumstances. His greatness is unchanging and sometimes we allow our fears to keep us from continually holding onto it. This quote gives us a practical way to live in the greatness of God.

"Beloved, I say, let your fears go, lest they make you fainthearted.
Stop inspiring fear in those around you and now take your stand in faith.
God has been good and He will continue to manifest His goodness.
Let us approach these days expecting to see the goodness of the Lord manifest.
Let us be strong and of good courage, for the Lord
will fight for us if we stand in faith".
—Francis Frangipane

Our highest thoughts of God do not do justice to His greatness. His greatness is truly great, other things that are quantified by this term are infinitely left lacking in His presence. Centering on His greatness leads us to follow His example of giving and loving others. Oh that this would be our lot in life, to love so deeply and display kindness as our expression of love to our great God! Great is our God and greatly to be praised!

December 30

1 Samuel 12:22
For the LORD will not abandon His people on account of His great name, because the LORD has been pleased to make you a people for Himself.

Isaiah 12:6
Shout aloud and sing for joy, people of Zion,
for great is the Holy One of Israel among you."

1 Chronicles 16:25 ♥ Jeremiah 10:6 ♥ Psalm 47:2
Luke 1:49

Willing Offering

As the year comes to a close, most will look back over the past and at the same time think about what lies ahead in the New Year. In doing both, there is a tremendous comfort in knowing that God is with us. At the end of the year, sometimes we are inclined to look negatively at the past and let disappointment and failure blare at our hearts but, instead what if we looked at all that God has done. Every blessing and the way He has helped us get through when we may have wondered if we could make it. There was a time in the history of the Israelites walked through some very difficult times. Afterwards, God called them to build the Tabernacle. He had some pretty specific instructions for them to follow but before they could even start, there were materials that were needed to complete the construction. As the plan was unfolded and people realized that they had in their possession certain items that were needed, the Bible tells us in Exodus 35 that there was a willingness about those who contributed to the building of the place where God's presence would dwell. Instead of looking at their past, and living in defeat, they looked ahead to all that God had promised in spite of their failures. Again and again in this chapter, the Word of God tells us of one after another that were "willing" to come and bring to God what was needed. Today, there is not a tabernacle built of human hands where the presence of God dwells. The Bible tells us that we are that place. He dwells now in the hearts of men and women that have, as those in the Old Testament, willingly yielded their whole heart to Him. As we live each day, we have the constant assurance that when we are willing to surrender what is precious to us, those things that we treasure in our hearts to God, He will take them and make something beautiful out of them. He will dwell in the tabernacle of our hearts to help us in every moment and circumstance. He has the design and He has a plan for the tabernacle of your heart. May we just be willing to be used and held in His hands? Lay aside striving and walk in childlike faith with Him into a new year. Those that were willing gave of themselves before they saw the completed beauty of the tabernacle that God was constructing. If they had held out on God, and selfishly held onto their stuff, they would not have been a part of the beauty that came together by God's design. We may just expect that God will provide the means for what He wants to do in and through us in this New Year, but perhaps our greatest gift to Him will be our willingness. We have the same decision today, to be generous unto God for the beauty of living in His presence as He designs a tabernacle of us for His dwelling place. We can be an offering to the Lord in this New Year.

1 Chronicles 29:9
Then the people rejoiced because they had offered so willingly, for they made their offering to the LORD with a whole heart, and King David also rejoiced greatly.
Exodus 35:5-9 ♥ Exodus 35:21 ♥ Exodus 35:29
Jeremiah 38:20

You can buy the first Devotional, *Enthroningf Him*
by Susan League on Amazon.com

Index

Index (continued)

9 781098 084158